Modern Hindu Thought

Modern Hindu Thought

The Essential Texts

ARVIND SHARMA

OXFORD

UNIVERSITY PRESS

OXFORD

UNIVERSITY PRESS

YMCA Library Building, Jai Singh Road, New Delhi 110 001

Oxford University Press is a department of the University of Oxford. It furthers the University's objective of excellence in research, scholarship, and education by publishing worldwide in

Oxford   New York

Athens   Auckland   Bangkok   Bogota   Buenos Aires   Calcutta
Cape Town   Chennai   Dar es Salaam   Delhi   Florence   Hong Kong   Istanbul
Karachi   Kuala Lumpur   Madrid   Melbourne   Mexico City   Mumbai
Nairobi   Paris   Sao Paulo   Singapore   Taipei   Tokyo   Toronto   Warsaw

with associated companies in   Berlin   Ibadan

Oxford is a registered trade mark of Oxford University Press
in the UK and in certain other countries

Published in India
By Oxford University Press, New Delhi

ISBN 019 565315 7

Typeset in Goudy by Eleven Arts, Keshav Puram, Delhi 110035
Printed in India by Sai Printopack Pvt. Ltd., New Delhi 110020
Published by Manzar Khan, Oxford University Press
YMCA Library Building, Jai Singh Road, New Delhi 110 001

for

Professor G.C. Pande

in esteem

Contents

Introduction

A fundamental religious and cultural corollary of British Rule over India—and India's eventually successful struggle against it— was the cultural encounter between the two countries and the religious encounter between Christianity and Hinduism. This cultural and religious encounter, with its horizon extended to the end of the twentieth century, and when viewed through the lens of Hinduism, constitutes the theme of this book.

Historians have identified four broad categories of responses in the context of this civilizational encounter between Britain and India—a classification which, upon reflection, would appear applicable to civilizational encounters in general. A civilization, in a state of encounter with one more powerful than it, may display a wide range of reactions: (1) acceptance, (2) rejection, (3) resistance, and (4) selective adaptation. These, of course, are not likely to be found as pure types. Different constituencies within the reactive civilization will display different aspects of this fourfold response in different degrees.

The focus of this source book lies in its attempt to foreground the pattern of 'selective adaptation', without overlooking the other three elements in the Hindu response to this encounter. I hope that students in the three fields of history, religion and culture will find this approach useful.

Any historical account, no matter how objective it claims or pretends to be, is subject to an inherent limitation which inevitably entails a bias—although some accounts could arguably be said to be more or less biased than others. This limitation is constituted by the fact that any such account must always limit itself to the presentation of certain facts, views, or explanations, and *leave others out*. The other option—that of encyclopedism, or including everything— is not a viable option, even, or perhaps especially, in this age of information explosion. Every fact presented has its opportunity cost—the fact *not* presented.

This *implicit* limitation of all historical accounts becomes *explicit* in a source book such as this for it highlights that fact of selection, which a historical account otherwise conceals. The subjects who feature in such a source book have to be *selected*, as also the facts through which their life is related, as well as the passages through which their thought is conveyed. This feature of historical presentations, implicit in all historical writing and explicit in a source book such as this, may point to a limitation but it also provides the justification of this source book. This book makes such selections from out of the vast mass of available data as might shed light on contemporary concerns.

Thus although earlier selections of source material already exist, either for the modern period of Hinduism by itself, or as part of a larger selection from the history of Hinduism, this particular selection too, I hope, will have its takers.

The reader has only to look at the selections under Rammohun Roy and Mahatma Gandhi to realize how tantalizingly different the selections are, compared to those in other books of a similar kind. And for good reason: contemporary Indians will relate to different aspects of Roy's or Gandhi's vision as compared to those of an earlier age. Roy's advocacy of British rule is less relevant now, his views on the nature of democracy perhaps more so. Similarly, although Gandhi's passion for non-violence now is not less relevant, its possible limitations as a technique of choice, which could not be as clearly identified earlier as now, require greater attention. And so on.

It is in this spirit that the selections included herein have been made. They must be biased like all selections—but one concludes with the lingering hope that they have the right bias, and that they foreground what might be relevant for our times in the thought of modern Hindu thinkers from Roy to Krishnamurti.

Raja Rammohun Roy
(1772/74–1833)

Life

Raja Rammohun Roy, who may well be among the first persons to have used the word 'Hinduism',[1] was one of the first major thinkers of modern Hinduism. Not much is known about his early life. An incident in later life, when he was insulted by a British magistrate, curiously furnishes some first-hand biographical information. In his letter to Lord Minto, whom he petitioned against this insult, he remarks:

> Your petitioner's grandfather was at various times, Chief of Administration under his Highness the Nawab Mohabut Jung, and your petitioner's father for several years, rented a farm from Government the revenue of which was lakhs of rupees. The education which your petitioner has received, as well as the particulars of his birth and parentage, will be made known to your Lordship by a reference to your principal officers of the Sudder Dewani Adawlats and the college of Fort William, and many of the gentlemen in the service of the Hon'ble company . . .[2]

It is also apparent that although Roy's lifestyle was that of a nobleman of his times, he was not without pride in his Brahmin ancestry.

> The Brahmins have a tradition from God that they have strict orders from God to observe their ceremonies and hold their faith for ever. There are many injunctions about this from the divine authority in the Sanskrit language, and I, the humblest creature of God, having been born amongst them, have learnt the language and got those injunctions by heart, and this nation (the Brahmanas) having confidence in such divine injunctions cannot give them up, although they have been subjected to many troubles

and persecutions and were threatened to be put to death by the followers of Islam.[3]

This, however, did not prevent Rammohun Roy from striking out on a path of his own. In a remarkable if extended passage, interspersed with sentiments which might touch a chord in the reader, he refers to how he became modern India's first major Hindu reformer.

> The physical powers of man are limited, and when viewed comparatively, sink into insignificance; while, in the same ratio, his moral faculties rise in our estimation, as embracing a wide sphere of action, and possessing a capability of almost boundless improvement. If the short duration of human life be contrasted with the great age of the universe, and the limited extent of bodily strength with the many objects to which there is a necessity of applying it, we must necessarily be disposed to entertain but a very humble opinion of our own nature; and nothing perhaps is so well calculated to restore our self-complacency as the contemplation of our more extensive moral powers, together with the highly beneficial objects which the appropriate exercise of them may produce.
>
> On the other hand, sorrow and remorse can scarcely fail, sooner or later, to be the portion of him who is conscious of having neglected opportunities of rendering benefit to his fellow-creatures. From considerations like these it has been that I (*although born a Brahman, and instructed in my youth in all the principles of that sect*), being thoroughly convinced of the lamentable errors of my countrymen, have been stimulated to employ every means in my power to improve their minds, and lead them to the knowledge of a purer system of morality. Living constantly amongst Hindoos of different sects and professions, I have had ample opportunity of observing the superstitious puerilities into which they have been thrown by their self-interested guides, who, in defiance of the law as well as of common sense, have succeeded but too well in conducting them to the temple of idolatry; and while they hid from their view the true substance of morality, have infused into their simple hearts a weak attachment for its mere shadow . . .[4]

The consequences of his actions were also not entirely unpredictable. For he wrote again in 1816:

> By taking the path which conscience and sincerity direct, I, born a Brahman, have exposed myself to the complainings and reproaches even of some of my relations, whose prejudices are strong, and whose temporal advantage depends upon the present system. But these, however accumulated, I can tranquilly bear, trusting that a day will arrive when my humble endeavours will be viewed with justice—perhaps acknowledged

with gratitude. At any rate, whatever men may say, I cannot be deprived of this consolation: my motives are acceptable to that Being who beholds in secret and compensates openly![5]

The early life of Rammohun Roy is clouded by some measure of obscurity and even controversy.[6] His life comes into clearer focus by the time he is thirty. By then his father, with· whom he is believed to have had some differences, had died (in 1803). He was already proficient in Persian and Arabic. Early retirement after a period of gainful employment with the East India Company enabled him to settle down in Calcutta and from the age of forty onwards, he was active in public life.

The reformist criticisms that Roy levelled against Hinduism even led some to doubt whether he remained a Hindu any longer. His wives would have nothing to do with him. He is said to have contracted a special marriage with a Muslim woman with Shaiva rites,[7] and when the Hindus got together to start an educational institution along Western lines, some were reluctant to accept Roy's contribution towards it. This is apparent from the following account of one of the pioneers:

Talking afterwards with several of the company, before I proceeded to open the business of the day, I found that one of them in particular, a Brahmin of good caste, and a man of wealth and influence, was mostly set against Rammohun Roy, son of (a *pattanidar* under) the Raja of Burdwan, a Brahmin of the highest caste, and of great wealth and rank (who has lately written against the Hindu idolatry, and upbraids his countrymen pretty sharply). He expressed a hope that no subscription would be received from Rammohun Roy. I asked 'why not?' 'Because he has chosen to separate himself from us, and to attack our religion.' 'I do not know', I observed, 'what Rammohun's religion is (I have heard it is a kind of Unitarianism)—*not being acquainted or having had any communication with him*; but I hope that my being a Christian, and a sincere one, to the best of my ability, will be no reason for your refusing my subscription to your undertaking.' This I said in a tone of gaiety; and he answered readily in the same style, 'No, not at all; we shall be glad of your money; but it is a different thing with Rammohun Roy, who is a Hindu, and yet has publicly reviled us, and written against us and our religion; and I hope there is no intention to change our religion.' I answered, that 'I knew of no intention of meddling with their religion; that every object of the establishment would be avowed, and a committee appointed by themselves to regulate the details, which would enable themselves to guard against everything they should disapprove of; that their own committee would accept or refuse subscription from whom they pleased.[8]

In the context of modern Hinduism, Rammohun Roy was among the first figures to make the sacred texts freely available to people both in the original and with translations, and who, taking his stand on them, questioned image worship, worked for the abolition of *Suttee*, and threw his weight in favour of the introduction of Western science. He learned English in later life and was soon defending his version of Hinduism against attacks on it by Christian missionaries. These public religious activities culminated in the founding of a place of worship in 1828, called the Brahmo Sabha, where worship proceeded as follows:

> Two Telugu Brahmins used to recite the Vedas in a side-room, screened from the view of the congregation, where non-Brahmins would not be admitted; Utsavananda would read texts of the Upanisads, which were afterwards explained in Bengali by Pandit Ramchandra Vidyavagish, who would then preach or read the sermons, some of which were written by Rammohun Roy. Singing of hymns terminated the ceremony.[9]

This ultimately led to the founding of the Brahmo Samaj, when the arrangement was formalized in 1830 through a trust-deed. It read in part as follows:

> And that in conducting the said worship or adoration no object, animate or inanimate, that has been, or is, or shall hereafter become, or be recognized, as an object of worship, by any man or set of men, shall be reviled or slightingly or contemptuously spoken of or alluded to either in preaching, praying, or in the hymns, or other mode of worship that may be delivered or used in the said message or building.
>
> And that no sermon, preaching, discourse, prayer, or hymn be delivered, made, or used in such worship but such as have a tendency to the promotion of the contemplation of the Author and Preserver of the Universe, to the promotion of charity, morality, piety, benevolence, virtue, and to the strengthening of the bonds of union between men of all religious persuasions and creeds.[10]

Roy died at Bristol in UK in 1833 with the sacred Hindu syllable *om* on his lips.

A Tribute

F. Max Mueller was involved in many things associated with India with one singular omission: he never visited it. When reproached for this fact and accused of forming 'too favourable a view of Indian character' as a result of encountering only its 'most distinguished sons and daughters' he remarked: 'But where is the harm? I have seen what the Indian character can be, I have learnt what it ought to be, and I hope what it will be though we cannot expect a whole nation of Rammohun Roys . . .' It's a longer list, but it begins with Rammohun Roy!

And yet I like to call Rammohun Roy a great man, using that word, not as a cheap, unmeaning title, but as conveying three essential elements of manly greatness, namely, unselfishness, honesty and boldness. Let us see whether Rammohun Roy possessed in a high degree these three essentials . . .

There is a quiet courage, a simple straightforwardness in all of Rammohun Roy's acts. Some of his friends have misunderstood him, and claimed him for a Mohammedan, or a Christian. He said himself, just before he set out for Europe, that on his death each sect, the Christian, the Hindu and the Mohammedan, would claim him as their own, but that he belonged to none of them. His real religious sentiments are embodied in a pamphlet, written and printed in his lifetime, but, according to his injunction, not published till after his death. This work discloses his belief in the unity of the Deity, his infinite power, his infinite goodness, and in the immortality of the soul.

With such a faith nothing would have been easier for him than to do what so many of his countrymen, even the most enlightened, are still content to do, to remain silent on doctrines which do not concern them; to shrug their shoulders at miracles and legends; and to submit to observances which, though distasteful to themselves, may be looked upon as possibly useful to others.

With such an attitude towards religion, he might have led a happy, quiet, respectable, useful life, and his conscience need not have smitten him more that it seems to have smitten many others. But he would not. He might part with his old mother in silent love and pity, but towards the rest of the world he wished to appear as what he was. He would not say that he believed in three Gods when he believed in One God only; he would not call idols symbols of the Godhead; he would not have ritual, because it helped the weak; he would not allow *Suttee*, because it was a time-hallowed custom, springing from the true love of a wife for a dead husband. He would have no compromising, no economizing, no playing with words, no shifting of responsibility from his own shoulders to others. And therefore, whatever narrow-minded critics may say, I say once more that Rammohun Roy was an unselfish, an honest, a bold man,—a great man in the highest sense of the word.[11]

Natural Theism

In Roy's very first book, which was composed in Persian with a preface in Arabic, entitled Tuhfat-ul-Muwahhidin *(1803) or* A Gift to the Monotheists, *Rammohan Roy developed the idea of a natural theism, almost in the manner of the tenth-century Hindu thinker Udayana, as follows:*

I travelled in the remotest parts of the world, in plains as well as in hilly lands, and found the inhabitants thereof agreeing generally in the personality of one Being, who is the source of all that exists and its governor, and disagreeing in giving peculiar attributes to that Being and in holding different creeds consisting of the doctrines of religion and precepts of *haram* (forbidden) and *halal* (lawful). From this induction it has been known to me that turning generally towards one eternal Being is like a natural tendency in human beings and is common to all individuals of mankind equally.

The followers of different religions, sometimes seeing the paucity of the number of believers in one God in the world, boast that they are on the side of the majority. It is to be seen that the truth of a saying does not depend upon the multiplicity of the sayers, and the non-reliability of a narration cannot arise simply out of the paucity of the number of the narrators. For it is admitted by the seekers of truth that truth is to be followed, although it is against the majority of the people.

It is strange to say that after the lapse of hundreds of years from the time of these religious leaders, with whom the prophetic mission is said to be closed, Nanak and others, in India and other countries, raised the flag of prophetic mission and induced a large number of people to become their followers and were successful.

Oh God! Notwithstanding implicit faith in the orders of the *mujtahid* or the doctors of religion, there is always such an innate faculty existing in the nature of mankind that if any person of sound mind, before or after assuming the doctrines of any religion, makes an impartial and just inquiry into the nature of the principles of religious doctrines of different nations, there is a strong hope that he will be able to distinguish truth from untruth and true propositions from fallacious ones, and also that he, becoming free from the useless restraints of religion, which sometimes become sources of prejudice of one against another and causes of physical and mental troubles, will turn to the one Being, who is the fountain of the harmonious organization of the universe, and will pay attention to the good of society.[12]

Opposition to Idolatry

That such a God should be worshipped through images was a position Roy could not countenance. He was convinced that image worship was a deviation from the pure theism of Hinduism, a practice to which Hindus had fallen prey through ignorance. This he tried to dispel by vigorously pointing to the chasm which seemed to him to separate pure from popular Hinduism.

To the Believers of the only True God

The greater part of Brahmans, as well as of other sects of Hindoos, are quite incapable of justifying that idolatry which they continue to practise. When questioned on the subject, in place of adducing reasonable arguments in support of their conduct, they conceive it fully sufficient to quote their ancestors as positive authorities! And some of them are become very ill disposed towards me, because I have forsaken idolatry for the worship of the true and eternal God! In order, therefore, to vindicate my own faith, and that of our early forefathers, I have been endeavouring, for some time past, to convince my countrymen of the true meaning of our sacred books, and to prove that my aberration deserves not the opprobrium which some unreflecting persons have been so ready to throw upon me.

The whole body of the Hindoo theology, law, and literature is contained in the Veds [Vedas], which are affirmed to be coeval with the creation! These works are extremely voluminous; and being written in the most elevated and metaphorical style, are, as may be well supposed, in many passages seemingly confused and contradictory. Upwards of two thousand years ago, the great Byas [Vyāsa Bādarāyaṇa], reflecting on the perpetual difficulty arising from these sources, composed with great discrimination a complete and compendious abstract of the whole, and also reconciled those texts, which appeared to stand at variance. This work be termed *The Vedant* [Vedānta], which, compounded of two Sungscrit [Sanskrit] words, signifies *The resolutions of all the Veds*. It has continued to be most highly revered by all the Hindoos, and, in place of the more diffuse arguments of the Veds, is always referred to as equal authority. But, from its being concealed within the dark curtain of the Sungscrit language, and the Brahmans permitting themselves alone to interpret, or even to touch any book of the kind, the Vedant, although perpetually quoted, is little known to the Public; and the practice of few Hindoos indeed bears the least accordance with its precepts!

In pursuance of my vindication, I have, to the best of my abilities, translated this hitherto unknown work, as well as an abridgement thereof, into the Hindoostanee and Bengalee languages, and distributed them, free of cost, among my own countrymen as widely as circumstances have possibly allowed. The present is an endeavour to render an abridgement of the same into English, by which I expect to prove to my European friends that the superstitious practices which deform the Hindoo religion have nothing to do with the pure spirit of its dictates!

I have observed, that, both in their writings and conversation, many Europeans feel a wish to palliate and soften the features of Hindoo idolatry, and are inclined to inculcate that all objects of worship are considered by their votaries as emblematical representations of the Supreme Divinity! If this were indeed the case, I might perhaps be led into some examination of the subject, but the truth is, the Hindoos of the present day have no such views of the subject, but firmly believe in the real existence of innumerable gods and goddesses, who possess, in their own departments, full and independent power; and to propitiate them, and not the true *God*, are Temples erected, and ceremonies performed. There can be no doubt, however, and it is my whole design to prove, that every rite has its derivation from the allegorical adoration of the true Deity; but, at the present day, all this is forgotten; and among many it is even heresy to mention it!

I hope it will not be presumed, that I intend to establish the preference of my faith over that of other men. The result of controversy on such a subject, however multiplied, must be ever unsatisfactory. For the reasoning faculty which leads men to certainty in things within its reach produces no effect on questions beyond its comprehension. I do no more than assert that if correct reasoning and the dictates of common sense induce the belief of a wise, uncreated Being who is the supporter and ruler of the boundless universe, we should also consider him, the most powerful and supreme existence, far surpassing our powers of comprehension or description. And although men of uncultivated minds and even some learned individuals (but in this one point blinded by prejudice) readily choose as the object of their adoration any thing which they can always see and which they pretend to feed, the absurdity of such conduct is not, thereby, in the least degree diminished.

My constant reflections on the inconvenient or, rather, injurious rites introduced by the peculiar practice of Hindoo idolatry, which, more than any other pagan worship destroys the texture of society, together with compassion for my countrymen, have compelled me to use every possible effort to awaken them from their dream of error; and by making them acquainted with their scriptures, enable them to contemplate, with true devotion, the unity and omnipresence of nature's God.[13]

Rammohun Roy and Christianity

Roy was one of the first educated Hindus to react to Christianity and set the general tone of the Hindu reaction to it in the modern period. In the sections below one detects, in that order, his admiration of Christ, his rejection of dogmatic Christianity in his sarcastic refutation of trinitarianism, and his defence of Hinduism against Christian attacks.

Introduction

A conviction in the mind of its total ignorance of the nature and of the specific attributes of the Godhead, and a sense of doubt respecting the real essence of the soul, give rise to feelings of great dissatisfaction with our limited powers, as well as, with all human acquirements which fail to inform us on these interesting points—on the other hand, a notion of the existence of a supreme superintending power, the Author and Preserver of this harmonious system, who has organised and who regulates such an infinity of celestial and terrestrial objects; and a due estimation of that law which teaches that man should do unto others as he would wish to be done by, reconcile us to human nature and tend to render our existence agreeable to ourselves and profitable to the rest of mankind. The former of these sources of satisfaction, viz., a belief in God, prevails generally, being derived either from tradition and instruction, or from the attentive survey of the wonderful skill and contrivance displayed in the works of nature. The latter, although, it is partially taught also in every system of religion with which I am acquainted, is principally inculcated by Christianity. This essential characteristic of the Christian religion, I was for a long time unable to distinguish as such, amidst the various doctrines I found insisted upon in the writings of Christian authors, and in the conversation of those teachers of Christianity with whom I have had the honour of holding communication. Amongst these opinions, the most prevalent seems to be that no one is justly entitled to the appellation of Christian who does not believe in the divinity of Christ and of the Holy Ghost as well as in the divine nature of God, the father, of all created beings.

I feel persuaded that by separating from the other matters contained in the New Testament, the moral precepts found in that book, these will be more likely to produce the desirable effect of improving the hearts and minds of men of different persuasions and degrees of understanding. For, historical and some other passages are liable to the doubts and disputes of free thinkers and anti-Christians, especially, miraculous relations, which are much less wonderful than the fabricated tales handed down to the natives of Asia, and consequently would be apt, at best, to carry little weight with them. On the contrary, moral doctrines, tending evidently to the maintenance of the peace and harmony of mankind at large, [are] beyond the reach of metaphysical perversion, and intelligible alike to the learned and to the unlearned. This simple code of religion and morality is so admirably calculated to elevate men's ideas to high and liberal notions of one God, who has equally subjected all living creatures, without distinction of caste, rank, or wealth, to change, disappointment, pain and death, and has equally admitted all to be partakers of the bountiful mercies which he has lavished over nature, and is also so well fitted to regulate the conduct of the human race in the discharge of their various duties to themselves and to society, that I cannot but hope the best effects from its promulgation in the present forum.[14]

MISSIONARY: . . . But (addressing the 3rd convert) perverse as your two brethren are, you appear worse than they: what can you possibly mean by answering there are no Gods?

3RD CONVERT: I heard you talk of three, but I paid more particular attention to what you said on the point of there being only one. This I could understand; the other I could not; and as my belief never reaches above my understanding (for you know I am no learned Mandarin) I set it down in my mind that there was but one God, and that you take your name of Christian from him.

MISSIONARY: There is something in this; but I am more and more astonished at your answer—'None'.

3RD CONVERT: (Taking up the Swanpan) Here is one. I remove it. There is none.

MISSIONARY: How can this apply?

3RD CONVERT: Our minds are not like yours in the West; or you would not ask me. You told me again and again, that there never was but one God, that Christ was the true God, and that a nation of merchants living at the head of the Arabian gulf, put him to death upon a tree, about eighteen hundred years ago. Believing you, what other answer could I give than 'None'?

MISSIONARY: I must pray for you . . . .[15]

If by the 'ray of intelligence' for which the Christian says we are indebted to the English, he means the introduction of useful mechanical arts, I am ready to express my assent and also my gratitude; but with respect to *science, literature,* or *religion,* I do not acknowledge that we are placed under any obligation. For by a reference to History it may be proved that the world was indebted to *our ancestors* for the first dawn of knowledge, which sprang up in the East, and thanks to the Goddess of Wisdom, we have still a philosophical and copious language of our own which distinguishes us from other nations who cannot express scientific or abstract ideas without borrowing the language of foreigners . . . .

Before 'A Christian' indulged in a tirade about persons being 'degraded by *Asiatic* effeminacy' he should have recollected that almost all the ancient prophets and patriarchs venerated by Christians, nay even Jesus Christ himself, a Divine Incarnation and the *founder* of the Christian Faith, were Asiatics. So that if a Christian thinks it degrading to be born or to reside in Asia, he directly reflects upon them . . . .

It is unjust in the Christian to quarrel with Hindoos because (he says) they cannot comprehend the sublime mystery of his religion [the Doctrine of the Trinity]; since he is equally unable to comprehend the sublime mysteries of ours, and since both these mysteries equally transcend the human understanding, one cannot be preferred to the other.[16]

Roy and the Rights of Women

Roy took an active interest in ameliorating the lot of women. He attacked Sati as the most visible form of their disempowerment and then attacked that view of womanhood which provided the psychological justification for their subordination. Finally, he opposed legal encroachments on their rights.

ADVOCATE: I alluded in page 18, line 18, to the real reason for our anxiety to persuade widows to follow their husbands, and for our endeavours to burn them pressed down with ropes; namely, that women are by nature of inferior understanding, without resolution, unworthy of trust, subject to passions, and void of virtuous knowledge; they, according to the precepts of the Shastru [shastra], are not allowed to marry again after the demise of their husbands, and consequently despair at once of all worldly pleasure; hence it is evident that death to these unfortunate widows is preferable to existence, for the great difficulty which a widow may experience by living a purely ascetic life as prescribed by the Shastrus is obvious; therefore if she does not perform concremation, it is probable that she may be guilty of such acts as may bring disgrace upon her paternal and maternal relation, and those that may be connected with her husband. Under these circumstances we instruct them from their early life in the idea of concremation, holding out to them heavenly enjoyments in company with their husbands, as well as the beatitude of their relations, both by birth and marriage, and their reputation in this world. From this many of them, on the death of their husbands, become desirous of accompanying them; but to remove every chance of their trying to escape from the blazing fire, in burning them we first tie them down to the pile.

OPPONENT: The reason you have now assigned for burning widows alive is indeed your true motive, as we are well aware; but the faults which you have imputed to women are not planted in their constitution by nature. It would be therefore grossly criminal to condemn that sex to death merely from precaution. By ascribing to them all sorts of improper conduct, you have indeed successfully persuaded the Hindoo community to look down upon them as contemptible and mischievous creatures, whence they have been subjected to constant miseries. I have therefore to offer a few remarks on this head. Women are in general inferior to men in bodily strength and energy; consequently the male part of the community, taking advantage of their corporeal weakness, have denied to them those excellent merits that they are entitled to by nature, and afterwards they are apt to say that women are naturally incapable of acquiring those merits. But if we give the subject consideration, we may easily ascertain whether or not your accusation against them is consistent with justice. As to their inferiority in point of understanding, when did you ever afford them a fair opportunity of exhibiting their natural capacity? How then can you accuse them of want of understanding? If after instruction in knowledge and wisdom a person cannot comprehend or retain what has been taught him, we may consider him as deficient; but as you keep women generally void of education and acquirements, you cannot therefore in justice pronounce on their inferiority. On the contrary, Leelavutee [Lilāvatī], Bhanoomutee [Bhānumatī](the wife of the Prince of Kurnat) and that of Kalidas, are celebrated for their thorough knowledge of the Shastrus: moreover in the Vrihudarunyuk Oopunishad [Bṛhadārāṇyaka Upaniṣad] of the Ujoor Ved [Yajur Veda] it is clearly stated, that Yagnuvulkyu [Yājñavalkya] imparted divine knowledge of the most difficult nature to his wife Muitreyee [Maitreyī], who was able to follow and completely attain it!

Secondly. You charge them with want of resolution, at which I feel exceedingly surprised. For we constantly perceive in a country where the name of death makes the male shudder, that the female from her firmness of mind offers to burn with the corpse of her deceased husband; and yet you accuse those women of deficiency in point of resolution.

Thirdly. With regard to their trustworthiness, let us look minutely into the conduct of both sexes, and we may be enabled to ascertain which of them is the most frequently guilty of betraying friends. If we enumerate such women in each village or town as have been deceived by men, and such men as have been betrayed by women, I presume that the number of deceived women would be found ten times greater than that of the betrayed men. Men are in general able to read and write and manage public affairs, by which means they easily promulgate such faults as women occasionally commit, but never consider as criminal the misconduct of men towards women. One fault they have, it must be acknowledged; which is, by considering others equally void of duplicity as themselves to give their confidence too readily, from which they suffer much misery, even so far that some of them are misled to suffer themselves to be burnt to death.

In the fourth place, with respect to their subjection to the passions, this may be judged of by the custom of marriage as to the respective sexes; for one man may marry two or three, sometimes even ten wives and upwards; while a woman, who marries but one husband, desires at his death to follow him, forsaking all worldly enjoyments, or to remain leading the austere life of an ascetic.

Fifthly. The accusation of their want of virtuous knowledge is an injustice. Observe what pain, what slighting, what contempt, and what afflictions their virtue enables them to support! How many Kooleen [Kulīna] Brahmans are there who marry ten or fifteen wives for the sake of money, that never see the greater number of them after the day of marriage, and visit others only three or four times in the course of their life. Still amongst those women, most, even without seeing or receiving any support from their husbands, living dependent on their fathers or brothers, and suffering much distress, continue to preserve their virtue. And when Brahmans or those of other tribes bring their wives to live with them, what misery do the women not suffer? At marriage the wife is recognized as half of her husband, but in after conduct they are treated worse than inferior animals. For the woman is employed to do the work of a slave in the house, such as in her turn to clean the place very early in the morning, whether cold or wet, to scour the dishes, to wash the floor, to cook night and day, to prepare and serve food for her husband, father, and mother-in-law, sisters-in-law, brothers-in-law, and friends and connections! (For amongst Hindoos more than in other tribes relations long reside together, and on this account quarrels are more common amongst brothers respecting their worldly affairs.) If in the preparation or serving up of the victuals they commit the smallest fault, what insult do they not receive from their husband, their mother-in-law, and the younger brothers of their husband? After all the male part of the family have satisfied themselves, the women content themselves with what may be left, whether sufficient in quantity or not. Where Brahmans or Kayustus [Kāyasthas] are not wealthy, their women are obliged to attend to their cows, and to prepare the cow dung for firing. In the afternoon they fetch water from the river or tank, and at night perform the office of menial servants in making the beds. In case of any fault or omission in the performance of those labours, they receive injurious treatment. Should the husband acquire wealth, he indulges in criminal amours to her perfect knowledge and almost under her eyes, and does not see her perhaps once a month. As long as the husband is poor she suffers every kind of trouble and when he becomes rich she is altogether heartbroken. All this pain and affliction their virtue alone enables them to support. Where a husband takes two or three wives to live with him, they are subjected to mental miseries and constant quarrels. Even this distressed situation they virtuously endure. Sometimes it happens that the husband, from a preference for one of his wives, behaves cruelly to another. Amongst the lower classes, and those even of the better class who have not associated with good company, the wife on the slightest fault, or even on bare suspicion of her misconduct, is chastised as a thief. Respect to virtue and their reputation generally makes them forgive even this treatment. If, unable to bear such cruel usage, a wife leaves her husband's house to live separately from him, then the influence of the husband with the magisterial authority is generally sufficient to place her again in his hands; when, in revenge for her quitting him, he seizes every pretext to torment her in various ways, and sometimes even puts her privately to death. These are facts occurring every day, and not to be denied. What I lament is, that seeing the women thus dependent and exposed to every misery, you feel for them no compassion, that might exempt them from being tied down and burnt to death.[17]

Rammohun Roy, The Condition of Women and Human Rights

The world is now accustomed to using the term human rights, perhaps too frequently. Scholars have expressed surprise at the ease with which Indians could switch from the idiom of duty to the idiom of rights in modern discourse.[18] This is already apparent in Roy.

Brief Remarks Regarding Modern Encroachments on the Ancient Rights of Females According to the Hindu Law of Inheritance

With a view to enable the public to form an idea of the state of civilization throughout the greater part of the empire of Hindustan in ancient days, and of the subsequent gradual degradation introduced into its social and political constitution by arbitrary authorities, I am induced to give as an instance, the interest and care which our ancient legislators took in the promotion of the comfort of the female part of the community; and to compare the laws of female inheritance which they enacted, and which afforded that sex the opportunity of enjoyment of life, with that which moderns and our contemporaries have gradually introduced and established, to their complete privation, directly or indirectly of most of those objects that render life agreeable.

All the ancient lawgivers unanimously awarded to a mother an equal share with her son in the property left by her deceased husband, in order that she may spend her remaining days independently of her children, as is evident from the following passages:

YAJNAVALKYA: After the death of a father, let a mother also inherit an equal share with her sons in the division of the property *left by their father.*

KATYAYANA: The father being dead, the mother should inherit an equal share with the son.

NARADA: After the death of husband, a mother would receive a share equal to that of each of his sons.

VISHNU THE LEGISLATOR: Mothers should be receivers of shares according to the portion allowed to the sons.

VRIHASPATI: After his (the father's) death a mother, the parent of his sons, should be entitled to an equal share with his sons; their step-mothers also to equal shares: but daughters to a fourth part of the shares of the sons.

VYASA: The wives of a father by whom he has no male issue, are considered as entitled to equal shares with his sons, and all the grand-mothers (*including the mothers and step-mothers of the father*), are said to be entitled as mothers.

This Muni seems to have made this express *declaration of rights* of step-mothers, omitting those of mothers, under the ideas that the latter were already sufficiently established by the direct authority of preceding lawgivers.

We come to the moderns.

The author of the Dayabhaga and the writer of the Dayatattwa, the modern expounders of Hindu law (whose opinions are considered by the natives of Bengal as standard authority in the division of property among heirs) have thus limited the rights allowed to widows by the above ancient legislators. When a person is willing to divide his property among his heirs during his lifetime, he should entitle only those wives by whom he has no issue, to an equal share with his sons; but if he omit such a division, those wives can have no claim to the property he leaves. These two modern expounders lay stress upon a passage of Yajnavalkya, which requires a father to allot equal shares to his wives, in case he divides his property during his life, whereby they connect the term 'of a father,' in the above quoted passage of Vyasa, *viz.* 'the wives of a father, &c.,' with the term 'division' understood, that is, the wives by whom he has no son, are considered in the division made by a father, as entitled to equal shares with his sons; and that when sons may divide property among themselves after the demise of their father, they should give an equal share to their mother only, neglecting step-mothers in the division. Here the expounders did not take into their consideration any proper provision for step-mothers, who have naturally less hope of support from their step-sons than mothers can expect from their own children.

In the opinion of these expounders even a mother of a single son should not be entitled to any share. The whole property should, in that case, devolve on the son; and in case that son should die after the succession to the property, his son or wife should inherit it. The mother in that case should be left totally dependent on her son or on her son's wife. Besides, according to the opinion of these expounders, if more than one son should survive, they can deprive their mother of her title, by continuing to live as a joint family (which has been often the case) as the right of a mother depends, as they say, on division, which depends on the will of the sons.

Some of our contemporaries (whose opinion is received as a verdict by Judical Courts) have still further reduced the right of a mother to almost nothing, declaring, as I understand, that if a person die, leaving a widow and a son or sons, and also one or more grandsons, whose father is not alive, the property so left is to be divided among his sons and his grandsons, his widow in this case being entitled to no share in the property, though she might have claimed an equal share, had a division taken place among those surviving sons and the father of the grandson while he was alive. They are said to have founded their opinion on the above passage, entitling a widow to a share when property is to be divided among *sons*.

In short a widow, according to the exposition of the law, can receive nothing when her husband has no issue by her; and in case he dies leaving only one son by his wife, or having had more sons, one of whom happened to die leaving issue, she shall, in these cases, also have no claim to the property; and again, should any one leave more than one surviving son, and they, being unwilling to allow a share to the widow, keep the property undivided, the mother can claim nothing in this instance also. But when a person dies, leaving two or more sons, and all of them survive and be inclined to allot a share to their mother, her right is in this case only valid. Under these expositions, and with such limitations, both step-mothers and mothers have, in reality, been left destitute in the division of their husband's property, and the right of a widow exists in theory only among the learned, but unknown to the populace.

The consequence is, that a woman who is looked up to as the sole mistress by the rest of a family one day, on the next, becomes dependent on her sons, and subject to slights of her daughters-in-law. She is not authorized to expend the most trifling sum or dispose of an article of the least value, without the consent of her son or daughter-in-law, who were all subject to her authority but the day before. Cruel sons often wound the feelings of their dependent mothers, deciding in favour of their own wives, when family disputes take place between their mother and wives. Step-mothers, who often are numerous on account of polygamy being allowed in these countries, are still more shamefully neglected in general by their step-sons, and sometimes dreadfully treated by their sisters-in-law who have fortunately a son or sons by their husband.

It is not from religious prejudices and early impressions only, that Hindu widows burn themselves on the piles of their deceased husbands, but also from their witnessing the distress in which widows of the same rank in life are involved, and the insults and slights to which they are daily subjected, that they become in a great measure regardless of their existence after the death of their husbands: and this indifference, accompanied with the hope of future reward held out to them, leads them to the horrible act of suicide. These restraints on female inheritance encourage, in a great degree, polygamy, a frequent source of the greatest misery in native families; a grand object of Hindus being to secure a provision for their male offspring, the law, which relieves them from the necessity of giving an equal portion to their wives, removes a principal restraint on the indulgence of their inclinations in respect to the number they marry. Some of them, especially Brahmans of higher birth, marry ten, twenty or thirty women, either for some small consideration, or merely to gratify their brutal inclinations, leaving a great many of them, both during their life-time and after their death, to the mercy of their own paternal relations. The evil consequences arising from such polygamy, the public may easily guess, from the nature of the fact itself, without my being reduced to the mortification of particularising those which are known by the native public to be of daily occurrence.

To these women there are left only three modes of conduct to pursue after the death of their husband. 1st. To live a miserable life as entire slaves to others, without indulging any hope of support from another husband. 2ndly. To walk in the paths of unrighteousness for their maintenance and independence. 3rdly. To die on the funeral pile of their husbands, loaded with the applause and honour of their neighbours. It cannot pass unnoticed by those who are acquainted with the state of society in India, that the number of female suicides in the single province of Bengal, when compared with those of any other British provinces, is almost ten to one: we may safely attribute this disproportion chiefly to the greater frequency of a plurality of wives among the natives of Bengal, and to their total neglect in providing for the maintenance of their females.

This horrible polygamy among Brahmans is directly contrary to the law given by ancient authors; for Yajnavalkya authorizes second marriages, while the first wife is alive, only under eight circumstances: 1st. The vice of drinking spirituous liquors. 2ndly. Incurable sickness. 3rdly. Deception. 4thly. Barrenness. 5thly. Extravagance. 6thly. The frequent use of offensive language. *7thly*. Producing only female offsprings. Or, *8thly*. Manifestation of hatred towards her husband.

> MANU, ch. 9, v. 80: A wife who drinks any spirituous liquors, who acts immorally, who shows hatred *to her lord*, who is *incurably diseased*, who is mischievous, who wastes his property, may at all times be superseded by another wife.

> v. 81: A barren wife may be superseded by another in the eighth year; she, whose children are all dead, in the tenth; she, who brings forth *only* daughters, in the eleventh; she, who is accustomed to speak unkindly, without delay.

> v. 82: But she, though afflicted with illness, is beloved and virtuous, must never be disgraced, though she may be superseded by another wife with her own consent.

Had a magistrate or other public officer been authorized by the rulers of the empire to receive applications for his sanctions to a second marriage during the life of a first wife, and to grant his consent only on such accusations as the foregoing being substantiated, the above Law might have been rendered effectual, and the distress of the female sex in Bengal, and the number of suicides, would have been necessarily very much reduced.

According to the following ancient authorities, a daughter is entitled to one-fourth part of the portion which a son can inherit.

> VRIHASPATI: The daughters should have the fourth part of the portion to *which the sons are entitled*.

> VISHNU: The rights of unmarried daughters shall be proportioned according to the shares allotted to the sons.

> MANU, ch. 9, v. 118: To the unmarried daughters let their brothers give portions out of their own allotments respectively. Let each give a fourth part of his own distinct share, and they who feel disinclined to give this shall be condemned.

> YAJNAVALKYA: Let such brothers as are already purified by the essential rites of life, purify by the performance of those rites the brothers that are left *by their late father* unpurified; let them also purify the sisters by giving them a fourth part of their own portion.

> KATYAYANA: A fourth part is declared to be the share of unmarried daughters, and three-fourth of the sons; if the fourth part of the property is *so* small *as to be inadequate to defray the expenses attending their marriage, the sons have an exclusive* right to the property, *but shall defray the marriage ceremony of the sisters*.

But the commentator on the Dayabhaga sets aside the right of the daughters, declaring that they are not entitled to any share in the property left by their fathers, but that the expenses attending their marriage should be defrayed by the brothers. He founds his opinion on the foregoing passage of Manu and that of Yajnavalkya, which as he thinks, imply mere donation on the part of the brothers from their own portions for the discharge of the expenses of marriage.

In the practice of our contemporaries a daughter or a sister is often a source of emolument to the Brahmans of less respectable caste (who are most numerous in Bengal) and to the Kayasthas of high caste. These so far from spending money on the marriage of their daughters or sisters, receive frequently considerable sums, and generally bestow them in marriage on those who can pay most. Such Brahmans and Kayasthas, I regret to say, frequently marry their female relations to men having natural defects or worn-out by old age or disease, merely from pecuniary considerations, whereby they either bring widowhood upon them soon after marriage or render their lives miserable. They not only degrade themselves by such cruel and unmanly conduct, but violate entirely the express authorities of Manu and all other ancient law-givers, a few of which I here quote.

MANU, ch. 3, v. 51: Let no father, who knows the law, receive a gratuity, however small, for giving his daughter in marriage; since the man, who, through avarice, takes a gratuity *for that purpose*, is a seller of his offspring.

ch. 9, v. 98: But even a man of the servile class ought not to receive a gratuity when he gives his daughter in marriage, since a father who takes a fee *on that occasion*, tacitly sells his daughter.

v. 100: Nor, even in former births, have we heard the *virtuous approve* the tacit sale of a daughter for a price, under the name of nuptial gratuity.

KASAPA: Those who, infatuated by avarice, give their own daughters in marriage, for the sake of a gratuity, are the sellers of their daughters, the images of sin, and the perpetrators of a heinous iniquity.

Both common sense, and the law of the land designate such a practice as an actual sale of females; and the humane and liberal among Hindus, lament its existence, as well as the annihilation of female rights in respect of inheritance introduced by modern expounders. They, however, trust, that the humane attention of Government will be directed to those evils which are the chief sources of vice and misery and even of suicide among women; and to this they are encouraged to look forward by what has already been done in modifying, in criminal cases, some parts of the law enacted by Muhammadan Legislators, to the happy prevention of many cruel practices formerly established.

How distressing it must be to the female community and to those who interest themselves on their behalf, to observe daily that several daughters in a rich family can prefer no claim to any portion of the property, whether real or personal, left by their deceased father, if a single brother be alive: while they (if belonging to a Kulin family or Brahman of higher rank) are exposed to be given in marriage to individuals who have already several wives and have no means of maintaining them.

Should a widow or a daughter wish to secure her right of maintenance, however limited, by having recourse to law, the learned Brahmans, whether holding public situations in the courts or not, generally divide into two parties, one advocating the cause of those females and the other that of their adversaries. Sometimes in these or .other matters respecting the law, if the object contended for be important, the whole community seems to be agitated by the exertions of the parties and of their respective friends in claiming the verdict of the law against each other. In general, however, a consideration of the difficulties attending a law suit, which a native woman, particularly a widow, is hardly capable of surmounting, induces her to forego her right: and if she continue virtuous, she is obliged to live in a miserable state of dependence, destitute of all the comforts of life; it too often happens, however, that she is driven by constant unhappiness to seek refuge in vice.

At the time of the decennial settlement in the year 1793, there were among European gentlemen so very few acquainted with Sanskrit and Hindu law that it would have been hardly possible to have formed a committee of European oriental scholars and learned Brahmans, capable of deciding on points of Hindu law. It was, therefore, highly judicious in Government to appoint Pandits in the different Zillah Courts of Appeal, to facilitate the proceedings of Judges in regard to such subjects. But as we can now fortunately find many European gentlemen capable of investigating legal questions with but little assistance from learned Natives, how happy would it be for the Hindu community, both male and female, were they to enjoy the benefits of the opinion of such gentlemen, when disputes arise, particularly on matters of inheritance.

Lest any one should infer from what I have stated, that I mean to impeach, universally, the character of the great body of learned Hindus, I declare positively, that this is far from my intention. I only maintain, that the Native community place greater confidence in the honest judgment of European gentlemen than in that of their own countrymen. But, should the Natives receive the same advantages of education that Europeans generally enjoy, and be brought up in the same notions of honour, they will, I trust, be found, equally with Europeans, worthy of the confidence of their countrymen and the respect of all men.[19]

Roy, The Future of India and Indian Independence in the Future

Rammohun Roy's views about British rule over India possessed a dimension perhaps pragmatic in his times, though unlikely to endear him to his countrymen now. R.C. Majumdar remarks: 'Rammohun practically reconciled his love of freedom in the abstract with India's subservience to the British rule. The philosophy behind it was clearly expounded by Rammohun to Victor Jacquemont. "Is not," he asked Jacquemont "this fiery love of national independence a chimera?"'[20] Then he added:

Conquest is very rarely an evil when the conquering people are more civilized than the conquered, because the former bring to [the] latter the benefits of civilisation. India requires many more years of English domination so that she may not have many things to lose while she is reclaiming her political independence.[21]

He was, however, not oblivious of that prospect, as when he wrote:

Supposing that one hundred years hence the native character becomes elevated from constant intercourse with Europeans and the acquirement of general and political knowledge as well as of modern arts and sciences, is it possible, that they [Indians] will not have the spirit as well as the inclination to resist effectually any unjust and oppressive measures serving to degrade them in the scale of society? It should not be lost sight of that the position of India is very different from that of Ireland, to any quarter of which an English fleet may suddenly convey a body of troops that may force its way in the requisite direction and succeed in suppressing every effort of a refractory spirit. Were India to share one-fourth of the knowledge and energy of that country, she would prove from her remote situation, her riches and her vast population, either useful and profitable as a willing province, an ally of the British empire, or troublesome and annoying as a determined enemy.

In common with those who seem partial to the British rule from the expectation of future benefits arising out of the connection, I necessarily feel extremely grieved in often witnessing acts and regulations passed by government without consulting or seeming to understand the feelings of its Indian subjects and without considering that this people have had for more than half a century the advantage of being ruled by and associated with an enlightened nation, advocates of liberty and promoters of knowledge.[22]

Roy's Stand Against Sati

The following passage is an abridged account of Roy's brief against Sati.

Abstract of the Argument, & C.

Several Essays, Tracts, and Letters, written in defence of or against the practice of burning Hindu widows alive have for some years past attracted the attention of the public. The arguments therein adduced by the parties being necessarily scattered, a complete view of the question cannot be easily attained by such readers as are precluded by their immediate avocations from bestowing much labour in acquiring information on the subject. Although the practice itself has now happily ceased to exist under the government of Bengal, nevertheless it seems still desirable that the substance of those publications should be condensed in a concise but comprehensive manner, so that enquirer may with little difficulty, be able to form a just conclusion, as to the true light in which this practice is viewed in the religion of Hindus. I have, therefore, made an attempt to accomplish this object, hoping that the plan pursued may be found to answer this end.

The first point to be ascertained is, whether or not the practice of burning widows alive on the pile and with the corpse of their husbands, is imperatively enjoyed by the Hindu religion? To this question even the staunch advocates for Concremation must reluctantly give a negative reply, and unavoidably concede the practice to the option of widows. This admission on their part is owing to two principal considerations, which it is now too late for them to feign to overlook. First, because Manu in plain terms enjoins a widow to '*continue till death* forgiving all injuries, performing austere duties, avoiding every sensual pleasure, and cheerfully practising the incomparable rules of virtue which have been followed by such women as were devoted to one only husband.' (ch. v., v. 158.) So Yajnavalkya inculcates the same doctrine: 'A widow shall live under care of her father, mother, son, brother, mother-in-law, father-in-law, or uncle; since, on the contrary, she shall be liable to reproach.' (*Vide* Mitakshara, ch. i.) Secondly, because an attempt on the part of the advocates for Concremation to hold out the act as an incumbent duty on widows, would necessarily bring a stigma upon the character of the living widows, who have preferred a virtuous life to Concremation, as charging them with a violation of the duty said to be indispensible. These advocates, therefore, feel deterred from giving undue praise to a few widows, choosing death on the pile, to the disgrace of a vast majority of that class preferring a virtuous life. And in consideration of these obvious circumstances, the celebrated Smartta Raghunandana, the latest commentator on Hindu Law in Bengal, found himself compelled to expound the following passage of Angira, 'there is no other course for a widow besides Concremation,' as 'conveying exaggerated praise of the adoption of that course.'

The second point is, that in case the alternative be admitted, that a widow may either live a virtuous life, or burn herself on the pile of her husband, it should next be determined whether both practices are esteemed equally meritorious, or one be declared preferable to the other. To satisfy ourselves on this question, we should first refer to the Vedas whose authority is considered paramount, and we find in them a passage most pointed and decisive against Concremation, declaring that 'From a desire, during life, of future fruition, life ought not to be destroyed.' (*Vide* Mitakshara, ch. i.) While the advocates of Concremation quote a passage from the Vedas, of a very abstruse nature, in support of their position, which is as follows: 'Oh fire, let these women, with bodies anointed with clarified butter, eyes coloured with collyrium and void of tears, enter thee, the parent of water, that they may not be separated from their husbands, themselves sinless, and jewels amongst women.' This passage (if genuine) does not, in the first place, enjoin widows to offer themselves as sacrifices, secondly, no allusion whatever is made in it to voluntary death by a widow *with the corpse of her husband*; thirdly, the phrase 'these women' in the passage, literally implies women then present; fourthly, some commentators consider the passage as conveying an allegorical allusion to the constellations of the moon's path, which are invariably spoken of in Sanskrit in the feminine gender:— butter implying the milky path, collyrium meaning unoccupied space between one star and another, husbands signifying the more splendid of the heavenly bodies, and entering the fire, or, properly speaking, ascending it, indicating the rise of the constellations through the south-east horizon, considered as the abode of fire. Whatever may be the real purport of this passage, no one ever ventured to give it an interpretation as *commending* widows to burn themselves on the pile and with the corpse of their husbands.

We next direct attention to the Smriti, as next in authority to the Vedas. Manu, whose authority supersedes that of other lawgivers, adjoins widows to live a virtuous life, as already quoted. Yajnavalkya and some others have adopted the same mode of exhortation. On the other hand, Angira recommends the practice of Concremation, saying, 'That a woman who, on the death of her husband, *ascends the burning pile* with him, is exalted to heaven, as equal to Arundhati.' So Vyasa says, 'A pigeon devoted to her husband, after his death, *entered the flames*, and, ascending to heaven, she there found her husband.' 'She who follows her husband to another world, shall dwell in a region of glory for so many years as there are hairs in the human body, or thirty-five millions.' Vishnu, the saint, lays down this rule, 'After the death of her husband, a wife should live as an ascetic or ascend his pile.' Harita and others have followed Angira in recommending Concremation.

The above quoted passages, from Angira and others, recommend Concremation on the part of widows, as means to obtain future carnal fruition; and, accordingly, previous to their ascent on the pile, all widows invariably and solemnly declare future fruition as their object in Concremation. But the Bhagavadgita, whose authority is considered the most sacred by Hindus of all persuasions, repeatedly condemns rites performed for fruition. I here quote a few passages of that book. 'All those ignorant persons who attach themselves to the words of the Sastras that convey promises of fruition, consider those extravagant and alluring passages as leading to real happiness, and say, besides them there is no other reality. Agitated in their minds by these desires, they believe the abodes of the celestial gods to be the chief object, and they devote themselves to those texts which treat of ceremonies and their fruits, and entice by promises of enjoyment. Such people can have no real confidence in the Supreme Being.' 'Observers of rites, after the completion of their rewards, return to earth. Therefore they, for the sake of rewards, repeatedly ascend to heaven and return to the world, and cannot obtain eternal bliss.'

Manu repeats the same. 'Whatever act is performed for the sake of gratification in this world or the next, is called Pravartak, as leading to temporary enjoyment of the mansions of gods; and those which are performed according to the knowledge respecting God are called Nivartak, as means to procure release from the five elements of this body; that is, they obtain eternal bliss.'

The author of the Mitakshara, a work which is considered as a standard of Hindu Law throughout Hindustan, referring on the one hand to the authority of Manu, Yajnavalkya, the Bhagavadgita, and similar sacred writings, and to the passages of Angira, Harita and Vyasa on the other hand, and after having weighed both sides of the question, declared that 'The widow who is not desirous of eternal beatitude, but who wishes only for a perishable and small degree of future fruition, is authorized to accompany her husband.' So that the Smartta Raghunandana, the modern expounder of Law of Bengal, classes Concremation among the rites holding out promises of fruition; and this author thus inculcates: 'Learned men should not endeavour to persuade the ignorant to perform rites holding out promises of fruition.' Hence, Concremation in their opinion, is the least virtuous act that a widow can perform.

The third and the last point to be ascertained is whether or not *the mode* of Concremation prescribed by Harita and others was ever duly observed. The passages recommending Concremation is quoted by these expounders of law, require that a widow, resolving to die after the demise of her husband, should *voluntarily ascend and enter the flames to destroy her existence*; allowing her, at the same time, an opportunity of retracting her resolution, should her courage fail from the alarming sight or effect of the flames, and of returning to their relatives, performing a penance for abandoning the sacrifice, or bestowing the value of a cow on a Brahman. Hence, as *voluntarily ascending* upon and *entering into the flames* are described as indispensably necessary for a widow in the performance of this rite, the violation of one of these provisions renders the act mere suicide, and implicates, in the guilt of female murder, those that assist in its perpetration, even according to the above quoted authorities, which are themselves of an inferior order. But no one will venture to assert, that the provisions, prescribed in the passages adduced, have ever been observed; that is, no widow has ever voluntarily *ascended* on and *entered* into the *flames* in the fulfilment of this rite. The advocates for Concremation have been consequently driven to the necessity of taking refuge in *usage*, as justifying both suicide and female murder, the most heinous of crimes.

We should not omit the present opportunity of offering up thanks to Heaven, whose protecting arm has rescued our weaker sex from cruel murder, under the cloak of religion, and our character, as a people, from the contempt and pity with which it has been regarded, on account of this custom, by all civilized nations on the surface of the globe.[23]

Roy as Trendsetter in Hindu Studies

Roy, in many ways, set trends in motion which characterized the Hindu renaissance. This is well known. He also set certain other trends whose association with him is less obvious. One such is the trend among educated Indians who at times applaud and at other times fault Western Indology. In the selection below, he applauds William Jones first and then criticizes him. In another extract he criticizes Colebrooke.

While translating this essay on the Gayatri, I deemed it proper to refer to the meaning of the text as given by Sir William Jones, whose talents, acquisitions, virtuous life, and impartial research, have rendered his memory an object of love and veneration to all. I feel so much delighted by the excellence of the translation, or rather the paraphrase, given by that illustrious character, that with a view to connect his name and his explanation of the passage with this humble treatise, I take the liberty of quoting it here.

The interpretation in question is as follows:

The Gayatri, or Holiest Verse of the Vedas
Let us adore the supremacy of that divine sun, the god-head who illuminates all, who recreates all, from whom all proceed, to whom all must return, whom we invoke to direct our understandings aright in our progress toward his holy seat.[24]

Manu, the most ancient authority, thus defines their limits. 'The lands lying as far as the eastern and as far as the western oceans, *and* between the mountains just mentioned (Himalaya and Vindhya) are known to the wise by the name of "Aryavarta" or the land inhabited by respectable people.' Ch. II, v. 22.

In his translation of this passage, Sir William Jones, by omitting to refer to the commentary, which substitutes the copulative Sanskrit particle 'Cha' for 'Eba,' has thus translated this passage: 'As far as the eastern and as far as the western oceans, between the two mountains just mentioned, lies the tract which the wise have named Aryavarta.' This rendered the description obscure, if not wholly unintelligible; since the countries lying between these two ranges of mountains, are scarcely situated between the eastern and western seas.[25]

To the Editor of the Bengal Hurkaru and Chronicle.
Sir,
Your learned correspondent, 'A Hindoo' introduces the subject of a last Will and Testament in his letter which appeared in your journal

of the 5th instant, questioning the validity of such instruments, on the authority of the following language of Mr Colebrooke: 'A last Will and Testament is *unknown to the Hindu* Law, but it has been introduced in this country *since the establishment of the British power*, and we only admit its validity wherein we see no discrepancies with the Hindoo Law.' I much regret that Mr Colebrooke, an eminent scholar, and diligent student of Hindu Law, while offering the above opinion, should have overlooked the very first part of the gloss on the Dayabhaga, by Sri Krishna, which he 'chiefly and preferably used,' and which, in the preface to his translation of that work (page 6) he characterises as 'the most celebrated of the glosses on the text.' 'Its authority has been long gaining ground in the schools of law throughout Bengal, and it has almost banished from them the other expositions of the Dayabhaga, being ranked, in general estimation, next after the treatises of Jimutavahana and of Raghunandana.' The passage I allude to is to be found in that celebrated gloss, expounding the purport of Sec. 38, Ch. I of the Dayabhaga.

Nor does this learned gentleman seem to have recollected his own translation of the same passage, which runs in these words: 'But when he, for the sake of obviating disputes among his sons, determines their respective allotments, continuing, however, the exercises of power over them, that is not partition, for his property still subsists, since there has been no relinquishment of it on his part. Therefore the use of the term partition, in such an instance, is lax and indeterminate.' That is, in this instance the father *does not separate his sons from himself with allotments*; he only declares what certain portion of his property each son is to enjoy immediately after the extinction of his ownership by death, civil or natural; such previously determined division, therefore, cannot in reality be styled *partition* during the life of the father, which implies separation, and consequently does not fall within that only case in which his privileges over ancestral property are restricted.

To shew the priority of Sri Krishna's era to the British conquest of India I beg to refer to the Preface to the translation of the Dayabhaga, by Mr Colebrooke, (page 7 and the note therein contained) giving an account of the probable periods at which Sri Krishna and some other commentators of the Dayabhaga lived. They shew clearly that Sri Krishna, whose authority is esteemed next to that of Jimutavahana, existed and died before the *establishment of British power* in India. How then, Mr Editor, could Sri Krishna declare the *law* on the point, if the practice of a father's prescribing the manner of distributing his property after his ownership should be extinct, was unknown at his time?[26]

Roy, however, also seems to be following in William Jones' Indo-European footsteps when he states the following, though what he says is purely speculative.

The first term 'Om' bears a striking similarity, both in sound and application, to the participle *wv* of the verb *Elul to be*, in Greek; and it is therefore not very improbable that one might have had its origin from the other. As to the similarity in sound, it is too obvious to require illustration; and a reference to the Septuagint will shew that *wv* like 'Om' is applied to Jehova the ever existing God. Exodus iii. 14.[27]

Roy offers the following explanation of how the spiritual and temporal realms came to be assigned to the Brāhmaṇas and the Kṣatriyas respectively. This attempt to extract history from the mine of myth also set a trend which continues to this day.

At an early age of civilization, when the division into castes was first introduced among the inhabitants of India, the second tribe who were appointed to defend and rule the country, having adopted arbitrary and despotic practices, the others revolted against them; and under the personal command of the celebrated Parasuram, defeated the Royalists in several battles, and put cruelly to death almost all the males of that tribe. It was at last resolved that the legislative authority should be confined to the first class who could have no share in the actual government of the state, or in managing the revenue of the country under any pretence, while the second tribe should exercise the executive authority. The consequence was, that India enjoyed peace and harmony for a great many centuries. The Brahmans having no expectation of holding an office, or of partaking of any kind of political promotion, devoted their time to scientific pursuits and religious austerity, and lived in poverty. Freely associating with all the other tribes they were thus able to know their sentiments, and to appreciate the justness of their complaints, and thereby to lay down such rules as were required, which often induced them to rectify the abuses that were practised by the second tribe. But after the expiration of more than two thousand years, an absolute form of government came gradually again to prevail. The first class having been induced to accept employments in political departments, became entirely dependent on the second tribe, and so unimportant in themselves, that they were obliged to explain away the laws enacted by their fore-fathers, and to institute new rules according to the dictates of their contemporary princes. They were considered as merely nominal legislators, and the whole power whether legislative or executive, was in fact exercised by the Rajputs. This tribe exercised tyranny and oppression for a period of about a thousand years, when Musulmans from Ghuznee and Ghore, invaded the country, and finding it divided among hundreds of petty princes, detested by their respective subjects, conquered them all successively, and introduced their own tyrannical system of government, destroying temples, universities and all other sacred and literary establishments. At present the whole empire (with the exception of a few provinces) has been placed under the British power, and some advantages have already been derived from the prudent management of its rulers, from whose general character a hope of future quiet and happiness is justly entertained. The succeeding generation will, however, be more adequate to pronounce on the real advantages of this government.[28]

As a reformist too Roy set another trend connected with Hinduism. This involves the selective use of scriptural verses in discourse or prayer, a practice made famous by Mahatma Gandhi. Although most scholars trace this tradition of selecting appropriate texts from various scriptures for liturgical use to Devendranath Tagore,[29] the following sample suggests that this tradition could perhaps be traced back to Roy. Therein, for each answer, Roy provides a scriptural prooftext in Sanskrit.

Religious Instructions Founded on Sacred Authorities

The following Treatise, in the form of questions and answers, contains a brief account of the worship enjoined in the sacred writings, as due to that Being who is pure as well as eternal, and to whose existence Nature gives testimony; that the faithful may easily understand and become successful in the practice of this worship. The proof of each doctrine may be found, according to the figures, in the end of the work.

As this subject is almost always expounded, in the sacred writings, by means of questions and answers, that it may be more easily comprehended, a similar plan is adopted in this place also.

1 QUESTION: What is meant by worship?

ANSWER: Worship implies the act of one with a view to please another; but when applied to the Supreme Being, it signifies a contemplation of his attributes.

2 Q: To whom is worship due?

A: To the Author and Governor of the universe, which is incomprehensibly formed, and filled with an endless variety of men and things; in which, as shown by the zodiac, in a manner far more wonderful than the machinery of a watch, the sun, the moon, the planets and the stars perform their rapid courses; and which is fraught with animate and inanimate matter of various kinds, locomotive and immoveable, of which there is not one particle but has its functions to perform.

3 Q: What is he?

A: We have already mentioned that he is to be worshipped, who is the Author and Governor of the universe; yet, neither the sacred writings nor logical argument, can define his nature.

4 Q: Are there no means of defining him?

A: It is repeatedly declared in the sacred writings, that he cannot be defined either by the intellect or by language. This appears from inference also; for, though the universe is visible, still no one can ascertain its form or extent. How then can we define the Being whom we designate as its Author and Governor?

5 Q: Is any one, on sufficient grounds, opposed to this worship?

A: To this worship no one can be opposed on sufficient grounds; for, as we all worship the Supreme Being, adoring him as the Author and Governor of the universe, it is impossible for anyone to object to such worship; because each person considers the object whom he worships as the Author and Governor of the universe; therefore, in accordance with his own faith, he must acknowledge that this worship is his own. In the same manner, they, who consider Time or Nature, or any other Object, as the Governor of the universe, even they cannot be opposed to this worship, as bearing in mind the Author and Governor of the universe. And in China, in Tartary, in Europe, and in all other countries, where so many sects exist, all believe the object whom they adore to be the Author and Governor of the universe; consequently, they also must acknowledge, according to their own faith, that this our worship is their own.

6 Q: In some places in the sacred writings it is written that the Supreme Being is imperceptible and unexpressible; and in others, that he is capable of being known. How can this be reconciled?

A: Where it is written that he is imperceptible and undefinable, it is meant, that his likeness cannot be conceived; and where it is said that he is capable of being known, his mere existence is referred to, that is, that there is a God, as the indescribable creation and government of this universe clearly demonstrate: in the same manner, as by the action of a body, we ascertain the existence of a spirit therein called the sentient soul, but the form or likeness of that spirit which pervades every limb and guides the body, we know not.

7 Q: Are you hostile to any other worship?

A: Certainly not; for, he who worships, be it whomsoever or whatsoever it may, considers that object as the Supreme Being, or as an object containing him; consequently, what cause have we to be hostile to him?

8 Q: If you worship the Supreme Being, and other persons offer their adoration to the same Divine Being, but in a different form, what then is the difference between them and you?

A: We differ in two ways; first, they worship under various forms and in particular places, believing the object of their worship to be the Supreme Being; but we declare that he, who is the Author of the universe, is to be worshipped; besides this, we can determine no particular form or place. Secondly, we see that they who worship under any one particular form, are opposed to those who worship under another; but it is impossible for worshippers of any denomination to be opposed to us; as we have shown in the answer to the 5th question.

9 Q: In what manner is this worship to be performed?

A: By bearing in mind that the Author and Governor of this visible universe is the Supreme Being, and comparing this idea with the sacred writings and with reason. In this worship it is indispensably necessary to use exertions to subdue the senses, and to read such passages as direct attention to the Supreme Spirit. Exertion to subdue the senses, signifies an endeavour to direct the will and the senses, and the conduct in such a manner as not only to prevent our own or others' ill, but to secure our own and others' good; in fact, what is considered injurious to ourselves, should be avoided towards others. It is obvious that as we are so constituted, that without the help of sound we can conceive no idea; therefore, by means of the texts treating of the Supreme Being, we should contemplate him. The benefits which we continually receive from fire, from air and from the sun, likewise from the various productions of the earth, such as the different kinds of grain, drugs, fruits and vegetables, all are dependent on him: and by considering and reasoning on the terms expressive of such ideas, the meaning itself is firmly fixed in the mind. It is repeatedly said in the sacred writings, that the theological knowledge is dependent upon truth; consequently, the attainment of truth will enable us to worship the Supreme Being, who is Truth itself.

10 Q: According to this worship, what rule must we establish with regard to the regulation of our food, conduct, and other worldly matters?

A: It is proper to regulate our food and conduct agreeably to the sacred writings; therefore, he who follows no prescribed form among all those that are promulgated, but regulates his food and conduct according to his own will, is called self-willed; and to act according to our own wish, is opposed both by the Scriptures and by reason. In the Scriptures it is frequently forbidden. Let us examine it by reason. Suppose each person should, in nonconformity with prescribed form, regulate his conduct according to his own desires, a speedy end must ensue to established societies; for to the self-willed, food, whether fit to be eaten or not, conduct proper or improper, desires lawful or unlawful, all are the same; he is guided by no rule; to him an action, performed according to the will, is faultless: but the will of all is not alike; consequently, in the fulfilment of our desires, where numerous opinions are mutually opposed, a quarrel is the most likely consequence; and the probable result of repeated quarrels is the destruction of human beings. In fact, however, it is highly improper to spend our whole time in judging of the propriety and impropriety of certain foods, without reflecting on science or Divine truth; for be food of whatever kind it may, in a very short space of time it undergoes a change into what is considered exceedingly impure, and this impure matter is, in various places, productive of different kinds of grain; therefore, it is certainly far more preferable to adorn the mind than to think of purifying the belly.

11 Q: In the performance of this worship, is any particular place, quarter, or time, necessary?

A: A suitable place is certainly preferable, but it is not absolutely necessary; that is to say, in whatever place, towards whatever quarter, or at whatever time the mind is best at rest, that place, that quarter, and that time is the most proper for the performance of this worship.

12 Q: To whom is this worship fit to be taught?

A: It may be taught to all, but the effect being produced in each person according to his state of mental preparation, it will be proportionably successful.[30]

Roy's Prototypical Experiences of Racism

Roy had many positive things to say about British rule in India but he also had a foretaste of its bitter side: racial discrimination both personal and institutional. The experience he narrates here is similar to that of Gandhi's ejection from the train, the only difference being one of degree.

Extract from a letter to J. Crawford, dated August 18, 1828.
Quoted by Miss Collett.

In his famous Jury Bill, Mr Wynn, the late President of the Board of Control, has by introducing religious distinctions into the judicial system of this country, not only afforded just grounds for dissatisfaction among the Natives in general, but has excited much alarm in the breast of everyone conversant with political principles. Any Natives, either Hindu or Mohamedan, are rendered by this Bill subject to judicial trial by Christians, either European or Native, while Christians, including Native Converts are exempted from the degradation [of] being tried either by a Hindu or Mussulman juror, however high he may stand in the estimation of Society. This Bill also denies both to Hindus and Mussulmans the honour of a seat in the Grand Jury even in the trial of fellow Hindus or Mussulmans. This is the sum total of Mr Wynn's late Jury bill, of which we bitterly complain.[31]

(Collected by Sj. Brojendranath Banerjee)
Letter to Lord Minto

To

The Right Honourable Lord Minto, Governor-General, etc., etc.
The humble petition of Rammohun Roy.

Most humbly sheweth:

That your petitioner, in common with all the native subjects of the British Government, looks up to your Lordship as the guardian of the just rights and dignities of that class of your subjects against all acts which have a tendency either directly or indirectly to invade those rights and dignities, and your petitioner more especially appeals to your Lordship as, from the nature of the treatment, however degrading, which he has experienced and from the nature of the existing circumstances with reference to the rank and destination of the gentleman from whom it proceeded, your petitioner is precluded from any other means of obtaining redress.

Confiding therefore in the impartial justice of the British Government and in the acknowledged wisdom which governs and directs all its measures in the just spirit of an enlarged and liberal policy, your petitioner proceeds with diffidency and humility to lay before your Lordship, the following circumstances of severe degradation and injury, which he has experienced at the hands of Sir Frederick Hamilton.

On the 1st of January last, your petitioner arrived at the Ghaut of the river of Bhaugulpur, and hired a house in that town. Proceeding to that house at about 4 o'clock in the afternoon, your petitioner passed in his palanquin through a road on the left side of which Sir Frederick Hamilton was standing among some bricks. The door of the palanquin being shut to exclude the dust of the road, your petitioner did not see that gentleman nor did the peon who preceded the palanquin, apprize your petitioner of the circumstance, he not knowing the gentleman, much less supposing that, that gentleman (who was standing alone among the bricks), was the Collector of the district. As your petitioner was passing, Sir Frederick Hamilton repeatedly called out to him to get out of his palanquin, and that with an epithet of abuse too gross to admit of being stated here without a departure from the respect due to your Lordship. One of the servants of your petitioner who followed in the retinue, explained to Sir Frederick Hamilton, that your petitioner had not observed him in passing by; nevertheless that gentleman still continued to use the same offensive language, and when the palanquin had proceeded to the distance of about 300 yards from the spot where Sir Frederick Hamilton had stood, that gentleman overtook it on horseback. Your petitioner then for the first time understood that the gentleman who was riding alongside of his palanquin, was the collector of the district, and that he was required a form of external respect, which, to whatever extent it might have been enforced under the Mogul Government, your petitioner had conceived from daily observation, to have fallen under the milder, more enlightened and more liberal policy of the British Government, into entire disuse and disesteem. Your petitioner then, far from wishing to withhold any manifestation of the respect due to the public officers of a Government which he held in the highest veneration, and not withstanding the novelty of the form in which that respect was required to be testified, alighted from his palanquin, and saluted Sir Frederick Hamilton, apologizing to him for the omission of that act of public respect on the grounds that in point of fact, your petitioner did not see him before, on account of the doors of his palanquin being nearly closed. Your petitioner stated however at the same time that even if the doors had been open, your petitioner would not have known him, nor would have supposed him to be the Collector of the district. Upon this, Sir Frederick asked your petitioner how the servant of the latter came to explain to him already, with your petitioner's salam, the reason of your petitioner's not having alighted from his palanquin. Your petitioner's servants stated in reply to the observations of Sir Frederick Hamilton that, he had not been desired by your petitioner, had gone on, and knowing that the doors of the palanquin were almost shut, he had explained the circumstance to Sir Frederick Hamilton in the hope of inducing that gentleman to discontinue his abusive language, but that he the servant had not expressed your petitioner's salam as he had no communication with your petitioner on the subject; Sir Frederick Hamilton then desired your petitioner to discharge the servant from his service and went away. In the course of that conversation, calculated by concession and apology to pacify the temper of Sir Frederick Hamilton, that gentleman still did not abstain from harsh and indecorous language. The intelligence of your petitioner's having been thus disgraced has been spread over the town and your Lordship's humane and enlightened mind will easily conceive, what must be the sensations of any native gentleman under a public indignity and disgrace, which as being inflicted by an English gentleman, and that gentleman an officer of Government, he is precluded from resenting, however strong the conviction of his own mind that such ill-treatment he has unmerited, wanton and capricious. If natives, therefore, of caste and rank were to be subjected to treatment which must infallibly dishonour and degrade them, not only within the pale of their own religion and society, but also within the circle of English Societies of high respectability into which they have the honour of being most liberally and affably admitted, they would be virtually condemned to close confinements within their house from the dread of being assaulted in the streets with every species of ignominy and degradation. Your petitioner is aware that the spirit of the British laws would not tolerate an act of arbitrary aggression, even against the lowest class of individuals, but much less would it continue an unjust degradation of persons of respectability, whether that respectability be derived from the society in which they move or from birth, fortune, or education; that your petitioner had some pretensions to urge on this point, the following circumstances will shew . . . .[32]

Roy's Historical and Political Views

Roy had an uncanny insight into Indian character, especially its political weakness. His historical comments, so close to the firm establishment of British rule, were already remarkably astute. One may begin with his capsule account of Indian history.

In consequence of the multiplied divisions and sub-divisions of the land into separate and independent kingdoms, under the authority of numerous princes hostile towards each other, and owing to the successive introduction of a vast number of castes and sects, destroying every texture of social and political unity, the country (or, properly speaking, such parts of it as were contiguous to foreign lands), was at different periods invaded, and brought under temporary subjection to foreign princes, celebrated for power and ambition.

About 900 years ago, the Mahommedan princes, advancing by the north-west began to ravage and overrun the country; and after con-tinued efforts, during several centuries, they succeeded in conquering the best parts of India. Their rule was transferred in succession from one dynasty of conquerors to another (Ghazni, Ghor, and Afghan), till 1525 of the Christian era, when prince Babar, a descendant of Timur (or Tamerlane), in the fifth generation, established his throne in the centre of Hindustan. His offspring (the Moghul dynasty) exercised the uncontrolled sovereignty of this empire for nearly two centuries (with the exception of about sixteen years), under a variety of changes, according to the rise or decrease of their power.

In the year 1712, the star of the Moghul ascendancy inclined towards descent, and has since gradually sunk below the horizon. The princes oftener consulted their own personal comfort than the welfare of the state, and relied for success on the fame of their dynasty, rather than on sound policy and military valour. Not only their crowns, but their lives also, depended on the goodwill of the nobles, who virtually assumed independence of the sovereign power, and each sought his own individual aggrandisement.

At present, all the southern and eastern, as well as several of the western provinces of the empire, have gradually fallen into the possession of the English. The army they employed chiefly consisted of the natives of India, a country into which the notion of patriotism has never made its way. Those territories were in fact transferred to British possession from the rule of a number of the rebellious nobility. While the greatest part of the northern provinces beyond the river Sutlej has fallen into the hands of Runjeet Singh, the chief of a tribe commonly called *Sikhs*.

Akbar the Second, present heir and representative of the imperial house of Timur, enjoys only the empty title of 'King of Delhi,' without either royal prerogative or power,

Runjeet Singh, sovereign of north-western India (consisting of Lahore, Multan, Cashmere, and Eastern Cabul), is considered highly gifted with prudence and moderation, and apparently inclined towards liberal principles; judicious in the discharge of public duties, and affable in private intercourse. The idea of constitutional government being entirely foreign to his mind, he has necessarily followed the same system of arbitrary rule which has been for ages prevailing in the country. The government he has established, although it be purely military, is nevertheless mild and conciliatory.

With regard to the circumstances under which a body of respectable English merchants (commonly) known by the name of the Honourable East India Company first obtained their Charter of Privileges in 1600, during the reign of Queen Elizabeth, to carry on trade with the East Indies; and with respect to the particulars of their success in procuring from the Emperor of Hindustan (Jahangir), and from several of his successors permission to establish commercial factories, as well as the enjoyment of protection and various privileges in that country; with relation further to their conquests, which commencing about the middle of the 18th century have extended over the greater part of India— conquests principally owing to the dissensions and pusillanimous conduct of the native princes and chiefs, as well as to the ignorance existing in the East, of the modern improvements in the art of war, combined with the powerful assistance afforded to the Company by the naval and military forces of the crown of England—I refer the reader to the modern histories of India, such particulars and details being quite foreign to the object which I have for the present in view.[33]

His political assessment of the Hindus follows. It was to remain unchanged until the 1930s.

Extract from a letter, dated January 18, 1828

I agree with you that in point of vices the Hindus are not worse than the generality of Christians in Europe and America; but I regret to say that the present system of religion adhered to by the Hindus is not well calculated to promote their political interest. The distinction of castes, introducing innumerable divisions and sub-divisions among them has entirely deprived them of patriotic feeling, and the multitude of religious rites and ceremonies and the laws of purification have totally disqualified them from undertaking any difficult enterprise. . . . It is, I think, necessary that some change should take place in their religion, at least for the sake of their political advantage and social comfort. I fully agree with you that there is nothing so sublime as the precepts taught by Christ, and that there is nothing equal to the simple doctrines he inculcated . . . .[34]

Roy never thought that India would one day be a Christian nation, even if Europeans settled in India in large numbers. While recounting the advantages of European settlement, he writes:

Ninthely: If, however, events should occur to effect a separation between the two countries, then still the existence of a large body of respectable settlers (consisting of Europeans and their descendants, professing Christianity, and speaking the English language in common with the bulk of the people, as well as possessed of superior knowledge, scientific, mechanical, and political) would bring that vast Empire in the east to a level with other large Christian countries in Europe, and by means of its immense riches and extensive population, and by the help which may be reasonably expected from Europe, they (the settlers and their descendants) may succeed sooner or later in enlightening and civilizing the surrounding nations of Asia.[35]

Roy was tremendously impressed by the West, a legacy which still survives.

From occasionally directing my studies to the subjects and events peculiarly connected with Europe, and from an attentive though partial, practical observation in regard to some of them, I felt impressed with the idea, that in Europe literature was zealously encouraged and knowledge widely diffused; that mechanics were almost in a state of perfection, and politics in daily progress; that moral duties were, on the whole, observed with exemplary propriety notwithstanding the temptations incident to a state of high and luxurious refinement; and that religion was spreading, even amid scepticism and false philosophy.

I was in consequence continually making efforts for a series of years, to visit the Western World, with a view to satisfy myself on those subjects by personal experience. I ultimately succeeded in surmounting the obstacles to my purpose, principally of a domestic nature; and having sailed from Calcutta on the 19th of November, 1830, I arrived in England on the 8th of April following. The particulars of my voyage and travels will be found in a Journal which I intend to publish together with whatever has appeared to me most worthy of remark and record in regard to the intelligence, riches and power, manners, customs,and especially the female virtue and excellence existing in this country.[36]

Roy's Universal Vision

When in Europe, Roy was shocked to learn that a passport was required to enter a country! He dreamt of a world sans frontiers, as his letter to the Minister of Foreign Affairs makes abundantly clear.

London
December 20th, 1831
(Endorsed).
28th December, 1831.
Rajah Rammohun Roy
Transg., copy of an intended communication to the Foreign Minister of France. Private note from Mr. Villiers to Rammohun Roy, January, 4, 1832.

To
    The Minister of Foreign Affairs of France, Paris.

Sir,

You may be surprised at receiving a letter from a Foreigner, the Native of a country situated many thousand miles from France, and I assuredly would not now have trespassed on your attention, were I not induced by a sense of what I consider due to myself and by the respect I feel towards a country standing in the foremost rank of free and civilized nations.

2nd: For twelve years past I have entertained a wish (as noticed, I think, in several French and English Periodicals) to visit a country so favoured by nature and so richly adorned by the cultivation of arts and sciences, and above all blessed by the possession of a free constitution. After surmounting many difficulties interposed by religious and national distinctions and other circumstances, I am at last opposite your coast, where, however, I am informed that I must not place my foot on your territory unless I previously solicit and obtain an express permission for my entrance from the Ambassador or Minister of France in England.

3rd: Such a regulation is quite unknown even among the Nations of Asia (though extremely hostile to each other from religious prejudices and political dissensions), with the exception of China, a country noted for its extreme jealousy of foreigners and apprehensions of the introduction of new customs and ideas. I am, therefore, quite at a loss to conceive how it should exist among a people so famed as the French are for courtesy and liberality in all other matters.

4th: It is now generally admitted that not religion only but unbiased common sense as well as the accurate deductions of scientific research lead to the conclusion that all mankind are one great family of which numerous nations and tribes existing are only various branches. Hence enlightened men in all countries must feel a wish to encourage and facilitate human intercourse in every manner by removing as far as possible all impediments to it in order to promote the reciprocal advantage and enjoyment of the whole human race.

5th: It may perhaps be urged that during the existence of war and hostile feelings between any two nations (arising probably from their not understanding their real interests), policy requires of them to adopt these precautions against each other. This, however, only applies to a state of warfare. If France, therefore, were at war with surrounding nations or regarded their people as dangerous, the motive for such an extraordinary precaution must have been conceived.

6th: But as a general peace has existed in Europe for many years, and there is more particularly so harmonious an understanding between the people of France and England and even between their present Governments, I am utterly at a loss to discover the cause of a regulation which manifests, to say the least, a want of cordiality and confidence on the part of France.

7th: Even during peace the following excuses might perhaps be offered for the continuance of such restrictions, though in my humble opinion they cannot stand a fair examination.

Firstly: If it be said that persons of bad character should not be allowed to enter France; still it might, I presume, be answered that the granting of passports by the French Ambassador here is not usually founded on certificates of character or investigation into the conduct of individuals. Therefore, it does not provide a remedy for that supposed evil.

Secondly: If it be intended to prevent felons escaping from justice: this case seems well-provided for by the treaties between different nations for the surrender of all criminals.

Thirdly: If it be meant to obstruct the flight of debtors from their creditors: in this respect likewise it appears superfluous, as the bankrupt laws themselves after a short imprisonment set the debtor free even in his own country; therefore, voluntary exile from his own country would be, I conceive, a greater punishment.

Fourthly: If it be intended to apply to political matters, it is in the first place not applicable to my case. But on general grounds I beg to observe that it appears to me, the ends of constitutional Government might be better attained by submitting every matter of political difference between two countries to a Congress composed of an equal number from the Parliament of each; the decision of the majority to be acquiesced in by both nations and the Chairman to be chosen by each Nation alternately, for one year, and the place of meeting to be one year, within the limits of one country and next within those of the other; such as at Dover and Calais for England and France.

8th: By such a Congress all matters of difference, whether political or commercial, affecting the Natives of any two civilized countries with constitutional Governments, might be settled amicably and justly to the satisfaction of both and profound peace and friendly feelings might be preserved between them from generation to generation.

9th: I do not dwell on the inconvenience which the system of passports imposes in urgent matters of business and in cases of domestic affliction. But I may be permitted to observe that the mere circumstance of applying for passport seems a tacit admission that the character of the applicant stands in need of such a certificate or testimonial before he can be permitted to pass unquestioned. Therefore, any one may feel some delicacy in exposing himself to the possibility of refusal which would lead to an inference unfavourable to his character as a peaceable citizen.

My desire, however, to visit that country is so great that I shall conform to such conditions as are imposed on me, if the French Government, after taking the subject into consideration, judge it proper and expedient to continue restrictions contrived for a different state of things, but to which they may have become reconciled by long habit; as I should be sorry to set up my opinion against that of the present enlightened Government of France.

> I have the honour to be,
> Sir,
> Your most obedient servant,
> Rammohun Roy.[37]

Criticism of the Brahmins

Rammohun Roy, although he himself came from the same stock, was extremely critical of the Brahmins, the hereditary priestly caste of Hinduism. The Brahmins are described as deliberately preying on the weak and the ignorant by perpetuating them in that state even as they cater to them.

Should be it said, 'It still remains un-accountable, that notwithstanding the Vedas and Puranas repeatedly declare the unity of the Supreme Being, and direct mankind to adore him alone, yet the generality of Hindus have a contrary faith, and continue to practice idolatry,' I would in answer request attention to the foundation on which the practical part of the Hindu religion is built. Many learned Brahmans are perfectly aware of the absurdity of idolatry, and are well informed of the nature of the purer mode of divine worship. But as in the rites, ceremonies, and festivals of idolatry, they find the source of their comforts and fortune, they not only never fail to protect idol-worship from all attacks, but even advance and encourage it to the utmost of their power, by keeping the knowledge of their scripture concealed from the rest of the people. Their followers, too, confiding in these leaders, feel gratification in the idea of the Divine Nature residing in a being resembling themselves in birth, shape, and propensities; and are naturally delighted with a mode of worship agreeable to the senses, though destructive of moral principles, and fruitful of prejudice and superstition.

Some Europeans, imbued with high principles of liberality, but unacquainted with the ritual part of Hindu idolatry, are disposed to palliate it by an interpretation which, though plausible, is by no means well founded. They are willing to imagine, that the idols which the Hindus worship, are not viewed by them in the light of gods or as real personifications of the divine attributes, but merely as instruments for raising their minds to the contemplation of those attributes which are respectively represented by different figures. I have frequently had occasion to remark, that many Hindus also who are conversant with the English language, finding this interpretation a more plausible apology for idolatry than any with which they are furnished by their own guides, do not fail to avail themselves of it, though in repugnance both to their faith and to their practice. The declarations of this description of Hindus naturally tend to confirm the original idea of such Europeans, who from the extreme absurdity of pure unqualified idolatry, deduce an argument against its existence. It appears to them impossible for men, even in the very last degree of intellectual darkness, to be so far misled as to consider a mere image of wood or of stone as a *human being*, much less as divine existence. With a view, therefore, to do away [with] any misconception of this nature which may have prevailed, I beg leave to submit the following considerations.

Hindus of the present age, with a very few exceptions, have not the least idea that it is to the attributes of the Supreme Being, as figuratively represented by shapes corresponding to the nature of those attributes, they offer adoration and worship under the denomination of gods and goddesses. On the contrary, the slightest investigation will clearly satisfy every inquirer, that it makes a material part of their system to hold as articles of faith all those particular circumstances, which are essential to belief in the independent existence of the objects of their idolatry as deities clothed with divine power.[38]

He often associates the Brahmins with idolatry as in the following passage.

Murder, theft, or perjury, though brought home to the party by a judicial sentence, so far from inducing loss of caste, is visited in their society with no peculiar mark of infamy or disgrace.

A trifling present to the Brahman, commonly called *Prayaschit*, with the performance of a few idle ceremonies, are held as a sufficient atonement for all those crimes; and the delinquent is at once freed from all temporal inconvenience, as well as all dread of future retribution.

My reflections upon these solemn truths have been most painful for many years. I have never ceased to contemplate with the strongest feelings of regret, the obstinate adherence of my countrymen to their fatal system of idolatry, inducing, for the sake of propitiating their supposed Deities, the violation of every humane and social feeling. And this in various instances; but more especially in the dreadful acts of self-destruction and the immolation of the nearest relations, under the delusion of conforming to sacred religious rites. I have never ceased, I repeat, to contemplate these practices with the strongest feelings of regret, and to view in them the moral debasement of a race who, I cannot help thinking, are capable of better things; whose susceptibility, patience, and mildness of character, render them worthy of a better destiny. Under these impressions, therefore, I have been impelled to lay before them genuine translations of parts of their scripture, which inculcates not only the enlightened worship of one God, but the purest principles of morality, accompanied with such notices as I deemed requisite to oppose the arguments employed by the Brahmans in defence of their beloved system. Most earnestly do I pray that the whole may, sooner or later, prove efficient in producing on the minds of Hindus in general, a conviction of the rationality of believing in and adoring the Supreme Being only; together with a complete perception and practice of that grand and comprehensive moral principle—*Do unto others as ye would be done by.*[39]

For Roy, however, idolatry was an evil in itself, and something one could take recourse to only as a last resort.

During the intervals between my controversial engagements with idolaters as well as with advocates of idolatry, I translated several of ten Upanishads, of which the Vedanta or principal part of the Vedas consists, and of which the Sariraka-Mimansa, commonly called the Vedanta-Darsana, composed by the celebrated Vyasa, is explanatory; I have now taken the opportunity of further leisure to publish a translation of the Mundaka-Upanishad. An attentive perusal of this as well as of the remaining books of the Vedanta will, I trust, convince every unprejudiced mind, that they, with great consistency, inculcate the unity of God; instructing men, at the same time, in the pure mode of adoring him in spirit. It will also appear evident that the Vedas, although they tolerate idolatry as the last provision for those who are totally incapable of raising their minds to the contemplation of the invisible God of nature, yet repeatedly urge the relinquishment of the rites of idol-worship, and the adoption of a purer system of religion, on the express ground that the observance of idolatrous rites can never be productive of eternal beatitude. These are left to be practised by such persons only as, notwithstanding the constant teaching of spiritual guides, cannot be brought to see perspicuously the majesty of God through the works of nature.

The public will, I hope, be assured that nothing but the natural inclination of the ignorant towards the worship of objects resembling their own nature, and to the external forms of rites palpable to their grosser senses, joined to the self-interested motives of their pretended guides, has rendered the generality of the Hindoo community (in defiance of their sacred books) devoted to idol-worship—the source of prejudice and superstition and of the total destruction of moral principle, as countenancing criminal intercourse, suicide, female murder, and human sacrifice. Should my labours prove in any degree the means of diminishing the extent of those evils, I shall ever deem myself most amply rewarded.[40]

Roy argues that the honour bestowed on the Brahmins is contrary to the very texts from which they seek to derive it.

According to the authority of Manu (text 155, chap. 2nd), respect and distinction are due to a Brahman, merely in proportion to his knowledge; but on the contrary amongst modern Hindoos, honour is paid exclusively to certain families of Brahmans, such as the Kulins, &c., however void of knowledge and principle they may be. This departure from law and justice was made by the authority of a native prince of Bengal, named Ballalsen, within the last three or four hundred years. And this innovation may perhaps be considered as the chief source of that decay of learning and virtue, which, I am sorry to say, may be at present observed. For wherever respectability is confined to birth only, acquisition of knowledge, and the practice of morality, in that country, must rapidly decline.[41]

Vices of Hinduism

Roy saw the various Hindu practices such as idolatry, polygamy, Sati and others as interconnected, and as constituting a noxious nexus. This is apparent from parts of his observations as distinguished from the texts cited, and in his Brief Remarks Regarding Modern Encroachments on the Ancient Rights of Females. *Roy also perceived a connection between idolatry and immorality in general.*

To these authorities a thousand others might be added. But should the learned gentleman require some practical grounds for objecting to the idolatrous worship of the Hindoos, I can be at no loss to give him numberless instances, where the ceremonies that have been instituted under the pretext of honouring the all-perfect Author of Nature, are of a tendency utterly subversive of every moral principle.

I begin with Krishna as the most adored of the incarnations, the number of whose devotees is exceedingly great. His worship is made to consist in the institution of his image or picture, accompanied by one or more females, and in the contemplation of his history and behaviour, such as his perpetration of murder upon a female of the name of Putana; his compelling a great number of married and unmarried women to stand before him denuded; his debauching them and several others, to the mortal affliction of their husbands and relations; his annoying them, by violating the laws of cleanliness and other facts of the same nature. The grossness of his worship does not find a limit here. His devotees very often personify (in the same manner as European actors upon stages do) him and his female companions, dancing with indecent gestures, and singing songs relative to his love and debaucheries. It is impossible to explain in language fit to meet the public eye, the mode in which Mahadeva, or the destroying attribute, is worshipped by the generality of the Hindoos: suffice it to say, that it is altogether congenial with the indecent nature of the image, under whose form he is most commonly adored.

The stories respecting him which are read by his devotees in the Tantras, are of a nature that, if told of any man, would be offensive to the ears of the most abandoned of either sex. In the worship of Kali, human sacrifices, the use of wine, criminal intercourse, and licentious songs are included: the first of these practices has become generally extinct; but it is believed that there are parts of the country where human victims are still offered.

Debauchery, however, universally forms the principal part of the worship of her followers. Nigam and other Tantras may satisfy every reader of the horrible tenets of the worshippers of the two latter deities. The modes of worship of almost all the inferior deities are pretty much the same. Having so far explained the nature of worship adopted by Hindoos in general, for the propitiation of their allegorical attributes, in direct opposition to the mode of pure divine worship inculcated by the Vedas, I cannot but entertain a strong hope that the learned gentleman, who ranks even monotheistical songs among carnal pleasures, and consequently rejects their admittance in worship, will no longer stand forward as an advocate for the worship of separate and independent attributes and incarnations.[42]

Roy noticed that Europeans had a tendency to extenuate idolatry by interpreting the idols as symbols, as indicated earlier. He considered these charitable sentiments misplaced and points out:

The circumstances alluded to in p. 168 of this treatise, relative to the wicked conduct of their supposed deities, are perfectly familiar to every individual Hindoo. But those Europeans who are not acquainted with the particulars related of them, may perhaps feel a wish to be in possession of them. I, therefore, with a view to gratify their curiosity and to vindicate my assertion, beg, to be allowed to mention a few instances in point, with the authorities on which they rest. As I have already noticed the debauchery of Krishna, and his gross sensuality, and that of his fellow-deities, such as Siva and Brahma, in the 147th, 148th and 150th pages of my reply to the observations of Sankar Sastri, instead of repeating them here, I refer my readers to that reply, also to the tenth division of the Bhagavata, to the Harivansa or last division of the Maha-Bharata, and to the Nigams, as well as to the several Agams, which give a detailed account of their lewdness and debauchery. As to falsehood, their favourite deity Krishna is more conspicuous than the rest. Jara-Sandha, a powerful prince of Behar, having heard of the melancholy murder of his son-in-law perpetrated by Krishna, harassed, and at last drove him out of the place of his nativity (Mathura) by frequent military expeditions. Krishna, in revenge, resolved to deprive that prince of his life by fraud, and in a most unjustifiable manner. To accomplish his object, he and his two cousins, Bhima and Arjuna, declared themselves to be Brahmans and in that disguise entered his palace; where, finding him weakened by a religious fast, and surrounded only by his family and priests, they challenged him to fight a duel. He accordingly fought Bhima, the strongest of the three, who conquered and put him to death—*Vide Sabha Parba or second book of the Maha-Bharata.* Krishna again persuaded Yudhisthira, his cousin, to give false evidence in order to accomplish the murder of Drona, their spiritual father—*Vide Drona Parba, or seventh book of the Maha-Bharata.*

Vishnu and others combined in a conspiracy against Bali, a mighty emperor; but finding his power irresistible, that deity was determined to defeat him by stratagem, and for that purpose appeared to him in the shape of a dwarf, begging alms. Notwithstanding Bali was warned of the intention of Vishnu, yet, impressed with a high sense of generosity, he could not refuse a boon to a beggar; that a grateful deity in return not only deprived him of his whole empire, which he put himself in possession of by virtue of the boon of Bali, but also inflicted on him the disgrace of bondage and confinement in Patal—*Vide latter part of the Hari-vansa or last book of the Maha-Bharata.*

When the battle of Kurukshetra was decided by the fatal destruction of Duryodhana, the remaining part of the army of his rival, Yudhisthira, returned to the camp to rest during the night, under the personal care and protection of Mahadeva. That deity having, however, been cajoled by the flattery offered him by Aswatthama, one of the friends of the unfortunate Duryodhana, not only allowed him to destroy the whole army that was asleep under the confidence of his protection, but even assisted him with his sword to accomplish his bloody purpose—*Vide Saushuptika Parba, or eleventh book of the Maha-Bharata.*

When the Asuras, at the churning of the ocean, gave the pitcher of *the water of immortality* in charge to Vishnu, he betrayed his trust by delivering it to their step-brothers and enemies, the celestial gods—*Vide first book or Adi Parba of the Maha-Bharata.*

Instances like these might be multiplied beyond number: and crimes of a much deeper dye might easily be added to the list, were I not unwilling to stain these pages by making them the vehicle of such stories of immorality and vice. May God speedily purify the minds of my countrymen from the corruptness which such tales are too apt to produce, and lead their hearts to that pure morality which is inseparable from the true worship of Him![43]

Roy's Religious Epistemology

Although Roy does not often consciously address this issue, his interest in the scriptures of all the religions he knew, as well as the evidence of his sturdy common sense, suggests that he saw both revelation and reason as playing a role in the determination of religious truth. In the following paragraph we obtain as clear a statement of his view on this point as we can ever hope to find.

I have often lamented that, in our general researches into theological truth, we are subjected to the conflict of many obstacles. When we look to the traditions of ancient nations, we often find them at variance with each other; and when, discouraged by this circumstance, we appeal to reason as a surer guide, we soon find how incompetent it is, alone, to conduct us to the object of our pursuit. We often find that, instead of facilitating our endeavours or clearing up our perplexities, it only serves to generate a universal doubt, incompatible with principles on which our comfort and happiness mainly depend. The best method perhaps is, neither to give ourselves up exclusively to the guidance of the one or the other; but by a proper use of the lights furnished by both, endeavour to improve our intellectual and moral faculties, relying on the goodness of the Almighty Power, which alone enables us to attain that which we earnestly and diligently seek for.[44]

The following passage provides a good example of the operation of this principle.

The argument which is frequently alleged in support of idolatry is that 'those who believe God to be omnipresent, as declared by the doctrines of the Vedanta, are required by the tenets of such belief to look upon all existing creatures as God, and to shew divine respect to birds, beasts, men, women, vegetables, and all other existences; and as practical conformity to such doctrines is almost impossible, the worship of figured gods should be admitted.' This misrepresentation, I am sorry to observe, entirely serves the purpose intended, by frightening Hindus in general from attending to the pure worship of the Supreme Regulator of the universe. But I am confident that the least reflection on the subject will clear up this point beyond all doubt; for the Vedanta is well known as a work which inculcates only the unity of God; but if every existing creature should be taken for a god by the followers of the Vedanta, the doctrines of that work must be admitted to be much more at variance with that idea than those of the advocates of idolatry, as the latter are contented with the recognition of only a few millions of gods and goddesses, but the Vedanta in that case must be supposed to admit the divinity of every living creature in nature. The fact is, that the Vedanta by declaring that 'God is everywhere, and everything is in God,' means that nothing is absent from God, and nothing bears real existence except by the volition of God, whose existence is the sole support of the conceived existence of the universe, which is acted upon by him in the same manner as a human body is by a soul. But god is at the same time quite different from what we see or feel.[45]

Roy on Maya

The way the word Maya is understood became quite consequential in later Hindu thought. Roy's views on it will not be without interest.

I reply—The world, as the Vedanta says, is the effect of Maya, and is material; but God is mere spirit, whose particular influences being shed upon certain material objects are called souls in the same manner as the reflections of the sun are seen on water placed in various vessels. As these reflections of the sun seem to be moved by the motion of the water of those vessels without effecting any motion in the sun, so souls, being, as it were, the reflections of the Supreme Spirit on matter, seem to be affected by the circumstances that influence matter, without God being affected by such circumstances. As some reflections are bright from the purity of the water on which they are cast, while others seem obscure owing to its foulness, so some souls are more pure from the purity of the matter with which they are connected, while others are dull owing to the dullness of matter.

As the reflections of the sun, though without light proper to themselves, appear splendid from their connection with the illuminating sun, so the soul, though not true intellect, seems intellectual and acts as if it were real spirit from its actual relation to the Universal Intellect: and as from the particular relations of the sun to the water placed in different pots, various reflections appear resembling the same sun in nature and differing from it in qualities; and again as these cease to appear on the removal of the water, so through the peculiar relation of various material objects to one Supreme Spirit numerous souls appear and seem as performing good and evil works, and also receiving their consequences; and as soon as that relation ceases, they, at that very minute cease to appear distinctly from their original. Hence God is one, and the soul, although it is not in fact of a different origin from God, is yet liable to experience the consequences of good and evil works; but this liability of the soul to reward or punishment cannot render God liable to either . . . .

Moreover, you say the Vedanta teaches that as bubbles arise from and again are absorbed in water; in like manner through the influence of Maya the world repeatedly proceeds from, depends upon, and is absorbed into God; and hence you infer that, according to this doctrine, the reproach of God's being under the influence of Maya attaches to the Deity. I reply, that the resemblance of the bubbles with the world is maintained by the Vedanta only in two respects: 1st, as the bubbles receive from water through the influence of the wind, their birth and existence, so the world takes by the power of God, its original existence from the Supreme Being and depends upon him; and 2ndly, that there is no reality in the existence either of bubbles or of the world. When we say such a one is like a lion, we mean resemblance only in respect of courage and strength and not in every respect, as in point of shape, size, &c. In like manner the resemblance of the world to bubbles, in this instance, lies in point of dependence and unreality. Were the similarity acknowledged in every respect we must admit God to be an insensitive existence like a portion of water and the world as a bubble to be a small part of God moving sometimes on the surface of the Deity and again uniting with him. Those who look only after faults, may think themselves justified in alleging that in consequence of the comparison of the world to bubbles of water and of Maya to the wind, as found in the Vedanta, God is supposed to be influenced by Maya.

Maya is the power of God through which the world receives its birth, existence and changes; but no men of learning who are not biased by partiality, would infer from these opinions an idea of the inferiority of God to Maya, his attribute. For as men of every tribe and of every country whatsoever acknowledge God to be the Cause of the world, they necessarily consider him possessed of the power through which he creates the world. But no one is from this concluded to believe that God is subordinate to that power. God pardons the sins of those that sincerely repent, through his attribute of mercy: this cannot be taken as an admission of the Deity's subjection to his own mercy. The followers of the Vedanta say, that Maya is opposed to knowledge, for when a true knowledge of God is obtained, the effect of Maya, which makes the soul appear distinct from God, does immediately cease.

The term Maya implies, primarily, the power of creation, and secondarily, its effect, which is the Universe. The Vedanta, by comparing the world with the misconceived notion of a snake, when a rope really exists, means that the world, like the supposed snake, has no independent existence, that it receives its existence from the Supreme Being. In like manner the Vedanta compares the world with a dream: as all the objects seen in dream depend upon the motion of the mind, so the existence of the world is dependent upon the being of God, who is the only object of supreme love; and in declaring that God is all in all and that there is no other substance except God, the Vedanta means that existence in reality belongs to God alone. He is consequently true and omnipresent; nothing else can bear the name of true existence. We find the phrases, God is all and in all, in the Christian books; and I suppose they do not mean by such words that pots, mats, &c., are gods. I am inclined to believe that by these terms they mean the omnipresence of God. Why do you attempt, by cavils, to find fault with the Vedanta?[46]

Rammohun Roy's Religious Beliefs

It would perhaps be fair to conclude this selection of Roy's statements with a clear statement of Roy's own religious position.

I shall now, in a few words, for the information of the Missionary Gentlemen, lay down our religious creed. In conformity with the Precepts of our ancient religion, contained in Holy Vedanta, though disregarded by the generality of moderns, we look up to One Being as the animating and regulating principle of the whole collective body of the universe, and as the origin of all individual souls which in a manner somewhat similar, vivify and govern their particular bodies; and we reject Idolatry in every form and under whatsoever veil of sophistry it may be practised, either in adoration of an artificial, a natural, or an imaginary object. The divine homage which we offer, consists solely in the practice of *Daya* or benevolence towards each other, and not in a fanciful faith or in certain motions of the feet, legs, arms, head, tongue or other bodily organs, in pulpit or before a temple. Among other objects, in our solemn devotion, we frequently offer up our humble thanks to God, for the blessings of British Rule in India and sincerely pray, that it may continue in its beneficent operation for centuries to come.

Shivuprusad Surma.*

Calcutta, November 15, 1823.
*The Raja's Pandit, under whose name he brought out this Magazine. Rammohun Roy was fond of using pseudonyms—Ed.[47]

A more formal statement on why he was a unitarian is also available.

Answer of a Hindoo

To the question, 'Why do you frequent a Unitarian place of worship, instead of the numerously attended established Churches?'

I. Because the prayers read, worship offered, and sermons preached in the Unitarian place of worship remind me of the infinitely wise Ruler of this infinite universe, without ascribing to him as Churchmen do, fellow-creators or co-operators equal in power and other attributes. My plain understanding, though it can comprehend the idea of fellow-creatures, is incapable of forming a notion of one or more fellow-creators each equally possessed of omnipotence and omnipresence.

II. Because Unitarian prayer, worship, and preaching constantly put me in mind of the beneficial design kept in view by the wise and benevolent Author of all, in organizing the members of the animal body, such as bones, veins, vessels, limbs, &c., and in preparing the manifold necessaries of life for our maintenance, as proofs of his gratuitous blessing and free grace; while in those Churches he is declared to have refused mercy and salvation to mankind until innocent blood was offered him to appease his wrath.

III. Because the Unitarian mode of worship exhibits how that infinite and Supreme author has designedly stationed the heavenly bodies, in systematic order, capable of producing and nourishing all the animal and vegetable objects under his divine control; while in those Churches that infinite being is represented as occupying a small space in this limited world, lying in a still smaller space in the womb of a virgin, subject to the control of his parents, though for a season, and daily performing the various animal functions.

IV. Because I feel already weary of the doctrine of 'Man-God' or

'God-Man' frequently inculcated by the Brahmans, in pursuance of their corrupt traditions: the same doctrine of Man-God, though preached by another body of priests better dressed, better provided for and eminently elevated by virtue of conquest, cannot effectually tend to excite my anxiety or curiosity to listen to it.

V. Because I have expressed my disgust, when I heard from the Brahmans the incredible story that God appeared in the form of a party-coloured kite (sic), to accomplish certain purposes. While I maintain the same reverence for Divine Being, I must be excused believing a similar doctrine held forth in those Churches, as to the appearance of God, on another occasion, in the bodily shape of a dove. I wonder to observe, that from a denial of the existence of God some are stigmatized with the term atheist; while others are highly respected, though they do not scruple, under the shield of religion, to bring the Deity into ridicule, by representing him in the form even of a common bird.

VI. Because having been taught in the schools, where the doctrine of the Incarnations of a two-fold or even of a three-fold nature has been solemnly preached, I perceive no novelty in the idea of a two-fold nature, divine and human, as entertained and expressed in those Churches.

VII. Because in those Churches, the Holy Ghost is represented as the very God and not as the miraculous power of the Deity, at the same time that the language applied there to this person of the God-head; such as 'she was found with child of the Holy Ghost,' 'The Holy Ghost shall come upon thee' fully corresponds to the words and ideas used for the deity in the western and eastern heathen mythologies, and consequently must be offensive to the feelings of those who ascribe to God purity and perfection.

VIII. Because the doctrine of the trinity inculcated in those Churches, consisting of God the Father, God the Son, and God the Holy Ghost, is defensible on the plea of mystery; while the Trinity preached to us by the Brahmans is a representation of the three principle attributes of the deity in an allegorical sense, and does therefore deserve some momentary attention. The mind which rejects the latter as a production of the fancy, cannot be reasonably expected to adopt the former.

IX. Because Unitarians reject polytheism and idolatry under every sophistical modification, and thereby discountenance all the evil consequences resulting from them.

X. Because Unitarians believe, profess, and inculcate the doctrine of the divine unity—a doctrine which I find firmly maintained both by the Christian Scriptures and by our most ancient writings commonly called the Vedas.

Such are my reasons for attending the Unitarian place of worship instead of the established Churches.[48]

Notes

1. Richard King, 'Orientalism and the Modern Myth of "Hinduism"', *Numen* 46 (1999), p. 165.
2. Kalidas Nag and Debajyoti Burman, eds., *The English Works of Raja Rammohun Roy* (Calcutta: Sadharan Brahmo Samaj, 1947), Part IV, pp. 110–11.
3. Cited by Kalidas Nag, 'The Brahmo Samaj', in Haridas Bhattacharyya, ed., *The Cultural Heritage of India* (Calcutta: The Ramakrishna Mission Institute of Culture, 1956), Vol. IV, p. 617.
4. Nag and Burman, Part II, p. 51, emphasis added.
5. Ibid., p. 61.
6. Ajit Kumar Ray, *The Religious Ideas of Rammohun Roy: A Survey of his Writings on Religion Particularly in Persian, Sanskrit, and Bengali* (New Delhi: Kanak Publications [Book India Project], 1976), p. 78.
7. Ramesh Chandra Majumdar, *On Rammohun Roy* (Calcutta: Asiatic Society, 1972), p. 51, note 41.
8. Ibid., pp. 25–6.
9. Nag, p. 624.
10. Ibid., pp. 624–5.
11. F. Max Mueller, *Rammohan to Ramakrishna* (Calcutta: S. Gupta, 1952), pp. 17–18. For the parenthetical citation at the beginning see p. 12.
12. Ibid., pp. 615–16. Also see Ray, p. 24, note 2.
13. Rammohun Roy, *Translation of an Abridgement of The Vedant or the Resolution of all Vedas; the most celebrated and revered work of Brahmunical theology; establishing the unity of the Supreme Being; and that He Alone is the object of propitiation and worship* (Calcutta: 1816). See Nag and Burman, Part II, pp. 59–61.
14. These passages constitute Roy's introduction to: *the precepts of Jesus The Guide to Peace and Happiness; extracted from the Books of the New Testament, ascribed to the four evangelists. With translations into Sungscrit and Bengalee* (Calcutta: 1820). See Nag and Burman, Part V, pp. 3–4. The translations into Sanskrit and Bengali are no longer traceable (ibid., p. iv).
15. Ibid., Part IV, pp. 77–9.
16. Extracted from Wm. Theodore de Bary, ed., *Sources of Indian Tradition* (New York and London: Columbia University Press, 1958), Vol. II, p. 28.
17. Nag and Burman, Part III, pp. 124–7.

18. John B. Carman, 'Duties and Rights in Hindu Society' in Leroy S. Rouner, ed., *Human Rights and the World's Religions* (Notre Dame, Indiana: University of Notre Dame Press, 1988), pp. 120–1.
19. Nag and Burman, Part I, pp. 1–7.
20. Majumdar, p. 47.
21. Ibid., p. 47.
22. Nag and Burman, Part IV, p. 103.
23. Ibid., Part III, pp. 131–36.
24. Ibid., Part II, p. 80.
25. Ibid., Part III, p. 4 footnote.
26. Ibid., Part I, pp. 49–50.
27. Ibid., Part II, p. 78 footnote.
28. Ibid., Part I, p. 1 footnote.
29. R. C. Zaehner, *Hinduism* (London: Oxford University Press, 1962), p. 201.
30. Nag and Burman, Part II, pp. 129–32. For Sanskrit see pp. 132–4.
31. Ibid., Part IV, pp. 102–3.
32. Ibid., pp. 108–10.
33. Ibid., Part III, pp. 5–6.
34. Ibid., Part IV. pp. 95–6.
35. Ibid., Part III, pp. 82–3.
36. Ibid., Part III. p. 8.
37. Ibid., Part IV, pp. 126–8.
38. Ibid., Part II, pp. 44–5.
39. Ibid., p. 52.
40. Ibid., Introduction.
41. Ibid., p. 114.
42. Ibid., pp. 92–3.
43. Ibid., pp. 117–19.
44. Ibid., pp. 14–15.
45. Ibid., pp. 46–7.
46. Ibid., pp. 145–6.
47. Ibid., pp. 188–9.
48. Ibid., pp. 193–4.

Devendranath Tagore
(1817–1905)

Life

Devendranath Tagore was the son of Dwarkanath Tagore, an associate of Rammohun Roy. The Brahmo Samaj, which institutionalized the legacy of Roy, languished after his death, partly because a more radical attitude towards reform was beginning to develop among the youth of Bengal, the consequences of which were destined to be felt by the Brahmo Samaj movement, but not as yet.

Devendranath Tagore had become spiritually inclined after the death of his grandmother (Didima), which had profoundly affected him. He deals with this event in his autobiography at some length, which also describes the somewhat dramatic manner in which he became acquainted with the Upaniṣads.[1] These passages are excerpted later in the chapter. At this point, the following remark by his biographer will not fail to interest us:

> The incident of the Maharshi's first chance acquaintance with the Upanishads had happened around the years of 1835–36. Chronologically it was before his grandmother's death, which took place in 1838. But the two facts got so intertwined that it is difficult to extricate the one from the other while discussing the factors leading to his break from the traditional forms of worship and falling back upon a mode from which idolatrous beliefs and practices were expunged. Since that period onwards he literally underwent a metamorphosis so far as his religious conviction was concerned.[2]

As a consequence of this metamorphosis Devendranath started an organization called the Tattvabodhini Sabha in 1839. Gradually the realization dawned on him that the aims of this society were not very different from those of the Brahmo Samaj and the two merged in 1843, thereby reviving the Brahmo Samaj.

Within a few years, however, Devendranath's life was destined to be buffeted by crises which lasted almost a decade (1846–56), precipitated by the demise of his father Dwarkanath who, like Rammohun, died in England, in 1846. This personal crisis was followed by a financial one, which could have been averted by resorting to chicanery, but which he faced with honesty to the point that in one particular instance,

> A list was being read out to the creditors in which assets of Devendranath and his two brothers had been mentioned item by item to the minutest detail. But through a mistake one item had not been included therein. Devendranath immediately corrected the mistake by declaring that the diamond ring that he was wearing had not been entered into the list through inadvertence but ought to be entered because it was also a part of their assets.[3]

These setbacks forced Devendranath to simplify his life, a change which he seems to have welcomed for he remarks: 'In short, I became a Sannyasin while in household.'[4]

Finally, in the year 1857, Devendranath set out on a tour of the Himalayas, where the natural splendour of his surroundings made a lasting impression on him. Devendranath's autobiography ends with his return from the Himalayas on 15 November 1858, when he was only forty-one years old, although it was written much later. It has been surmised that the rest of the story might have been too contentious for his sagely disposition to recall, as upon his return he probably found that the Brahmo Samaj had changed in complexion with the radical wing gaining at the expense of the conservative elements, a development which in due course led to a confrontation between the two groups.

After returning from the Himalayas, Devendranath Tagore made the acquaintance of a young man to whom he had offered support when the youth's own family had refused to countenance his reforming zeal. His name was Keshub Chunder Sen. Keshub had joined the Brahmo Samaj in 1857 and was looked upon with great favour by Devendranath. Under the influence of Keshub's reforming zeal, who, unlike Devendranath, was not a Brahmin, the officials of the Samaj were first encouraged and then required to discard the sacred thread, a mark of caste status. Such steps ultimately led to a breach in 1864 between Keshub and Devendranath. On account of a meteorological disturbance, the services of the Samaj temporarily began to be held at the house of Devendranath, who was less vigorous in pursuing the issue of divestiture of the sacred thread. Keshub thereupon founded his own Samaj.

It seems that throughout this period of extreme tension Devendranath maintained a most dignified deportment, for within a year of the formal break in 1867, 'The title of "Maharshi" was conferred on him by the same Brahmo Samaj of India [as the splinter group was known], the members of which had only the other day been his adversaries.'[5]

As we shall see later, Brahmo Samaj of India itself underwent a schism in 1872. Although these differences did lead to a dissociation between Devendranath and Keshub at the formal level, it is perhaps a tribute to them both that Devendranath was by Keshub's side when he passed away in 1884.

Devendranath became less active in public life after the schism in the Samaj, but pursued his own spiritual interests until he passed away at the venerable age of eighty-eight, to be remembered for his sageliness and by his various writings which include *Atmajivani* (autobiography), *Brahmo Dharmer Byakhyan* (the interpretation of the Brahmo Dharma), *Brahmo Dharmah* (an anthology), and *Atmatattvavidya* (self-knowledge).

Spiritual Transformation

Two experiences are said to have 'changed the course of Devendranath's life'.[6] The first was the experience he had at the age of fourteen when he was overcome by the sight of the star-studded sky, an experience whose power Kant has made us all aware of. He recalls it in the context of a subsequent attempt to fathom the mystery of God, when he scoured the thought of both East and West to find an answer to his questions.

What can we hope for, whom can we trust? Again I thought, as things are reflected on a photographic plate by the rays of the sun, so are material objects manifested to the mind by the senses; this is what is called knowledge. Is there any other way but this of obtaining knowledge? These were the suggestions that Western philosophy had brought to my mind. To an atheist this is enough, he does not want anything beyond Nature. But how could I rest fully satisfied with this? (My endeavour was to obtain God, not through blind faith but by the light of knowledge.) And being unsuccessful in this, my mental struggles increased from day to day. Sometimes I thought I could live no longer.

Suddenly, as I thought and thought, a flash as of lightning broke through this darkness of despondency. I saw that knowledge of the material world is born of the senses and the objects of sight, sound, smell, touch, and taste. But together with this knowledge, I am also enabled to know that I am the knower. Simultaneously with the facts of seeing, touching, smelling, and thinking, I also come to know that it is I who see, touch, smell, and think. With the knowledge of objects comes the knowledge of the subject; with the knowledge of the body comes the knowledge of the spirit within. It was after a prolonged search for truth that I found this bit of light, as if a ray of sunshine had fallen on a place full of extreme darkness. I now realised that with the knowledge of the outer world we come to know our inner self. After this, the more I thought over it, the more did I recognise the sway of wisdom operating throughout the whole world. For us the sun and moon rise and set at regular intervals, for us the wind and rain are set in motion in the proper seasons. All these combine to fulfil the one design of preserving our life. Whose design is this? It cannot be the design of matter, it must be the design of mind. Therefore this universe is propelled by the power of an intelligent being.

I saw that the child, as soon as born, drinks at its mother's breast. Who taught it to do this? He alone Who gave it life. Again, who put love into the mother's heart? Who but He that put milk into her breast. He is that God Who knows all our wants, Whose rule the universe obeys. When my mind's eye had opened thus far, the clouds of grief were in a great measure dispelled. I felt somewhat consoled.

One day, while thinking of these things, I suddenly recalled how, long ago, in my early youth, I had once realised the Infinite as manifested in the infinite heavens. Again I turned my gaze towards this infinite sky, studded with innumerable stars and planets, and saw the eternal God, and felt that this glory was His. He is Infinite Wisdom. He from Whom we have derived this limited knowledge of ours, and this body, its receptacle, is Himself without form. He is without body or senses. He did not shape this universe with His hands. By His will alone did He bring it into existence. He is neither the Kali of Kalighat, nor the family Shaligram. Thus was the axe laid at the root of idolatry. In studying the mechanism of creation, we find evidences of the wisdom of the Creator. On looking at the starry sky, we feel that He is infinite. By the help of this slender thread, His attributes became clearer to my mind. I saw that no one could frustrate the will of Him Who is Infinite Wisdom. Whatever He wills comes to pass. We collect all the necessary materials, and then make a thing; He by His will creates all the materials necessary for the making of things. He is not only the maker of the world, but what is more, He is its Creator. All created things are transient, corruptible, changeable, and dependent. The Perfect Wisdom that has created them and is guiding them; that alone is eternal, incorruptible, unchangeable, and self-dependent. That eternal, true and perfect Being is the source of all good, and the object of all worship. After debating in my mind for days and days I made sure of this much; after continuous and strenuous endeavour I arrived at this conclusion. And yet my heart kept trembling. The path of knowledge is beset with difficulties. (Who would bear me up, cheer and encourage me along this path?) Who would give his assent to the conclusion I had arrived at? Do you know what kind of assent I mean? Like that which I received from a boatman of the Padma.[7]

The other was the death of his grandmother seven years later, already alluded to. Such accounts are a significant feature of modern Hinduism. By contrast we possess only a few first-hand accounts of spiritual transformations or spiritual encounters from the earlier phases in the history of Hinduism.[8]

On the night before Didima's death I was sitting at Nimtola Ghat on a coarse mat near the shed. It was the night of the full moon; the moon had risen, the burning ground was near. They were singing the Holy Name to Didima:

Will such a day ever come, that while uttering the name of Hari, life will leave me?

The sounds reached my ears faintly, borne on the night-wind; at this opportune moment a strange sense of the unreality of all things suddenly entered my mind. I was as if no longer the same man. A strong aversion to wealth arose within me. The coarse bamboo-mat on which I sat seemed to be my fitting seat, carpets and costly spreadings seemed hateful, in my mind was awakened a joy unfelt before. I was then eighteen years old.

Up to this time I had been plunged in a life of luxury and pleasure. I had never sought after spiritual truths. What was religion? What was God? I knew nothing, had learnt nothing. My mind could scarcely contain the unworldly joy, so simple and natural, which I experienced at the burning-ghat. Language is weak in every way: how can I make others understand the joy I felt? It was a spontaneous delight, to which nobody can attain by argument or logic. God Himself seeks for the opportunity of pouring it out. He had vouchsafed it unto me in the fullness of time. Who says there is no God? This is proof enough of His existence. I was not prepared for it; whence then did I receive this joy?

With this sense of joy and renunciation, I returned home at midnight. That night I could not sleep. It was this blissful state of mind that kept me awake. Throughout the night my heart was suffused with a moonlight radiance of joy. At daybreak I went again to the river-side to see Didima. She was then drawing her last breaths. They had carried her into the water of the Ganges, and were fervently crying aloud, 'Ganga Narayan Brahma.' Didima breathed her last. I drew near and saw that her hand was placed on her breast, with the fourth finger pointing upwards. Turning her finger round and round, and crying 'Haribol,' she passed into the next world. When I saw this it seemed to me that at the time of death she pointed out to me with uplifted finger, 'That is God, and the Hereafter.' As Didima had been my friend in this life, so was she the guide to the next.

Her Shraddha ceremony was celebrated with great pomp. Anointing ourselves with oil and turmeric, we went and planted the *vrisha kashtha* of the Shraddha on the banks of the Ganges. These few days passed in a whirl of excitement and confusion. Then I tried to recover the joy of the night previous to Didima's death. But I never got it back. At this time the state of my mind was one of continued despondency and indifference to the world. On that night the indifference had been coupled with delight. Now, in the absence of that delight, a deep gloom settled on my mind. I longed for a repetition of that ecstatic feeling. I lost all interest in everything else.

Devendranath then proceeds to provide a Pauranic parallel of his experience.

There is a story in Bhagavata, which might furnish a parallel to my case. Narada is talking about himself thus to Vedavyasa. 'In my former birth I was the son of a certain Rishi's maidservant. During the rainy season, many holy people used to come and seek refuge in that Rishi's hermitage. I used to minister to their wants. In course of time divine wisdom dawned upon me, and my mind was filled with a single-hearted devotion to Hari. Then when those holy men were about to leave the hermitage they, in the goodness of their heart, taught me the mysteries of philosophy, which enabled me to understand clearly the glory of Hari. My mother was the Rishi's maidservant and I was her only son. It was only for her sake that I could not leave the Rishi's *asrama*. One night she went out to milk the cows. On the way she was bitten by a black serpent that she had trod on, and she died. But I looked upon this event as a great opportunity for the fulfilment of my desire, and alone I entered a huge and terrible forest, shrill with the voice of cicadas. In the course of my wanderings I felt very hungry and thirsty. I relieved my fatigue by drinking and bathing in a pool of water. Then I went and sat underneath an *ashvattha* tree, and according to the teaching of the saints began meditating on the Spirit of God dwelling within the soul. My mind was flooded with emotion, my eyes were filled with tears. All at once I saw the shining vision of Brahma in the lotus core of my heart. A thrill passed through my whole body, I felt a joy beyond all measure. But the next moment I could see Him no more. On losing sight of that beatific vision which destroys all sorrow, I suddenly rose from the ground. A great sadness came over my spirit. Then I tried to see Him again by force of contemplation, but found Him not. I became as one stricken with disease, and would not be comforted. Meanwhile I suddenly heard a voice in the air, 'In this life thou shalt see Me no more. Those whose hearts have not been purified, who have not attained the highest Yoga, cannot see Me. It was only to stimulate thy love that I once appeared before thee.'

I was exactly in the same position. For want of the joy of that night, my heart was sore distressed. But it was that which awakened my love of God. Only in one point did my case differ from this story of Narada's. His heart had first obtained love and faith by hearing the praise of Hari from the lips of the Rishis, and afterwards he received from them much instruction regarding the knowledge of Brahma. But I had had no opportunity of my love and faith being aroused by any such praises of Hari, nor had any one deigned to impart to me the truths of divine wisdom. The fair winds of luxury and pleasure were blowing all around me day and night. Yet in spite of these adverse circumstances, God in His mercy gave me the spirit of renunciation, and took away from me my attachment to the world. And then He Who is the source of all joy gave me new life by pouring streams of joy into my mind. This mercy of His is beyond compare. He alone is my Guru. He alone is my Father.[9]

From Spiritual Transformation to Religious Organization

The story of the formation of the religious organization is best told in Devendranath's own words.

When I was in this depressed state of mind, one day all of a sudden I saw a page from some Sanskrit book flutter past me. Out of curiosity I picked it up, but found I could understand nothing of what was written on it. I said to Shyamacharan Bhattacharya, who was sitting by me, 'I will come home soon, after attending to the business of the Union Bank. In the meantime you decipher the meaning of the verses on this page, so that you can explain it all to me on my return from office.' Saying this I hurried off to the Bank. At that time I had a post in the Union Bank. My youngest uncle, Ramanath Tagore, was the cashier, and I his assistant. I had to stay there from 10 o'clock until the day's work was over. It took us up to 10 o'clock at night to make up the accounts. But on that day, as I was to have the page out of the Sanskrit book explained to me by Shyamacharan Bhattacharya, I could not brook the delay of balancing accounts; so with my uncle's permission I came home early. I hurried up to the *boythakkhana* on the third storey, and asked Shyamacharan Bhattacharya to explain to me what was written on the printed page. He said, 'I have been trying hard all this time, but cannot make out its meaning.' This astonished me. English scholars can understand every book in the English language; why then cannot Sanskrit scholars understand every Sanskrit book? 'Who can make it out then?' I asked. He said, 'This is what the Brahma Sabha talks about. Ramchandra Vidyavagish of the Sabha could probably explain it.' 'Then call him,' said I. Soon afterwards Vidyavagish came to me. On reading the page he said, 'Why, this is the *Isopanishat.*'

When I learnt the explanation of '*Isavasyamidam sarvam*' from Vidyavagish, nectar from paradise streamed down upon me. I had been eager to receive a sympathetic response from men; now a divine voice had descended from heaven to respond in my heart of hearts, and my longing was satisfied. I wanted to see God everywhere, and what did I find in the Upanishads? I found, 'If the whole world could be encompassed by God, where would impurity be? Then all would be pure, the world would be full of sweetness.' I got just what I wanted. (I had never heard my most intimate thoughts expressed like this anywhere else.) Could men give any such response? The very mercy of God Himself descended into my heart; therefore I understood the deep significance of *Isavasyamidam sarvam*. Oh! what words were those that struck my ears! '*Tena tyaktena bhunjitha.*' 'Enjoy that which He has given unto thee.' What is it that He has given? He has given Himself. Enjoy that untold treasure; leave everything else and enjoy that supreme treasure. Cleave unto Him alone and give up all else. Blessed beyond measure is he who cleaves unto Him alone. This tells me that which I have long desired.

The keenness of my sorrow lay in this, that I was dead to all happiness, earthly and divine; I could take no delight in the things of this world, I could feel no joy in God.

But when the divine voice declared that I should renounce all desire of worldly pleasure and take my delight in God alone, I obtained what I had wished for, and was utterly flooded with joy. It was not the dictum of my own poor intellect, it was the word of God Himself. Glory be to that Rishi in whose heart this truth was first revealed! My faith in God took deep root; in lieu of worldly pleasure I tasted divine joy. Oh! what a blessed day was that for me—a day of heavenly happiness! Every word of the Upanishads tended to enlighten my mind. With their help I daily advanced along my appointed path. All the deepest significances began to be revealed to me. One by one I read with Vidyavagish the *Isa*, *Kena*, *Katha*, *Mundaka*, and *Mandukya* Upanishads, and the remaining six with other pundits. What I read each day, I at once committed to memory, and repeated the next day to Vidyavagish. Hearing my enunciation of the Vedas, he would ask, 'Whence did you learn this pronunciation? I must say we cannot pronounce like that.' I had learnt the pronunciation of the Vedas from a Dravidian Vedic Brahman.

When I had thoroughly entered into the Upanishads, and when my intellect began to be daily illumined by the light of truth, I felt a strong desire to spread the true religion. As a beginning I proposed to form an association with my brothers, friends, and relatives. There was a small room near the tank in our grounds, which I had whitewashed and cleaned. Meanwhile the Durga Puja season commenced. All the other members of our family gave themselves up to the excitement of this festival. Should we alone remain with empty hearts? On that *Krishna-chaturdasi* we founded an association, with hearts full of enthusiasm. We all bathed early in the morning, and in a purified state went and sat in that clean little room by the tank. It seemed as if Faith entered my heart as soon as I took my seat there with the others. As I looked around, each face was animated with reverence. The whole room was filled with an atmosphere of purity. After invoking the Deity with a fervid heart, I discoursed upon this text of the *Kathopanishad*:

> The Hereafter is hidden from the eyes of the foolish and of those blinded by riches.
>   Those who think that this world alone exists and there is no future existence, they come again and again under my yoke (that of Death).

Everybody listened to my discourse in a sacred and solemn mood. This was my first sermon. When it was over, I proposed that this Sabha should be called the 'Tatwaranjini Sabha,' and should be made permanent. All agreed to this. The object of this association was to gain the knowledge of God. The evening of the first Sunday in every month was the time appointed for the meeting of the assembly. At the second meeting Ramchandra Vidyavagish was invited, and I ordained him *acharya* (chief minister) of this Sabha. He named it 'Tatwabodhini' instead of 'Tatwaranjini.' Thus the Tatwabodhini Sabha was founded on Sunday, the fourteenth day of the dark fortnight, the 21st Ahswin, 1761 Shaka (6th October 1839).[10]

The Discarding of the Sacred Thread: An Incident

Social changes sometimes take a personal toll. As history they have an impersonal quality; as biography they are different.

I engaged eight or nine boats and took over all the Brahmas to this garden from Calcutta. This was the occasion of a great Brahma festival, where their goodwill, affection, and enthusiasm had full play. In the early morning, with the rising of the sun, we raised a paean of praise to Brahma; and sitting in the shade of a tree adorned with fruit and flowers, we delighted and sanctified ourselves by worshipping God with all our heart. At the conclusion of the service Rakhaldas Haldar proposed that: 'It is fit and proper that Brahmas should discard the sacred thread. As we have all become worshippers of the one and only God, it is better not to have any caste-distinctions. The Sikh community, worshippers of *Alakh Niranjan*, having all become one nation by giving up caste and adopting the surname of 'Singh,' obtained such strength of unity that, defeating such a dauntless Badshah of Delhi as Aurangzebe himself, they founded an independent kingdom.' When Rakhaldas Haldar's father heard of his son's proposal to renounce the sacred thread, he immediately tried to stab himself in the heart with a knife.[11]

The Source of Religious Authority

Belief in the infallibility of the Vedas is a basic tenet of orthodox Hinduism. It, however, was called into question with the introduction of Western education. Devendranath, after an initial phase of confidence in the doctrine, gradually 'had to admit against himself that some of these [Upaniṣads] contained passages that were irrational and did not square up with their belief in God as an Infinite, Immutable, Unsearchable, Eternal Being.'[12] He then located the seat of spiritual knowledge in the heart, but did not discard the Hindu scriptures, the way Keshub was to later when he gave an unexpected extension to this idea in his doctrine of Inspiration.[13]

I had started with the idea that there were eleven Upanishads in all, and their commentaries had been written by Shankaracharya. I now found that there were several Upanishads which had not been annotated by Shankaracharya. On investigation I found there were 147 Upanishads. Those ancient ones that Shankaracharya had commented upon were the most authentic. In them were contained teachings about the knowledge and worship of Brahma, and the way of salvation.

When these Upanishads came to be revered everywhere as the head and front of the Vedas and the choicest of all the *shastras*, then the Vaishnava and Shaiva sects began to disseminate works by the name of Upanishads in which they inculcated the worship of their own respective divinities, in place of the Supreme Soul. Then was composed the Gopal Tapani Upanishad, in which the Supreme Being's place was occupied by Sri Krishna. In that Gopal Tapani Upanishad Mathura is designated as Brahmapura and Sri Krishna as Parabrahma. Again there is a Gopinchandana Upanishad, in which instructions are given as to how the *tilaka* is to be made. In this way the Vaishnavas proclaimed the glory of their own deity. On the other hand, the Shaivas proclaimed the glory of Shiva in another book called the Skandopanishad. There are also the Sundari Tapani Upanishad, Devi Upanishad, Kaulopanishad, and others, in all of which only Sakti is glorified. Eventually anybody and everybody began to publish anything and everything with the name of Upanishad. In the days of Akbar an Upanishad was again composed with the object of converting Hindus into Musulmans—and it was called Allopanishad.

How strange! Formerly I did not know of the existence of this thorny tangle of Upanishads: only eleven Upanishads were known to me, with the help of which I had started the propagation of Brahma Dharma, making them its foundation. But now I saw that even this foundation was shaky and built upon sand; even here I did not touch firm ground. First I went back to the Vedas, but could not lay the foundation of the Brahma Dharma there; then I came to the eleven authentic Upanishads, but how unfortunate! Even there I could not lay the foundation. Our relation with God is that of worshipper and worshipped—this is the very essence of Brahmaism. When we found the opposite conclusion to this arrived at in Shankaracharya's *Sarirak mimamsa* of the Vedanta Darsana, we could no longer place any confidence in it; nor could we accept it as a support of our religion. I had thought that if I renounced the Vedanta Darsana and accepted the eleven Upanishads only, I would find a support for Brahmaism; hence I had relied entirely upon these, leaving aside all else. But when in the Upanishads I came across 'I am He' and 'Thou art That,' then I became disappointed in them also.

These Upanishads could not meet all our needs; could not fill our hearts. Then what was to be done now? What hope was there for us? Where should we week a refuge for Brahmaism? It could not be founded on the Vedas, it could not be founded on the Upanishads. Where was its foundation to be laid?

I came to see that the pure heart, filled with the light of intuitive

knowledge—this was its basis. Brahma reigned in the pure heart alone.
The pure, unsophisticated heart was the seat of Brahmaism. We could
accept those texts only of the Upanishads which accorded with that
heart. Those sayings which disagreed with the heart we could not
accept. These were the relations which were now established between
ourselves and the Upanishads, the highest of all *shastras*. In the
Upanishad itself we read that God is revealed through worship to the
heart illumined by an intellect free from all doubt. To the soul of the
righteous is revealed the wisdom of God. The Rishi of old who by
means of contemplation and the grace of wisdom had seen the Perfect
Brahma in his own pure heart, records his experience in these words:
'The pure in spirit, enlightened by wisdom, sees the holy God by means
of worship and meditation.'

These words accorded with experience of my own heart, hence I
accepted them.[14]

Criticism of Advaita

*Devendranath was a theist through and through, and unlike Rammohun Roy, he
vigorously repudiated Śakara's non-dualism.*

After this I used to go nearly every morning to Prasanna Kumar Tagore,
show him the accounts, and talk over money matters. Whenever I went,
I used to see his favourite boon companion, Naba Banerjee, by his side,
with a white *morassa* turban on. As the sheriff is to the judge's court, so
was Naba Banerjee to his *darbar*. In all matters he would take counsel
with him. Naba Banerjee was the only man he trusted. One day, in the
presence of Prasanna Kumar Tagore, this Naba Banerjee said to me,
'The *Tatwabodhini Patrika* is an excellent paper. I sit in Babu's library
and read it; it imparts knowledge and arouses one's faculties; from it
one gains wisdom.' 'Do you read the *Tatwabodhini?*' said I. 'Don't read
it, don't read it.' 'Why?' asked Prasanna Kumar Tagore. 'What happens
if you read the *Tatwabodhini?*' I said, 'Reading the *Tatwabodhini* brings
one to such a plight as mine.' He said, 'I say, Devendra has come out
with a confession, he has made a real confession!' and broke out into
loud laughter. 'Well,' said he to me, 'can you prove to me that God
exists?' 'Can you prove to me that wall is there?' I replied. He laughed
and said, 'Upon my word, what a question! I can see that the wall is
there; what is there to prove?' I said, 'I see that God is everywhere;
what is there to prove?' 'As if God is the same as the wall!' he answered.

'Ha, ha! what is Devendra saying?' I said, 'God is something even nearer to me that this wall—He is within me, within my soul. The sacred books speak ill of those who do not believe in God. "The *asuras* cling to falsehood, they say there is no God in this world."' He said, 'But I revere this saying of the Scriptures above all others, "I am the Supreme Deity, eternal, free and self-existent; I am none other."'

If he had put forward some other proud claim such as, 'I am wealthy, I am lord over many: who is there equal to me?'—then there would have been some sense in his claim. But that I myself am the Supreme Deity—such vaunting is the source of much evil; one feels ashamed at the very idea. Bound as we are by a thousand worldly coils—steeped as we are in decay and sorrow, sin and evil—what is more strange than that we should consider ourselves eternal, free, and self-existent? Shankacharya had turned India's head by preaching the doctrine of Monism; the identity of God and man. Following his teachings, both ascetics and men of the world are repeating this senseless formula, 'I am that Supreme Deity.'[15]

Selective Use of Scriptures

Although this trend can be traced to Roy, it is in Devendranath that we find the evolution of a scriptural strategy which became a characteristic feature of modern Hinduism[16]—namely, the selective use of scriptural sources, to the extent of even combining different verses to produce a new one. Brahmo Dharma I.12.109, which is reproduced below, combines Bṛhadāraṇyaka Upaniṣad II.4.3 and I.3.28 from the same source, with Aitareya (Benediction) and concludes with Śvetāśvatara IV.21.[17]

> Yenaham namrita syam kimaham tena kuryyam
> Asato ma sad gamaya
> Tamaso ma jyotir gamaya
> Mrityormamritam gamaya
> Avir avir ma edhi
> Rudra yatte dakshinam mukham tena mam pahi nityam

> What should I do with that by which I do not become immortal.
> From unreal lead me to the real.
> From darkness lead me to light.
> From death lead me to immortality.
> O thou manifest one, be manifest for me.
> O Rudra, may your face which is gracious protect me forever.[18]

The Divinity of Beauty

The aesthetic instinct is close to the religious—and some have a deeper appreciation of this than others. Gandhi saw God clothed in morality, Rabindranath saw Him also clothed in beauty; so did his father Devendranath.

A servant who was with me gave me the flowering branch of a creeper. I had never seen such a beautiful flowering creeper before. My eyes were opened, and my heart expanded; I saw the Universal Mother's hand resting on those small white blossoms. Who was there in this forest to inhale the scent of these flowers or see their beauty? Yet with what loving care had she endowed them with sweet scent and loveliness, moistened them with dew, and set them upon the creeper! Her mercy and tenderness became manifest in my heart. Lord! when such is Thy compassion for these little flowers, what must be the extent of Thy mercy for us?

Thy mercy will endure in my heart and soul for ever and ever.
Thy mercy has pierced my soul so deeply, that even though I were to lose my head, it would never depart from within my heart.

I repeated this verse of Hafiz aloud the whole day on my way, and remained steeped in the waters of His mercy till evening, when shortly before sunset I reached a peak called Sunghri. How and when the day passed away I knew not. From this high peak I was enchanted with the beauty of two mountain ranges facing each other. One of the hills contained a deep forest, the abode of bears and suchlike wild animals. Another hill was coloured gold from top to bottom with ripe fields of wheat. Scattered upon it at long distances were villages consisting of ten or twelve huts grouped together, shining in the sun. Some hills, again, were covered with short grasses from head to foot. Other hills, by their very nakedness, heightened the beauty of their wooded neighbours. Each mountain was standing serenely in the pride of its own majesty, without fear of any one. But the wayfarers on its bosom were in a state of continual fear, like the servants of a king—one false step meant destruction. The sun set, and darkness began gradually to steal across the earth. Still I sat alone on that peak. From afar the twinkling lights here and there upon the hills alone gave evidence of human habitation.[19]

Visit to Amritsar

A fraternal attitude towards other religions of Indian origin is an important dimension of modern Hinduism, although not without its problems.

Devendranath's visit to Amritsar offers not only a glimpse of how someone belonging to the oldest living religion of India relates to the youngest but also something more. It offers the reflections of the leader of a later reform movement within Hinduism, loosely defined, upon an earlier reform movement—movements whose relationship to Hinduism have assumed different configurations over time.

Although I had come to Amritsar, yet my heart was set on that other Amritsar, that lake of immortality, where the Sikhs worship the Alakh Niranjan or Inscrutable Immortal One. Quite early in the morning, I hurried through the town to see that holy shrine of Amritsar. After wandering through several streets, I at last asked a passerby where Amritsar was. He stared at me in surprise and said, 'Why, this is Amritsar.' 'No,' said I; 'where is that Amritsar where God is worshipped with sacred chanting?' He replied, 'The Gurudwara? Oh, that is quite near; go this way.'

Taking the road indicated, and going past the bazar of red cloth shawls and scarves, I saw the golden spire of the temple shining in the morning sun. Keeping this in view, I arrived at the temple, and saw a big tank, four or five times the size of the Laldighi in Calcutta. This was the lake. It is replenished by the waters of the river Iravati, flowing through the canal of Madhavapur. Guru Ramdas had this fine tank dug here, and called it Amritsar. Formerly it was called 'Chak.'

In the midst of the lake, like an islet, there is a white marble temple, which I entered by passing over a bridge. In front there was a huge pile of books covered over with a parti-coloured (sic) silk cloth. One of the chief Sikhs of the temple was waving a plume over it. On one side, singers were chanting from the sacred books. Punjabi men and women came and walked round the temple, and having made their salutations with offerings of shells and flowers, went away. Some stayed, and sang with devotion. Here all may come and go when they please; nobody asks them to come, nobody tells them not to. Christians and Mahomedans, all may come here; only according to the rules none may enter the bounds of the Gurudwara with shoes on. All the Sikhs felt deeply humiliated and aggrieved by this rule being transgressed by the Governor-General, Lord Lytton.

I again went to the temple in the evening, and saw that the *arati* of vesper ceremony was being performed. A Sikh was standing in front of the Books, with five-wick lamp in hand, performing the arati. All the other Sikhs stood with joined hands, repeating with him in solemn tones:

In the disc of the sky,
The sun and the moon shine as lamps;
The galaxy of stars glitter like pearls,
The zephyr is incense, the winds are as fans,
All the woods are bright with flowers.
Oh Saviour of the world, Thine arati
Is wonderful indeed! Loud sounds the drum,
And yet no hand doth beat it!
My soul is ever panting and athirst for the honey of Hari's lotus-feet;
Give the waters of Thy mercy to the *chatak* Nanak, so that I may dwell in
Thy Name.

At the close of the arati, *kada bhog* (a kind of sweetmeat) was
distributed to all. The worship of God is carried on thus in the temple
night and day for twenty-one hours; prayers being suspended for the
last three hours of the night in order to cleanse the temple. In the
Brahma-Samaj, we have prayers for two hours in the week only; and
in the Sikh temple of Hari, there is worship night and day. If any one
feels restless and distressed, he can go there even at night, and pray,
and find peace. This good example should be followed by the Brahmas.

The Sikhs have no Guru or spiritual perceptor now. Their books
occupy his place. Their tenth and last Guru was Guru Govinda. It
was he that broke up the caste system of the Sikhs, and introduced
the custom of initiation amongst them which goes by the name of
'pahal,' and is still in existence. He who wants to became a Sikh must
first perform the pahal. This custom is as follows: Sugar is thrown
into a vessel filled with water, which is then stirred with a sword or
knife, and sprinkled on those who are to become Sikhs. They all then
drink this sugared water out of the same cup. Brahman, Kshatriya,
and Sudra, all may become Sikhs without distinction of caste.
Mahomedans also can become Sikhs. Whoever becomes a Sikh is
given the surname Singh. There is no image in this temple of the
Sikhs; for Nanak has said, 'He cannot be placed anywhere, none can
make Him; He is the Self-existent stainless One.' But strange to say,
having received these noble teachings of Nanak—and worshipping
as they do the formless Brahma—the Sikhs have yet founded a temple
of Shiva within the precincts of the Gurudwara. They also believe in
the goddess Kali. It is no easy matter for anybody to keep this Brahmic
vow—'I shall not worship any created thing, thinking it to be the
supreme Deity.' A great festival takes place in this temple during Holi.
The Sikhs then give themselves up to drink. They take liquor, but do
not smoke; [they] do not even touch the *hookah* or *chillum*.

Many Sikhs used to come to my rooms, and I used to learn the Gurumukhi language and their religious doctrines from them. I did not find much religious zeal amongst them. I met one zealous Sikh, who said to me, 'If one died weeping, without having tasted the immortal nectar, what then?' I said weeping and mourning for him would not have been in vain.[20]

The Educational Defence of Hinduism

Devendranath Tagore, though immersed in spiritual life, was not oblivious of the practical dimension of it. When one Umeshchandra Sarkar and his young wife were forcibly converted by Duff against the protests of their relatives, the conscience of the Hindu community of Calcutta was roused to its depths.[21] That included Devendranath:

One morning, in the month of Byśakh 1767 (AD 1845), I was reading the papers, when a clerk of our Bank, Rajendranath Sircar, came to me with tears in his eyes. He said, 'Last Sunday my wife and the wife of my youngest brother Umeschandra were going to a party in a carriage, when Umeschadra came and took his wife out of the carriage by force, and they both went off to Dr Duff's house to become Christians. My father, after much fruitless effort to bring them back from there, filed a complaint in the Supreme Court. That complaint was dismissed. But I went to Dr Duff, and, telling him that we would again file a complaint, entreated him not to baptize my brother and sister-in-law until the second judgment was given. But he has been deaf to my entreaties and has baptized them last evening.' And Rajedranath fell to weeping.

At this I felt greatly indignant and distressed. They are making Christians even of our Zenana ladies! Wait a bit, I am going to put a stop to this. So saying, I was up. I immediately set Akshay Kumar Datta's pen in motion, and a spirited article appeared in the *Tatwabodhini Patrika*: 'Even the ladies of our Zenana are falling away from their own religion and adopting that of others. Are we not to be roused even by the direct evidence of such dreadful calamities? How much longer are we going to remain overpowered by the sleep of inaction? Behold, our religion is being altogether destroyed, our country is on the road to ruin, and our very Hindu name is about to wiped out for ever . . . . Therefore, if you desire your own welfare and that of your family, if you hope for the advancement of our country and have regard for truth, then keep your boys aloof from all contact with missionaries. Give up sending your sons to their schools, and take immediate steps to enable them to cultivate their minds with due vigour. Perhaps you will say, where else can the children of the poor receive education except in mission schools? But is not this a crying shame? In order to spread their own religion the Christians have set at naught the waves of the deep sea, and entering India are founding schools in every town and every village; whereas we have not got a single good school of our own where our children can be taught. If we all combine could we not set up schools as good as theirs or ten times better? What object is there which cannot be achieved by unity?'

Akshay Kumar Datta's article was published in the *Patrika*, and after that I went about in a carriage every day from morning till evening to all the leading and distinguished men in Calcutta, and entreated them to adopt measures by which Hindu children would no longer have to attend missionary schools and might be educated in schools of our own. Raja Radhakanta Deb and Raja Satyacharan Ghosal on the one hand, on the other hand Ramgopal Ghose—I went to each and all of them, and incited them all. They were all fired by my enthusiasm. This did away with the rivalry between the Dharma sabha and the Brahma sabha, and all their disagreement with each other. All were ranged on the same side, and tried their best to prevent children going to Christian schools and missionaries making Christian converts. A large meeting was convened on the 13th Jaishtha, at which nearly a thousand people assembled. It was resolved that, as missionaries had their free schools, so we also should have a school where children would be taught free of charge. We were waiting subscription-book in hand to see what each one would subscribe, when Ashutosh Deb and Pramathanath Deb took the book and put down ten thousand rupees against their names. Raja Satyacharan Ghosal subscribed three thousand, Brajanath Dhar two thousand, and Raja Radhakanta Deb one thousand. In this manner forty thousand rupees were raised then and there. Then we knew that our labours were crowned with success. As a result of this meeting an educational institution called the *Hindu-hitarthi* was founded, and Raja Radhakanta Deb Bahadur was appointed president to carry on its work. Harimohun Sen and I became the secretaries. Babu Bhudeb Mukhopadhaya was the first teacher appointed in this free school. Thenceforward the tide of Christian conversion was stemmed, and the cause of the missionaries received a serious blow.[22]

A Meditation

Devendranath's autobiography testifies to a life of austerity, but rich in interiority, of which the following meditation might provide a fitting example:

Even in the cold of Pausha and Magha I would not allow the fire to be lighted in my room. I followed this rule in order to find out for myself how much cold the human body is capable of bearing, and to acquire habits of endurance and fortitude. At night I used to leave my bedroom windows open; and I enjoyed the cold night wind very much indeed. Wrapping myself in a blanket, and sitting up in bed oblivious of all else, I spent half the night reciting hymns and the verses of Hafiz. It is the holy man who keeps awake, not the man of pleasure nor the sick man. 'He who knows Brahma, who contemplates Brahma, who drinks the nectar of delight in Brahma, who loves Brahma—he it is that wakes.'

The lamp that turns night into day, in whose chamber is that lamp?
It has burnt my life to ashes; to whom, I ask, has it brought delight?

Those nights in which I felt His intimate companionship I repeated aloud in ecstasy:

Do not bring a lamp into my audience-hall to-day.
To-night, that full moon my Friend is shining here.[23]

The nights I spent thus delightfully, and in the daytime remained plunged in deep mediation. Every day till noon I sat rigidly with folded limbs, and concentrated my mind on the consideration and examination of the first principles of the soul. Finally, I came to this conclusion, that thoughts which were opposed to first principles could not be entertained in the mind at all. The latter were not any man's individual way of thinking; they were universally true for all time. The authenticity of first principles did not depend on anything else; they were self-evident, and proved themselves, since they were founded on spiritual consciousness. Relying on these first principles the ancient sages of the Upanishads have said:

This is the glory of that Supreme Deity, by Whom the wheel of this universe is made to revolve.

Deluded by ignorance, some thinkers say it is by the laws of nature— by the blind force of matter—that this wide world goes round; or others say that it is without any cause, by the force of Time alone. But I say—it is the glory of that Supreme Deity alone, by Whom this universal wheel is being turned:

> The whole world has come forth from the Living God. It exists by the power of the Living God.
> This divine Being, Maker of the Universe, Supreme Soul, dwells for ever in the hearts of men.

These irrefutable truths concerning first principles have overflowed from the pure hearts of the Rishis.

The tree that stands in front of us we see and touch; but we can neither see nor touch the space in which it stands. In course of time the tree puts forth branches and leaves, and bears flowers and fruit; we see all this, but cannot see the thread of time which runs through all. We see the power of the life-force by which the tree is enabled to draw sap from its roots and nourish itself, the force which operates in every vein of its leaves; but that force we cannot see. That conscious Being, by Whose will the tree has received this life-force—He Himself pervades the tree through and through, but Him we cannot see:

> This secret Spirit exists in all creatures and in all things; but He is not revealed.
> The senses perceive only outward things, they cannot perceive that which is within. This is their shame:
> The self-existent God has made senses face outwards; hence they see outward things alone, not the soul within.
> Sometimes a wise man, desirous of immortality, closes his eyes and sees a Spirit dwelling in all things.

Hearing this precept, laying it to heart, and pondering deeply upon it, I saw God, not with fleshly eyes, but with the inner vision, from these Himalayan Hills, the holy land of Brahma. This was given me by the Upanishads. They say, 'All things are enveloped in God.' I enveloped all things with God, 'Now I have come to know that great sun-coloured Being beyond this darkness.'

> Henceforward I shall radiate light from my heart upon the world;
> For I have reached the Sun, and darkness has vanished.[24]

Notes

1. *The Autobiography of Maharshi Devendranath Tagore* (trans. Satyendranath Tagore and Indira Devi. London: MacMillan & Co Ltd, 1914), pp. 38ff.
2. Narayan Chaudhuri, *Maharshi Devendranath Tagore* (New Delhi: Sahitya Akademi, 1973), p. 20.
3. Ibid., p. 32.
4. Ibid., p. 33.
5. Ibid., p. 54.

6. Chaudhuri, p. 13.
7. *The Autobiography of Maharshi Devendranath Tagore*, p. 51.
8. Ibid., pp. 38–40.
9. Ibid., pp. 40–3.
10. Ibid., pp. 56–61.
11. Ibid., pp. 82–3.
12. Chaudhuri, p. 39.
13. D.S. Sarma, *Hinduism Through the Ages* (Bombay: Bharatiya Vidya Bhavan, 1956), p. 77.
14. *The Autobiography of Maharshi Devendranath Tagore*, pp. 159–62.
15. Ibid., pp. 198–9.
16. See Troy Wilson Organ, *The Hindu Quest for the Perfection of Man* (Athens: Ohio University Press, 1970), p. 345, note 46.
17. Chaudhuri, p. 42.
18. S. Radhakrishnan, ed., *The Principal Upaniṣads*, (Atlantic Highlands, NJ: Humanities Press, 1996), pp. 162, 195–6, 514, 737.
19. *The Autobiography of Maharshi Devendranath Tagore*, pp. 240–41.
20. Ibid., pp. 215–19.
21. Chaudhuri, p. 26.
22. *The Autobiography of Maharshi Devendranath Tagore*, pp. 98–101. Glyn Richards has this to say about the incident: 'He attracted many able young men to the movement including Keshub Chunder Sen and showed great enthusiasm for the purification of the Hindu religion and for the education of children. In 1845 he joined the campaign against Christian conversions through education provided in Christian schools and to combat this practice sought to establish a school for Hindu children where they might receive education free of charge. At a meeting in Calcutta attended by almost a thousand people it was resolved to found such a school and it was called the Hind-hitarthi (the well-wisher of Hindus). While Tagore approved of the efforts of Christians for the welfare of his fellow countrymen he did not believe that they had much to offer that would help India to develop its own religious heritage.' (*A Source-book of Modern Hinduism* [London: Curzon Press, 1985], p. 24). For a recent allusion to this incident see Sumit Sarkar, 'Conversion and Politics of Hindu Right', *Economic and Political Weekly*, 26 June 1999, p. 1695.
23. This and the earlier verse above are from Hafiz.
24. *The Autobiography of Maharshi Devendranath Tagore*, pp. 251–3.

Keshub Chunder Sen
(1838–1884)

Life

Keshub Chunder Sen, who belonged to the Vaidya caste, hailed from one of the leading families of Bengal and his education had a strong Western orientation. 'He never learnt Sanskrit'—a deficiency Dayananda did not fail to remind him of[1]—and 'his knowledge of the Hindu scriptures was very much inferior to his extremely thorough knowledge of, and ability to quote from, the Bible.'[2]

The religious impulse manifested itself early in his life. As a result he abjured meat in his fourteenth year. As the urge to pray surfaced, idolatry fell by the wayside. We owe these details to his autobiographical accounts, delivered in the form of sermons between July and December 1882, in Bengali (even though English came more naturally to him) and compiled under the title *Jivanbed* or the Veda of Life.

After experimenting with the formation of a religious society, Keshub joined the Brahmo Samaj when he discovered that its tenets accorded with his own. This occurred in 1857 and after Devendranath's return from the hills in 1858 they gravitated towards each other.

Three incidents strengthened this bond: Keshub spending the day he was to be initiated by the family *guru*, but did not want to, at Devendranath's house; Keshub accompanying Devendranath, a Brahmin who had lost caste, across the seas one was forbidden to cross, to Ceylon; and Keshub taking his wife along, against the rules of female seclusion, to join him in the festivities on his appointment as an *ācārya* in the Brahmo Samaj in 1862.[3] By now he had also quit his job and with the help of providence and patrimony, was engaged entirely in the affairs of the Samaj.

Keshub's rise in the Samaj was rapid but led to a schism in 1867, over the question of the appointment of *ācāryas* (namely, whether formal Brahmin *ācāryas* should be retained). More broadly, it reflected a clash between the reformist elements led by Keshub, and more conservative elements (although the differences were really over the pace rather than the fact of reform). The Brahmin *acaryas* were first removed but then reinstated. The Brahmo Samaj could not survive the convulsion intact.

The new Brahmo Samaj of India (the original body now being known as Adi Brahmo Samaj) was highly successful under Keshub's leadership, and underwent a period of consolidation and expansion from 1866–69, culminating in Keshub's trip to England in 1870. During this trip he met Max Mueller, who wrote in a letter to his wife: 'We soon got into a warm discussion, and it was curious to see how we almost made him confess himself a Christian.' When asked by Max Mueller why he did not publicly declare himself one, Keshub said: 'Suppose that fifty years hence people found out that I was a disciple of Christ, what would be the harm? *Only were I to profess myself a Christian now, all my influence would be gone at once.*'[4] To Mueller also we owe the following account of his meeting with Dr Pusey:

> Dr. Pusey was at first reserved till the conversation turned on prayer. Keshub Chunder Sen, while defending his own position towards Christianity, burst out into an eloquent panegyric on prayer which ended with the words, 'I am always praying.' This touched Pusey's heart, and he said, 'Then you cannot be far wrong.'[5]

Keshub epitomized the impact of his visit to England thus:

> . . . as I came here an Indian, I go back a confirmed Indian; I came here a Theist, I return a confirmed Theist. I have learnt to love my own country more and more. English patriotism has by a sort of electric process quickened my own patriotism. I came here a believer in the Fatherhood of God and the Brotherhood of Man, and I shall return confirmed in this belief. I have not accepted one single new doctrine that God had not put into my mind before; I have not accepted new dogmas or doctrines, but I have tried as far as possible to imbibe the blessed influence of Christian lives. I have placed myself at the feet of Christians of all shades of opinion, and tried to gather from their lives and examples all that was calculated to enlighten me and to purify me, and to sanctify my native land; and I have been amply repaid for all my exertions. I am now, thank God, a man of the world, and can say that England is as much my Father's house as India . . . .[6]

A major accomplishment of Keshub, upon returning from England, was the passage of the Native Marriage Act in 1872, which legalized Brahmo marriages as distinct from Hindu marriages. However, during the period from 1871–77, Keshub in general became more moderate in relation to traditional Hinduism and even began to use Bengali.

The Marriage Act just referred to was destined to cause another schism. Through a series of events too tedious to detail, Keshub's own daughter came to be betrothed to the prince of Cooch Bihar, before she had reached the minimum age of 14, as specified in the very Act Keshub had piloted. Although this was technically not a Brahmo marriage, the Samaj felt let down. Keshub, who was originally opposed to the match, finally consented, claiming to have heard the word of God.

This led to a schism in 1878, after which Keshub proclaimed the New Dispensation in 1879. Thereafter Keshub plunged into a vortex of activity until he passed away in 1884.

> On his sickbed he received visits from Debendranath, Ramakrishna and the bishop of Calcutta. On his death he was supposed to have cried out 'Mother', 'Mother of Buddha', and to have asked for a hymn about Christ's sufferings in Gethsemane. After prolonged suffering he eventually died of diabetes on 8 January 1884. His body was cremated on 13 January according to the reformed rites of his own *Nava Samhita*. The Memorial Meeting in the Town Hall was attended by over 2,000 people from the Muslim, Hindu, Brahmo and Christian communities, overlooking their differences to unite in mourning the loss of a man whom Max Mueller described as India's 'greatest son'.[7]

The New Dispensation

The New Dispensation, or Naba Bidhan (Nava Vidhāna in Sanskrit) as it was called, places Keshub's syncretic vision in a biblical background. It was meant as a gospel and a church on the same level as the Jewish and Christian dispensations; as the fulfilment of Christ's prophecy; as the harmonization of all scriptures and all religions; and as a message of love which proscribed every distinction between Brahmins and Śūdras, Asiatics and Europeans. Its universal character is illustrated by his description of it as 'the celestial court where around enthroned Divinity shine the lights of all heavenly saints and prophets. Its uniqueness for him lay in its insistence on direct worship with no mediator between God and man.'[8]

> What I accept as the New Dispensation in India neither shuts out God's light from the rest of the world, nor does it run counter to any of those marvellous dispensations of His mercy which were made in ancient times. It only shows a new adaptation of His eternal goodness, an Indian version and application of His universal love.

Is this new gospel a Dispensation, or is it simply a new system of religion, which human understanding has evolved? I say it stands upon the same level with the Jewish dispensation, the Christian dispensation, and the Vaishnava dispensation through Chaitanya. It is a divine Dispensation, fully entitled to a place among the various dispensations and revelations of the world.

My individuality is lost in the community that forms my Church. This dispensation will not tolerate any form of egotism. It hides me in my brother-apostles.... We are lost in each other, and all distinctive personality is merged in the unity of the common Church.... While other dispensations have their special mediatorial agencies between God and a sinful world, here we have no such thing, no intercessor, no mediator .... Upon every theist the new gospel imposes the inviolable vow of direct worship. This is the peculiarity of the present dispensation, and in this, more perhaps than in anything else, it differs from all other dispensations.

Besides immediacy there is another characteristic of the present dispensation which distinguishes it from all other religions. It is inclusive, while they are more or less exclusive. They exclude each other. But this includes all religions. This dispensation shuns altogether the old-path of exclusivism, and establishes for itself the new character of an all-embracing and all-absorbing eclecticism. No one can be true to the New Dispensation who indulges in sectarian hatred and bigotry, and lives in a strait church which excludes the rest of the world.

We are the fulfilment of Moses. He was simply the incarnation of Divine conscience. But there was no science in his teachings, that science which in modern times is so greatly honoured. Let Moses grow into modern science, and you have the New Dispensation, which may be characterized as the union of conscience and science. As for Christ, we are surely among his honoured ambassadors. We are a deduction and corollary from his teachings. The New Dispensation is Christ's prophecy fulfilled.

Paul was raised by God to break caste, and level the distinctions of race and nationality; and nobly did he fulfil his mission. The Jew and the Gentile he made into one body. The modern Pauls of the New Dispensation are carrying on a similar crusade against caste in India. The obnoxious distinctions between Brahmin and Sudra, between Hindu and Yavana, between Asiatic and European, the new gospel of love thoroughly proscribes .... In this anti-caste movement, which daily brings Jew and Gentile, Hindu and Christian, nearer and nearer in spiritual fellowship, the chief workers are verily spiritual descendants of Moses, Jesus, and Paul.

Such is the New Dispensation. It is the harmony of all scriptures and prophets and dispensations. It is not an isolated creed, but the science which binds and explains and harmonizes all religions. It gives to history a meaning, to the action of Providence a consistency, to quarrelling churches a common bond, and to successive dispensations a continuity. It shows marvellous synthesis how the different rainbow colours are one in the light of heaven. The New Dispensation is the sweet music of diverse instruments. It is the precious necklace in which are strung together the rubies and pearls of all ages and climes. It is the celestial court where around enthroned Divinity shine the lights of all heavenly saints and prophets. It is the wonderful solvent, which fuses all dispensations into a new chemical compound. It is the mighty absorbent, which absorbs all that is true and good and beautiful in the objective world. Before the flag of the New Dispensation bow ye nations, and proclaim the Fatherhood of God and the Brotherhood of man.[9]

God and India

Like most leading Indians, Keshub too felt that God had a special dispensation for India.

God's Special Dispensation in India
Chinsurah, 26 October 1879

India's God, cause Thy grace to descend upon us that we may prove true to Thee and to our Motherland. All-Perfect, All-Holy God, fill us with Thy holy presence, inspire my lips with Thy holy wisdom that I, Thy humble servant, may speak words of faith and hope. Father, give us Thy grace.

Fellow-countrymen, I believe that God has given us a special Dispensation. He has selected this country to save it. He has kindled in India a holy fire that will disperse all the moral and spiritual gloom that has for centuries covered the face of the country. India is now under the benign influences of God's special grace. All seers and prophets of old India are before us. We see in India the relics of fallen greatness. We have heard a voice from God to establish His kingdom in India. We are in a time of prophetic wisdom. We have seen strange things and we have received communications from Heaven. The prophets of bygone ages studied Nature, and through Nature they received inspiration. Our forefathers contemplated God on the heights of the Himalayas. They saw with eyes raised upward the Spirit of God; they saw the beauty of God in flowers, in rivers, and everywhere. All the scientists of these days acknowledge the existence of a mighty uncreated force under all these natural phenomena; but they dare not call it God. They have contaminated and sophisticated themselves by false philosophy. They are wallowing in the mire of scepticism. They would not admit that God's communications are made to us now as directly as they were made in olden times to the ancient seers and prophets. To the ancient prophets all Nature was full of God. Some of them used to baptize their followers with water. They used the plain crystal water for human sanctification. Water is Nature's high priest. There in every drop of water is the indwelling presence of God. But we are forgetful of God; we do not behold Him although He encircles us on all sides. God is everywhere or He is nowhere. If my soul is infidel I can see him nowhere. Faith beholds Him in every grain of corn or in every blade of grass. Do you sincerely believe in God? Is He not present to-day as He was present a thousand years back? Is not God's inspiration universal and everlasting? India's God is not confined to this place or that place. Did not your prophet Chaitanya behold God everywhere? Know ye not that ye are the temples of the Living God? Upon the pedestal of your own heart I wish to establish God's throne. Why should we undertake a pilgrimage to Brindaban or Benares when God is with us? Have sincere and earnest belief in the Real God of the universe. Books will never cure your atheism. What do you see in India to-day? Civilization on one side, and on the other scepticism and dissipation. O degraded Bengal, how long will you swallow the abominable infidelity of Western civilization? Ah! our fathers were simple. They used to learn the wisdom and love of God at the feet of the Ganges and trees. The modern civilized hypocrites are splendid book-worms. They forsake yonder trees. But if you can spurn that little blade of grass you are not a scientist. If you really seek true wisdom you must convert yourselves into *Dhrubo* or *Prahlada*, and have unswerving faith in the saving efficacy of God. You will not need books or earthly instructors to teach you true wisdom; but simply pray to the Living God and He will inspire you with divine wisdom. There is not a drop of blood in your body which does not come from God's feet. There is not a drop of water which you drink which does not come fresh from God. And God dwells concealed in every radiant flame. There is God in every flash of lightning as well as in a vast conflagration. When the sun rises it brings to us the gladdening messages of God's radiance. Study the sun, the moon, the human body, and then come and say whether you live in an atheistic universe. The beautiful volume of Nature is before you. It incessantly proclaims the Great God who is the Father of all nations. Imbue your heart with God's loving wisdom. Every little child whom the mother presses to her bosom is prophetic and poetic. Why should we not be like these little children? Those who are full of the conceit of the world, and delight only in carnal pleasures, cannot behold God in Nature. There is vile infidelity in them. But the men of simple faith, who have no other language but that of prayer, know no one else but their Mother God. The child only wants to know who is its mother. The child is perfectly happy when it has learnt to love its mother, who is its saviour, protector, and teacher.

So you will enjoy perfect happiness if you only trust the Supreme Mother of the universe. Why should you ask me to-night which religion is true? My business is with God and not with controversial theology. For a quarter of a century I have lived in and for Him. He is my life and vitality, and He is my habitation where I will dwell for ages without end. O my countrymen, see the real God of India, and your eyes shall be pure. Show that you are pushing your energies uphill. I am full of hope for the future of India. Behold these two flags. One says, 'Truth will triumph.' The other says, 'Come, all nations, unto the true God.' The Kingdom of heaven will certainly be established in India. True religion will sweep off all the accumulated errors and sins of India.

One word more. The Lord God is not only the world's Saviour but Salvation. See Him, hear Him, and touch His feet. Here is our God, our Friend.

O God, India's God, ancient India's God, modern India's God, so many are gathered under Thy feet; in the plenitude of Thy mercy tear our bonds of sin, that all India may ascribe to Thee glory for ever. India knows Thee alone. O Lord God, do Thou save India.[10]

State of England

Indians had a strange love-hate relationship with England. The one thing they could not do was to ignore it. What they did do was to both admire and revile it. That even such a Westernized and virtually Christianized Indian as Keshub Chunder Sen should display both these streaks takes one by surprise.

Englishmen and their Dinners

Would you like to eat and drink in the English way? I really think it is barbarous. (*Laughter and applause.*) A vegetarian in the midst of carnivorous England! (*Applause.*) I am sure if the people of India were to see the horrors of the meat market in London they would never send their little children to England. (*Laughter.*) Certainly horrid English beef is a horror. I was invited to many dinner parties, and what did I invariably see there? Why, the dining room appeared to be more like a Zoological garden; there were all sorts of fowls of the air, the beasts of the wilderness, and fishes of the sea and creeping things laid on the table. (*Laughter.*) They were about to start into a new life as it were. (*Shrieks of laughter.*) I need not say I could not positively say whether they were alive or dead. These are the things which our English friends eat. I am glad I have run away from England. (*Laughter.*) But English fashions and dinners! These are really two things that are barbarous. Excuse my saying so, but I honestly believe they are barbarous. (*Laughter.*)

Protest Against English Fashions and Dinners

I think there ought to be a protest against what is called 'fashion' in England. It is a dangerous thing and makes frightful progress. The tails of the ladies' dresses should be protested against and the horrors of English dinners ought to be protested against, and if you, my countrymen, are really anxious to promote the welfare of your country, avoid these two things. (*Laughter.*) Import into your country all that is good in England but not these horrid things.

English Poverty and English Charity

Do not allow yourselves to be carried away by the idea that every thing that pertains to that country is grand and glorious. (*Applause.*) No, there are the worst men in England—(*applause*)—as there are the best everywhere. The worst, the lowest, the most wicked are to be found in it. Destitution, poverty in its worst and most frightful phases is found in the streets of London—ignorance, frightful and appalling, pervade the masses of the people. These know not their God; they are worse than those whom Christians denounce as heathen. There is a large quantity of heathenism—too much, I may say—in Christian England—there is much ignorance, much spiritual destitution. And what does all this show? That, how, even in the centres of civilization there are such bad things; and when you see these with your own eyes pray do not indiscriminately censure the whole community for the more degraded. The more lost, the more appalling the disease, the greater the antidote—the greater the amount of intellectual darkness, the greater is the anxiety to promote education among the masses of the people—the more there is of wickedness, the more pure-hearted earnestness there is in order to send out what are called biblewomen and missionaries, and readers, and moral and religious teachers, of all shades of opinion and all positions in society, in order to elevate the spiritual sufferings and supply the spiritual wants of those people. (*Applause.*) So England by her own destitution has made herself immensely charitable. The ignorance and wickedness of some of the people have made a large body of philanthropists, ready even now to sacrifice their blood for the glory and redemption of England—and not only to England are their energies confined, but you see them in all parts of the world. All I have to request English residents in India to do is this—let them help us to have English charity here. There are many who have fallen into the lowest depths of sin, ignorance, and superstition. Let us, then, have the thousands of charitable institutions you have in England transplanted into our country. Such we like and must have. While we guard our nationality, let us bring from England the charitable institutions—let all good and charitable men and women come out to regenerate this country. Against denationalization I have protested, but do not understand me to say that you shall keep back the tide of trade and civilization—that you shall say to the wave of the refining sea of true refinement and philanthropy coming from the West to the East, 'Thus far shalt thou come and no further'—but you must allow the advancing wave to come and encroach on our land—to break down the multitudinous evils that have been allowed to accumulate in the course of centuries, and break down the embankments of superstition, idolatry and caste. Let us be prepared for that—let it be proved to God and the world that England has nobly fulfilled her mission in India—(*applause*)—and that all India is now freed from ignorance and prejudice. Oh, what a glorious day that will be when we shall see throughout the length and breadth of our country such pious, charitable, and Christian ladies as we see in England, and such disinterested, generous, Christian-minded men as we see in England. There are some men and women of this character in India, I must say. Oh, may their number multiply—may the number of those who come to India simply for the sake of money be less and less, and may those who come to India for nothing but the glory and redemption of India be greater day by day. (*Applause.*)[11]

Notes

1. J.T.F. Jordens, *Dayānanda Sarasvatī: His Life and Ideas* (Delhi: Oxford University Press, 1978), p. 82.
2. Meredith Borthwick, *Keshub Chunder Sen: A Search for Cultural Synthesis* (Calcutta: Minerva Associates [Publications] Pvt. Ltd., 1977), p. 8.
3. Ibid., pp. 24–5.
4. Ibid., p. 110, emphasis added.
5. Ibid., p. 111.
6. Ibid., p. 128.
7. Ibid., p. 228.
8. Glyn Richards, *A Source-Book of Modern Hinduism* (London: Curzon Press, 1985), p. 38.
9. Ibid., pp. 42–4.
10. *Keshub Chunder Sen's Lectures in India* (London: Cassell and Company Limited, 1904), pp. 429–33.
11. Ibid., pp. 292–6.

Rāmakṛṣṇa Paramahaṃsa
(1836–1886)

Life

Rāmakṛṣṇa was born at a time when, under the impact of modern European civilization, the Indian mind was 'perhaps' 'for the first time . . . thrown off its balance. Even the devastating Muslim invasions and conquests had not produced a result of this kind.'[1] That it regained its balance, at least the spiritual dimension of it, was largely due to an illiterate mystic Rāmakṛṣṇa and his famous disciple Vivekānanda (1863–1902). Rāmakṛṣṇa, earlier known as Gadādhar, came to Calcutta to serve as a priest in a temple dedicated to Kālī, built by a rich widow. He undertook his vocation with the utmost seriousness, raising it from a priestly to a spiritual level. Rāmakṛṣṇa was seized with an intense longing to have a vision of Kālī until it became unbearable. He was to tell his disciples later:

> There was then an intolerable anguish in my heart because I could not have Her vision. Just as a man wrings a towel forcibly to squeeze out all the water from it, I felt as if somebody caught hold of my heart and mind and was doing so with them. Greatly afflicted with the thought that I might never have Mother's vision, I was dying of despair. Being in an agony I thought that there was then no use in living this life. My eyes suddenly fell upon the sword that was there in the Mother's temple. I made up my mind to put an end to my life with it that very moment. Like one mad, I ran and caught hold of it, when suddenly I had the wonderful vision of the Mother, and fell down unconscious. I did not know what happened then in the external world—how that day and the next slipped away. But, in my heart of hearts, there was flowing a current of intense bliss, never experienced before, and I had the immediate knowledge of the Light that was Mother.[2]

Thus commenced a career of dazzling spiritual versatility, during the course of which Rāmakṛṣṇa not only crossed many a threshold of Hinduism but even went beyond it. He successfully experienced divinity, according to his biographies, in the various devotional modes specified in Hinduism and also gained the results of Tantrika *sādhānā* under the guidance of a woman adept.[3] From the point of view of subsequent developments, Rāmakṛṣṇa's initiation into the non-dual mode of realization holds considerable importance. He followed this mode of spiritual disciple under Totā Purī, nicknamed 'the naked one' for obvious reasons.

> After initiating me, the naked one taught me many dicta conveying the conclusion of the Vedanta, and asked me to make my mind free of function in all respects and merge in the meditation of the Self. But, it so happened with me that when I sat for meditation I could by no means make my mind go beyond the bounds of name and form and cease functioning. The mind withdrew itself easily from all other things but, as soon as it did so, the intimately familiar form of the universal Mother, consisting of the effulgence of pure consciousness, appeared before it as living and moving and made me quite oblivious of the renunciation of names and forms of all descriptions. When I listened to the conclusive dicta and sat for meditation, this happened over and over again. Almost despairing of the attainment of the Nirvikalpa Samadhi, I then opened my eyes and said to the naked one, 'No, it cannot be done; I cannot make the mind free from functioning and force it to dive into the Self'. Scolding me severely, the naked one said very excitedly, 'What, it can't be done! What utter defiance!' He then looked about in the hut and finding a broken piece of glass took it in his hand and forcibly pierced with its needle-like pointed end my forehead between the eye-brows and said, 'Collect the mind here to this point'. With a firm determination I sat for meditation again and, as soon as the holy form of the divine Mother appeared now before the mind as previously, I looked upon knowledge as a sword and cut it mentally in two with that sword of knowledge. There remained then no function in the mind, which transcended quickly the realm of names and forms, making me merge in Samadhi.[4]

The nature of Rāmakṛṣṇa's Advaitic or non-dual experience[5] and the significance[6] to be attached to it, continue to be matters of debate. However, from the perspective of the Ramakrishna Mission itself, this constituted the culmination of his spiritual enterprise, which would continue with many lateral manifestations but would not be surpassed vertically. According to the received account:

> After his guru left Dakshineswar, Sri Ramakrishna was determined to remain in a state of absolute identity with Brahman. He accordingly

meditated and entered into *nirvikalpa samadhi* again. Referring to this period of his life, he used to say, 'For six months at a stretch I remained in that state whence ordinary men can never return—the body falling off after twenty-one days like a seared leaf. I was not conscious of day and night; flies would enter my mouth and nostrils just as they do in a dead body, but I did not feel them; the hair became matted with accretions of dust. There was no chance for the body to survive, and it would certainly have perished but for the kind ministrations of a monk who was present at Dakshineswar at the time. He realized the state of my mind and also understood that this body must be kept alive at any cost, since it was to be of immense good to the world. He therefore busied himself in preserving this body. He would bring food regularly to me and try in various ways to bring my mind down to the consciousness of the relative world, even by beating me with a stick. As soon as he found me to be a little conscious, he would press some food into my mouth, only a bit of which reached the stomach; and there were days in which all his efforts would be in vain. Six months passed in this way. At last I received the Mother's command, "Remain on the threshold of relative consciousness (*bhavamukha*) for the sake of humanity." Then I was laid up with a terrible attack of dysentery; and excruciating pain in the stomach tortured me day and night; it went on for six months. Thus only did the mind gradually come down to a lower level and to consciousness of the body. I became a normal man; but before that at the slightest opportunity the mind would take a transcendental flight and merge in the *nivikalpa samadhi*.' . . .

Sri Ramakrishna . . . had thus gone through the whole range of Hindu disciplines in the course of twelve years, from his eighteenth year to his thirtieth. He had become a Paramahamsa.[7]

It is also to be a matter of great significance that Rāmakṛṣṇa subsequently had Christian and Islamic mystical experiences as well and was therefore able to testify to the validity of these paths through his own personal experience. This might be a matter of tangential interest to these traditions themselves, but is a matter of central importance for modern Hinduism, as it provides, in the eyes of the Hindus, the experiential proof of the neo-Hindu doctrine of the validity of all religions.[8] As Rāmakṛṣṇa himself said:

I have practised all religions—Hinduism, Islam, Christianity—and I have also followed the paths of the different Hindu sects. I have found that it is the same God toward whom all are directing their steps, though along different paths. You must try all beliefs and traverse all the different ways once. Wherever I look, I see men quarrelling in the name of religion— Hindus, Mohammedans, Brahmos, Vaishnavas, and the rest. But they never reflect that He who is called Krishna is also called Siva, and bears the name of the Primal Energy, Jesus, and Allah as well—the same Rama with a thousand names. A lake has several ghats. At one the Hindus take water in pitchers and call it 'jal'; at another the Mussalmans take water in leather bags and call it 'pani'. At a third the Christians call it 'water'. Can we imagine that it is not 'jal', but only 'pani' or 'water'? How ridiculous! The substance is One under different names, and everyone is seeking the same substance; only climate, temperament, and name create differences. Let each man follow his own path. If he sincerely and ardently wishes to know God, peace be unto him! He will surely realize Him.[9]

In due course Rāmakṛṣṇa was joined by his wife. His marriage to her had been arranged earlier in the hope of maintaining his sanity, when his family thought he was about to go over the edge in his passionate pursuit of God. The marriage was never consummated; she became his first disciple. Many others followed. The story of his favourite disciple, Naren, who later became known as Vivekānanda will be covered in a later chapter. Rāmakṛṣṇa's reputation as a God-intoxicated saint soon spread and we possess accounts of his meetings with major contemporary figures such as Keshub, the Theosophists and Dayānanda Sarasvatī. Out of these, his encounter with Keshub was by far the most consequential.

Rāmakṛṣṇa passed away at the age of fifty, after suffering from cancer of the throat, with a halo of sanctity attached to his name. In his own life he was hailed as an Incarnation and is expected to appear again in our midst according to the accounts we possess.[10]

Rāmakṛṣṇa on God

The Hindu tradition, since time immemorial, has adopted two approaches towards the ultimate reality we often refer to as God: the absolutistic and the theistic. In the following passage Rāmakṛṣṇa addresses this dual approach:

But you should remember that the heart of the devotee is the abode of God. He dwells, no doubt, in all beings, but He especially manifests Himself in the heart of the devotee. A landlord may at one time or another visit all parts of his estate, but people say he is generally to be found in a particular drawing-room. The heart of the devotee is the drawing-room of God.

He who is called Brahman by the jnanis is known as Atman by the yogis and as Bhagavan by the bhaktas. The same brahmin is called priest when worshipping in the temple, and cook, when preparing a meal in the kitchen. The jnani, sticking to the path of knowledge, always reasons about the Reality, saying, 'Not this, not this'. Brahman is neither 'this' nor 'that; It is neither the universe not its living beings. Reasoning in this way, the mind becomes steady. Then it disappears and the aspirant goes into samadhi. This is the Knowledge of Brahman. It is the unwavering conviction of the jnani that Brahman alone is real and the world illusory. All these names and rooms are illusory, like a dream. What Brahman is cannot be described. One cannot even say that Brahman is a Person. That is the opinion of the jnanis, the followers of Vedanta philosophy.

But the bhaktas accept all the states of consciousness. They take the waking state to be real also. They don't think the world to be illusory, like a dream. They say that the universe is a manifestation of God's power and glory. God has created all these—sky, stars, moon, sun, mountains, ocean, men, animals. They constitute His glory. He is within us, in our hearts. Again, He is outside. The most advanced devotees say that He Himself has become all this—the twenty-four cosmic principles, the universe, and all living beings. The devotee of God wants to eat sugar, not to become sugar.[11]

God, Devotion and Philanthropy

Rāmakṛṣṇa's teachings at several points run counter to our firmly ingrained popular beliefs that it is good to help others, that such charity represents a commendable exercise of moral volition and that obviously we possess volition which we should exercise in ways God will approve. Rāmakṛṣṇa does not deny these points directly but they end up becoming moral molehills before the metaphysical mountains he sets up beside them.

But no spiritual progress is possible without the renunciation of 'woman and gold'. I renounced these three: land, wife, and wealth. Once I went to the Registry Office to register some land, the title of which was in the name of Raghuvir. The officer asked me to sign my name; but I didn't do it, because I couldn't feel that it was 'my' land. I was shown much respect as the guru of Keshab Sen. They presented me with mangoes, but I couldn't carry them home. A sannyasi cannot lay things up.

How can one expect to attain God without renunciation? Suppose one thing is placed upon another; how can you get the second without removing the first?

One must pray to God without any selfish desire. But selfish worship, if practised with perseverance, is gradually turned into selfless worship. Dhruva [a model devotee] practised tapsaya [austerities] to obtain his kingdom, but at last he realized God. He said, 'Why should a man give up gold if he gets it while searching for glass beads?'

God can be realized when a man acquires sattva [goodness]. Householders engage in philanthropic work, such as charity, mostly with a motive. That is not good. But actions without motives are good. Yet it is very difficult to leave motives out of one's actions.

When you realize God, will you pray to Him, 'O God, please grant that I may dig reservoirs, build roads, and found hospitals and dispensaries?' After the realization of God all such desires are left behind.

Then mustn't one perform acts of compassion, such as charity to the poor? I do not forbid it. If a man has money, he should give it to remove the sorrows and sufferings that come to his notice. In such an event the wise man says, 'Give the poor something.' But inwardly he feels: 'What can I do? God alone is the Doer. I am nothing.'

The great souls, deeply affected by the sufferings of men, show them the way to God. Sankaracharya kept the 'ego of Knowledge' in order to teach mankind. The gift of knowledge and devotion is far superior to the gift of food. Therefore Chaitanyadeva distributed bhakti to all, including the outcaste. Happiness and suffering are the inevitable characteristics of the body. You have come to eat mangoes. Fulfil that desire. The one thing needful is jnana and bhakti. God alone is Substance; all else is illusory.

It is God alone who does everything. You may say that in that case man may commit sin. But that is not true. If a man is firmly convinced that God alone is the Doer and that he himself is nothing, then he will never make a false step.[12]

Śiva-Liṅga

Just as the Eucharist may seem cannibalistic to the outsider but never to the Christian celebrant, the most popular symbol of God Śiva appears phallic in shape and nature to the outsider but not to the devotee of Śiva. Moreover, the shape of its base further seems to add to its sexual dimension by appearing like its female counterpart. In the following remark Rāmakṛṣṇa accepts this explanation but sublimates its significance remarkably.

Do you know the significance of the Śiva emblem? It is the worship of the symbols of fatherhood and motherhood. The devotee worshipping the image prays, 'O Lord, please grant that I may not be born into this world again; that I may not have to pass again through a mother's womb.'[13]

Kālī's Colour

The common depiction of Goddess Kālī as black in colour similarly acquires an unsuspected spiritual potency in Rāmakṛṣṇa's explanation of it.

Is Kali, my Divine Mother, of a black complexion? She appears black because She is viewed from a distance; but when intimately known She is no longer so. The sky appears blue at a distance; but look at it close by and you will find that it has no colour. The water of the ocean looks blue at a distance, but when you go near and take it in your hand, you find that it is colourless.[14]

Englishmen

The English figure now and then in Rāmakṛṣṇa's conversations almost like symbols waiting to be deciphered. Once he went into a trance on seeing an English boy who reminded him of Kṛṣṇa. Here are two other samples of references to Englishmen and what he associated with them in his conversations.

How many other visions I saw while meditating during my sadhana! Once I was meditating under the bel-tree when 'Sin' appeared before me and tempted me in various ways. He came to me in the form of an English soldier. He wanted to give me wealth, honour, sex pleasure, various occult powers, and such things. I began to pray to the Divine Mother. Now I am telling you something very secret. The Mother appeared. I said to Her, 'Kill him, Mother!' I still remember that form of the Mother, Her world-bewitching beauty. She came to me taking the form of Krishnamayi.[15] But it was as if her glance moved the world.[16]

It is God *alone* who has planted in man's mind *what the 'Englishman' calls free will.* People who have not realized God would become engaged in more and more sinful action if God had not planted in them the notion of free will. Sin would have increased if God had not made the sinner feel that he alone was responsible for his sin.[17]

Rāmakṛṣṇa and Keshub

The following reminiscence of Rāmakṛṣṇa about Keshub and his followers provides an insight into the nature of their relationship.

Keshab Sen used to come here frequently. As a result he changed a great deal. Of late he has become quite a remarkable man. Many a time he came here with his party; but he also wanted to come alone. In the earlier years of his life Keshab didn't have much opportunity to live in the company of holy men.

I visited him at his house in Colootola Street. Hriday was with me. We were shown into the room where Keshab was working. He was writing something. After a long while he put aside his pen, got off his chair, and sat on the floor with us. But he didn't salute us or show us respect in any other way.

He used to come here now and then. One day in a spiritual mood I said to him: 'One should not sit before a sadhu with one leg over the other. That increases one's rajas [active ego].' As soon as he and his friends arrived, I would salute them before they bowed to me. Thus they gradually learnt to salute a holy man, touching the ground with their foreheads.

I said to Keshab: 'Chant the name of Hari. In the Kaliyuga [present degenerate age] one should sing the name and glories of God.' After that they began to sing the name of God with drums and cymbals.

Do you know how my faith in the name of Hari was all the more strengthened? Holy men, as you know, frequently visit the temple garden. Once a sadhu from Multan arrived. He was waiting for a party going to Gangasagar. (*Pointing to* M.)[18] The sadhu was of his age. It was he who said to me, 'The way to realize God in the Kaliyuga is the path of bhakti as prescribed by Narada.'

One day Keshab came here with his followers. They stayed till ten at night. We were all seated in the Panchavati [a grove]. Pratap and several others said they would like to spend the night here. Keshab said: 'No, I must go. I have some work to do.' I laughed and said: 'Can't you sleep without the smell of your fish-basket? Once a fishwife was a guest in the house of a gardener who raised flowers. She came there with her empty basket, after selling fish in the market, and was asked to sleep in a room where flowers were kept. But, because of the fragrance of the flowers, she couldn't get to sleep for a long time. Her hostess saw her condition and said, 'Hello! Why are you tossing from side to side so restlessly?' The fishwife said: 'I don't know, friend. Perhaps the smell of the flowers has been disturbing my sleep. Can you give me my fish-basket? Perhaps that will put me to sleep.' The basket was brought to her. She sprinkled water on it and set it near her nose. Then she fell sound asleep and snored all night.'

At this story the followers of Keshab burst into loud laughter.

Keshab conducted the prayer that evening at the bathing-ghat on the river. After the worship I said to him: 'It is God who manifests Himself, in one aspect, as the scriptures; therefore one should worship the sacred books, such as the Vedas, the Puranas, and the Tantras. In another aspect He has become the devotee. The heart of the devotee is God's drawing-room. One can easily find one's master in the drawing-room. Therefore, by worshipping His devotee, one worships God Himself.'

Keshab and his followers listened to my words with great attention. It was a full-moon night. The sky was flooded with light. We were seated in the open court at the top of the stairs leading to the river. I said, 'Now let us all chant, "Bhagavata—Bhakta—Bhagavan."' All chanted in unison, 'Bhagavata—Bhakta—Bhagavan'. Next I said to them, 'Say, "Brahman is verily Sakti; Sakti is verily Brahman."' Again they chanted in unison. 'Brahman is verily Sakti; Sakti is verily Brahman.'

I said to them: 'He whom you address as Brahma is none other than She whom I call Mother. Mother is a very sweet name.'

Then I said to them, 'Say, "Guru—Krishna—Vaishnava."' At this Keshab said 'We must not go so far, sir. If we do that, then all will take us for orthodox Vaishnavas.'

I used to tell Keshab now and then: 'He whom you address as Brahma is none other than She whom I call Sakti, the Primal Energy. It is called Brahman in the Vedas when It transcends speech and thought and is without attributes and action. I call It Sakti, Adyasakti, and so forth, when I find It creating, preserving and destroying the universe.'

I said to Keshab: 'It is extremely difficult to realize God while leading a worldly life. How can a typhoid patient be cured if he is kept in a room where tamarind, pickle, and jars of water are kept? Therefore one should go into solitude now and then to practise spiritual discipline. When the trunk of a tree becomes thick and strong, an elephant can be tied to it; but a young sapling is eaten by cattle.' That is why Keshab would say in his lectures, 'Live in the world after being strengthened in spiritual life.'

(*To the devotees*) You see, Keshab was a great scholar. He lectured in English. Many people honoured him. Queen Victoria herself talked to him. But when Keshab came here he would be bare-bodied and bring some fruit, as one should when visiting a holy man. He was totally free from egotism.[19]

Notes

1. D. S. Sarma, *Hinduism Through the Ages* (Bombay: Bharatiya Vidya Bhayan, 1956), p. 62.
2. Swami Saradananda, *Sri Ramakrishna: The Great Master* (trans. Swami Jagadananda) (Madras: Sri Ramakrishna Nath, 1952), p. 140. This account may be supplemented with the following (ibid., p. 141): 'On another occasion the Master described to us in detail his wonderful vision spoken of before. He said, 'It was as if houses, doors, temples and all other things vanished altogether; as if there was nothing anywhere! And what I saw was a boundless infinite conscious sea of light! However far and in whatever direction I looked, I found a continuous succession of effulgent waves coming forward, raging and storming from all sides with a great speed. Very soon they fell on me and made me sink to the unknown bottom. I panted, struggled, and fell unconscious.' The Master told us that at the time of his first vision he saw a conscious sea of light. But what about the divine Mother's form consisting of pure consciousness only—the form of Hers with hands that give boons and freedom from fear? Did the Master then have the vision of that form also in that sea of light? It appears that he had, for as soon as he had the slightest consciousness at the time of his first vision, he, we are told, uttered repeatedly the word 'Mother' in a plaintive voice.'
3. See Claude Alan Stark, *God of All* (Cape Cod, Mass.: Claude Stark, Inc., 1974), passim.
4. Saradananda, p. 250.
5. Stark, pp. 57ff.
6. Ibid., pp. 189–90.
7. Swami Ghanananda, as cited in Stark, p. 66.
8. Arvind Sharma, *Ramakrishna and Vivekananda: New Perspectives* (New Delhi: Sterling Publishers Private Ltd., 1989), chapter 2.
9. Swami Nikhilananda, tr., *The Gospel of Sri Ramakrishna* (New York: Ramakrishna–Vivekananda Center, 1952), p. 35.
10. Arvind Sharma, chapter 13.
11. Nikhilananda, p. 133.
12. Ibid., p. 374.
13. Ibid., p. 604.
14. Ibid., pp. 135–6.
15. Daughter of an acquaintance.
16. Nikhilananda, p. 746.
17. According to Swami Nikhilananda, 'Sri Ramakrishna used this word [Englishman] to denote Europeans in general, and also those whose ways and thoughts were largely influenced by Western ideas.' (ibid., p. 378.)
18. The initial of the name of the diarist who has provided this account, translated by Swami Nikilananda, p. vii.
19. Ibid., pp. 433–4.

Swami Vivekānanda
(1863–1902)

Life

Swami Vivekānanda was a disciple of Rāmakṛṣṇa and in many ways he, and his guru, Rāmakṛṣṇa, are a study in contrast: Rāmakṛṣṇa was from the country, Vivekānanda from the city; Rāmakṛṣṇa was a Brāhmaṇa, Vivekānanda a Śūdra; Rāmakṛṣṇa was barely literate, Vivekānanda had a Western education; Rāmakṛṣṇa worshipped Kālī, Vivekānanda, at least initially, had his doubts about image-worship; Rāmakṛṣṇa never left the shores of India, Vivekānanda returned from the West a cultural hero. But they turned out to be excellent foils for each other and the movement which Vivekānanda founded in the name of his Master was (until recently) a byword for modern Hinduism.

Vivekānanda was led to Rāmakṛṣṇa by his English teacher who, while discussing Wordsworthian mysticism, cited Rāmakṛṣṇa as a living mystic. An early encounter between the two has since become legendary. There are several accounts of it. The one given below is in Vivekānanda's own words:

> I heard of this man and I went to hear him. He looked just like an ordinary man, with nothing remarkable about him. He used the most simple language and I thought, 'Can this man be a great teacher?'—crept near to him and asked him the question which I had been asking others all my life: 'Do you believe in God, Sir?' 'Yes.' 'How?' 'Because I see Him just as I see you here, only in a much intenser sense.' That impressed me at once. For the first time I found a man who dared to say that he saw God, that religion was a reality, to be felt, to be sensed in an infinitely more intense way than we can sense the world.[1]

The turning point in their relationship came when Vivekānanda's father died suddenly and the family's financial fortunes plummeted. It was during this time of trial, at the end of which Vivekānanda renounced the world, that he finally 'accepted' Kālī. We have an account of this from his Western disciple, Sister Nivedita, which contains a curious undeciphered element:

> 'How I used to hate Kali!' he said, 'and all Her ways! That was the ground of my six years' fight,—that I would not accept Her. But I had to accept Her at last! Ramakrishna Paramahamsa dedicated me to Her, and now I believe that She guides me in every little thing I do, and does with me what She will . . . . Yet I fought so long! I loved him, you see, and that was what held me. I saw his marvellous purity . . . . I felt his wonderful love . . . . His greatness had not dawned on me then. All that came afterwards, when I had given in. At that time I thought him a brain sick baby, always seeing visions and the rest. I hated it. And then I too had to accept Her!
>
> *No, the thing that made me do it is a secret that will die with me.* I had great misfortunes at that time . . . . It was an opportunity . . . . She made a slave of me. Those were the very words—"a slave of you." And Ramakrishna Paramahamsa made me over to her . . . . Strange! He lived only two years after doing that, and most of the time he was suffering. Not more than six months did he keep his own health and brightness.'[2]

This account may be supplemented with the following, again in his own words. It harks back to the same dark days that followed the sudden death of his father.

> I began going from place to place now as before and made various kinds of efforts. I worked in the office of the attorney and translated a few books, as a result of which I earned a little money and the household was being managed somehow. But these were all temporary jobs; and in the absence of any permanent work no smooth arrangement for the maintenance of mother and brothers could be made. I remembered a little later: 'God grants the Master's prayers. I shall make him pray for me so that the suffering of my mother and brothers for want of food and clothing might be removed; he will never refuse to do so for my sake.' I hurried to Dakshineswar [temple] and asked persistently that he must pray to the Mother that the pecuniary difficulty of my mother and brothers might be removed. The Master said to me affectionately, 'My child, I cannot say such words, you know. Why don't you yourself pray? You don't accept the Mother; that is why you suffer so much.' I replied, 'I have no knowledge of the Mother; please pray to Mother yourself for my sake. Pray you must; I will not leave you unless you do so.' The Master said with affection, 'I prayed to Mother many times indeed to remove your sufferings. But as you do not accept Mother, She does not grant the prayer. Well, today is Tuesday, a day especially sacred to Mother. Mother will, I say, grant you whatever you would ask for. Go to the temple

tonight and, bowing down to Her, pray for a boon. My affectionate Mother is the Power of Brahman; She is pure consciousness embodied. She has given birth to the universe according to Her will; what can She not do, if She wills?'

A firm faith arose in my mind that all the sufferings would certainly come to an end as soon as I prayed to the Mother, inasmuch as the Master had said so. I waited for the night in great expectancy. The night arrived at last. Three hours of the night had elapsed when the Master asked me to go to the holy temple. As I was going, a sort of profound inebriation possessed me; I was reeling. A firm conviction gripped me that I should actually see Mother and hear Her words. I forgot all other things, and became completely merged in that thought alone. Coming in the temple, I saw that Mother was actually pure Consciousness, was actually living and was really the fountain-head of infinite love and beauty. My heart swelled with loving devotion; and, beside myself with bliss, I made repeated salutations to Her, praying, 'Mother, grant me discrimination, grant me detachment, grant me divine knowledge and devotion; ordain that I may always have unobstructed vision of you.' My heart was flooded with peace. The whole universe completely disappeared and Mother alone remained filling my heart.

No sooner had I returned to the Master than he asked, 'Did you pray to Mother for the removal of your worldly wants?' Startled at his question, I said, 'No, sir; I forgot to do so. So, what should I do now?' He said, 'Go quickly again and pray to Her.' I started for the temple once more, and, coming to Mother's presence, became inebriated again. I forgot everything, bowed down to Her repeatedly and prayed for the realization of divine knowledge and devotion, before I came back. The Master smiled and said, 'Well, did you tell Her this time?' I was startled again and said, 'No, sir; hardly had I seen Mother when I forgot everything on account of the influence of an indescribable divine Power and prayed for knowledge and devotion only. What's to be done now?' The Master said, 'Silly boy, could you not control yourself a little and make that prayer? Go once more, if you can and tell Her those words. Quick!' I started a third time; but as soon as I entered the temple a formidable sense of shame occupied my heart. I thought what a trifling thing have I come to ask of Mother? It is, as the Master says, just like the folly of asking a king, having received his grace, for gourds and pumpkins. Ah! how low is my intellect! Overpowered with shame and aversion I bowed down to Her over and over again saying, 'I don't want anything else, Mother; do grant me divine knowledge and devotion only.' When I came out from the temple, it occurred to me that it was certainly the play of the Master, otherwise how was it that I could not speak the words though I came to pray to Her as many as three times? Afterwards I insisted that he must ensure my mother's and brothers' freedom from lack of food and clothing, saying, 'It is certainly you who made me intoxicated that way.' He said affectionately to me, 'My child, I can never offer such a prayer for anyone; it does not indeed come out of my mouth. You would, I told you, get from Mother whatever you wanted. But you could not ask Her for it; you are not meant for worldly happiness. What am I to do?' I said, 'That won't do, sir. You must utter the prayer for my sake; it is my firm conviction that they will be free from all sufferings if you only say so.' As I kept on persisting, he said, 'Well, they will never be in want of plain food and clothing.'³

This episode is cited at some length as it serves to illustrate several points: the relationship of Kālī to Rāmakṛṣṇa, of Rāmakṛṣṇa to Vivekānanda, of Vivekānanda to his family, and the mystery in which it is enveloped. It also forces one to ask a very uncomfortable question: Did Rāmakṛṣṇa or/and Kālī keep the promise? 'It was at Almora, as we now know,' after he had renounced the world 'that news reached him of the death, in pitiful extremity, of the favourite sister of his childhood, and he had fled into the wilder mountains, leaving no clue.'⁴ Do we have any?

Great then, was the cost, in personal terms, of Vivekānanda's decision to renounce the world. For several years he almost dropped out of sight, travelling throughout India until we find him making his way to the World's Parliament of Religions at Chicago in 1893, against heavy odds.

This Parliament had been organized as part of the Great Columbian Exhibition to celebrate the 400th anniversary of the discovery of America by Columbus. Swami Vivekānanda made his mark at this Parliament, gained a following in the West, established several Vedanta Centres and was hailed as a hero when he returned to India in 1897. The rest of his life was devoted to revitalizing Hinduism until he died in 1902.

In the 1970s Professor Philip H. Ashby surveyed the students at the University of Andhra at Waltair on several aspects of Hinduism. He writes:

> For me one of the most unexpected results of our study was elicited by the request that the students name the Hindu religious thinker(s) and/or leader(s) each admired most. Forty percent gave as their first or only choice Swami Vivekananda, the founder and organizer of the Ramakrishna Vedanta Society at the end of the nineteenth century. Many saw in him the proper, heroic attitude necessary on the part of Hindus today. Vivekananda was praised as the man who gave Hindus a basis for pride in their own culture and tradition and, equally if not more importantly, demonstrated that Hindu religion had a message for all mankind. Many were convinced that the West, and America in particular, still vividly remembers the dramatic appearance of the dynamic swami before the Parliament of Religions at the Chicago World's Fair in 1893. The next most frequently mentioned names were those of Sankara, Gandhi, and Ramakrishna, each being cited as the first or only choice by about 12 percent of the students.⁵

At the Parliament: First Address

Swami Vivekānanda's response to the welcome given him on 11 September 1893 at the World's Parliament of Religions at Chicago has stirred the imagination of the Hindus over the years, perhaps even more than that of the original audience of around 6000 people to whom it was delivered.

Sisters and Brothers of America,

It fills my heart with joy unspeakable to rise in response to the warm and cordial welcome which you have given us. I thank you in the name of the most ancient order of monks in the world; and I thank you in the name of the mother of religions; and I thank you in the name of millions and millions of Hindu people of all classes and sects.

My thanks, also, to some of the speakers on this platform who, referring to the delegates from the Orient, have told you that these men from far-off nations may well claim the honour of bearing to different lands the idea of toleration. I am proud to belong to a religion which has taught the world both tolerance and universal acceptance. We believe not only in universal toleration, but we accept all religions as true. I am proud to belong to a nation which has sheltered the persecuted and the refugees of all religions and all nations of the earth. I am proud to tell you that we have gathered in our bosom the purest remnant of the Israelites, who came to Southern India and took refuge with us in the very year in which their holy temple was shattered to pieces by Roman tyranny. I am proud to belong to the religion which has sheltered and is still fostering the remnant of the grand Zoroastrian nation. I will quote to you, brethren, a few lines from a hymn which I remember to have repeated from my earliest boyhood, which is every day repeated by millions of human beings: '*As the different streams having their sources in different places all mingle their water in the sea, so, O Lord, the different paths which men take through different tendencies, various though they appear, crooked or straight all lead to Thee.*'

The present convention, which is one of the most august assemblies ever held, is in itself a vindication, a declaration to the world of the wonderful doctrine preached in the Gita: '*Whosoever comes to Me, through whatsoever form, I reach him; all men are struggling through paths which in the end lead to me.*' Sectarianism, bigotry, and its horrible descendant, fanaticism, have long possessed this beautiful earth. They have filled the earth with violence, drenched it often and often with human blood, destroyed civilisation and sent whole nations to despair.

Had it not been for these horrible demons, human society would be far more advanced than it is now. But their time has come; and I fervently hope that the bell that tolled this morning in honour of this convention may be the death-knell of all fanaticism, of all persecutions with the sword or with the pen, and of all uncharitable feelings between persons wending their way to the same goal.[6]

At the Parliament: Why We Disagree

A persistent theme in the talks of Swami Vivekānanda is that of religious tolerance. The note struck in the inaugural response found an echo in what he had to say on 15 September 1893.

I will tell you a little story. You have heard the eloquent speaker who has just finished saying, 'Let us cease from abusing each other,' and he was very sorry that there should be always so much variance.

But I think I should tell you a story which would illustrate the cause of this variance. A frog lived in a well. It had lived there for a long time. It was born there and brought up there, and yet was a little, small frog. Of course the evolutionists were not there then to tell us whether the frog lost its eyes or not, but, for our story's sake, we must take it for granted that it had its eyes, and that it every day cleansed the water of all the worms and bacilli that lived in it with an energy that would do credit to our modern bacteriologists. In this way it went on and became a little sleek and fat. Well, one day another frog that lived in the sea came and fell into the well.

'Where are you from?'

'I am from the sea.'

'The sea! How big is that ? Is it as big as my well?' and he took a leap from one side of the well to the other.

'My friend,' said the frog of the sea, 'how do you compare the sea with your little well?'

Then the frog took another leap and asked, 'Is your sea so big?'

'What nonsense you speak, to compare the sea with your well!'

'Well, then,' said the frog of the well, 'nothing can be bigger than my well; there can be nothing bigger than this; this fellow is a liar, so turn him out.'

That has been the difficulty all the while.

I am a Hindu. I am sitting in my own little well and thinking that the whole world is my little well. The Christian sits in his little well and thinks the whole world is his well. The Mohammedan sits in his little well and thinks that is the whole world. I have to thank you of America for the great attempt you are making to break down the barriers of this little world of ours, and hope that, in the future, the Lord will help you to accomplish your purpose.[7]

At the Parliament: Paper on Hinduism

On 19 September 1893 Swami Vivekānanda delivered a substantial paper on Hinduism. After he had finished speaking, Sister Nivedita was to comment later: 'Hinduism had been created.' That is to say, his pronouncements were to become normative for Hindu identity in modern times. A few pages are excerpted below to convey its flavour.

Paper on Hinduism
Read at the Parliament on 19th September, 1893

Three religions now stand in the world which have come down to us from time prehistoric—Hinduism, Zoroastrianism and Judaism. They have all received tremendous shocks and all of them prove by their survival their internal strength. But while Judaism failed to absorb Christianity and was driven out of its place of birth by its all-conquering daughter, and a handful of Parsees is all that remains to tell the tale of their grand religion, sect after sect arose in India and seemed to shake the religion of the Vedas to its very foundations, but like the waters of the seashore in a tremendous earthquake it receded only for a while, only to return in an all-absorbing flood, a thousand times more vigorous, and when the tumult of the rush was over, these sects were all sucked in, absorbed, and assimilated into the immense body of the mother faith.

From the high spiritual flights of the Vedanta philosophy, of which the latest discoveries of science seem like echoes, to the low ideas of idolatry with its multifarious mythology, the agnosticism of the Buddhists, and the atheism of the Jains, each and all have a place in the Hindu's religion.

Where then, the question arises, where is the common centre to which all these widely diverging radii converge? Where is the common basis upon which all these seemingly hopeless contradictions rest? And this is the question I shall attempt to answer.

The Hindus have received their religion through revelation, the Vedas. They hold that the Vedas are without beginning and without end. It may sound ludicrous to this audience, how a book can be without beginning or end. But by the Vedas no books are meant. They mean the accumulated treasury of spiritual laws discovered by different persons in different times. Just as the law of gravitation existed before its discovery, and would exist if all humanity forgot it, so is it with the laws that govern the spiritual world. The moral, ethical, and spiritual relations between soul and soul and between individual spirits and the Father of all spirits, were there before their discovery, and would remain even if we forgot them.

The discoverers of these laws are called Rishis, and we honour them as perfected beings. I am glad to tell this audience that some of the very greatest of them were women. Here it may be said that these laws as laws may be without end, but they must have had a beginning. The Vedas teach us that creation is without beginning or end. Science is said to have proved that the sum total of cosmic energy is always the same. Then, if there was a time when nothing existed, where was all this manifested energy? Some say it was in a potential form in God. In that case God is sometimes potential and sometimes kinetic, which would make Him mutable. Everything mutable is a compound, and everything compound must undergo that change which is called destruction. So God would die, which is absurd. Therefore there never was a time when there was no creation.

If I may be allowed to use a simile, creation and creator are two lines, without beginning and without end, running parallel to each other. God is the ever active providence, by whose power systems after systems are being evolved out of chaos, made to run for a time and again destroyed. This is what the Brahmin boy repeats every day: 'The sun and the moon, the Lord created like the suns and moons of previous cycles.' And this agrees with modern science.

Here I stand and if I shut my eyes, and try to conceive my existence, 'I', 'I', 'I', what is the idea before me? The idea of a body. Am I, then, nothing but a combination of material substances? The Vedas declare, 'No'. I am a spirit living in a body. I am not the body. The body will die, but I shall not die. Here am I in this body; it will fall, but I shall go on living. I had also a past. The soul was not created, for creation means a combination which means a certain future dissolution. If then the soul was created, it must die. Some are born happy, enjoy perfect health, with beautiful body, mental vigour and all wants supplied. Others are born miserable, some are without hands or feet, others again are idiots and only drag on a wretched existence. Why, if they are all created, why does a just and merciful God create one happy and another unhappy, why is He so partial? Nor would it mend matters in the least to hold that those who are miserable in this life will be happy in a future one. Why should a man be miserable even here in the reign of a just and merciful God?

In the second place, the idea of a creator God does not explain the anomaly, but simply expresses the cruel fiat of an all-powerful being. There must have been causes, then, before his birth, to make a man miserable or happy and those were his past actions.

Are not all the tendencies of the mind and the body accounted for by inherited aptitude? Here are two parallel lines of existence—one of the mind, the other of matter. If matter and its transformations answer for all that we have, there is no necessity for supposing the existence of a soul. But it cannot be proved that thought has been evolved out of matter, and if philosophical monism is inevitable, spiritual monism is certainly logical and no less desirable than a materialistic monism; but neither of these is necessary here.

We cannot deny that bodies acquire certain tendencies from heredity, but those tendencies only mean the physical configuration, through which a peculiar mind alone can act in a peculiar way. There are other tendencies peculiar to a soul caused by its past actions. And a soul with a certain tendency would by the laws of affinity take birth in a body which is the fittest instrument for the display of that tendency. This is in accord with science, for science wants to explain everything by habit, and habit is got through repetitions. So repetitions are necessary to explain the natural habits of a new-born soul. And since they were not obtained in this present life, they must have come down from past lives.

There is another suggestion. Taking all these for granted, how is it that I do not remember anything of my past life? This can be easily explained. I am now speaking English. It is not my mother tongue, in fact no words of my mother tongue are now present in my consciousness; but let me try to bring them up, and they rush in. That shows that consciousness is only the surface of the mental ocean, and within its depths are stored up all our experiences. Try and struggle, they would come up and you would be conscious even of your past life.

This is direct and demonstrative evidence. Verification is the perfect proof of a theory, and here is the challenge thrown to the world by the Rishis. We have discovered the secret by which the very depths of the ocean of memory can be stirred up—try it and you would get a complete reminiscence of your past life.

So then the Hindu believes that he is a spirit. Him the sword cannot pierce—him the fire cannot burn—him the water cannot melt—him the air cannot dry. The Hindu believes that every soul is a circle whose circumference is nowhere, but whose centre is located in the body, and that death means the change of this centre from body to body. Nor is the soul bound by the conditions of matter. In its very essence it is free, unbounded, holy, pure, and perfect. But somehow or other it finds itself tied down to matter, and thinks of itself as matter.

Why should the free, perfect, and pure being be thus under the thraldom of matter, is the next question. How can the perfect soul be deluded into the belief that it is imperfect? We have been told that the Hindus shirk the question and say that no such question can be there. Some thinkers want to answer it by positing one or more quasi-perfect beings, and use big scientific names to fill up the gap. But naming is not explaining. The question remains the same. How can the perfect become the quasi-perfect; how can the pure, the absolute, change even a microscopic particle of its nature? But the Hindu is sincere. He does not want to take shelter under sophistry. He is brave enough to face the question in a manly fashion; and his answer is: 'I do not know. I do not know how the perfect being, the soul, came to think of itself as imperfect, as joined to and conditioned by matter.' But the fact is a fact for all that. It is a fact in everybody's consciousness that one thinks of oneself as the body. The Hindu does not attempt to explain why one thinks one is the body. The answer that it is the will of God is no explanation. This is nothing more than what the Hindu says, 'I do not know.'

Well, then, the human soul is eternal and immortal, perfect and infinite, and death means only a change of centre from one body to another. The present is determined by our past actions, and the future by the present. The soul will go on evolving up or reverting back from birth to birth and death to death. But here is another question: Is man a tiny boat in a tempest, raised one moment on the foamy crest of a billow and dashed down into a yawning chasm the next, rolling to and fro at the mercy of good and bad actions—a powerless, helpless wreck in an ever-raging, ever-rushing, uncompromising current of cause and effect; a little moth placed under the wheel of causation which rolls on crushing everything in its way and waits not for the widow's tears or the orphan's cry? The heart sinks at the idea, yet this is the law of Nature. Is there no hope? Is there no escape?— was the cry that went up from the bottom of the heart of despair. It reached the throne of mercy, and words of hope and consolation came down and inspired a Vedic sage, and he stood up before the world and in trumpet voice proclaimed the glad tidings: 'Hear, ye children of immortal bliss! even ye that reside in higher spheres! I have found the Ancient One who is beyond all darkness, all delusion: knowing Him alone you shall be saved from death over again.' 'Children of immortal bliss'—what a sweet, what a hopeful name! Allow me to call you, brethren, by that sweet name—heirs of immortal bliss—yea, the Hindu refuses to call you sinners. Ye are the Children of God, the sharers of immortal bliss, holy and perfect beings. Ye divinities on earth—sinners! It is a sin to call a man so; it is a standing libel on human nature. Come up, O lions, and shake off the delusion that you are sheep; you are souls immortal, spirits free, blest and eternal; ye are not matter, ye are not bodies; matter is your servant, not you the servant of matter.

Thus it is that the Vedas proclaim not a dreadful combination of unforgiving laws, not an endless prison of cause and effect, but that at the head of all these laws, in and through every particle of matter and force, stands One 'by whose command the wind blows, the fire burns, the clouds rain, and death stalks upon the earth.'

And what is His nature?

He is everywhere, the pure and formless One, the Almighty and the All-merciful. 'Thou art our father, Thou art our mother, Thou art our beloved friend, Thou art the source of all strength; give us strength. Thou art He that beareth the burdens of the universe; help me bear the little burden of this life.' Thus sang the Rishis of the Vedas. And how to worship Him? Through love. 'He is to be worshipped as the one beloved, dearer than everything in this and the next life.'

This is the doctrine of love declared in the Vedas, and let us see how it is fully developed and taught by Krishna, whom the Hindus believe to have been God incarnate on earth.

He taught that a man ought to live in this world like a lotus leaf, which grows in water but is never moistened by water; so a man ought to live in the world—his heart to God and his hands to work.

It is good to love God for hope of reward in this or the next world, but it is better to love God for love's sake, and the prayer goes: 'Lord, I do not want wealth, nor children, nor learning. If it be Thy will, I shall go from birth to birth, but grant me this, that I may love Thee without the hope of reward—love unselfishly for love's sake.' One of the disciples of Krishna, the then Emperor of India, was driven from his kingdom by his enemies and had to take shelter with his queen in a forest in the Himalayas, and there one day the queen asked him how it was that he, the most virtuous of men, should suffer so much misery. Yudhishthira answered, 'Behold, my queen, the Himalayas, how grand and beautiful they are; I love them. They do not give me anything, but my nature is to love the grand, the beautiful, therefore I love them. Similarly, I love the Lord. He is the source of all beauty, of all sublimity. He is the only object to be loved; my nature is to love Him, and therefore I love. I do not pray for anything; I do not ask for anything. Let Him place me wherever He likes. I must love Him for love's sake. I cannot trade in love.'

The Vedas teach that the soul is divine, only held in the bondage of matter; perfection will be reached when this bond will burst, and the word they use for it is therefore, Mukti—freedom, freedom from the bonds of imperfection, freedom from death and misery.

And this bondage can only fall off through the mercy of God, and this mercy comes on the pure. So purity is the condition of His mercy. How does that mercy act? He reveals Himself to the pure heart; the pure and the stainless see God, yea, even in this life; then and then only all the crookedness of the heart is made straight. Then all doubt ceases. He is no more the freak of a terrible law of causation. This is the very centre, the very vital conception of Hinduism. The Hindu does not want to live upon words and theories. If there are existences beyond the ordinary sensuous existence, he wants to come face to face with them. If there is a soul in him which is not matter, if there is an all-merciful universal Soul, he will go to Him direct. He must see Him, and that alone can destroy all doubts. So the best proof a Hindu sage gives about the soul, about God is: 'I have seen the soul; I have seen God.' And that is the only condition of perfection. The Hindu religion does not consist in struggles and attempts to believe a certain doctrine or dogma, but in realising—not in believing, but in being and becoming.

Thus the whole object of their system is by constant struggle to become perfect, to become divine, to reach God and see God, and this reaching God, seeing God, becoming perfect even as the Father in Heaven is perfect, constitutes the religion of the Hindus.

And what becomes of a man when he attains perfection? He lives a life of bliss infinite. He enjoys infinite and perfect bliss, having obtained the only thing in which man ought to have pleasure, namely God, and enjoys the bliss with God.

So far all the Hindus are agreed. This is the common religion of all the sects of India; but, then, perfection is absolute, and the absolute cannot be two or three. It cannot have any qualities. It cannot be an individual. And so when a soul becomes perfect and absolute, it must become one with Brahman, and it would only realise the Lord as the perfection, the reality, of its own nature and existence, the existence absolute, knowledge absolute, and bliss absolute. We have often and often read this called the losing of individuality and becoming a stock or a stone.

He jests at scars that never felt a wound.

I tell you it is nothing of the kind. If it is happiness to enjoy the consciousness of this small body, it must be greater happiness to enjoy the consciousness of two bodies, the measure of happiness increasing with the consciousness of an increasing number of bodies, the aim, the ultimate of happiness being reached when it would become a universal consciousness.

Therefore, to gain this infinite universal individuality, this miserable little prison-individuality must go. Then alone can death cease when I am one with life, then alone can misery cease when I am one with happiness itself, then alone can all errors cease when I am one with knowledge itself; and this is the necessary scientific conclusion. Science has proved to me that physical individuality is a delusion, that really my body is one little continuously changing body in an unbroken ocean of matter; and Advaita (unity) is the necessary conclusion with my other counterpart, soul.[8]

At the Parliament: Religion Not the Crying Need of India

On 20 September 1893 Swami Vivekānanda spoke again. He had come to the West in the hope that perhaps Western material prosperity and Hindu spiritual riches could be fruitfully exchanged to mutual benefit. But disappointment was already setting in.

Christians must always be ready for good criticism, and I hardly think that you will mind if I make a little criticism. You Christians, who are so fond of sending out missionaries to save the soul of the heathen— why do you not try to save their bodies from starvation? In India, during the terrible famines, thousands died from hunger, yet you Christians did nothing. You erect churches all through India, but the crying evil in the East is not religion—they have religion enough— but it is bread that the suffering millions of burning India cry out for with parched throats. They ask us for bread, but we give them stones. It is an insult to a starving people to offer them religion; it is an insult to a starving man to teach him metaphysics. In India a priest that preached for money would lose caste and be spat upon by the people. I came here to seek aid for my impoverished people, and I fully realised how difficult it was to get help for heathens from Christians in a Christian land.[9]

At the Parliament of World Religions: Address at the Final Session

Many of the themes Vivekānanda was to expand on in his subsequent talks surfaced at the Parliament. For instance, on 26 September 1893, he spoke on 'Buddhism, the fulfilment of Hinduism'. The question of the relationship of the various religions of India was a theme he would advert to repeatedly. In his final address on 27 September 1893, he proposed a way of dealing with religious pluralism which has remained the most popular Hindu response.

The World's Parliament of Religions has become an accomplished fact, and the merciful Father has helped those who laboured to bring it into existence, and crowned with success their most unselfish labour.

My thanks to those noble souls whose large hearts and love of truth first dreamed this wonderful dream and then realised it. My thanks to the shower of liberal sentiments that has overflowed this platform. My thanks to this enlightened audience for their uniform kindness to me and for their appreciation of every thought that tends to smooth the friction of religions. A few jarring notes were heard from time to time in this harmony. My special thanks to them, for they have, by their striking contrast, made general harmony the sweeter.

Much has been said of the common ground of religious unity. I am not going just now to venture my own theory. But if any one here hopes that this unity will come by the triumph of any one of the religions and the destruction of the others, to him I say, 'Brother, yours is an impossible hope.' Do I wish that the Christian would become Hindu? God forbid. Do I wish that the Hindu or Buddhist would become Christian? God forbid.

The seed is put in the ground, and earth and air and water are placed around it. Does the seed become the earth, or the air, or the water? No. It becomes a plant, it develops after the law of its own growth, assimilates the air, the earth, and the water, converts them into plant substance, and grows into a plant.

Similar is the case with religion. The Christian is not to become a Hindu or a Buddhist, nor a Hindu or a Buddhist to become a Christian.

But each must assimilate the spirit of the others and yet preserve his individuality and grow according to his own law of growth.

If the Parliament of Religions has shown anything to the world it is this: It has proved to the world that holiness, purity and charity are not the exclusive possessions of any church in the world, and that every system has produced men and women of the most exalted character. In the face of this evidence, if anybody dreams of the exclusive survival of his own religion and the destruction of the others, I pity him from the bottom of my heart, and point out to him that upon the banner of every religion will soon be written, in spite of resistance: 'Help and not Fight,' 'Assimilation and not Destruction,' 'Harmony and Peace and not Dissension.'[10]

Hinduism and Conversion

That Vivekānanda was opposed to conversion is widely known. It is less widely known that he was not opposed to the reconversion of those Indians to Hinduism who had been weaned away from the parent religion in Hinduism's times of troubles.

On the Bounds of Hinduism
(*Prabuddha Bharata*, April 1899)

Having been directed by the Editor, writes our representative, to interview Swami Vivekānanda on the question of converts to Hinduism, I found an opportunity one evening on the roof of a Ganges houseboat. It was after nightfall, and we had stopped at the embankment of the Ramakrishna Math, and there the Swami came down to speak with me.

Time and place were alike delightful. Overhead the stars, and around—the rolling Ganga; and on one side stood the dimly lighted building, with its background of palms and lofty shade-trees.

'I want to see you, Swami,' I began, 'on this matter of receiving back into Hinduism those who have been perverted from it. Is it your opinion that they should be received?'

'Certainly,' said the Swami, 'they can and ought to be taken.'

He sat gravely for a moment, thinking, and then resumed. 'Besides,' he said, 'we shall otherwise decrease in numbers. When the Mohammedans first came, we are said—I think on the authority of Ferishta, the oldest Mohammedan historian—to have been six hundred millions of Hindus. Now we are about two hundred millions. And then every man going out of the Hindu pale is not only a man less, but an enemy the more.

'Again, the vast majority of Hindu converts to Islam and Christianity are converts by the sword, or the descendants of these. It would be obviously unfair to subject these to disabilities of any kind. As to the case of born aliens, did you say? Why, born aliens have been converted in the past by crowds, and the process is still going on.

'In my own opinion, this statement not only applies to aboriginal tribes, to outlying nations, and to almost all our conquerors before the Mohammedan conquest, but also to all those castes who find a special origin in the Puranas. I hold that they have been aliens thus adopted.

'Ceremonies of expiation are no doubt suitable in the case of willing converts, returning to their Mother Church, as it were; but on those who were alienated by conquest—as in Kashmir and Nepal—or on strangers wishing to join us, no penance should be imposed.'

'But of what caste would these people be, Swamiji?' I ventured to ask. 'They must have some, or they can never be assimilated into the great body of Hindus. Where shall we look for their rightful place?'

'Returning converts', said the Swami quietly, 'will gain their own castes, of course. And new people will make theirs. You will remember', he added, 'that this has already been done in the case of Vaishnavism. Converts from different castes and aliens were all able to combine under that flag and form a caste by themselves—and a very respectable one too. From Ramanuja down to Chaitanya of Bengal, all great Vaishnava Teachers have done the same.'

'And where should these new people expect to marry?' I asked.

'Amongst themselves, as they do now,' said the Swami quietly.

'Then as to names,' I enquired, 'I suppose aliens and perverts who have adopted non-Hindu names should be named newly. Would you give them caste-names, or what?'

'Certainly,' said the Swami, thoughtfully, 'there is a great deal in a name!' and on this question he would say no more.

But my next enquiry drew blood. 'Would you leave these new-comers, Swamiji, to choose their own form of religious belief out of many-visaged Hinduism, or would you chalk out a religion for them?'

'Can you ask that?' he said. 'They will choose for themselves. For unless a man chooses for himself, the very spirit of Hinduism is destroyed. The essence of our Faith consists simply in this freedom of the Ishta.'

I thought the utterance a weighty one, for the man before me has spent more years than any one else living, I fancy, in studying the common bases of Hinduism in a scientific and sympathetic spirit— and the freedom of the Ishta is obviously a principle big enough to accommodate the world.

But the talk passed to other matters, and then with a cordial good night this great teacher of religion lifted his lantern and went back into the monastery, while I, by the pathless paths of the Ganga, in and out amongst her crafts of many sizes, made the best of my way back to my Calcutta home.[11]

The Future of Hinduism

Vivekānanda's vision of the future of Hinduism was almost startling in its boldness. The reader should realize that these words were uttered at a time when not even a glimmer of hope regarding India's future, as other than as a British colony, could be seen or even foreseen on the horizon.

Thus India is working upon the world, but one condition is necessary. Thoughts like merchandise can only run through channels made by somebody. Roads have to be made before even thought can travel from one place to another, and whenever in the history of the world a great conquering nation has arisen, linking the different parts of the world together, then has poured through these channels the thought of India and thus entered into the veins of every race. Before even the Buddhists were born, there are evidences accumulating every day that Indian thought penetrated the world. Before Buddhism, Vedanta had penetrated into China, into Persia, and the Islands of the Eastern Archipelago. Again when the mighty mind of the Greek had linked the different parts of the Eastern world together there came Indian thought; and Christianity with all its boasted civilisation is but a collection of little bits of Indian thought. Ours is the religion of which Buddhism with all its greatness is a rebel child, and of which Christianity is a very patchy imitation. One of these cycles has again arrived. There is the tremendous power of England which has linked the different parts of the world together. English roads no more are content like Roman roads to run over lands, but they have also ploughed the deep in all directions. From ocean to ocean run the roads of England. Every part of the world has been linked to every other part, and electricity plays a most marvellous part as the new messenger. Under all these circumstances we find again India reviving and ready to give her own quota to the progress and civilisation of the world. And that I have been forced, as it were, by nature, to go over and preach to America and England is the result. Every one of us ought to have seen that the time had arrived. Everything looks propitious, and Indian thought, philosophical and spiritual, must once more go over and conquer the world. The problem before us, therefore, is assuming larger proportions every day. It is not only that we must revive our own country—that is a small matter; I am an imaginative man—and my idea is the conquest of the whole world by the Hindu race.[12]

Song of the Sannyāsin

Vivekānanda's approach to life is said to have been characterized by a 'burning renunciation', the spirit of which finds an ecstatic, lyrical expression in the following poem. The fact that its 'handwritten original was discovered (long after his passing in 1902) hidden in a wall during the 1943 restoration of the retreat where Swamiji had spent the summer and given Darshan and discourse to Western seekers'[13] perhaps adds to its appeal.

The burden of the song: om tat sat also appears in the Bhagavadgītā (XVII.23).

Wake up the note! The song that had its birth
Far off, where worldly taint could never reach,
In mountain caves and glades of forest deep,
Whose calm no sigh for lust or wealth or fame
Could ever dare to break; where rolled the stream
Of knowledge, truth, and bliss that follows both.
Sing high that note, *sannyāsin* bold! Say,
'Om Tat Sat, Om!'

Strike off thy fetters! Bonds that bind thee down,
Of shining gold, or darker, baser ore—
Love, hate; good, bad; and all the dual throng.
Know slave is slave, caressed or whipped, not free;
For fetters, though of gold, are not less strong to bind.
Then off with them, *sannyāsin* bold! Say,
'Om Tat Sat, Om!'

Let darkness go; the will-o'-the-wisp that leads
With blinking light to pile more gloom on gloom.
This thirst for life forever quench; it drags

From birth to death, and death to birth, the soul.
He conquers all who conquers self.
Know this and never yield, *sannyāsin* bold! Say,
'Om Tat Sat, Om!'

'Who sows must reap,' they say, 'and cause must bring
The sure effect: good, good; bad, bad; and none
Escapes the law. But whoso wears a form
Must wear the chain.' Too true; but far beyond
Both name and form is *ātman*, ever free.
Know thou art That, *sannyāsin* bold! Say,
'Om Tat Sat, Om!'

They know not truth who dream such vacant dreams
As father, mother, children, wife and friend.
The sexless Self—whose father He? Whose child?
Whose friend, whose foe, is He who is but One?
The Self is all in all—none else exists;
And thou art That, *sannyāsin* bold! Say,
'Om Tat Sat, Om!'

There is but One: the Free, the Knower, Self,
Without a name, without a form or stain.
In Him is *māyā* , dreaming all this dream.
The Witness, He appears as nature, soul.
Know thou art That, *sannyāsin* bold! Say,
'Om Tat Sat, Om!'

Where seekest thou? That freedom, friend, this world
Nor that can give. In books and temples, vain
Thy search. Thine only is the hand that holds
The rope that drags thee on. Then cease lament.
Let go thy hold, *sannyāsin* bold! Say,
'Om Tat Sat, Om!'

Say, 'Peace to all. From me no danger be
To aught that lives. In those that dwell on high,
In those that lowly creep—I am the Self in all!
All life, both here and there, do I renounce,
All heavens and earths and hells, all hopes and fears.'
Thus cut thy bonds, *sannyāsin* bold! Say,
'Om Tat Sat, Om!'

Heed then no more how body lives or goes.
Its task is done: let *karma* float it down.
Let one put garlands on, another kick
This frame: say naught. No praise or blame can be
Where praiser, praised, and blamer, blamed, are one.
Thus be thou calm, *sannyāsin* bold! Say,
'Om Tat Sat, Om!'

Truth never comes where lust and fame and greed
Of gain reside. No man who thinks of woman
As his wife can ever perfect be;
Nor he who owns the least of things, nor he
Whom anger chains, can ever pass through *māyā's* gates.
So, give these up, *sannyāsin* bold! Say,
'Om Tat Sat, Om!'

Have thou no home. What home can hold thee, friend?
The sky thy roof, the grass thy bed, and food
What chance may bring—well cooked or ill, judge not.
No food or drink can taint that noble Self
Which knows Itself. Like rolling river free
Thou ever be, *sannyāsin* bold! Say,
'Om Tat Sat, Om!'

Few only know the truth. The rest will hate
And laugh at thee, great one; but pay no heed.
Go thou, the free, from place to place, and help
Them out of darkness, *māyā's* veil. Without
The fear of pain or search for pleasure, go
Beyond them both, *sannyāsin* bold! Say,
'Om Tat Sat, Om!'

Thus day by day, till *karma's* power's spent,
Release the soul forever. No more is birth,
Nor I, nor thou, nor God, nor man. The 'I'
Has All become, the All is 'I' and Bliss
Know thou art That, *sannyāsin* bold! Say,
'Om Tat Sat, Om!'[14]

Notes

1. Sailendra Nath Dhar. *A Comprehensive Biography of Swami Vivekananda* (Madras: Vivekananda Prakashan Kendra, 1975), Part I, p. 90.
2. *The Complete Works of Sister Nivedita* (Calcutta: Ramakrishna Sarada Mission, 1967), Vol. I, p. 119, emphasis added.
3. Swami Vivekananda, *Ramakrishna and His Message* (Calcutta : Advaita Ashrama, 1972), pp. 79–82.
4. *The Complete Works of Sister Nivedita*, Vol. I, p. 61.
5. Philip H. Ashby, *Modern Trends in Hinduism* (New York and London: Columbia University Press, 1974), p. 68.
6. *The Complete Works of Swami Vivekananda* (Mayavati Memorial Edition: Calcutta: Advaita Ashrama, 1970), Vol. I, pp. 3–4.
7. Ibid., pp. 4–5.
8. Ibid., pp. 6–14.

9. Ibid., p. 20.
10. Ibid., pp. 23–4.
11. Ibid., Vol. V, pp. 233–5.
12. Ibid., pp. 276–7.
13. *Sivaya Subramuniya Swami, Merging with Śiva* (Hawaii, USA: Himalayan Academy, 1999), p. 1121. *Swamiji* is an honorific form of Swami and *darshan*, which literally means 'seeing', signifies perceptual interaction.
14. Ibid., pp. 1119–21.

Swami Dayānanda Saraswatī (1824–1883)

Life

Swami Dayānanda was born in 1824 in what is now the state of Gujarat in India,[1] in a Śaiva family.[2] Two events in his early life proved significant. When in his teens, he was asked by his father to maintain an all-night vigil on the night of Śiva-rātri, a night sacred to Śiva. But not only did the young Mulaji (for that was his given name) see his father doze off, he also saw a rat desecrate the offerings lying in front of the emblem of Śiva, the Śiva-liṅga. How could a God who is helpless against rodents protect others, he wondered. This experience of paternal hypocrisy and divine impotence undermined Mulaji's faith in conventional religion. The second event was the death of his dear sister, which made him lose interest in worldly life. So when he overheard his parents making plans for his marriage, Mulaji fled home at the age of twenty-one, a flight which culminated in his initiation as a monk on the banks of the Narmada river.[3] He now became Dayānanda Sarasvatī.

While leading his life as an itinerant monk, Dayānanda reached Mathura, where he met his guru Virajānanda in 1860, under whom he spent three years intensively studying the Vedas. Virajānanda drew a sharp distinction between the original Vedic texts, which were authentic and the later texts of Hinduism which were not.[4] He was a staunch upholder of original Vedic authority, and it was this torch which he passed on to Dayānanda. When, at the completion of his course, Dayānanda asked his blind guru what dakṣiṇā (tuition fees in secular parlance) he could offer in return for the pedagogical services received, he met with a rather unconventional response:

> I demand of you something else as dakṣiṇā. Take a vow before me that so long as you live, you will work incessantly to spread true knowledge of the

Vedas and the Arshagranthas and condemn works which teach false doctrines and tenets; and that you will even give your life if necessary in reestablishing Vedic religion.[5]

Dayānanda may have done just that, for his 'revolutionary teachings evoked the wrath of the orthodox and numerous attempts were made on Dayānanda's life. His great physical strength saved him from swordsmen, thugs, and cobras, but the last of many attempts to poison him succeeded. Like John the Baptist, he accused a princely ruler of loose living, and the woman in question instigated his death by having ground glass put in his milk.'[6]

But we have gave ahead of our story. If the period from 1824–45 covers the early life of Dayānanda, and 1845–63 that of his wanderings and studies, then the period from 1863–83 constitutes the period of his public ministry, which was brought to an end in the tragic manner just alluded to.[7] The year 1875 marks the high point of this ministry. It was in this year that Dayānanda published his most influential work, the Satyārtha Prakash.[8] It was written in Hindi and is one of the few major works of modern Hinduism originally not composed in English. The Arya Samaj, the institution for the propagation of his teachings, was also founded in 1875 at Bombay.

Dayānanda, through his example and teachings, contributed in a major way to the rise of Hindu nationalism. It is interesting to reflect that the challenge posed to Hinduism by the British rule and Western culture was led, on the spiritual front, by a mystic like Rāmakṛṣṇa, who had no formal education and, on the intellectual front, by someone literate only in Sanskrit and Hindi. It is equally significant that their followers had to resort to English and Western modes of operation to spread their message—but it was with a Hindu tinge; and for Dayānanda it even involved reconverting those Indians who had been initiated into Christianity or Islam by the process of śuddhi or purification.[9]

A Tribute

Dayānanda's somewhat pugnacious campaign against pious fraud in all religions, including Hinduism, has given him the somewhat dubious and in my view unjustified reputation of being intolerant in matters religious. It may therefore be useful to share with the reader a tribute offered by no less a person than Sir Sayyid Ahmad Khan (1817–98) himself, who played such a major role in the evolution of Muslim identity on the subcontinent.

Swami Dayānand Saraswatī was a profound scholar of Sanskrit and a critical student of the Vedas. Besides being a learned scholar he was a man of distinctly noble and spiritual nature. His disciples honoured him like a God. And undoubtedly he deserved that honour. He brought about certain reforms in the Hindu religion. He was vehemently against idol worship; and he was triumphant in discussions with pandits on the contention that there was no idol worship sanctioned by the Vedas. He did not consider it right to worship any other God than the formless One. He also strove to establish that the Vedas do not advocate the worship of the elements. I was very well acquainted with the late Swami Dayānand Saraswatī, and I always showed great respect to him simply because he was such an excellent and learned man that it behoved men of all religions to respect him. I may be wrong but I understand that Swamiji's belief was that 'matter' by which he meant Maya was meaningless and eternal. Had he not had this belief there would have been full agreement between him and the Muslims on the nature of God.

In any case, he was such a great man as has no equal in India. Everyone, therefore, should mourn his death and feel sorry that such an unparalleled man has passed away from our midst.[10]

Record of a Debate

During the early part of his career Dayānanda would actively seek opportunities to debate religious topics with representatives of other religions, as well as his own. After his visit to Calcutta in 1872, he relied less on combative engagement and more on the direct promotion of one's cause. What follows is a record of a typical debate.

As time was short, after some talk it was decided that the question 'What is salvation and how to attain it?' should be discussed. As both the Christians and the Muslims declined to open the debate, Swamiji opened it. He said:

'Mukti or salvation means deliverance; in other words, to get rid of all suffering, and to realize God, to remain happy and free from re-birth. Of the means to attain it, the first is to practise truth, that is truth which is approved both by one's conscience and God. That is truth, in uttering which, one gets encouragement, happiness, and fearlessness. In uttering untruth, fear, doubt, and shame are experienced. As the third mantra of the fortieth chapter of Yajurveda says, those who violate God's teachings, that is, those who speak, act, or believe against one's conscience are called Asur, Rakhshas, wicked and sinful. The second means to attain salvation is to acquire knowledge of the Vedas and follow truth. The third means is to associate with men of truth and knowledge. The fourth is by practising Yoga, to eliminate untruth from the mind and the soul, and to fix it in truth. The fifth is to recite the qualities of God and meditate on them. The sixth is to pray to God to keep one steadfast in truth (gyana), realization of the reality and dharma, to keep one away from untruth, ignorance and adharma, and to free one from the woes of birth and death and obtain mukti. When a man worships God wholeheartedly and sincerely, the merciful God gives him happiness. Salvation, dharma, material gain and fulfillment of desires, and attainment of truth are the results of one's efforts, and not otherwise. To act according to the teaching of God is dharma and violation of it is adharma. Only rightful means should be adopted to attain success and prosperity. Injustice, untruth and unrighteous means should not be made use of to gain happiness.'

Rev. Scott said:

'Salvation does not mean deliverance from woes. Salvation only means to be saved from sins and to obtain Heaven. God had created Adam pure, but he was misled by Satan and committed sin which made all his descendants sinful. Man commits sin of his own accord as the clock works by itself, that is to say, one cannot avoid committing sin by one's own effort and so cannot get salvation. One can obtain salvation only by believing in Christ. Wherever Christianity spreads, people are saved from sin. I have attained salvation by believing in Christ.'

Maulvi Muhammad Hasim said:

'God does what he wishes to do; whom He wishes He gives salvation, just as a judge acquits those with whom he is pleased and punishes those with whom he is displeased. God does what He likes. He is beyond our control. We must trust whoever is the ruler for the time being. Our Prophet is the ruler of the present time. We can get salvation by putting our trust in Him. With knowledge we can do good work, but moksha or salvation lies in His hands.'

Swamiji replied that:

'Suffering is the necessary result of sin; whoever avoids sin will be saved from suffering. The Christians believe God to be powerful; but to believe that Satan misled Adam to commit sin is to believe that God is not All powerful; for, if God had been All powerful, Satan could not have misled Adam, who had been created pure by God. No sensible man can believe that Adam committed sin and all his descendants became sinful. *He alone undergoes suffering who commits sin; no one else.* You say that Satan misleads everyone, I therefore ask you who misled Satan. If you say no one misled him, then as Satan misled himself, so must Adam have done it. Why believe in Satan then? If you say, somebody else must have misled Satan, then the only one who could have done it was God. In that case when God himself misleads and gets others to commit sin, then how can He save people from sin. Satan disturbs and spoils God's creation, but God neither punishes him nor imprisons him, nor puts him to death. This proves that God is powerless to do so. Those who believe in Satan cannot avoid committing sins, for they believe that Satan gets them to commit sin and they themselves are not sinful. Again, if God's only son suffered crucifixion for the sins of all people, then the people need not be afraid of being punished for their sins and they can go on committing sins with impunity. The illustration of the clock given by the Padree sahib is also inappropriate. The clock works only as its *maker has given it the power* to do . . . Then again how can you continue to live in Paradise. Adam was misled there by Satan into eating wheat. Will you not eat wheat and be expelled from Paradise? You gentlemen believe God to be like a man. Man has limited knowledge and does not know everything, he therefore stands in need of recommendation of someone who possesses knowledge. But God is All-knowing and All-powerful. He does not stand in need of any recommendation or help from any prophet or anyone else; otherwise, where would be the difference between God and man? Nor does He according to you remain just, for He does not do justice, if he pardons the culprit on the recommendations of anybody. If God is present everywhere, He cannot have a body; for if he has a body, He will be subject to limitation and will not be infinite, and then he must be subject to birth and death. Is God incapable of saving his worshippers without Christ's intervention? Nor has God any need of a prophet. It is true that where there are good people in a country, people improve because of good men's teachings. As regards the Maulvi sahib, he is wrong in saying that God does what He likes, because then He does not remain just. As a fact, he gives salvation only to those whose works deserve it. Without sin and righteousness there can be no suffering and no happiness. God is the ruler for all time. If God gives salvation on the recommendation of others, he becomes dependent. God is All-powerful. It is a matter of surprise that though the Mussalmans believe God to be one and without a second, yet they made the prophet take part with God in bestowing salvation.'[11]

The Arya Samaj

Dayānanda institutionalized his teachings through the formation of the Ārya Samāj in 1875 in Bombay, with the help of a list of twenty-eight rules.[12] These were reduced to ten by the time the chapter was founded in Lahore in 1877.[13] They are given below in one of their English versions.

1. Of all true knowledge and whatever is known from knowledge, the primary cause is God.
2. God is an embodiment of truth, intelligence and bliss, and one without form, all powerful, just, kind, unborn, infinite, unchangeable, beginningless, incomparable, supporter of all, lord of all, all-pervading, omniscient, undeteriorable, immortal, fearless, eternal, holy and creator of the universe. He alone is worthy of worship.
3. The *Vedas* are the books of all true knowledge. It is the paramount duty of all Aryas to read them, to teach them, to hear them and to preach them.
4. We should be ever ready to accept truths and renounce untruth.
5. Everything should be done according to *dharma*, i.e., after considering what is truth and what is untruth.
6. The chief object of the Arya Samaj is to do good to the world, i.e., to make physical, spiritual and social improvement.
7. We should treat all with love, and justice according to their desserts.
8. We should dispel ignorance and diffuse knowledge.
9. Nobody should remain contented with his personal progress. One should count the progress of all as one's own.
10. Everyone should consider oneself as bound in obeying social and all benefiting rules, but everyone is free in matters pertaining to individual well-being.

Hence if you are anxious for the advancement of your country, you would do well to join the *Arya Samaj* and conduct yourself in accordance with its aims and objects. Otherwise, you (will simply waste your lives) and gain nothing in the end. It behoves us all to lovingly devote ourselves with all our heart, with all our wealth, and aye even with our lives, to the good of our country, the land of our birth, the land of the products of which we have lived, the land which sustains us still and will continue to do so in the future. No other *Samaj* or Society can equal the *Arya Samaj* in its power to raise *Aryavarta*. It will be a very good thing, indeed, if you would all help this *Samaj*, as the capability of a *Samaj* or Society to do good depends not on any single individual, but on all the members that support it.[14]

Beliefs and Disbeliefs

We possess a clear statement of Dayānanda's beliefs and disbeliefs in his own words, which was published from Benaras in 1875. It remains a comprehensive statement of his position, although it is of course possible that his views may have changed on some points before he passed away in 1883. The twelfth belief introduces a new wrinkle in the Hindu doctrine of Mokṣa.

That faith (*dharma*) alone is really worthy of credence which is accepted by the *Apta*, i.e., the persons who are true in word, deed and thought, and who promote public good, and are impartial and learned. Similarly, what is discarded by such men (i.e., the *Apta*) is unworthy of belief and is not authoritative. It is not at all my purpose to found a new system or religion. My sole object is to believe in what is true, and help others to believe in it, and to reject what is untrue and help others to do the same. If I had been partial, I would have championed any one of the religions prevailing in India, but neither do I accept the demerits of different faiths whether Indian or alien, nor reject what is good in them.

He alone is entitled to be called a human being who, keeping his mind cool, feels for the happiness and unhappiness, profit and loss, of others, in the same way as he does for his own self, who does not fear the unjust, however, powerful he may be, but fears the virtuous though weak. And not only this: he should always exert himself to his utmost to protect and promote the cause of the virtuous people even if they are extremely poor and weak and to discourage, suppress and destroy those who are wicked and unrighteous, even though they be the mightiest sovereigns of the whole world. In other words, a man should, as far as it lies in his power, constantly endeavour to undermine the power of the unjust and to strengthen the power of the just, even at the cost of great suffering. He should perform this duty which devolves on him as a man, and which he should never shirk, even if he has to sacrifice his life.

I subjoin here some relevant verses which *Bhartrihari* and others have written in this regard:

'The worldly-wise may praise them or censure them; fortune may smile on them or frown on them; death may overtake them today or after ages, but wise men do not swerve from the path of justice.'

'Let no man ever renounce *dharma* (righteousness) either through lust of through fear or through greed or even for the sake of his life. *Dharma* is eternal while pleasure and pain are transitory. The soul is eternal, while the body is perishable.'

'*Dharma* is the friend that follows one even after death. All else perishes with the body.'

'Truth alone conquers; untruth never. It is the path of rectitude alone that men of learning and piety have followed; and it is by treading this path that the great sages of righteous desire have reached the highest citadel of truth.'

'Verily there is no virtue higher that Truth ; no sin greater than falsehood. Verily, there is no knowledge higher than Truth; let a man, therefore follow truth.'

Every one should hold convictions in accordance with the teachings of the above verses.

I now proceed to describe briefly various things as I believe them to be. Their detailed expositions have been given in my books (*Satyaratha Prakash* etc.).

1. There are many names of God, such as *Brahma* (the most High), *Parmatma* (the Supreme Spirit), etc., and He possesses the attributes of Existence, Consciousness, Bliss, etc. His attributes, work and characteristics are pure. He is Omniscient, Formless, All-pervading, Unborn, Infinite, Almighty, Merciful and Just. He is the maker of the whole universe and is its sustainer and dissolver. He awards with absolute justice to all souls the fruits of their deeds as they deserve, and is possessed of the like attributes. Him alone I believe to be the Great God.

2. I hold that the four *Vedas* (the Divine revealed knowledge and Religious Truth comprising the *Samhita* or *Mantras*) as infallible and as authority by their very nature. In other words, they are self-authoritative and do not stand in need of any other book to uphold their authority; just as the sun or a lamp by its light is self-luminous and illuminates the earth and other objects, even so are the *Vedas*. I hold the four *Brahmanas* of the four *Vedas*, the six *Angas*, and *Upangas*, the four *Up-Vedas*, and the eleven hundred and twenty seven *Shakhas* of the *Vedas* as books composed by *Brahma* and other *Rishis*, as commentaries on the *Vedas*, and having authority of a dependent character. In other words, they are authoritative in so far as they are in accord with the *Vedas*; whatever passages in these words are opposed to the *Vedas*, I hold them as unauthoritative.

3. I accept as *Dharma*, whatever is in full conformity with impartial justice, truthfulness and the like (virtues); that which is not opposed

to the teachings of God as embodied in the *Vedas*. Whatever is not free from partiality and is unjust, partaking of untruth and the like (vices), and as opposed to the teachings of God as embodied in the *Vedas*—that I hold as *Adharma*.

4. I hold the soul as that eternal entity which possesses the attributes of desire and hatred, repulsion, feelings of pleasure and pain, and as possessing limited knowledge and such other things.

5. God and the souls are distinct entities, being different in nature and characteristics: they are, however, inseparable being related as the pervader and the pervaded, and having certain attributes in common. Just as a material object has never been and shall never be, separable from the space in which it exists; nor has it ever been or shall ever be one and the same or identical with it; even so, I hold that God and the souls are related as the pervader and the pervaded, worshipped and worshipper, father and son, and having other similar relations.

6. There are three things beginningless: namely, God, Souls and *Prakriti* or the material cause of the universe. These are also ever-existing. As they are eternal, their attributes, works and nature are also eternal.

7. Substances, attributes and works come into existence by combination, cease to exist after dissolution. But the power by which they first integrated is eternally inherent in them, and it will lead to similar unions by succession.

8. *Creation* is that which results from the combination of different substances in various forms in an intelligent manner and according to design.

9. The object of creation is the exercise or fulfilment of the creative energy, activity, and nature of the deity. When a person asked another, 'what is the use of the eyes', the other person replied, 'to see with', similarly, the fulfilment of God's creative energy is in creating the universe, and in making the souls reap the fruits of their deeds properly.

10. *The world is a creation*, and its Creator is the aforesaid God. From the display of design in the universe and the fact that dead inert matter is incapable of moulding itself into seeds and other various requisite forms, it follows that the world must have a Creator.

11. Bondage (of the soul) has a cause. This is ignorance. All sinful acts such as worship of objects other than God result in suffering, which has to be borne though no one desires it. Hence it is called *bondage*.

12. *Moksha* or salvation is the emancipation of the soul from all woes

and sufferings, and to live bondfree, a life of liberty and free movement in the all-pervading God and His creation, and resumption of the earthly life after the expiration of a fixed period of enjoying salvation.

13. The means to attain salvation are, contemplations of God, i.e., practice of *yoga*, performance of virtuous deeds, acquisition of knowledge, practising *brahmacharya*, associating with wise and pious men, true knowledge, purity of thought, a life of (benevolent) activity and the like.

14. *Artha* or true wealth is that which is righteously acquired; while that which is acquired or achieved by vicious means is called *anartha*.

15. *Kama* or enjoyment of legitimate desires is that which is achieved by righteousness or *dharma* and honestly acquired wealth or *artha*.

16. I hold that the *varna* (caste or class or order of an individual) is determined by his merits (qualifications) and actions.

17. He alone deserves the title of a *raja* or king, who is illumined with excellent qualities, works and disposition, who follows the dictates of impartial justice, who treats his subjects like a father; considering them as his own children, always strives for promoting their advancement and happiness.

18. *Praja* or subjects are those who, by cultivating excellent qualities, works and disposition, and by following the dictates of impartial justice, and being ever engaged in furthering public good, are loyal to the sovereign whom like children they regard as a parent.

19. He, who after careful thinking, is ever ready to accept truth and reject falsehood; who puts down the unjust and promotes just things, and strives for the happiness of others as he does for his own self, him I call the Just.

20. I hold that *devas* are those men who are wise and learned; *asuras* are those who are ignorant; *rakhshasas* are those who are sinful; *pishachas* are those who are wicked in their acts.

21. *Devapuja* consists in showing honour to the wise and the learned, to one's father, mother and preceptor, to preachers of truth, to a just ruler, to righteous persons, to women who are devoted to their husbands, to men who are devoted to their wives. The opposite of this is called *Adevapuja*. I hold that worship is due to these living persons and not to the inert images of stone, etc.

22. *Shiksha* or education is that which promotes knowledge, culture, righteousness, self-control and such other virtues, and eradicates evils like ignorance.

23. I hold that the *Puranas* are the *Brahmanas* such as *Aittiriya* and others written by *Brahma* and others. They are also called *Itihas, Kalpa, Gatha,* and *Narashansi,* but not the *Bhagwat* and other books of that sort.

24. *Tirtha* is that by means of which the ocean of misery is crossed: in other words I hold that *tirthas* are good works such as speaking the truth, acquisition of knowledge, society of the wise and the good, practice of the *yamas* and (other stages) of *Yoga,* life of activity, spreading knowledge and similar other good works. *No places of water of rivers are tirthas.*

25. Activity is superior to destiny since the former is the maker of the latter, and also because if the activity is well directed, all is well but if it is wrongly directed, all goes wrong.

26. I hold that it is commendable for a man to treat all others in the same way as he does his own self; sympathise with them in their happiness and sorrows, their losses and gains. It is reprehensible to behave otherwise.

27. *Sanskara* (ritual) is that which contributes to the physical, mental, and spiritual improvement of man. From conception to cremation there are sixteen *sanskaras.* I hold their performance as obligatory. Nothing should be done for the dead, after their remains have been cremated.

28. *Yajna* consists in showing due respect to the wise and the learned; in the proper application of the principles of physical and mechanical sciences and chemistry; in the dissemination of knowledge and culture and the performance of *agnihotra* which, by contributing to the purification of air, rain, water and medicine plants, promotes the well-being of all sentient creatures. I hold its performance as highly commendable.

29. The word *Arya* means virtuous man, and *Dassue* a wicked man. I hold the same opinion.

30. This country is called *Aryavarta,* because it has been the abode of the *Aryas* from the dawn of creation. It is, however, bounded on the north by the Himalayas, on the south by the Vindhyachala mountains, on the west by the river Attock and on the east by the river Brahmaputra. The people who have been living in it from time immemorial are called *Aryas.*

31. One is called *Acharya,* who teaches his pupils the science of the *Vedas* with their *Angas* and *Upangas* and helps them to adopt right conduct and relinquishment of wrong conduct.

32. One is termed as *shishya* (pupil) who is fit for acquiring true culture and knowledge, possesses a virtuous character, is eager to learn, and is devoted to his preceptor.
33. By the term *guru* is meant father, mother and any one who imparts truth and makes one reject falsehood.
34. He is a *Purohita*, who wishes well to his *Yajman*, by preaching truth to him.
35. And *upadhayaya* (Professor) is one who can teach any portion of the *Vedas* or the *Angas*.
36. *Shishtachar* consists in leading a virtuous life in acquiring knowledge while observing *brahmacharya*, in testing truth by reasoning, such as direct cognition, and other ways, and then accepting truth and rejecting error. He who practises *shishtachar* is called a '*dhishta*' (gentleman).
37. I believe in the *eight kinds of evidence* (as described in the *Shastras*) such as direct cognition, etc.
38. I call him alone an *Apta* who always speaks the truth, is virtuous and strives for the good of all.
39. There are five kinds of tests of knowledge. The first is the attributes, works and nature of God, and the teachings of the *Veda*. The second is eight kinds of evidence such as direct cognition, etc. The third is 'Laws of Nature'. The fourth is conduct and practice of *aptas*; the fifth is purity and conviction of one's own conscience. Every man should sift truth from error with the help of these five tests, and accept truth and reject error.
40. I call that *paropkar* (philanthropy) which helps in freeing all men from their vices and sufferings, and promotes the practice of virtue and happiness.
41. The soul is a free agent in his works; but is dependent inasmuch as he has to enjoy and suffer the fruit of his works awarded by the justice of God. Likewise, God is independent in doing His good works.
42. *Swarga* (heaven) is the enjoyment of special happiness and the possession of the means thereof.
43. *Narka* (Hell) is undergoing great suffering and the means thereof.
44. *Janma* (birth) is the soul's assumption of the body which I hold to be three-fold, viz, past, present and future.
45. Birth is the name given to the union of the soul with the body, and Death is only their separation.
46. *Marriage* is the acceptance of the hand, through mutual consent, (of a person of the opposite sex) in a public manner and in accordance with laws or rules.

47. *Niyoga* is the temporary union of a person with another of the opposite sex, of the same or higher class, as a measure in exceptional or distressing conditions, for the raising of issue in widowhood, or when he or she is suffering from some permanent disease, like impotence or sterility.

48. *Stuti* (adoration) is reciting divine attributes or hearing them recited, and meditating on them. It results in love for God and similar pious feelings.

49. *Prarthana* (Prayer) is requesting God to grant knowledge (and similar other boons) which can come only from communion with Him and what is beyond one's own power and capacity after one has exerted his utmost. Its result is humility and similar things.

50. *Upasana* (Communion) consists in purifying our attributes, works and nature to become similar to those of God, and in feeling that God pervades us also, and that we are the pervaded. Also in realising through the practice of *yoga* that we are near to God and he is near to us. This results in the advancement of our knowledge.

51. *Saguna* and *nirguna stuti* consists in praising God as possessed of the attributes which are inherent in Him, and also as devoid of the attributes which are foreign to His nature.

    Saguna and nirguna prarthna (prayer) consists in praying for God's help for the attainment of virtuous qualities and elimination of vicious qualities.

    Saguna and *nirguna upasana* consists in resigning oneself to God and His will, realising Him as possessed of all good attributes and as devoid of all evils.

I have thus briefly explained my beliefs here: their detailed exposition is to be found in *Satyaratha Prakash* in their proper places, and is also given in other works such as *Rig Vedadi Bhashya Bhumika* (An Introduction to the Exposition of the *Vedas*).

In short, I accept universal maxims: for example, speaking of truth is commended by all, and speaking of falsehood is condemned by all. I accept all such principles. I do not approve of the wrangling of the various religions, against one another for they have, by propagating their creeds, misled the people and turned them into one another's enemy. My purpose and aim is to help in putting an end to this mutual wrangling, to preach universal truth, to bring all men under one religion so that they may, by ceasing to hate each other and firmly loving each other, live in peace and work for their common welfare. May this view through the grace and help of the Almighty God, and with the support of all virtuous and pious men, soon spread in the whole world so that all may easily acquire righteousness, wealth, gratification of legitimate desires and attain salvation, and thereby elevate themselves and live in happiness. This alone is my chief aim. May God, the Lord of Justice, the mightiest of all, the Lord of the Universe, the Omnipresent, be the giver of happiness to us. Salutations to Brahma, the Supreme Lord of infinite power, the Great God, whose true knowledge I have preached. I have spoken the Truth. You have, therefore, given protection to me, the Truth Speaker. May you, Lord, save us from three kinds of sufferings.[15]

Notes

1. K.C. Yadav, tr., *Autobiography of Swami Dayananda Saraswati* (Delhi: Manohar, 1976), p. 11. For a possibly conflicting date see D.N. Vasudeva, *Swami Dayananda Saraswati* (New Delhi: Dayanand Sansthan, 1973), p. 3.
2. J.T.F. Jordens, *Dayānanda Saraswati: His Life and Ideas* (Delhi: Oxford University Press, 1978), p. 4.
3. Ibid., p. 21.
4. Ibid., pp. 36–7.
5. Yadav, p. 44, note 100.
6. Wm. Theodore de Bary, ed., *Sources of Indian Tradition* (New York and London: Columbia University Press, 1958), Vol. II, p. 76.
7. See Jordens, p. 243.
8. Ibid., chapter V.
9. Ibid., pp. 169–70.
10. Bawa Chhajju Singh, *Life and Teachings of Swami Dayanand Saraswati* (New Delhi: Jan Gyan Prakāshan, 1971), p. 176.
11. de Bary, Vol. II, pp. 79–81.
12. Jordens, pp. 337–40.
13. Ibid., p. 340.
14. Glyn Richards, *A Source-Book of Modern Hinduism* (London: Curzon Press, 1985), pp. 60–1.
15. Yadav, pp. 54–65.

Jyotirao Phule
(1827–1890)

Life

The life of Mahatma Jyotirao Phule is significant for providing a very different perspective within modern Hindu thought. The overarching context of modern Hindu thought is provided by the British presence in India and, subsequently, by the struggle for national independence. Not everyone was, however, equally keen on driving the British away. This difference in attitude involved a basic difference in perspective. Almost all Hindus were agreed that India had to be economically, socially and politically regenerated but all were not agreed on the best way to achieve this.

The method proposed was related to the diagnosis of the problem. Most of the Hindu community came to believe in due course that the British were the problem. They were not indifferent to the problems found within Hindu society, and, in fact, worked assiduously for their amelioration but the central belief was that the solution of these problems was the task of the Hindus and that they could all be traced to their general backwardness, of which foreign rule itself was a symptom. Some constituents of the larger Hindu community, however, believed that the real problem lay not with imperialism but with Hinduism itself and that in its reform the imperial presence had a positive role to play, by safeguarding the interests of the less privileged sections within it, such as the *śūdras* and untouchables, and women in general.

Mahatma Jyotirao Phule held such a view and articulated it forcefully throughout his career. He came from the Mali or gardener caste and was educated at the Scottish Mission School, after having attended a small village school outside Pune from 1834–38.[1] He completed his secondary education in English at the Mission School in 1847 where he also befriended two Brahmins, S.B. Govande and M.V. Valavekar, who were destined to assist him in his future work up to a point.

When he left the school in 1847 the '20-year-old Phule and his friends are said to have been fired with the ideas of liberating their country from foreign rule by reading the lives of Shivaji and George Washington, and of the work of Thomas Paine, and by the influence of anti-British Brahmins'.[2] But Phule's views were about to change. In 1848 Phule was introduced to Thomas Paine's works by the Brahmins[3] of Pune, who sought to 'persuade the young students of the necessity of all castes uniting to win back the control of their own political affairs'.[4] However, that very year he underwent a rather disillusioning experience so far as solidarity across caste lines was concerned.

> He had been invited in 1848 to the marriage party of a Brahman friend. Whilst walking along with the marriage procession, at which he was one of the very few non-Brahmans present, he was recognised as a Mali and a *Shudra* and roughly rebuked for daring to take part in a Brahman ceremony. He returned home, deeply shaken, to question his father about the traditional social values that lay behind the incident. His father advised him that the relative degree of social liberty enjoyed by the lower castes was a very recent phenomenon, and recounted the punishments that such a social misdemeanour would have incurred under the rule of the Brahman peshwas. He also described the more general social disabilities then inflicted on the lower castes and untouchables, and advised his son not to take such risks again. If this story has a basis in fact, it has almost certainly been embroidered, both by Phule himself and his biographers. However, an incident of that kind would not be inconsistent with what we know of Phule's intellectual development during the year.[5]

During 1848–53, Phule was mainly concerned with spreading education as a cure for the malaise of Hindu society. He, with the help of his wife, opened a school for girls of low and untouchable castes, modelled after a missionary school he had seen at Amhadnagar. Phule was honoured for his efforts by the Board of Education, with 'a pair of shawls, a gift traditionally bestowing merit, in a public ceremony' in 1852.[6] In his expression of thanks he noted:

> What I may have done towards furthering the cause of educating native females is indeed too little and falls far short even of the demands of duty as one of the sons of the beloved land. It is to your benevolent and philanthropic desires to create a noble and generous ambition among the youths of this country and to see India raise her now abject head and occupy a place among the civilised nations of the earth that I owe these honours.[7]

In 1853 Phule constituted a 'Society for increasing education amongst Mahars, Mangs and others', with S.B. Govande as president, Valaveyar as secretary, S.Y. Paranjape, a school friend as treasurer and Phule as a member. The alliance did not last, however, and Rosalind O'Hanlon attributes its failure to a shift in Phule's views from emphasizing 'the general backwardness of Hindu society as the cause of the sufferings of the lower castes'[8] to the view that 'Brahmans as a caste might be held responsible both for the condition of the low castes, and for the backwardness of Hindu society itself'.[9] This was also accompanied by a change in the attitude towards the British presence. Phule felt that because of the 'predominance of Brahmans at the lower levels of administration', they were in a position to 'defuse the revolutionary potential'[10] generated by educational upliftment, and therefore one had to turn to the British for help. He declared:

> All of you Malis and Kunbis, even Mangs and Mahars should not fear the Brahmans for a moment. For this purpose, God has sent the English into your country.[11]

In 1858 Phule retired from teaching and turned his attention to social reform campaigns. In the course of these campaigns he proposed an alternative model of Indian history which consisted of the following basic propositions: (1) the so-called lower castes were really kṣatriyas, (2) they were reduced to their position through Brahminical hegemony, and (3) the stories of the destruction of kṣatriyas by Paraśurāma, and the humiliation of Bali by Viṣṇu in the form of a dwarf, provide historical evidence of this fact, just as the enslavement of the 'negros' by the whites in America provides a contemporary example. This situation, according to him, was legalized through Brahmanic law:

> In order to fulfil their plan that those people should remain perpetually in slavery, and that they should be able to live comfortably on what the Shudras earned by the sweat of their brow, the Brahmans set up the fiction of caste divisions, and made up several books on it for their own selfish ends.[12]

By contrast, the '"Golden Age" of India had been the pre-Aryan realm of kshatriyas. Under the benign rule of King Bali, the most important values of this society were those of the warrior and the peaceful landholder and cultivator. Their representatives were the Shudrās and ati-Shudrās, who united in their history the material and the agricultural pursuits.'[13]

These intellectual developments culminated in the foundation of the Satyashodhak Samaj or 'Truth-Seeking Society' in 1873. This Society, comparable in some ways to the Arya Samaj, the Prarthana Samaj, etc. was, however, uncompromisingly radical in being ideologically and materially oriented towards the lower classes. Some 700 families of lower castes joined the movement[14] and by 1875 marriages without Brahmin priests were also being performed.[15]

In that year, however, three years after its inception, the society was plagued by a struggle for leadership between Krishnarao Bhalelar, a young radical, and Phule, which continued until Phule's death in 1890.[16] This did not prevent the Society from launching rural campaigns against priestcraft in 1884[17] and in resisting what was felt to be a Brahminical appropriation of Shivaji.[18] Brahminical ritual dominance was also questioned. A proclamation issued by the Samaj in a case in which the right to conduct marriages without a Brahmin priest was challenged by Brahmin priests is particularly instructive in this respect.[19] Interestingly, while questioning Brahminical authority, the proclamation made it clear that the complaining castes did not yield to a lack of confidence in their Hindu identity and in fact argued their case on the basis of Hindu scriptural authority.

Jyotirao Phule authored numerous works during his career: *The Third Eye* (1855); *A Ballad on the Chatrapati Raja Shivaji Bhosale* (1869); *Priestcraft Exposed* (1869); *Memorial Addressed to the Education Commission* (1882); *The Cultivator's Whip-chord* (1882–83); *The Essence of Truth* (1885); *The Tale of the Untouchables* (1885); *All the Rites, Ceremonies and Verses Used in the Satyashodhak Samaj* (1887); and *A Book of True Religion for All* (1889).

The strand within modern Hindu thought represented by Phule is remarkable because it tests some of its common assumptions inasmuch as it was pro-reform without being anti-Christian and radical without being anti-British. Some modern low-caste-oriented political parties such as the Bahujan Samaj Party (BSP) seem to derive their ideology from Phule.

Priestcraft Exposed

In a ballad entitled Priestcraft Exposed, *Phule described how the Brahmins seized power.*

> Lawless men leagued together
> They made Brahma their chief
> They plundered and caused chaos
> Beating the people and bringing them to their knees
> Degrading them into slaves
> See, these are the Shudras
> The rest left over, a tiny number
> Rose up and challenged Parashuram
> They took care to remain united

Of their countrymen, their beloved brothers,
Many were slain
The Shudras no longer cared for unity
The maha-ari attacked Parashuram
Many women became widows
Parashuram routed the maha-ari
In constant fighting he broke their spirit
He did not spare pregnant women
He killed the newborn children
The great enemies of the twice-born
Came to the end of their strength
Thrust down and defeated
Those that were left were punished severely
Abused as Mangs and maha-aris, great enemies
See, these are the Kshatriyas of the olden days.[20]

Phule's Interpretation of Hindu Mythology and Indian History

For Phule, the Aryan Brahmins and their desire to dominate and exploit provides the master-key for understanding Hindu mythology and Indian history. The story of Bali and his dethronement by Viṣṇu in his incarnation as the dwarf (vāmana) and the killing of Kṣatriyas by Paraśurāma, another incarnation of Viṣṇu, are central to his understanding of Hindu mythology. Similarly, the relief from such oppression offered by Muslim and British rule figures prominently in his understanding of Indian history. The following excerpt elaborates some of these themes in the form of a dialogue:

YASHWANT JOTIRAO PHULE: Is caste distinction found among human beings?

JOTIRAO GOVINDRAO PHULE: Originally there was no caste-distinction among human beings.

YASHWANT: Why was there no caste-distinction among human beings?

JOTIRAO: If there is no caste-distinction among birds and beasts, how can there be such distinction among human beings only?

YASHWANT: Kindly explain, in some detail, your theory that there was originally no caste-distinction among human beings.

JOTIRAO: Birds and beasts differ from one another in point of their limbs etc. Biped human beings differ from quadruped animals considerably in point of their limbs etc. (The Aryan Brahmins maintain that) the *Aryan Brahmaji* created the four castes—namely the Brahmins, the Kshatriyās, the Vaishyās and the Shudrās, from (four) different parts of his body. Can you, then, show me (point out) who were the Brahmins among the (non-human) animals—such as donkeys, crows, jackals etc.?

YASHWANT: It is very difficult to prove who are the Brahmins among the (non-human) animals (beings) such as jackals, crows etc., because even the Aryan Brahmarishis also were practising non-vegetarians. From this we cannot prove that there was caste-distinction among birds and beasts. There are references in their (sacred) Scriptures to the effect that the four castes among human beings were created from the limbs of the (venerable) *Brahmaji*.

JOTIRAO: Then tell me from which parts (limbs) of the body of the four-mouthed Brahmadeo were the different birds and beasts (such as donkeys) created?

YASHWANT: We are making these statements on the authority of the (sacred) Scriptures of the Aryan Brahmins.

JOTIRAO: Have you ascertained and verified yourself all this from a personal perusal of the (sacred) books of the Aryan Brahmins?

YASHWANT: No, sir, because the Aryan Brahmins do not allow us even to see those books. And if we express a desire to hear (of the contents of) those books, the Brahmins do not permit us even to hear those contents (being read out to us).

JOTIRAO: So without personally verifying the truth contained in the (sacred) books of the Brahmins, why do you accept blindly the blasphemy of caste-distinction based on the fictions spread orally by them? This is sheer madness on the part of the Shudrās.

YASHWANT: Sir, the Brahmins are venerable and high-caste and we Shudrās are too low and insignificant. Try as we might, how is it possible for us Shudrās to become (as great as) the Brahmins? And how can the Brahmins be degraded to the low status of the Shudrās?

JOTIRAO: Granted for argument's sake, that Aryan Brahmins cannot be degraded to the low status of the Shudrās, then how is it that these self-same Brahmin earth-gods do not feel it below their dignity to partake of wine and bread and biscuits with the Ati-Shudrās (Mangs and Mahars) at the tables in the bungalows of the high Church dignitaries? And do they also not marry the girls belonging to the Ati-Shudrās (low-caste) foreigners and lead (peaceful) lives? From this you should challenge and defame the so-called sacred dictum that 'the Brahmin is venerable everywhere'. That should do the trick.

YASHWANT: So there are a number of different castes such as Dhangars (shepherds), Malis (gardeners, horticulturists), Kumbis (cultivators) in this unfortunate land of King Bali, never found elsewhere in the world. Do you mean to say that all of them are baseless (false)?

JOTIRAO: This thesis will prove to be baseless and false, on careful consideration. Suppose a person has three sons. One of them spends his lifetime in tending his flock of sheep; the second one plants saplings in his irrigated field and devotes himself to tending them (by removing the weeds therein) and the third one ploughs his field, sows corn in it, harvests it and he does this throughout his life-span. Would you, then, call the first one a shepherd, the second one a gardener and the third one a Kunbi (cultivator, farmer), and would you say that they belong to these three castes?

YASHWANT: How can we do that? (It would be wrong to do so.)

JOTIRAO: Suppose now that an Aryan Brahmin has three sons. The first one chooses the profession of playing on a 'tabla' to earn his livelihood; the second one adopts the profession of a physician (apothecary). Thus he prescribes and dispenses medicines to his patients and spends his time in dissecting the dead bodies, irrespective of caste-consideration; and the third one earns his livelihood by working as an humble cook for different families. Would you then say that the first one belongs to the 'gurav' (caste), the second one to the apothecary-caste and the third one to the cook's caste. (It would be quite wrong to term them so.)

YASHWANT: You are quite right, sir, we cannot state that they belong to those three castes. But does your theory not prove that the female scavenger belongs to the meanest caste as she is engaged all the time in performing a very dirty (unclean) job?

JOTIRAO: Just reflect, Yashwant, for a while. Our (venerable) mothers have performed the meanest duties of scavengers for us when we were just infants (in arms). Shall we be justified in condemning them as mean scavengers?

YASHWANT: Who will dare condemn our (venerable) mothers as scavengers for having performed the meanest duties (chores) of scavengers for us when we were infants in arms? It would be most difficult (for me) to find such an ungrateful wretch anywhere upon the surface of this earth. But tell me, Tātyāsaheb, can we not determine the different caste-distinctions based on the respective qualities or temperaments or dispositions or aptitudes (personal nature as a whole)? What have you to say about this?

JOTIRAO: We cannot determine the various caste distinction based on the temperaments or personal nature or personal qualities of different human beings. Some parents provide a fine liberal education to their children and as they are extremely intelligent or clever they turn out as well-behaved and well-trained, and thus become qualified to shoulder high responsibilities (positions). On the other hand there are other parents who take great pains (efforts) to provide their children with the best possible education, but they are extremely dull and unreceptive, and hence turn out to be 'learned fools' and vicious to boot, with the result that they tend to perform mean jobs. (You will also grant that) virtue or vice is not hereditary (which can be passed on by the parents to their children). For, we often find that the children of virtuous and profoundly learned parents do not turn out always as virtuous. Nor do the children of cunning (shrewd) Aryan Brahmins turn out to be as virtuous as the (original) Shankarāchārya himself. So an impartial and just gentleman can never say that if we choose intelligent children of the Ati-Shudra Chamars (shoe-makers) and train them properly they will not become scholars who will hold a candle even to Shankarāchārya himself.

YASHWANT: Kindly enlighten me about how the inveterately invidious (caste-distinctions) were first introduced in our unfortunate land of King Balirājā (a practice which is not found anywhere else in the world), and how the different castes such as Brahmins and Mahārs and Māngs came into existence in India. I am most curious to learn all about this.

JOTIRAO: The Kshatriyās in India (the land of Balirājā), that is, the original masters of the land here were known as Astiks, Pishāchās, Rakshasās, Ahirs, Kakatas, Bhuts, Kolis, Māngs, Mahars etc. They were extremely adept in fighting without the aid of arms (weapons) and were famed as brave and valiant warriors. They were of an epicurean (joyful) temperament and were given to the enjoyment of the good things of life. The kingdoms of most of these rulers (chiefs) were in a prosperous condition, and it would be no exaggeration to say that the land of *King Bali* was literally flowing with milk and honey. Just then the Aryans i.e. the Iranians discovered the useful and novel art of archery. So some adventurous, violent, covetous and ever avaricious Iranian Brahmins, Iranian Kshatriyās and Iranian Vaishyās banded together and invaded this land of King Bali, actuated by their greed for gold and harassed the gentle and well-behaved original inhabitants of this land a number of times and, it is rumoured that at the end of their campaigns, the Aryans flayed the skin off the bodies of the brave warriors of this land. (The Sanskrit words are *twacam kṛṣṇāmrandhayat.*) References to this barbarous practice are found in their so-called chronicles, namely the Vedās which they managed to conceal effectively from the brave inhabitants of our land. In sum, the Iranians drove away (banished) the brave warriors, the Kshatriyās of this land, to the nether world (Hades) i.e. America (this reference seems to be open to doubt) and began to call the remaining Kshatriyās by the pejorative names of Shudrās (Kshudra-insignificant), Ati-Shudrās, dasyus (slaves), plunderers etc. They further persecuted them in diverse ways, and converted (reduced) them into hereditary slaves, serfs, or helots. Finally the Aryans created a fourth category (class) comprising all the Shudrās in the land of Balirājā and assimilated them among the Iranian Brahmins, the Iranian Kshatriyās, and the Iranian Vaishyās. They (the Aryan Brahmins) further banned imparting of education (instruction) to the original (brave) Kshatriyās of this land of (Bali) i.e. the Shudrās and Ati-Shudrās here. In addition to this, some cunning (shrewd) Aryan Rishis (sages) incorporated strict regulations into their (spurious) books with the evil intention that the Shudrās and Ati-Shudrās should for ever be deprived of the healing balm of education. Saint Dnyaneshwar who is supposed to have performed the miracle of riding a stone-wall, and of having made a he-buffalo recite the verses from the Vedās, as also another saint Rāmdās (seventeenth century) who is supposed to have tested the loyalty of one of his disciples by using his mouth as a mortar (and pestle)—these and some other cunning and wicked Aryan Brahmin saints composed heaps and heaps of new religious books to augment the stocks of similar books written by equally cunning and wicked Rishis of yore. They took care not to expose the wicked stratagems of the Aryan Brahmins in having reduced the Shudrās and the Ati-Shudrās to the degrading status of serfs. On the contrary, they encouraged them to revere and worship various stone and metal images (icons) (or gods and goddesses invented by their fertile brains) and thus, entangled them in the imaginary snares (traps) of the trickery of Brahma. The cunning Aryan Brahmins also devised a most iniquitous code of regulations regarding the Māngs and Mahārs and enforced it most rigorously. That is why these wicked discriminating practices continued unabated among them. Not being content with this villainy, they practised hide and seek (i.e. a blatant deception) upon the all-powerful Creator of us all, styled themselves as earth-gods and incarnations of Lord Brahma Himself and systematically befooled the Shudrās and Ati-Shudrās skilfully, and made them dance and clap in (so-called) divine ecstasy.

YASHWANT: All the Brahmins, young and old alike, in India genuinely believe that the authentic Aryan Brahmins are to be found only in the land of King Bali (i.e. India) to-day. Their contention is that when the Aryan Parashurām (the chief of the Aryan Brahmins) vanquished the original Kshatriya warriors of this land, the Kshatriyās automatically lost all their (human) rights. The third category of Aryan Vaishyās were also wiped out automatically. They contend that the Aryan Brahmins and the Shudrās have survived in the land of Bali only in name. What have you to say about this contention of the Aryan Brahmins?

JOTIRAO: The contention of the Aryan Brahmins seems to be true. Some Aryans who came into the land of Bali along with the Aryan hordes, were adept in performing animal sacrifices. Those who were experts (well-versed) in conducting religious rites were called as Brahmins. Those Aryans who took up the profession of arms were known as Kshatriyās, while those Aryans who took to the pastoral life were called as Vaishyās. The original inhabitants of the land of Bali were called as Kshatriyās. The Aryan Brahmins, the Aryan Kshatriyās and the Aryan Vaishyās (of Iran) originally banded together and invaded this land of Bali a number of times, and, thus, destroyed the mastery of these original inhabitants of the land of Bali on their native land. Then these three classes of Iranians began to style themselves unanimously as Aryan Brahmins, and began to stigmatise the original inhabitants of this land whom they had managed to vanquish, by the pejorative and contemptuous name of Shudrās and Ati-Shudrās. The Iranians used to call their soldiers as 'Kshatriyās', whereas the inhabitants of the land of Bali used to call all the subjects (people) as Kshatriyās. As the term 'Kshatriyā' could be interpreted in both these senses (meanings), the cunning Iranians (Aryan Brahmins) could manage to create such a confusion (of nomenclature).

YASHWANT: From this it appears that the description of the natural (innate) qualities of a Brahmin given in the Gita of the Hindu religion (the Hindus) may have been a fiction incorporated in it in order to throw dust in the eyes of (deceive) the ignorant folk (masses). For instance: 'Peace-loving nature, self control, penance, purity (of character), forgiveness, humility (straight-forwardness), learning, deep self-knowledge (spiritual knowledge), and theism—all these are the natural (innate) qualities of a Brahmin.'

If this, indeed, be so, then why do the victorious, adventurous and cunning Aryan Brahmins regard the helpless, poor Shudrās and Ati-Shudrās whom they had vanquished (on the battlefield) as mean, contemptible and insignificant all this while, in all things (in all departments of life)? Why do they detest them heartily all the time and why do they prevent them from enjoying (all) human rights? This proves conclusively that the wicked and cunning Aryan Brahmins did not have even a modicum of pity (compassion) in their hearts (for their unfortunate compatriots). Let it be! (What baffles or surprises me most is), if our Creator is reputed to be an ocean of compassion and also extremely just, how is it that he did not feel like taking pity upon the Shudrās and the Ati-Shudrās who were oppressed and persecuted (by the Brahmins) in every conceivable way?

JOTIRAO: Our most compassionate Creator, in His infinite mercy, sent the Mohammedans who believe in Him as our common Creator and who has supplanted (destroyed) all invidious caste-distinctions among them, to this country in order to liberate the helpless (crippled) Shudrās and Ati-Shudrās from the trammels of the cunning, wicked Aryans' thraldom. But unfortunately the Mohammedans set at nought His commendable commands and were given to a luxurious way of life—such as song and dance, soft and enervating comforts of life and a taste for good and rich viands. Thus they were so intoxicated with power and luxury (pelf) that they imagined themselves to be in the seventh heaven. So incensed was our Creator with the Mohammedans that He cast them into the utmost straits and destroyed all their glory and grandeur.

YASHWANT: How is it that our Creator destroyed the grandeur of the overweening Mohammedans and preferred to remain absolutely quiet or idle afterwards?

JOTIRAO: He did not remain idle at all afterwards. (He did not keep quiet.) He saw to it that the English people rose to prominence and prosperity from a barbarous state, endowed them with many admirable qualities (of head and heart) such as bravery (valiance), and sent them (directed them) to our country to accomplish His mission of releasing the helpless (crippled) Shudrās and Ati-Shudrās in our land from the trammels of the cunning and wicked Aryan Brahmins' thraldom. There are some benevolent and enlightened Englishmen who, inspired by the good teachings of a truly holy man of their religion (*Christ*) have been constantly trying to free the Shudrās and Ati-Shudrās from the trammels of the Aryan Brahmins' wicked thraldom.

YASHWANT: May I know the name of the holy man whose noble teachings have inspired these Englishmen to liberate the helpless Shudrās and Ati-Shudrās from the trammels of the Aryan Brahmins' thraldom. I would be most grateful to you if you would kindly enlighten me about him and his teachings.

JOTIRAO: The name of their noble, enlightened and exalted holy man is 'Yashwant' (i.e. Jesus=Yeshu), and his noble teaching is as follows: 'Love your enemies and do good unto them!'

YASHWANT: If the deceitful and cunning Aryan Brahmins had heeded (respected) the good advice (gospel) of the great holy man—Jesus—and yet failed to discard (set aside) the teachings contained in their (spurious) books—enjoining them to treat the Shudrās and Ati-Shudrās as serfs and helots. And if they still continued to behave in a most arrogant and undignified manner—it will surely result in a great catastrophe for them in this world. Can you foretell (prophesy, presage) that disaster?

JOTIRAO: I would like to foretell (prophesy) as follows:—If the cunning Aryan Brahmins do not totally destroy their wicked books (Scriptures) which enjoin them to treat the Shudrās and Ati-Shudrās as serfs and helots, then the Almighty Himself who is justice incarnate and Omnipotent, will surely cause (enable) the Shudrās and Ati-Shudrās themselves to condemn and ridicule the cunning Aryan Brahmins and their spurious (heretical) scriptures in no time at all.

YASHWANT: From what you have told me, I begin to wonder whether the composers (writers, authors) of the four Vedās were gentlemen (men of honour and dignity) at all. I also begin to doubt their goodness (of heart). So if you happen to have any authentic knowledge about the said four Vedās, kindly impart it to me. The Shudrās and Ati-Shudrās will be most beholden unto you (for the same).

JOTIRAO: Once upon a time there was a great and good (enlightened) researcher (scholar) in our land, he has criticised the Vedās roundly. I shall quote just a little line from that celebrated work here, for your information (enlightenment): 'The authors (composers) of the three Vedās were deceitful, cunning and of a demoniac nature.'

YASHWANT: From this it is clear that some Aryan Brahmins have distinguished themselves as great scholars under the English rule (administration), and they are also highly qualified to occupy (adorn) positions of high responsibility (to shoulder high responsibilities) in the service of Government. It is also a patent fact that their ancestors defeated, vanquished and totally extirpated the poor helpless Shudrās and Ati-Shudrās, and thus confusion was worse confounded in their lives. Why do they (the highly educated Aryan Brahmins) not take any steps to remove this supreme confusion, root and branch, fruit and flower? Why does our Creator, (or *Jesus*) through whose palms strong iron nails were driven on the Cross, not remove the scales from the eyes of the Aryan Brahmins? Why does he not absolve them of their crimes and bring them back to the path of righteousness, in their own interest?

JOTIRAO: A careful study of the laws of operations of Nature proves that though the Rishi-like (saintly, sanctified, venerable) ancestors of the present Aryan Brahmins did not have to suffer the evil consequences of their villainous deeds in their own life-times, taking into consideration the villainous nature of their evil conduct (practices), their descendants (children, progeny) will most certainly have to suffer the evil consequences of the original villainy. (In the words of the Holy Bible 'The fathers have eaten the sour grapes and the children's teeth are set on edge.') But I make bold to say that the present-day learned Aryan Brahmins will never come to their senses and will never repent their past villainy. In order to escape from the disasters and catastrophes which are impending against them, they will establish (found) many spurious religious and political organizations, and will invent many devices (ruses) to throw dust into the eyes of the Government as also of the ignorant masses. But I dare say, all these devices (ruses, stratagems) are foredoomed to ignominious failure.[21]

Phule and British Education

In his submission before the Education Commission (popularly known as the Hunter Commission) of 1882, Phule cited from his English preface to a book in Marathi, in which he accuses the British of promoting the education of the upper classes rather than of the masses.

Perhaps a part of the blame in bringing matters to this crisis may be justly laid to the credit of the Government. Whatever may have been their motives in providing ampler funds and greater facilities for higher education, and neglecting that of the masses, it will be acknowledged by all that in justice to the latter, this is not as it should be. It is an admitted fact that the greater portion of the revenues of the Indian Empire are derived from the ryot's labour—from the sweat of his brow.

The higher and richer classes contribute little or nothing to the state exchequer. A well-informed English writer states that 'our income is derived, not from surplus profits, but from capital; not from luxuries, but from the poorest necessaries. It is the product of sin and tears.'

That Government should expend profusely a large portion of revenue thus raised, on the education of the higher classes, for it is these only who take advantage of it, is any thing but just or equitable. Their object in patronising this virtual high class education appears to be to prepare scholars who, it is thought, would in time vend learning without money and without price. If we can inspire, say they, the love of knowledge in minds of the superior classes, the result will be a higher standard of morals in the cases of the individuals, a large amount of affection for the British Government, and unconquerable desire to spread among their own countrymen the intellectual blessings which they have received.

Regarding these objects of Government the writer above alluded to, states that we have never heard of philosophy more benevolent and more Utopian. It is proposed by men who witness the wondrous changes brought about in the Western world, purely by the agency of popular knowledge, to redress the defects of the two hundred millions of India, by giving superior education to the superior classes and to them only. We ask the friends of Indian Universities to favour us with a single example of the truth of their theory from the instances which have already fallen within the scope of their experience. They have educated many children of wealthy men and have been the means of advancing very materially the worldly prospects of some of their pupils. But what contribution have these made to the great work of regenerating their fellowmen? How have they begun to act upon the masses? Have any of them formed classes at their own homes or elsewhere, for the instruction of their less fortunate or less wise countrymen? Or have they kept their knowledge to themselves, as a personal gift, not to be soiled by contact with the ignorant vulgar? Have they in any way shown themselves anxious to advance the general interests and repay the philanthropy with patriotism? Upon what grounds is it asserted that the best way to advance the moral and intellectual welfare of the people is to raise the standard of instruction among the higher classes? A glorious argument this for aristocracy, were it only tenable. To show the growth of the national happiness, it would only be necessary to refer to the number of pupils at the colleges and the lists of academic degrees. Each Wrangler would be accounted a national benefactor; and the existence of Deans and

Proctors would be associated, like the game laws and the ten-pound franchise, with the best interests of the constitution.

One of the most glaring tendencies of Government system of high class education has been the virtual monopoly of all the higher offices under them by Brahmins. If the welfare of the Ryot is at heart, if it is the duty of Government to check a host of abuses, it behoves them to narrow this monopoly day by day so as to allow a sprinkling of the other castes to get into the public services. Perhaps some might be inclined to say that it is not feasible in the present state of education. Our only reply is that if Government look a little less after higher education which is able to take care of itself and more towards the education of the masses there would be no difficulty in training up a body of men every way qualified and perhaps far better in morals and manners.

My object in writing the present volume is not only to tell my Shudra brethren how they have been duped by the Brahmins, but also to open the eyes of Government to that pernicious system of high class education, which has hitherto been so persistently followed, and which statesmen like Sir George Campbess, the present Lieutenant-Governor of Bengal, with broad universal sympathies, are finding to be highly mischievous and pernicious to the interests of Government. I sincerely hope that Government will ere long see the error of their ways, trust less to writers or men who look through highclass spectacles, and take the glory into their own hands of emancipating my Shudrā brethren from the trammels of bondage which the Brahmins have woven around them like the coils of a serpent. It is no less the duty of each of my Shudrā brethren as have received any education, to place before Government the true state of their fellowmen and endeavour to the best of their power to emancipate themselves from Brahmin thraldom. Let there be schools for the Shudrās in every village; but away with all Brahmin school-masters! The Shudras are the life and sinews of the country, and it is to them alone, and not to the Brahmins, that Government must ever look to tide over their difficulties, financial as well as political. If the hearts and minds of the Shudras are made happy and contented, the British Government need have no fear for their loyalty in the future.[22]

The Tenets of the Satya Samaj

Mahatma Jyotirao Phule founded the Satya Shodhak Samaj, or the Society of Seekers of Truth, on 24 September 1873.[23] Every member of the Samaj had to take a pledge of loyalty to the British.[24] The Samaj however was directed towards supporting humanism. This is brought home by the proceeding when it met as the Satya Samaj on 11 April 1911 in Poona under the chairmanship of Shri Ramayya Venkayya, when it took the following decisions.[25]

1. This 'Samaj' should be designated as 'Satya Samaj'.
2. (A) All human beings are the children of one God. He is the father of us all.

   (B) Just as no intermediary or broker is needed to entreat one's mother or to please one's father, so no intermediary or broker is needed for a devotee to know God in His true form and to propitiate him (such as a priest, or a religious preceptor or a guru).

   (C) He who accepts this tenet is a Satya Samajist.
3. Every Satya Samajist must take the following pledge:—

   All human beings are the children of one God. I shall always conduct myself, keeping in mind the common fraternal relations of us all.

   While worshipping God or offering devout prayers to Him or while performing any religious rites, I shall not seek the aid of any intermediary or broker. I shall try to persuade others also to behave in this manner. I shall not fail to educate my children. I shall be loyal to my rulers. I take this solemn pledge, invoking (remembering) the Almighty God who is Omnipresent and truth incarnate. May the Almighty God give me strength to realise this holy resolve (of mine) and to fulfil the *Summum bonum* of my life.[26]

Phule's Views on Enforced Widowhood

For Phule, the question of the position of women and that of the underprivileged classes was as closely connected as Siamese twins.

Now I touch upon the most delicate subject of enforced widowhood upon Brahmin women. The partial Aryan Institution inconsiderately allows polygamy to males, which causes them to fall into new habits of wickedness. When his lust is satisfied with his legal wives, he for novelty's sake haunts the houses of public women. He then contracts venereal diseases from them and is obliged to seek medical assistance at an exorbitant cost, for himself and his wives. When medical treatment ceases to cure him and his wives, he loses all hopes of getting children. In this deplorable condition of his life if the lewd husband finds his own wife to go out during night he suspects her of leading a vicious course and so, punishing her severely, turns her out. In old age in order to obliterate the stigma upon his character, the shameless fellow becomes a religious man and hires public harlots to dance and sing in the temples with a view to venerating the stone idols, for his own satisfaction. After the death of this wicked man, his young and beautiful wife is not allowed by the same Aryan Institution to remarry. She is stripped of her ornaments; she is forcibly shaved by her near relatives; she is not well fed; she is not properly clothed; she is not allowed to join pleasure parties, marriages or religious ceremonies. In fact she is bereaved of all the worldly enjoyments, nay, she is considered lower than a culprit or a mean beast.

Moreover, the Aryan Institution enjoins Brahmin males to marry even the lower class girls during the life-time of his first wife; but his real own sister is prohibited to remarry, after the demise of her first husband. Such partial and unjust prohibitions necessarily lead the helpless Aryan widow to commit horrible and heart-rending acts of atrocity. To prove the above assertion I insert the following instance. One of my Brahmin friends named Rao Saheb Sedashive Bullal Gowndey, who was an officer in the Inam Commission, employed in his house a Brahmin widow as cook, whose name was Kashibai. The poor Kashibai was a well-behaved and beautiful young woman of a respectable family. She was a chaste woman. She served several months in his house. But in his neighbourhood there lived a shrewd and cunning Shashtriboova of a Brahmin caste, who tried his utmost to mislead this ignorant woman. Kashibai at first resisted his inducement but at last she fell victim to his desire and immediately became pregnant. Afterwards by the persuasion of her paramour, she tried several poisonous drugs to commit abortion, but all her attempts failed. After nine months were completed, Kashibai gave birth to a beautiful son and for the sake of her disgrace she murdered the innocent infant with a knife and the corpse was thrown into the well behind the house of her master. Two days after she was arrested by the police on suspicion, tried before the Session Court in Poona and was sentenced to transportation for life. This crime Kashibai committed, that her character may not be spoilt among the Brahmin community. Her case brought to the notice of the public the unjust and partial character of the Aryan Institution, and so the people were struck with horror. Although my means were not sufficient to defray my expense, yet I was compelled to establish a fondling house, in my own compound in Poona, for the Brahmin community immediately after Kashibai's trial was over. The enclosed copy of printed notices was then pasted on the walls of the corners of streets, where the Brahmins reside. From its commencement up to the present time, thirty-five pregnant widows came to his [this?] house and were delivered of children, of whom five [were] living; thirty died by the injuries done to them while in the womb by the poisonous drugs which the mothers must have taken with a view to concealing their pregnancy. Many of the beautiful and helpless ignorant young widows of the respectable Brahmin families have turned out private and public prostitutes on account of this wretched system. How abominable and degrading is the system of Aryan Institution, which compels Brahmin widows to drag their lives in so miserable and shameless ways, that even modesty shrinks back to enter into particular details! In conclusion, I most respectfully crave the favour of your enlightened English Government to remove the tyranny of enforced widowhood, exercised upon the helpless women, by the relentless system of Aryan religious institution. I, therefore, propose that no barbers should be allowed to shave the unfortunate Brahmin widows. It is quite evident from the partial Aryan religious institution that, when it prohibits the widows from remarrying, why the widowers should be allowed to remarry? If the favour be shown to the latter then the poor widows must of necessity be permitted to remarry. There is no doubt that the selfish and wicked law-givers must have added such unjust and nonsensical clauses into their Shastras with malice towards the female sex.[27]

Notes

1. Rosalind O'Hanlon, *Caste, Conflict, and Ideology: Mahatma Jyotirao Phule and Low Caste Protest in Nineteenth Century Western India* (Cambridge: Cambridge University Press, 1985), p. 110.
2. Ibid.
3. Ibid., p. 111.
4. Ibid.
5. Ibid., p. 111.
6. Ibid., p. 118.
7. Ibid., pp. 118–19.
8. Ibid., p. 119.
9. Ibid., p. 120
10. Ibid., p. 127.
11. Cited, ibid., p. 129.
12. Cited, ibid., p. 142.

13. Ibid., p. 149. Incidentally, as O'Hanlon notes, 'These values represented all that was best in nineteenth-century society.'
14. Ibid., p. 230.
15. Ibid., p. 241.
16. Ibid., p. 243ff.
17. Ibid., p. 277ff.
18. Ibid., p. 295ff.
19. Ibid., p. 280. The case was decided in favour of the Samaj.
20. Ibid., pp. 142–3.
21. P.G. Patil, tr., *Collected Works of Mahatma Jyotirao Phule* (Bombay: Education Department, Government of Maharashtra, 1991), Vol. II, pp. 5–12.
22. Ibid., pp. 119–21.
23. Ibid., Vol I, p. xix.
24. Ibid.
25. Ibid., p. 86.
26. Ibid. Quoted at the end of the second edition of 'Slavery', published in 1911 by Shri Ramayya Vyankayya Ayyawaru.
27. Ibid., Vol. II, pp. 117–18.

Mahadev Govind Ranade
(1842–1901)

Life

The leading figures of modern Hinduism, whose lives and thoughts have been discussed so far, were from two ends of India. The first five—Roy, Tagore, Sen, Rāmakṛṣṇa and Vivekānanda—hailed from Bengal or eastern India, and equally significantly, Dayānanda Sarasvatī and Phule hailed from Gujarat and Maharashtra respectively, or western India. This shift in the geographical theatre is not without its historical logic. Bengal, in the east, was the first region of India to come under British rule (in 1757) in a major way, while Maharashtra in the west followed suit only later (in 1818). Indeed, religious developments within Hinduism in the east also had an enriching impact on the west.

This point is well illustrated by the circumstances which led to the founding of the Prarthana Samaj in Bombay.

> When Keshub Chander Sen visited Bombay in 1864 and roused the people by his impassioned lectures some earnest men decided to form an association with the four declared objects of (1) the disapproval of caste, (2) the introduction of widow-marriage, (3) the encouragement of women's education, and (4) the abolition of child marriage. After more meetings, it was further decided to make religious reform the basis of their programme of social reform and to organize the pure worship of the one true God. Accordingly a weekly prayer meeting was started. The first meeting took place on the 31st March 1867, in the house of Dr. Atmaram Pandurang. Four month later the articles of the new Society were drawn up, its rules were framed and its managing committee was appointed. This was the genesis of the Prarthana Samaj.[1]

M.G. Ranade is one of the more famous members of the Prarthana Samaj. He was born in Kolhapur in 1842, the eldest of three children, in a family of Chitpavan Brahmins, a caste which 'produced three leaders whose names were to be inscribed in Indian nationalism's hall of fame—Rānade, Gokhale, and Tilak'.[2] After an exceptionally bright academic career, both as a student[3] and a teacher at Elphinstone College, which lasted fourteen years, Ranade chose to enter law at the age of thirty and commenced his career as a subordinate judge at Poona. It culminated in his appointment as a judge of the Bombay High Court in 1893.[4] He died in harness in 1901.

During his career Ranade also became involved with several other associations, apart from the Prarthana Samaj. He was one of the founders of the Indian National Congress (1885).[5] In 1887 he founded the Indian National Social Conference (which met regularly with the Indian National Congress); and in 1890, the Industrial Association of India. He attended the annual meeting of the Congress and the Conference for eighteen years without interruption, until prevented by an illness, which eventually proved fatal. These institutions reflect the various dimensions of his personality: his interest in theism and reform, and in India's political and economic future, the latter interest earning him the distinction of being called the Father of Indian Economics.[6]

It is primarily in terms of his role in Hindu theological and reformist developments that he must be assessed in the present context. Herein the differences between his thought and that of someone like Keshub Chunder Sen are illuminating. D.S. Sarma summarizes these differences as follows: 'Under Ranade's able guidance, the Prarthana Samaj of Bombay avoided some of the errors of the Brahmo Samaj of Bengal. It did not cut itself off from the parent Hindu community and form a separate sect. It announced no New Dispensations, it did not play with Christianity. On the other hand, it tried to affiliate its Theism to the older Theisms of the Bhagavatas and the Saints of Maharashtra. While it concentrated its attention on social reform, it kept its religious beliefs rather undefined.'[7]

This latter tendency means that the theism of Ranade, which formally 'inclined to the Ramanuja school of Vedantism',[8] must be more generally viewed as 'continuing the religious tradition of the prophets and saints of Maharashtra, the tradition of Changdev and Jnanadev, of Eknath and Namdev, of Tukaram and Ramdas and of Janardanpant and Malopant'.[9] Ranade was inclined to compare their work with that of Luther and Calvin, and Latimer and Knox, which accounts for the title of one of the talks he delivered in 1895. It was called *Hindu Protestantism*.[10] This Hindu Protestantism, however, differed from Christian Protestantism in two significant ways: Hindu Protestantism was not as iconoclastic as its Christian counterpart, and its God was more accessible, more like 'a father or a mother, or a brother or a friend', than like 'a judge, or a chastiser or a ruler, the form God is more prone to assume in the Semitic religions compared with the Indic'.[11] In one respect, however, the movement represented by the Prarthana Samaj did not quite rise to the level of either the Protestant movement in Europe or the movement in Maharashtra he compared it with: it never became as widespread and popular.[12]

Ranade's reformist thought followed a middle course between the conservative orthodoxy of traditional Hinduism and the radical reformism of the Brahmo Samaj of India. For Ranade, one did not have to turn to the West but to one's past to seek inspiration for reform, once one had shifted one's vision 'from the more immediate past of our degradation to the most remote past of our glory'.[13] Thus although the theological position of the Prarthana Samaj was 'the same as that of the Sadharan Brahmo Samaj, it refused to identify itself with any of the Brahmo Samaj branches in Bengal. Hence there were no schisms, no unseemly quarrels in the Prarthana Samaj like those in the Brahmo Samaj'.[14] But Ranade could not entirely avoid an embarrassment similar to the one experienced by Keshub Chunder Sen. Although he was a staunch opponent of child marriage (and proponent of widow remarriage and caste intermarriage), 'within a month of the death of his first wife, Ranade, himself thirty-two, was married in the conventional way to a maiden girl of eleven'.[15] Small wonder then that:

> His second marriage at the age of 32 to a girl of 12 occasioned the criticism that he had betrayed the cause of social reform which he championed by distinguishing between precept and practice in his own life. The explanation that he had submitted unwillingly to the wishes of his father failed to satisfy his fellow reformers who expected him, as founder of the society for encouragement of widow remarriage, to adhere to his principles by choosing a suitable widow to remarry.[16]

This incident remained potentially embarrassing. The fact that he had not married a widow enabled 'a young zealot in the audience to denounce Ranade's presence as detrimental to the movement' even in 1899. Ranade then 'replied with a long discussion of his marriage to Ramabai, which he prefaced by stating, "We are lame and weak persons. So I say to my young friend: You lead us and we shall follow you with whatever strength and ability we possess in our frailty." '[17]

Ranade may not have been able to 'live up to the principle of widow remarriage. But he could pursue other principles; women's education for instance. He decided to educate his wife.'[18] Neither did his enthusiasm for the cause of widows diminish; he supported even Pandita Ramabai (who had converted to Christianity) until her attempts at proselytization were exposed by B.G. Tilak,[19] in comparison with whom he was a moderate. The two differed on many issues[20] but like Tilak, Ranade also moulded public opinion, though in constitutional rather than agitational ways. Ranade was instrumental in founding the Sarvajanik Sabha in 1870, which subsequently aroused the suspicions of the British government. One of its founding members, G.W. Joshi, 'was the first in India to practise and propagate the idea of Swadeshi; he attended the Durbar in Delhi in 1877 in Khadi dress.'[21] Nor did Ranade shy away from public confrontation when justified. When Swami Dayānanda Sarasvatī visited Poona in 1874, his public talks stirred the waters sufficiently for the opponents of his reforms to organize a demonstration designed to humiliate him. On the day Swami Dayānanda Sarasvatī was to be taken out in a procession, his opponents 'started another procession, that of a donkey with a yellow scarf round its head and a coloured cloth decorated over its body accompanied by noise-makers'. In the commotion that ensued Ranade's clothes got soiled.[22]

Ranade also believed in the uplift of the lower classes, but as a reformer rather than as a revolutionary. He was 'congenitally averse to intercaste conflict, and although he seems to have supported Jyotiba Phule's non-Brahmin movement privately and cautiously, he could never subscribe to the militantly expressed antagonisms on the part of the non-Brahmin leaders'.[23] His feelings on the issue were revealed in a curious context in which he was himself at the receiving end of racism. 'In 1894, when Ranade was returning to Bombay after attending the Congress at Madras, a young British ICS officer insulted him at the Solapur station. While Ranade had gone to the second class compartment to talk to his friends, the Englishman threw down his bedding in the first class carriage and usurped his seat. Ranade sat quietly on the berth nearby, on which Bhandarkar accommodated him. On arriving in Poona, the Englishman, who was an Assistant Judge, came to know that the gentleman he had insulted was a Judge of the High Court. He then wanted to apologize but Ranade turned away.'[24] Though Ranade did not retaliate, he felt the insult, for he later mused to Gokhale:

> Is our own conscience clear in these matters? How do we treat members of the depressed classes—our own countrymen—even in these days? At a time, when they and we must all work hand in hand for our common country, we are not prepared to give up the privileges of our old ascendency, and we persist in keeping them down-trodden. How can we, then, with a clear conscience, blame members of the ruling race, who treat us with contempt?[25]

Ranade's vision of Indian history contained an important religious component. He visualized its movement as essentially dialectical. Although this expression has now become fraught with all sorts of frightening possibilities in our own times, it can still be applied to Ranade in the sense that Indian history disclosed a movement of upward synthesis, in which, first of all, the races of India produced Hinduism, which then interacted with Islam in a mutually fecundating manner until Aurangzeb arrested the process, which brought the Marathas to power. The British presence in India was seen as continuing the process. But while Ranade 'recognized the benefits British rule bestowed on India',[26] he was also 'sufficiently patriotic to realize that the transfer of power from British to India was ultimately inevitable since millions of Indians could not be held permanently in a state of subjugation'.[27]

India and Providence

Like other leading Indians, Ranade did not fail to see the hand of providence in the fate of India. But his reading of the writing on the wall in one respect was unique: he saw Hinduism not in the context of Christianity but of Judaism! He declared in his address to the Social Conference in Lahore in 1893:

> I profess implicit faith in two articles of my creed. This country of ours is the true land of promise. This race of ours is the chosen race.[28]
>
> If the miraculous preservation of a few thousand Jews had a purpose, this more miraculous preservation of one-fifth of the human race is not due to mere chance.[29]

By the time he addressed the Social Conference at Calcutta in 1896 the imagery had flowered further.

> With a liberated manhood, with buoyant hope, with a faith that never shirks duty, with a sense of justice that deals fairly to all, with unclouded intellect and powers fully cultivated, and, lastly, with a love that overleaps all bounds, renovated India will take her proper rank among the nations of the world, and be the master of the situation and of her own destiny. This is the goal to be reached—*this is the promised land.*[30]

Hindus, Muslims and India's Providence

At the Social Conference in 1899 Ranade delivered an address entitled 'I am neither Hindu nor Mohamedan', the claim with which Guru Nanak used to surprise his audiences in the sixteenth century.

If the lessons of the past have any value, one thing is quite clear, viz., that in this vast country, no progress is possible unless both Hindus and Mahomedans join hands together, and are determined to follow the lead of the men who flourished in Akbar's time, and were his chief advisers and councillors, and sedulously avoid the mistakes which were committed by his great-grandson Aurangzeb. Joint action from a sense of common interest, and a common desire to bring about the fusion of the thoughts and feelings on men, so as to tolerate small differences and bring about concord—these were the chief aims kept in view by Akbar, and formed the principle of the new divine faith formulated in the Din-i-Ilahi. Every effort on the part of either Hindus or Mahomedans to regard their interests as separate and distinct, and every attempt made by the two communities to create separate schools and interests among themselves, and not to heal up the wounds inflicted by mutual hatred of caste, and creed, must be deprecated on all hands. It is to be feared that this lesson has not been sufficiently kept in mind by the leaders of both communities in their struggle for existence, and in the acquisition of power and predominance during recent years. There is at times a great danger of the work of Akbar being undone by losing sight of this great lesson which the history of his reign and that of his two successors is so well calculated to teach. The Conference which brings us together is especially intended for the propagation of this 'Din' or 'Dharma', and it is in connection with that message chiefly that I have ventured to speak to you today on this important subject. The ills that we are suffering are, most of them, self-inflicted evils, the cure of which is to a large extent in our own hands. Looking at the series of measures which Akbar adopted in his time to cure these evils, one feels how correct was his vision when he and his advisers put their hand on those very defects in our natural character, which need to be remedied first before we venture on higher enterprises. Pursuit of high ideals, mutual sympathy and co-operation, perfect tolerance, a correct understanding of the diseases from which the body politic is suffering, and an earnest desire to apply suitable remedies—this is the work cut out for the present generation. The awakening has commenced, as is witnessed by the fact that there are men in this place from such distances for joint consultation and action. All that is needed is that we must put our hands to the plough, and face the strife and the struggle . . . .

Both Hindus and Mahomedans have their work cut out in this struggle. In the backwardness of female education, in the disposition to overleap the bounds of their own religion, in matters of temperance, in their internal dissensions between castes and creeds, in the indulgence of impure speech, thought and action on occasions when they are disposed to enjoy themselves, in the abuses of many customs in regard to unequal and polygamous marriages, in the desire to be extravagant in their expenditure on such occasions, in the neglect of regulated charity, in the decay of public spirit in insisting on the proper management of endowments—in these and other matters both communities are equal sinners, and there is thus much ground for improvement on common lines.[31]

Reform or Revivalism

Ranade attacked revivalism as an enemy of reform, despite the fact that Dayānanda Sarasvatī's example pointed in the opposite direction.

On the other side, some of our orthodox friends find fault with us, not because of the particular reforms we have in view, but on account of the methods we follow. While the new religious sects condemn us for being too orthodox, the extreme orthodox section denounce us for being too revolutionary in our methods. According to these last, our efforts should be directed to revive, and not to reform. I have many friends in this camp of extreme orthodoxy, and their watchword is that Revival, and not Reform, should be our motto. They advocate a return to the old ways, and appeal to the old authorities, and the old sanctions. Here also, as in the instance stated above, people speak without realizing the full significance of their own words. When we are asked to revive our old institutions and customs, people seem to me to be very much at sea as to what it is they seek to revive. What particular period of our history is to be taken as the old—whether the period of the Vedas, of the Smritis, of the Puranas, or of the Mohamedans or the modern Hindu times. Our usages have been changed from time to time by a slow process of growth, and in some cases of decay and corruption, and you cannot stop at any particular period without breaking the continuity of the whole. When my revivalist friend presses his argument upon me he has to seek recourse to some subterfuge which really furnishes no reply to his own question. What shall we revive? Shall we revive the old habits of our people when the most sacred of our castes indulged in all the abominations, as we now understand them, of animal food and intoxicating drink, which exhausted every section of our country's Zoology and Botany . . . . Shall we revive the Niyoga system of propagating sons on our brother's wives when widowed? . . . Shall we revive the Shakti worship of the left hand, with its indecencies and practical debaucheries? Shall we revive the *Sati* and infanticide customs, or the flinging of living men into the rivers or over rocks, or hookswinging, or the crushing beneath the Jagannath car? Shall we revive the internecine wars of the Brahmins and Kshatriyas or the cruel persecution and degradation of the Aboriginal population? . . . These instances will suffice to show that the plan of reviving the ancient usages and customs will not work our salvation, and is not practicable. If these usages were good and beneficial, why were they altered by our wise ancestors? If they were bad and injurious, how can any claim be put forward for their restoration after so many ages? Besides, it seems to be forgotten that in a living organism, as society is, no revival is possible.

I think I have said more than enough to suggest to your reflecting minds what it is that we have to reform. All admit that we have been deformed. We have lost our stature, we are bent in a hundred places, our eyes lust after forbidden things, our ears desire to hear scandals about our neighbours, our tongue wants to taste forbidden fruit, our hands itch for another man's property, our bowels are deranged with indigestible food. We cannot walk on our feet, but require stilts or crutches. This is our present social polity, and now we want this deformity to be removed, and the only way to remove it is to place ourselves under the discipline of better ideas and forms such as those I have briefly touched above. Now this is the work of the reformer. Reforms in the matter of infant marriages and enforced widowhood, in the matter of temperance and purity, intermarriages between castes, the elevation of the low castes, and *the readmission of converts*, and the regulations of our endowments and charity are reforms, only so far and no further, as they check the influence of the old ideas and promote the growth of the new tendencies. The reformer has to infuse in himself the light and warmth of nature and he can do it by purifying and improving himself and his surroundings.[32]

The Bhakti Movement in Maharashtra

Ranade is credited with generating the present-day perspective of Indian history according to which a Maratha period intervenes between the period of Muslim and British rule over India, as against the earlier tendency to elide it. He argued persuasively for the emergence of a Maratha polity by locating the rise of Martha power in the context of the devotional movement in Maharashtra, and not as merely the product of military adventurism. He also associated the devotional movement with what in today's vocabulary might be called elements of a liberation theology.

We propose accordingly in this chapter to trace in rough outline the history of this religious upheaval in Western India. Our main sources of information will be the voluminous biographies of the saints and prophets of Maharashtra, written by one of our own poets, Mahipati, towards the close of the last century, long before the British influence was felt in these parts as a factor of any importance. Like the political struggle for independence, the religious upheaval was also not the work of a single man, or even of a single century. Its early commencement can be traced even anterior to the Mahomedan conquest of the Deccan. Under the rule of the Yadav kings of Devgiri, Dnyandev, the first saint and prophet of Maharashtra, wrote his famous commentary of the *Bhagavad Gita* in the spoken language of the country. Mukundraj, who lived under the Ballal Kings, also wrote his famous work, the first of the kind in Marathi in the twelfth century. The Mahomedan invasions for a time seem to have paralysed all activity but gradually the national spirit regained its healthy elasticity, and just about the time of the rise of the Maratha power we had a galaxy of saints and prophets, whose names have become household words with the people of the country. The stream continued to flow in full tide for two centuries, and then it appears to have dried up, and with its ebb, the political domination also became a thing of the past. Roughly speaking we may state that the history of this religious revival covers a period of nearly five hundred years, and during this period some fifty saints and prophets flourished in this land, who left their mark upon the country and its people so indelibly as to justify Mahipati in including them in his biographical sketches. A few of these saints were women, a few were Mahomedan converts to Hinduism, nearly half of them were Brahmans, while there were representatives in the other half from among all the other castes, Marathas, *kunbis*, tailors, gardeners, potters, goldsmiths, repentant prostitutes, and slave girls, even the outcaste *Mahars*. Much of the interest of this religious upheaval is centred in the facts we have noticed above, as they indicate plainly that the influence of higher spirituality was not confined to this or that class, but permeated deep through all strata of society, male and female, high and low, literate and illiterate, Hindu and Mahomedan alike. These are features which the religious history of few other countries can match or reproduce, unless where the elevating influence is the result of a widespread popular awakening. In Northern and Eastern India, a similar movement manifested itself much about the same time. Nanak stirred up the Punjab to rise, and made a supreme effort to reconcile Hinduism with Mahomedanism. Chaitanya in the far East sought to bring men back from the worship of *Shakti* and *Kali* to the faith of the *Bhagawat*; while Ramanand and Kabir, Tulsidas and Surdas, Jayadev and Rohidas, contributed each in his own way to the work of spiritual enlightenment. Their influence has no doubt been great and abiding, but it cannot be compared with the work done by the saints and prophets of Maharashtra. The names of Changdev and Dnyandev, Nivritti and Sopan, Muktabai and Jani, Akabai and Venubai, Namdev and Eknath, Ramdas and Tukaram, Shaik Mahomed and Shanti Bahamani, Damaji and Udhav, Bhanudas and Kurmdas, Bodhle Bawa and Santoba Powar, Keshv Swami and Jayaram Swami, Narasinha Saraswati and Rangnath Swami, Chokhamela and the two potters, Narahari Sonar and Savatia Mali, Bahiram Bhat and Ganesh Nath, Janardanpant and Mudhopant, and many others that might be cited, furnish an array which testifies to the superior efficacy of this movement in Maharashtra. The Brahmans in these parts furnished a much larger proportion of saints and prophets than was the case in any of the other parts of India where the *Kshatriya* and *Vaishya* castes furnished a much larger contingent than the Brahmans.

As is the case with all biographies of saints, the popular imagination attributes to these persons wonderful and miraculous powers, notably those of raising the dead to life, healing the sick and feeding the hungry. The stories which are told of the way in which they were helped by supernatural agency in their mission of love may or may not be accepted in these days of vigilant criticism. As Mr. Lecky has remarked, it is the atmosphere of child-like credulity which predisposes men to require and accept these wonders and miracles as events of ordinary occurrence. The saints and prophets themselves did not claim miraculous powers. They were meek and suffering men who placed their trust in Providence, and their trust was justified beyond their expectations, often-times to their own surprise. The moral interest of these biographies centres, however, not in their miraculous feats, but in their struggles and in the testimony their lives afforded in vindication of the eternal verities of the moral law and man's higher spiritual life. It is with this aspect of their life that we are more immediately concerned in the sequel, and we hope to show that in this respect the work they accomplished was priceless and blessed beyond all comparison.

There is a curious parallel between the history of the Reformation movement in Western Europe and the struggle represented by the lives and teachings and writings of these saints and prophets who flourished about the same time in Maharashtra. The European reformers of the sixteenth century protested strongly against the authority claimed by the priests and the clergy with the Roman Bishop at their head. The clergy and the Pope represented a tradition of authority which had come down from the remote past, and had done signal service in its own time in humanizing and civilizing the hordes of the barbarian conquerors who devastated the Roman provinces. In course of time, the priests, instead of being the servants, claimed to be masters and rulers, with temporal and spiritual powers, and intermediaries between God and man. The exercise of this intercession was hedged round by numberless rites and ceremonies, and in course of time many abuses crept in and alienated general sympathy. These abuses assumed their worst forms about the time that Luther rebelled against the authority which issued indulgences and levied Peter's Pence, not as charity, but as a tax to subserve the temporal power of intriguing Popes and their vicious cardinals. The Reformation in Western India had its counterpart in this respect. Ancient authority and tradition had been petrified here, not in an ambitious Bishop and his clergy, but in the monopoly of the Brahman caste, and it was against the exclusive spirit of this caste domination that the saints and prophets struggled most manfully to protest. They asserted the dignity of the human soul as residing in it quite independently of the accidents of its birth and social rank. The circumstances of their own birth and education naturally predisposed some of these preachers to take up such a position. As observed above, nearly half of them were of castes other than Brahmans, and some of them of very low castes indeed. Many of the Brahman reformers also had some stain in their inherited purity which led or forced them to rebel against all artificial restraints. Dnyandev and his brothers and sister were born to their father after he had retired from the world and become a *Sanyasi* monk. His spiritual guide, Ramanand, came to know that this *Sanyasi* had not obtained his wife's consent to a change of *Ashram*, and he ordered him to go back to his native place and live with his wife. The children so born to the *Sanyasi* became marked objects of caste aversion, and the Brahmans refused to perform the initiation ceremony when the brothers reached the proper age. The children remained in this unrecognized condition all their life, and were revered notwithstanding this defect in their caste respectability. Another saint, Malopant, was married to a low-caste girl, whose caste was not discovered till after the marriage, and the husband did not abandon her, but only held no intercourse with her, and, when on her death, he performed her death-rites as usual, a miracle was displayed which satisfied his worst enemies, that Malopant and his *Mahar* wife were both holy by nature. Jayaram Swami's master, Krishnadas, was similarly married to a barber girl, and the inferiority of her caste was discovered after marriage. The holy life of the man had, however, such an effect that at last, after much persecution, even the high priest Shankaracharya of the day raised no objection. Eknath, it is well known, made no secret of the little importance he attached to caste distinctions. He fed an hungry *Mahar* at his house, and, when out-casted, allowed himself to be taken to the river for purposes of purification, when a miracle took place by which the merit of feeding an hungry *Mahar* was proved to be far greater than that of feeding many hundred Brahmans, for the former merit cured a leper of his foul disease, when the latter failed to make any impression on him. A very common miracle is reported to have been performed by many of the saints notably by Dnyandev, Eknath, and Nagnath, when, on the refusal of the Brahmans to officiate on *Shraddha* ceremonies in their places for breach of caste regulations, the deceased fathers of the obstinate Brahmans were made to descend to earth, and shamed their incredulous sons into the belief that their caste exclusiveness was wholly out of place. In Namdev's biography, his God of Pandharpur, who had allowed Namdev to invite Brahmans to a feast and himself partook of that feast with the saint, was himself excommunicated, and then the story relates how Dnyandev, who was present in spirit, remonstrated with the Brahman persecutors.

He said: 'There was no high or low with God. All were alike to him. Never entertain the thought that I am high born, and my neighbour is low of birth. The Ganges is not polluted, nor is the wind tainted, nor the earth rendered untouchable, because the low born and high born bathe in the one, or breathe the other, or move on the back of the third.'

The most touching incident, however, is that which occurred in the persecution of the out-caste *Mahar* Chokhamela for his having dared to enter the temple of Pandharpur. When remonstrated with for his temerity, Chokhamela replied that his God took him inside by force, and he did not go of his own accord. He remonstrated with the Brahman worshippers of the temple in this strain—'What availeth birth in high caste, what availeth rites or learning, if there is no devotion, or faith? Though a man be of low caste, yet if he is faithful in heart, and loves God, and regards all creatures as though they were like himself, and makes no distinction between his own and other peoples' children, and speaks the truth, his caste is pure, and God is pleased with him. Never ask a man's caste when he has in his heart faith in God, and love of men. God wants in his children love and devotion, and he does not care for his caste.' The Brahmans, as might be expected, were not converted by this preaching of high wisdom, and they complained to the Musalman officer of the place, and he, like another Pilate of the Bible story, ordered Chokhamela to be punished by being tied to and driven by a team of bullocks, and tortured to death in this cruel fashion. God, however, miraculously delivered his worshipper, and baffled the oppressors, for the bullocks would not move from their place. The story of Bahiram Bhat is also interesting in this connection. Being a *Shastri*, he did not find rest in Brahmanism, and therefore became a Mahomedan under the impression that its monotheism would satisfy the cravings of his heart, but failing to find the satisfaction he desired, he returned back to Brahmanism. Both Brahmans and Mahomedans found fault with him for these changes of faith, but he disclaimed being either Hindu or Mahomedan. Bahiram Bhat challenged the Brahmans to make him a true Brahman as long as his circumcision mark was not removed, and he challenged the Mahomedans to fill up the hole in his ears, which showed that he was still a Hindu. The Mahomedan converts to Hinduism, represented by Shaik Mahomed's followers, even to this day observe the *Ramjan* fasts, and the *Ekadashi* fast, and make pilgrimages to Mecca as also to Pandharpur. There are many other saints of great renown who, like Kabir, Nanak and Manik Prabhu are claimed both by Hindus and Mahomedans as belonging to their respective communities, and worshipped and reverenced as such by both. These examples will suffice to show how the lives of these men have tended to elevate the national conception of man's spiritual nature, and shake the hold of caste intolerance.

The rest of all this elevated teaching is seen in the fact that caste exclusiveness now finds no place in the religious sphere of life, and it is relegated solely to the social concerns of men, and even there its restrictiveness is much relaxed, as any one can judge who compares the Brahmans of Southern India with their exclusive caste prejudices, and their abhorrence of even the shadow of the lower castes defiling Brahman streets, with the comparative indifference shown in such matters in the Deccan portion of Maharashtra. This feeling of indifference is most accentuated at the times of the annual pilgrim gatherings, and the mixed greetings with which the Lord's feast is celebrated on the last day. Just as in Europe, men ceased to believe that the priest was a necessary medium between God and man for [the] purpose of salvation, in this part of India, the domination of the Brahman caste as the Gods of creation, whom the other castes should serve and worship, lost much of its potency, and men and women, high and low, came to feel that they were free to attain salvation by faith and love in spite of their low origin.

The European reformers protested further against the institution of the monastic orders, and the celibacy of the clergy, and the unnatural retirement of women who exiled themselves from the world and became nuns. There was a counterpart of this same protest in the way in which our saints and prophets raised their voice against self-mortification and fasts, and meaningless penances and endless pilgrimages. The same spirit prompted them to condemn austerities practised by those who followed the *Yoga* system with a view of acquiring the power of working wonders which, it was supposed, the *Yogis* enjoyed in consequence. This contest between *Yoga* and *Bhakti* is well illustrated by the encounter of the proud Chagdev with Dnyandev, when the former, in reliance on his *Yoga* powers, rode on tigers, and used serpent whips, and was put to shame by Dnyandev riding on a wall. There was a similar encounter between Dnyandev and Namdev when the former, by the exercise of *Yoga* powers, became small in size, and drank the waters of a deep well, while Namdev, by his devotion, brought the waters to overflow the well for all time, so that all who passed by, and felt thirsty, might drink to their hearts' content. These stories most beautifully typify this feature of the teaching of the saints and prophets of Maharashtra.

The story of Kanoba Pathak, who was upbraided by a Brahman of Benares for his inordinate love of children, and astonished his critic by throwing away his child into a well with seeming indifference, illustrates the vanity of the vows of celibacy, which cannot by themselves produce equableness of mind, and indifference to pains and pleasures. Eknath all his life lived with his wife and children, and so did Tukaram and Namdev, though they were not blessed with sympathetic female relations. Bodhle Bawa, Chokhamela, Damajipant, Bhanusas, the two potter saints, and many others lived in the midst of their families. Dnyandev's father, who had become a *Sanyasi* without obtaining the free consent of his wife, was directed by Ramanand to return to his home, and live with his wife. All these incidents prove that a very high conception of the sanctity of family-life was realised by these saints and prophets, and they did their best to correct the national weakness which shrinks from trouble and anxiety by retiring from the world's conflict. The lives of the female saints have a special interest in this connection. The biographies relate that owing to their devotion and implicit faith, God helped them out of their difficulties by assisting them in their daily household work, and by assuming strange disguises, permitted them the freedom they wanted to serve him without being missed by their jealous relations. There is a danger in all such stories of making Providential intervention too cheap, but this fault is more than balanced by the high moral which underlies these accounts. The sanctity of married and family life was nobly vindicated by these saints and prophets, and this was a signal moral triumph over the past traditions of asceticism.

All students of modern European history are aware that the Reformers achieved their most permanent success in the liberation of the national intellect from the thraldom of scholastic learning, and the oppressive preponderance of the classical Latin in which all the best books were till then written. The Bible was, by the help of these Reformers, for the first time made accessible to all, high and low, and the monopoly of learning, till then enjoyed by the priests, was shaken to its foundations. Here in India, the process of liberation was carried out on the same lines. The professors of the old Sanskrit learning found for the first time to their great surprise that the saints and prophets addressed the people, both in speech and writing, in their own vernacular, and boldly opened the hitherto hidden treasures to all and sundry, men and women, Brahmans and Shudras, alike. The final victory was not achieved without much struggle and considerable suffering. Dnyandev was the first adventurer to stray into these forbidden regions, and his example was followed by Eknath and Ramdas, Namdev and Tukaram, Vaman Pandit and Mukteshwar, Shridhar and Moropant. These last four gifted men are more celebrated as authors and poets than as religious teachers, but they derived their inspiration from the same sources. It is true the *Vedas* and the *Shastras* were not translated as the Bible was, but there was a sufficient reason for this difference. These early Marathi writers knew that modern India, after the Buddhistic revolution, was less influenced by the *Vedas* and *Shastras* than by the *Ramayan* and *Mahabharata*, the *Bhagavad Purana* and the *Gita*, and these latter works were translated and made accessible to all. The pioneers in this field, Eknath and Tukaram, were each made to bear the brunt of Brahman opposition, their works were not burned as in

Europe, but they were ordered to be thrown into the water. The river gods, however, so the story runs, would not let them be destroyed, and their works remained dry and would not sink, and thus became more famous than ever. Vaman Pandit, was, when brought in contact with Ramdas, made to see the error of his ways; and a Brahman translator of the *Ramayan* named Salya Rasal, who was over-proud of his superior learning, was similarly put to shame by a message from his goddess that he should get the work corrected by submitting it to the revision of the tailor Namdev. Dnyandev also was made the instrument of preforming a miracle, by which a buffalo was said to have recited the *Vedas* by heart. This story is obviously an allegorical parody of the mental condition of those who prided themselves upon their ability to recite the *Vedas* without understanding their contents.

The struggle between the claims of the classical Sanskrit and the vernaculars, of which we hear so much in these days, is thus an old conflict, the issues in which were decided in favour of the vernacular or living languages long ago, and whatever scholars and antiquarians may urge to the contrary, there can only be one answer to the question— the answer which was given by the saints and prophets when they laid Sanskrit aside as useless for their work, and spent all their energies in the cultivation and growth of their mother tongue. It may safely be said that the growth of the modern vernaculars in India is closely the result of the labours of these saints and that the provinces, which showed most decided tendencies in the way of reform, also showed the most healthy development of their vernacular literature.[33]

The Clash Between Tradition and Reform in the Domestic Sphere: An Account

Allusion has already been made to the second marriage of Ranade. We have a unique account of how this came about from Ranade's wife, which offers an insightful glimpse into the field realities the reformers had to grapple with.

My Marriage

I was married in December of 1873. There was not much of a bridal procession. Actually, after the Vedic ceremony was over, we walked home.

My husband had not eaten anything at my mother's house. Even when he returned home, he spoke to no one. He went to his own room and locked himself in. He was in deep agony that day.

It was just a month since he had lost his first wife, who had been like a comrade to him. That great grief was yet fresh in his mind. To add to that, he had had to yield to his father's stern insistence and marry again entirely against his resolve. Two principles were sacred to him—never to go against the word of his father, and never to disturb the peace and well-being of his family. For this, he gave up a view which he had accepted as correct over a long period of time, the principle of the justice of widow remarriage. He gave up his valued friendships. He even flung away his self-respect and the esteem arising from it. For the sake of his principle of devotion to the parental word, he faced the ridicule and lasting calumny of society. It was but natural then, that the night of his sacred wedding should be one of agony for him.

Even today, so many feel that if there is any black spot in his life, it is the traditional character of his second marriage. But I for one feel that if there is any aspect in his life of self-sacrifice and large-heartedness which is nobler than others, it is this one. Whatever anyone might say, I have tremendous respect for the decision he took in this particular regard, and I am sure whoever thinks of his life with true understanding, will feel likewise.

For a fortnight before the wedding, he used to receive a number of letters from friends in Bombay. 'This is the time', they would say, 'when you must tell your father that you will not marry a young girl. You must announce to him that you will marry a widow.' The first few letters reached him directly. But when Mamanji [Ranade's father] came to know of them he grew watchful. As soon as the mail arrived, he would first take it himself. He would remove the letters and telegrams from Bombay and send the rest to my husband upstairs. No one in the family dared say a word against Mamanji. So no one mentioned it to my husband.

Mamanji came to Poona after the death of my husband's first wife and immediately started a hectic search for a new bride for him. He already knew that his son was a staunch supporter of widow remarriage and feared that he would now put his principle into practice. He decided not to give him a chance of being influenced by his friends in Bombay and to get him married again at once.

At this time, my father had also gone to Poona to look for a bridegroom for me. He already knew Mamanji. He met him and said, 'I am looking for a match for my daughter. But there is a tradition in our family that our girls do not go out of their home to be considered for marriage. You might be aware of this. My request to you, therefore,

is that you might send some one to see my daughter in her own home.
If she is considered suitable, she will be brought here. It will be highly
derogatory to our family if the girl is brought out for marriage and has
to return home without being married.'

Mamanji asked Vedamoorti Shri Balambhatji Watwe to go with
my father. That learned Brahmin had lived with us since he was ten
or twelve years old, and was like a member of the family. He lived a
clean life and was rigorous in his rituals and discipline. Manamji had
complete confidence in him. He came to our house with my father
and 'saw' me. He put me all the usual questions. He stayed with us the
whole day, perhaps to observe everything else about our family.

At night before he retired to bed, he said to my father, 'I approve
of the girl. We shall go with her tomorrow. You may send a telegram
and ask the family to come over, after the *muhurta* is fixed.'

When this was done, my father, Balambhatji and I left for Poona
by mail-tonga. In the meantime, my husband tried hard to make
Mamanji see his point of view. He said, 'I do not wish to marry. I am
not young any more. I am thirty-two years old. I can certainly lead a
life of thought and retirement. Durga [Ranade's sister] is younger than
I and has been a widow since she was twenty-one. You do not love
her less than you love me, in any way. And yet no one thinks of her.
Why am I being urged to marry? If you think it would be good for her
to lead a life of restraint, it should apply equally to me. If you are
afraid that I may marry a widow, I give you my word of honour that I
will not do so. You need have no anxiety on that score.'

He urged Mamanji in many ways. But it was of no avail. Arguments
only made Mamanji all the more furious. So my husband said, 'Even if
you are not willing to listen to me, I must obey you. But leave me free
for at least six months. I will go to England during that period.' Even
that Mamanji would not agree to. So my husband sent him a message
to this effect: 'You are going to force me to marry. But please do this
much. Do not select a girl from this place. She should be from another
place and she should belong to a family of good repute. It should also be
ascertained that the other antecedents and connections of the family
are decent. I do not wish to marry a girl from an ordinary family just for
the sake of her looks or age. Our relationship is likely to be a little more
happy if a good family is given preference over good looks.' A couple of
days after this, my father and I arrived in Poona.

Mamanji came to the place where we had put up, saw me, approved
of me and fixed up the *muhurta* for the next *ekadashi*. He, however,
asked my father to see the bridegroom himself and hear him out. 'If

he agrees to everything, well and good, if not, you may tell him that you have decided to give your daughter in marriage to our family', he said. My father agreed. In the evening he visited the house and went upstairs to see my husband.

My father had an impressive appearance. He looked dignified, respectable and firm, like one from a high and reputed family. My husband rose to receive him when he saw him and enquired about him and his business. My father told him that he was a *jagirdar* of such and such a place and gave very briefly the rest of the information about himself. Then he said, 'My daughter is of marriageable age. I have come to propose a match.'

My husband said, 'Why do you think I will be an appropriate match? You belong to an ancient *jagirdar* family. I am a reformer in favour of widow remarriage. I look hale and hearty but I have weak eyesight and am also hard of hearing. Besides, I am planning to go to England. I shall not undergo any *prayaschitta* after I return. You should consider all this and then decide.'

My father replied, 'I have known Bhausahib for years. He has told me everything and I have already taken my decision.'

After a long silence, my husband said, 'If that is so, I would like to propose that only an engagement should take place. The wedding might be postponed for a year.'

But my father urged that it would not be consistent with our family traditions. He requested him to consider the embarrassment to his family and so on. In the end my husband decided that they should both see what Bhausahib had to say and abide by it. At this my father left.

My husband persuaded himself that after he had conceded so many things to Bhausahib, he would certainly agree to postpone the marriage by six months. With that hope he went to his father, told him that my father, Annasahib Kurkelar, had seen him and gave him an account of the talk. Mamanji said, 'What was the decision, finally?'

'We have left it to you. We need not agree to everything he proposes. He should consider some of our points also. I have told him that I shall agree to everything, I shall marry, but not today. It should be postponed by a year or six months.'

My husband kept saying this, softly but again and again. Mamanji heard it all, but said nothing for a long time. After about two hours, Mamanji spoke. He first asked all the others who were there to go and to leave father and son alone for an hour or so. They all disappeared quickly, but my sister-in-law stayed nearby, unseen.

Mamanji said, 'I have heard all you have been saying and have thought over it deeply. But I do not think I can agree to what you say. I have never distrusted you; nor will I do so now. But don't you realise that you are now in a situation full of temptation? Even the most firm and thoughtful decisions may be defeated by a moment of temptation at this stage. I have a feeling that if I leave you free for a year or six months, I shall lose all my peace of mind in this declining age. I shall tell you why. Your friends in Bombay have sent you a number of letters and telegrams during the last fortnight. I have seen them all and kept them with me. Considering them all, I do not think I should agree to your proposal. You are already strongly inclined towards these new ideas, and your friends are encouraging you. You are also young. If you had any children, it might have held you back to some extent. If you were left utterly free, you would naturally be driven towards these new-fangled ideas. This is what I am afraid of. I am now quite old. You are stepping into the position of the master of the family. The women and children depend upon you. And you are worthy of the burden. I have put everything before you. You can think for yourself. You may do just what you think right. But I shall tell you what I have decided. If you do not marry now, I have vowed not to send the girl back. It will be derogatory to the family of Annasahib and it will be highly insulting to me too. But, if that has to be, you may take it that I shall leave for Karveer for good. Our bonds will be broken for ever. The rest will be in the hands of Providence.' Mamanji said all this, heaved a heavy sigh and got up. He washed his hands and feet and went for his *sandhya*. My husband got up and went upstairs. This account of what happened before our marriage was given to me by my sister-in-law.

And so, as decided by Mamanji, we were married on the eleventh day of the bright half of Margasheersha in Saka 1795 (December 1873) at the auspicious hour of dusk, the hour when the cattle return home. My husband went through the Vedic ritual, but did not allow the customary social ceremonies at all. He did not take leave even on the wedding day. Until he returned from the courts before the hour of the wedding, Mamanji was half afraid that one of his Bombay friends might seize the opportunity and take him away for a walk, just to make him miss the *muhurat*. At the same time, he was sure of his son. He knew that once he had given his word, he would never depart from it, however much it might be against his own wishes. Completely justifying that confidence, my husband came straight home from the courts, without going either for a walk or to the library as he was wont to.

After the wedding, my father returned home leaving me in my new home in Poona. I had come with him alone when the match was being considered. When it was decided and the *muhurat* was fixed, a telegram was to go for my mother, brothers, sisters-in-law, sisters and brothers and all the rest of the family. But the *muhurat* fixed up by Mamanji left no time for that. Besides, my husband declared that he would not allow any ceremonies other than the Vedic ritual. So my father thought it wiser not to send for the whole family and disappoint them with the bareness of the ritual.

The evening my father left, my husband called me upon the terrace after he had returned from the courts. He said, 'Has your father left?'

'Yes.'

'You are now married to me. Do you know who I am and what my name is?'

'Yes.'

'Then tell me. What is my name?'[34]

Notes

1. D.S. Sarma, *Hinduism Through the Ages* (Bombay: Bharatiya Vidya Bhavan, 1956), pp. 83–4. This association was preceded by the more radical Paramahamsa Sabha, see P.J. Jagirdar, *Mahadev Govind Ranade* (New Delhi: Government of India Publications Division, 1974), pp. 36, 47.
2. Wm. Theodore de Bary et al, *Sources of Indian Traditions* (New York and London: Columbia University Press, 1958), Vol. II, p. 129. For more on his early life see Jagirdar, pp. 1–23.
3. When his father decided to let him have an English education, his mother did not eat for three days for fear that he might end up a Christian (ibid., pp. 8–9).
4. Richard P. Tucker, *Ranade and the Roots of Indian Nationalism* (Bombay: Popular Prakashan, 1977), p. 278.
5. Glyn Richards, ed., *A Source-Book of Modern Hinduism* (London: Curzon Press, 1985), p. 92.
6. Ibid.
7. Sarma, p. 84.
8. Richards, p. 91.
9. Sarma, p. 85.
10. See Jagirdar, pp. 201–2.
11. Ibid., p. 87.
12. Ibid.
13. Cited in Sarma, p. 89. Even at the level of theology, Ranade considered the two articles of faith: fatherhood of God and brotherhood of man—as simplistic, since they did not address comprehensively religious difficulties human beings experience in life (ibid., p. 88).
14. Ibid., p. 84.

15. Jagirdar, p. 55.
16. Richards, p. 91.
17. Tucker, p. 305. Ranade's second wife has left behind an account of her life with Ranade.
18. Jagirdar, p. 59.
19. Ibid., pp. 112–13.
20. Ibid., pp. 162–73.
21. Ibid., p. 62.
22. Jagirdar, p. 76. A detailed account of this incident is provided by Ranade's wife, Ramabai, as follows (*Ranade: His Wife's Reminiscences* [Translated by Kusumavati Deshpande. New Delhi: Publications Division, Government of India, 1963], pp. 54–6):

About Dayanand Swami

When Swamiji came to Poona from Lahore, he used to deliver public lectures every evening in Bhide's Wada opposite Belbag in Budhwar Peth. My husband used to spend more than two hours every evening looking after the arrangements and attending the lecture. A few days before the end of the series, a meeting was held at our house and it was decided that before Dayanandji returned to his place, there would be a procession in his honour. The details of the programme were worked out. This was announced two or three days before the date fixed.

The opposition camp was greatly disturbed over this. Ramdixit Apte, one of the Shastris, was the leader of the opposite party. A large rabble of local *goondas* filled their ranks. Many others, who had never before taken the trouble to think of religion, seized this opportunity of joining and lending a helping hand in bringing disgrace and dishonour to Dayanandji and his followers. They discussed many plans and in the end they thought of a devilish device which was immediately approved by them all. They decided to put it into action the next day. They must indeed have been greatly tickled by their plan.

The Procession

Early next morning, before six o'clock, a strange procession came out. A well-decorated donkey was being taken around. It was preceded by a musical band and a score of *goondas*. This was the procession of Gardabhanand. It started from the Kala Howd and began to trail over the city. The whole place was filled with roaring laughter and fun. The news reached our house at about seven in the morning. Some of the eye-witnesses gave a vivid account of it. People of our group were also highly amused by it. But, realising that the opposition had become so active, they thought that special care had to be taken to see that no harm came to Dyanandji himself. Gangarambhau Mhaske suggested that a special police guard should be asked for. This was agreed to and he wrote to the Police Superintindent about it. The procession of Gardabhananda traversed every lane and byelane during the day and continued from six in the morning to six in the evening. The processionists shouted slogans of *Shri Gardabhananda Swami Ki*

Jai! after every few paces. How much Gardabhananda enjoyed these wanderings, one does not know. Nor does one know whether he really established himself the next day or whether he took *samadhi* and departed to the other world!

When it was about four-thirty, an audience began to assemble in Bhide's Wada, as usual. Swami Dayanandji was an eloquent and moving orator. He spoke in a solemn manner. He could hold his audience in rapt attention. He stood up to deliver his valedictory address. He thanked the audience for their keen attention and their cordiality towards him during all his lectures. He spoke in a pleasantly humorous manner. He was then garlanded and offered *pan-supari*. Swamiji and the whole audience came downstairs. An elephant and a palanquin were waiting in readiness on the road. The sacred books were placed in the palanquin and Dayanandji was helped to mount the elephant. The procession was just about to start when a crowd of people of the other group broke in. They began to shout and use foul language. Malicious scandal-mongers supporting that group stood at a little distance with an air of polite non-interference. But actually they encouraged the rowdyism of the group. It had rained heavily that day. The streets were full of wet mud. The procession continued solemnly, regardless of the rowdyism. This disappointed and irritated the rowdies. The incitement by the onlookers added to their irritation and they began flinging whatever was at hand at the people in the procession, those who could get nothing began to throw mud-balls at the processionists from behind. The people of our group walked along so solemnly that although mud-balls hit their backs and their legs, not one of them even turned round to look. They just paid no heed and walked on quietly. Although a *posse* of policemen accompanied them, they had been warned not to interfere until asked to do so. They were only to walk along as though only to add to the dignity of the procession. After a quarter of an hour of mud-slinging, from the Aditwar Square to the Daruwala Bridge, the rowdies began to fling stones and sticks. None of the important processionists were hurt, but a few followers were badly wounded. Then the police intervened. Immediately the rowdies took to their heels and the procession proceeded in peace. The wounded were sent to the hospital.

My husband returned home and changed his mud-soiled clothes. When someone in the family asked how mud had been thrown even at him when the police were there, he smiled and said, 'Why not, when I was with them all? Why should they think of whether an individual in opposition is big or small? It would be wrong of us to think of personal prestige in such a case.'

23. Tucker, p. 296.
24. Jagirdar, pp. 196–7.
25. Tucker, p. 297. Tucker goes on to remark: 'The incident is similar to the racial discrimination that the young Mohandas Gandhi was experiencing on trains in South Africa at the time. The two men's reactions were similar: a sharp sense of disillusionment that the British system had room for racist tendencies, combined with a heightened awareness that the Hindu caste system embodied similar evils. Gokhale relates that during the mid-1890s Ranade was corresponding

with Gandhi, although no trace of the correspondence survives. Ranade is also recorded as having pleaded with a Bombay audience in 1895, shortly before Gandhi's return, to see that the social degradation which was permitted by legal racial discrimination in South Africa was no worse that the social discrimination of the caste system in India.'

26. Richards, p. 91.
27. Ibid., p. 92.
28. Ibid., p. 90.
29. Ibid.
30. Ibid., p. 91, emphasis added. This parallel is intriguing, especially if one takes Martin Buber's correspondence with Mahatma Gandhi into account or considers S. Radhakrishnan's remark that 'For a religion like Hinduism, which emphasizes Divine Immanence, the chosen people embraces all mankind.' [*Eastern Religions and Western Thought*, (New York: Oxford University Press, 1959), p. 331; also see *The Hindu View of Life* (New York: Macmillan, 1929), p. 55]. The following comment by A. C. Bouquet is also relevant [*Hinduism* (London: Hutchinson University Library, 1969), p. 15]:

> Although it is not correct to identify Hindu culture with Indian culture, it is true, nevertheless, that Hinduism, taken as a whole, is a culture quite as much as a religion. It is so much woven into the social structure of its adherents that the orthodox Hindu like the Jew, if he should dare to give up his religion for any other, becomes by his choice an outcaste from his own people. It has recently been said that as long as one keeps out Christ, one can pack anything into Judaism. The remark not only shows how curiously alike in many respects are the Hindu and Jewish communities (though in others extremely unlike), but it may also be parodied by saying: 'So long as one keeps out the idea that the historical process as such has any value for religion, one can pack anything into Hinduism.' Yet it is impossible for a foreigner to become a Hindu without at the same time being made a member of some caste or other, and by this means included in the structure of a national social order as well.

31. Richards, pp. 100–1.
32. Ibid., pp. 98–9, emphasis added.
33. Verinder Grover, ed., *Political Thinkers of Modern India* (New Delhi: Deep & Deep Publications, 1990), Vol. III, pp. 214–22.
34. *Ranade: His Wife's Reminiscences*, pp. 32–7.

Gopal Krishna Gokhale
(1866–1915)

Life

Gopal Krishna Gokhale, like Bal Gangadhar Tilak and Mahadev Govind Ranade, was born in the community of Chitpavan Brahmins.[1] According to the mythology of the community,

> the community's patron deity, Parashurama, an avatar of Vishnu, had by his profuse slaughter of warriors become so defiled in the eyes of the then existing Brahmans that they refused to perform the ritual of purification for him. Incensed at this boycott, Parashurama took the bodies of fourteen ship-wrecked foreigners, which he found washed onto peninsular India's western shore, purified them in a pyre, and then restored the corpses to life. He subsequently taught these 'Chitpavans' the Brahmanic rituals which they in turn performed for their maker, absolving him of the sin of blood guilt.[2]

In history, the Chitpavan Brahmins were the *de facto* heads of the Maratha confederacy, the defeat of which by the British in 1818 signaled the effective establishment of the British Raj over India. The reaction of this community to the establishment of British rule over India, whether in loyalty or by opposition, played a significant factor not only in the rise of modern India, but also in shaping the contours of modern Hindu thought.

G.K. Gokhale is of special interest to students of Hindu thought on account of his close connection to Mahatma Gandhi. One comes across two views on this relationship. According to some Gandhi really inherited Tilak's mantle rather than Gokhale's, inasmuch as Gandhi challenged British rule like Tilak, instead of accepting it like Gokhale. Gandhi himself, however, acknowledged Gokhale as his guru,[3] on the basis of Gokhale's urge to 'spiritualize public life', a saying whose meaning Gandhi elaborated as follows: 'All of us can surely cultivate the virtues of fearlessness, truthfulness, courage, meekness (*sic*), fairness, straight forwardness, firmness and such like and devote them to the service of the country. This is the meaning of the great saying "Let us spiritualize politics."'[4] Mahatma Gandhi referred to Gokhale as 'Gokhale the Good' and wrote: 'Ghokale's political career served me as my ideal. I installed him in my heart of hearts as my teacher in politics.'[5]

G.K. Gokhale was born in 1866. His father died when Gokhale was thirteen and Gokhale's character, like Gandhi's, was apparently deeply influenced by his mother.

> After her husband's death, she had treasured an old garment of his as a memento which she would not part with in any event and at any cost. It is interesting to recall in this connection a similar story about Gokhale that Gandhiji has related. Gokhale had treasured a scarf with a gold border which he had received from Ranade as a gift which he very carefully preserved and used only on special occasions. While in South Africa, Gokhale used the scarf round his neck at the banquet given in his honour by the Johannesburg Indians. It had got creased and needed ironing. There was not enough time for sending it to the laundry. Gandhiji offered to wash and iron it for him. He said to Gandhiji 'I can trust your capacity as a lawyer, but not as a washerman. What if you should soil it? Do you know what it means to me?' Yet Gandhiji convinced him of his skill as even a washerman and won his certificate. Gokhale has obviously inherited his mother's devotion and paternal qualities of resolution, truthfulness, honesty of purpose and a spirit of independence.[6]

Again, like Gandhi, Gokhale displayed great honesty of character in his childhood, confessing with tears to having cheated at classwork.[7] He passed the matriculation examination successfully at fifteen but his academic future was threatened by the straitened circumstances of the family. The crisis was averted when his sister-in-law sold her jewellery,[8] a sacrifice he justified by ultimately graduating successfully in 1884 by dint of effort and the gift of a retentive memory. He finally chose a career in teaching over law and public administration, which culminated in his becoming a 'devoted "servant of India" rather than an Indian Civil Servant'.[9]

The decisive factor which turned his mind towards teaching and its promise was his proximity to a group of dedicated people who had founded the Deccan Education Society, which Gokhale joined in 1886. This brought him into close contact with Ranade, which continued for fourteen years until Ranade's death. According to Professor J.R. Raju:

> The story of this friendship is one of the most beautiful romances of modern Indian history. For years, they were engaged together in the close study of

the progress and destiny of nations, the inner meaning of public events, the far off results of action, the discipline of failure, service and sacrifice and the infinite play of human motive and passion, not only in profound treatises of political philosophy, but also in the ephemeral effusions of the daily press, and in ponderous Govenment publications. Surely, there is no fairer sight on earth than the close communion of two such kindred spirits and it has brought untold blessings in its train on us all.[10]

This association also gradually led to Gokhale's increased participation in public life as he 'began his long and fruitful apprenticeship under him [Ranade]—examining documents, weighting evidence, analysing fiscal data, and preparing comprehensive memoranda on public questions'.[11] In 1889 Gokhale criticized the reduction in government expenditure on education, testifying to his 'trust in its liberating power'. In 1893, he criticized the excessive burden of Home Charges borne by Indians. In 1899, he was elected to the Bombay Legislative Council (more on which later) and in 1901 to the Supreme Legislative Council in Calcutta. Several years later his career culminated in the founding of the Servants of India Society (which famously rejected Mahatma Gandhi's candidacy as too controversial years later). It came into being in 1905[12] as a result of Gokhale's conviction that while patriotism is a noble and exalted emotion, it is 'only an emotion. It has got to be directed into useful, fruitful channels and that can only be if every worker prepared himself by arduous study, patient survey of the realities of India's life and by an appreciation on the spot of the variety of things and circumstances of each particular locality.'[13] An interesting feature of the society was the disciple-like trust the candidate was to repose in the mentor for five years,[14] which aroused some criticism. Although the society was steeped in idealism, it never suffered from lack of funds as long as Gokhale was alive. Some of his financial supporters even 'handed him cheque books, with signatures in each folio, and Gokhale was authorized to put any figure according to his requirement'.[15]

No account of Gokhale's life can be complete without taking his differences with B.G. Tilak into account. They stemmed from the fact that both these patriots advocated somewhat different responses to the British presence in India. Very briefly, Gokhale stood for reform and Tilak for revolution. The withdrawal of Tilak from the Deccan Education Society in 1890 was an early anticipation of these differences.[16] The so-called apology incident of 1897 is more complex. It unfolded as follows. The British government had to use soldiers to control the plague epidemic at the time, which gave rise to the rumour that 'two women had been violated by these soldiers and that one of them had committed suicide a little later'.[17] Gokhale was then in England and mentioned this incident in an interview with *The*

Manchester Guardian, following it up with a letter.[18] This created a sensation both in India and Britain. He was, however, unable to substantiate it and thus apologized to the British authorities. For this

> The common people condemned Gokhale in unmeasured terms, vilified him, abused him and hooted him when he made his appearance in public. A typical occasion of this kind was the session of the Indian National Congress held at Amraoti at the end of December 1897. It is said that some people there did not want him even to be seated on the platform with other leaders of the Congress and had he been asked to move or second a resolution, as was customary in his case since 1889 till that year, they had planned to insult him. He was not asked to make any speech and curiously enough he did not figure as a speaker on the Congress platform since then till 1904. . . . There is no getting [away] from the fact that for some time his own countrymen made Gokhale's life a terrific burden for him.[19]

Tilak had feared that Gokhale might give too clean a chit to the government and invited complaints against the government's conduct in writing. But when he went to Bombay to receive Gokhale on his return form England, Tilak was arrested,[20] and released only after the publication of Gokhale's apology on 4 August 1897. In this case Tilak swung close to Gokhale. Tilak thought the government was out to 'humiliate Poona leaders'.[21] In 1899, however, both contested a position in the Bombay Legislative Council, which Gokhale won.[22]

Tilak's religiosity was more public than Gokhale's, but Gokhale was not devoid of it. 'Though he rarely spoke of his religious convictions and was for a time a self-proclaimed agnostic', Gokhale, in the course of his campaign for the seat in the assembly 'turned . . . to the all-encompassing Shri Guru Dattatreya, syncretic embodiment of Vishnu, Shiva and Brahma'.[23] In fact his statement on the occasion makes him sound like a (Hindu?) religious universalist missionary when he states:

> '. . . in all these assemblies I will try to do good to my country by all means in my power. I will try to become a preacher of the highest philosophical religion and I will preach it *to the whole* world.'[24]

The following incident sheds a flood of light on the differences between him and Tilak. Mrs Ray of the Brahmo Samaj revealed this incident in 1943:

> One incident in the discussions I will relate to you and it will prove to you Gokhale's intrinsic love of truth and his great virtue of owning his own errors. One evening after dinner, we were both trying to convince

each other of our respective theories. He gave precedence to political and I to social reform. I got rather angry and said, 'Now, Mr Gokhale, with all your ideals of unity of India and political freedom, tell me which of your men are sincere and truthful. You can't even give up your caste-system; you don't believe in idolatry and still your biggest political leaders go to Benaras, and do their *pinda* etc. according to the old rites; none of you political men can live up to your own convictions; yet want to unite India and govern. I am sure with all your liberal views, you have a sacred thread under your shirt to denote that you are a Brahman born. Even you have not got the strength of your convictions.' I saw him grow rather grave and thought probably I had overstepped my familiarity by personal attack. So I turned the conversation to other higher matters. Would you believe, the next morning comes to me a sealed envelope enclosing his sacred thread, cut into two pieces with the following words in a slip of paper: 'Many thanks for rousing me to order. I own that I had no business to wear my sacred thread when I did not believe in it. Henceforth, I shall try to act according to my convictions. Forgive.' I have kept that sacred thread in a little box with the slip of paper attached to it. It is very seldom in life you have the opportunity of meeting a man who loves truth and is strong enough to own an error.[25]

One can only imagine how Tilak would have acted under these circumstances, but one can be reasonably certain that it would have been different. Lest this leave the reader with the wrong impression, however, regarding the nature of the relationship between Gokhale and Tilak, it might be wise to include the following account:

After Friday, 19 February, 1915, Gopal Krishna himself could do no more. He had given all that he could give in the service of his country. As the pyre which consumed his mortal remains was lit, the old man whose life had been so strangely interwoven with his own appeared at the cremation ground on the bank of the Mula, and some of the youths who had gathered there cheered irreverently when the Lokamanya approached. Tilak silenced them bluntly. 'This is not a time for cheers,' he berated them. 'This is a time for shedding tears.' Whatever the differences which had divided them, and however bitter their conflicts had been Tilak was too great a man himself, and too much of a fighter, not to acknowledge freely the great merits of his rival. 'This is a time for expressing sorrow for the irreparable loss which we have sustained by the death of Mr. Gokhale,' he said in his stirring farewell tribute. 'This diamond of India, this jewel of Maharashtra, this prince of workers, is taking eternal rest on the funeral grounds. Look at him and try to emulate him. Mr. Gokhale has passed away from our midst, after having satisfactorily performed his duty.' The Lokamanya could have uttered no higher praise of any man, since duty was to him the highest religion. 'Will any one of you come forward to take his place?' he asked contemptuously of the callow youths in the now chastened crowd.[26]

The passions aroused by India's struggle for Independence against British rule are now so far in the past that Gokhale's attempt to fine-tune British policies in India might seem almost irrelevant. But they are not without significance. Tilak and Gokhale stood apart in this respect in their intensity. It is interesting that both the attitudes, as exemplified by Gokhale and Tilak, find a resonance in Gandhi, whose opposition to British rule gradually became more radical. He started out a Gokhale and ended a Tilak. This is how one might understand the now well-known historiographical comment that although Gandhi acknowledged Gokhale as his guru, it was the mantle of Tilak that fell on his shoulders.

On Depressed Classes

The question of untouchables, referred to here euphemistically as the depressed classes, was destined to play a very significant social and political role in the decades to come. If Gandhi acknowledged Gokhale as his socio-political guru, then his public efforts on the behalf of the untouchables, as distinguished from his private repugnance of which he showed signs even in his early teens, are perhaps traceable to the emphasis placed on this dimension of social reform by Gokhale, an emphasis embodied in the following resolution moved by Gokhale at the Dharwar Social Conference on 27 April 1903.

That this Conference holds that the present degraded condition of the low castes is in itself and from the national point of view unsatisfactory, and is of the opinion that every well-wisher of the country should consider it his duty to do all he can to raise the moral and social condition by trying to rouse self-respect in these classes and placing facilities for education and employment within their reach.

Gentlemen, I hope I am not given to the use of unnecessarily strong language and yet I must say that this resolution is not as strongly worded as it should have been. The condition of the low castes—it is painful to call them low castes—is not only unsatisfactory as this resolution says—it is so deeply deplorable that it constitutes a grave blot on our social arrangements; and, further, the attitude of our educated men towards this class is profoundly painful and humiliating. I do not propose to deal with this subject as an antiquarian; I only want to make a few general observations from the standpoint of justice, humanity, and national self-interest. I think all fair-minded persons will have to admit that it is absolutely monstrous that a class of human beings, with bodies similar to our own, with brains that can think and with hearts that can feel, should be perpetually condemned to a low life of utter wretchedness, servitude and mental and moral degradation, and that permanent barriers should be placed in their way so that it should be impossible for them ever to overcome them and improve their lot. This is deeply revolting to our sense of justice. I believe that one has only to put oneself mentally into their place to realise how grievous this injustice is. We may touch a cat, we may touch a dog, we may touch any other animal, but the touch of these human beings is pollution! And so complete is now the mental degradation of these people that they see nothing in such treatment to resent, that they acquiesce in it as though nothing better than that was their due . . . .

How can we possibly realise our national aspirations, how can our country ever hope to take her place among the nations of the world, if we allow large numbers of our countrymen to remain sunk in ignorance, barbarism, and degradation?[27]

Women and Education

Social reformers, from Vivekānanda onwards, had long recognized the liberating role of education in connection with social reform in general and its key role in the liberation of women in particular. In fact once women become educated the roles are reversed; it is women who turn into its keenest proponents, for no educated woman is going to allow her children to remain uneducated. In the ensuing passage Gokhale's remarks are restricted to what education does for women rather than what they might do for it.

A wide diffusion of female education in all its branches is a factor of the highest value to the true well-being of every nation. In India it assumes additional importance by reason of the bondage of caste and custom which tries to keep us tied down to certain fixed ways of life and fixed modes of thought, and which so often cripples all efforts at the most elementary reforms. One peculiarity of the Indian life of the present day is the manner in which almost every single act of our daily life is regarded as regulated by some religious notion or another. . . . All who know anything of Indian women know that the turn of their mind is intensely religious—a result due in no small measure to their being shut out from all other intellectual pursuits. And this combination of enforced ignorance and overdone religion not only makes them willing victims of customs unjust and hurtful in the highest degree, but it also makes them the most formidable, because the most effective, opponents of all attempts at change or innovation. It is obvious that, under the circumstances, a wide diffusion of education, with all its solvent influences, among the women of India, is the only means of emancipating their minds from this degrading thraldom to ideas inherited through a long past and that such emancipation will not only restore women to the honoured position which they at one time occupied in India, but will also facilitate, more than anything else, our assimilation of those elements of Western civilisation without which all thoughts of India's regeneration are mere idle dreams, and all attempts at it foredoomed to failure.[28]

Swadeshi

By Gokhale's time the Swadeshi movement had gained momentum. It was destined to have important consequences for future developments in India. It arose in protest against the partition of Bengal by Lord Curzon in 1905. As the Muslim population stayed away from it, the protest acquired a largely Hindu character.[29] It was also pronouncedly anti-British. It had two foci: the rejection of foreign goods in favour of indigenous goods and the increased production of indigenous goods. Gokhale saw more merit in its positive emphasis on indigenous production and much less in its hostility towards foreign goods.

Gentlemen, the true *Swadeshi* movement is both a patriotic and an economic movement. The idea of *Swadeshi* or 'one's own country' is one of the noblest conceptions that have ever stirred the heart of humanity . . . . The devotion to motherland, which is enshrined in the highest *Swadeshi*, is an influence so profound and so passionate that its very thought thrills and its actual touch lifts one out of oneself. India needs today above everything else that the gospel of this devotion should be preached to high and low, to prince and peasant, in town and in hamlet, till the service of motherland becomes with us as overmastering a passion as it is in Japan.

One of the most gratifying signs of the present times is the rapid growth of the Swadeshi sentiment all over the country during the last two years. I have said more than once here, but I think the idea bears repetition, that Swadeshism at its highest is not merely an industrial movement, but that it affects the whole life of the nation—that Swadeshism at its highest is a deep, passionate, fervent, all-embracing love of the mother land and that this love seeks to show itself, not in one sphere of activity only, but in all; it invades the whole man, and will not rest until it has raised the whole man . . . .

Now as our needs are various, so the *Swadeshi* cause requires to be served in a variety of ways, and we should be careful not to quarrel with others simply because they serve the cause in a different way from our own. Thus, whoever tries to spread in the country a correct knowledge of the industrial conditions of the world and points out how we may ourselves advance, is a promoter of the *Swadeshi* cause. Whoever again contributes capital to be applied to the industrial development of the country must be regarded as a benefactor of the country and a valued supporter of the *Swadeshi* movement. Then those who organise funds for sending Indian students to foreign countries for acquiring industrial or scientific education . . . are noble workers in the *Swadeshi* field. These three ways of serving the *Swadeshi* cause are, however, open to a limited number of persons only. But there is a fourth way, which is open to all of us, and in the case of most, it is, perhaps, the only way in which they can help forward the *Swadeshi* movement. It is to use ourselves, as far as possible, *Swadeshi* articles only and to preach to others that they should do the same. By this we shall ensure the consumption of whatever articles are produced in the country, and we shall stimulate the production of new articles by creating a demand for them . . . .

In this connection I think I ought to say a word about an expression which has, of late, found considerable favour with a section of my countrymen—'the boycott of foreign goods'. I am sure that most of those that speak of this 'boycott' mean by it only the use, as far as possible, of *Swadeshi* articles in preference to foreign articles. Now such use is really included in true *Swadeshi*; but unfortunately the word 'boycott' has a sinister meaning—it implies a vindictive desire to injure another, no matter what harm you may thereby cause to yourself. And I think we would do well to use only the word *Swadeshi* to describe our present movement, leaving alone the word 'boycott', which creates unnecessary ill-will against ourselves.[30]

Gokhale and British Rule Over India

Gokhale was a moderate when it came to opposition to British rule not only in practical politics but also in emotional reactions to it.

The fact that a small island at one end of the world had by an astonishing succession of events been set to rule over a vast country, inhabited by an ancient and civilized race, at the other end; the character of the new rulers as men who had achieved constitutional liberty for themselves, and who were regarded as friends of freedom all over the world; their noble declarations of policy in regard to India—these were well calculated to cast a spell on the Indian mind. . . . The spell, however, is already broken, and even the hold on the reason is steadily slackening. A tendency has set in to depreciate even those advantages which at one time were most cordially acknowledged. And the disadvantages of the situation—wounded self, inability to grow to the full height of one's stature, a steady deterioration in the manhood of the nation, and the economic evils of vast magnitude inseparable from such foreign domination—these evils which, while the spell lasted, had not been realised with sufficient clearness, have now already begun to appear as intolerable . . . .

The system under which India is governed at present is an unnatural system and however one may put up with it as a temporary evil, as a permanent arrangement it is impossible, for under such a system 'the noble, free, virile, fearlesslike', to use the words of a well-known American preacher, 'which is the red blood of any nation gradually becomes torpid', and nothing can compensate a people for so terrible a wrong.

But two things I wish to say for my countrymen. First, that because we came under the rule of foreigners, it does not mean that we are like some savage or semi-civilized people whom you have subjugated. The people of India are an ancient race who had attained a high degree of civilization long before the ancestors of European nations understood what civilization was. India has been the birth place of great religions. She was also the cradle and long the home of literature and philosophy, of science and arts. But God does not give everything to every people, and India in the past was not known for that love of liberty and that appreciation of free institutions which one finds to be so striking a characteristic of the West. Secondly, because the Indians are under the rule of foreigners, it does not follow that they are lacking in what is called the martial spirit; for some of the best troops that fight the battles of the Empire today are drawn from the Indians themselves. I mention these two things because I want you to recognize that though we have lost our independence, we have not, on that account, quite forfeited our title to the respect and consideration of civilized people . . . .[31]

Servants of India Society

Two precedents have been posited as the possible inspiration for the Servants of India Society founded by Gokhale: The Society of Jesus founded by Ignatius Loyola in Spain in the face of Catholicism's conflict with Protestantism and the 1100 centres established by Saint Ramdas in the seventeenth century for the protection of the Hindu faith.[32] The reader may wish to form his or her own judgement in the matter, in the light of the preamble to the constitution of the Servants of India Society. It reads as follows:

For some time past the conviction has been forcing itself on many earnest and thoughtful minds that a stage has been reached in the work of nation-building in India, when for further progress, the devoted labours of a specially trained agency, applying itself to the task in a true missionary spirit are required. The work that has been accomplished so far has indeed, been of the highest value. The growth during the last 50 years of a feeling of common nationality based upon common traditions and ties, common hopes and aspirations, and even common disabilities, has been most striking. The fact that we are Indians first and Hindus, Mahomedans, Parsees or Christians afterwards, is being realized in a steadily increasing measure and the idea of a united and renovated India, marching onwards to a place among the nations of the world, worthy of her great past, is no longer a mere idle dream of a few imaginative minds, but is the definitely accepted creed of those who form the brain of the community—the educated classes of the country. A creditable beginning has been made already in matters of education and of local self-government; and all classes of people are slowly but steadily coming under the influence of liberal ideas. The claims of public life are every day receiving wider recognition and attachment to the land of our birth is growing into a strong and deeply cherished passion of the heart. The annual meetings of the Congresses and Conferences, the work of public bodies and associations, the writings in the columns of the Indian Press—all bear witness to the new life that is coursing in the veins of the people. The results achieved so far are undoubtedly most gratifying, but they only mean that the jungle has been cleared and the foundations laid. The great work of rearing the superstructure has yet to be taken in hand and the situation demands on the part of workers devotion and sacrifices proportionate to the magnitude of the task.

The servants of India Society has been established to meet in some measure these requirements of the situation. Its members frankly accept the British connection as ordained in the inscrutable dispensation of Providence for India's good. Self-government within the Empire for their country and higher life generally for their countrymen is their goal. This goal, they recognize, cannot be attained without years of earnest and patient effort and sacrifices worthy of the cause. Much of the work must be directed towards building up in the country a higher type of character and capacity than is generally available at present and the advance can only be slow. Moreover, the path is beset with great difficulties; there will be constant temptations to turn back; bitter disappointments will repeatedly try the faith of those who have put their hand to the work. But the weary toil can have but one end, if only the workers grow not faint-hearted on the way. One essential condition of success in this work is that a sufficient number of our countrymen must now come forward to devote themselves to the cause in the spirit in which religious work is undertaken. Public life must be spiritualized. Love of country must so fill the heart that all else shall appear as of little moment by its side. A fervent patriotism which rejoices at every opportunity of sacrifice for the motherland; a dauntless heart which refuses to be turned back from its object by difficulty or danger; a deep faith in the purpose of Providence, which nothing can shake—equipped with these—the worker must start on his mission and reverently seek the joy which comes of spending oneself in the service of one's country.

The Servants of India Society will train men prepared to devote their lives to the cause of the country in a religious spirit, and will seek to promote by all constitutional means, the national interests of the Indian people. Its members will direct their efforts principally towards (1) creating among the people, by example and by precept, a deep and passionate love of the motherland, seeking its highest fulfilment in service and sacrifice; (2) organizing the work of political education and agitation basing it on a careful study of public questions and strengthening generally the public life of the country; (3) promoting relations of cordial good-will and co-operation among the different communities; (4) assisting educational movements especially those for the education of women, the education of backward classes and industrial and scientific education; (5) helping forward the industrial development of the country; and (6) the elevation of the depressed classes. The headquarters of the Society will be at Poona where it will maintain a Home for its members and attached to it, a Library for the study of subjects bearing on its work.[33]

Each member undertook to abide by certain vows upon admission.

Here are the seven vows that every member had to take at the time of admission: (1) that the country will always be the first in his thoughts and he will give to her service the best that is in him; (2) that in serving the country he will seek no personal advantage for himself; (3) that he will regard all Indians as brothers and will work for the advancement of all without distinction of caste or creed; (4) that he will be content with such provision for himself and his family if he has any, as the Society may be able to make. He will devote no part of his energies to earning money for himself; (5) that he will lead a pure personal life; (6) that he will engage in no personal quarrel with any one; (7) that he will always keep in view the aims of the Society and watch over its interests with the utmost zeal, doing all he can to advance its work. He will never do anything which is inconsistent with the objects of the Society.[34]

Srinivasa Sastri described his initiation into this society as follows:

I had been enjoined to bathe and not to break my fast till the ceremony was over. I remember being in a highly chastened mood although there had been no vigil or prayer the preceding night. Gokhale's deportment was solemn and inspired me with something like awe. As I pronounced the phrases of each vow after him, I was seized with terrible misgivings as to my being able to keep them in a tolerable degree. But the trial was quickly over. Next day I started on my travels of East Bengal which was then only beginning to recover from the effects of the partition agitation.[35]

Notes

1. Percival Spear, ed., *The Oxford History of India by the Late Vincent A. Smith C.I.E.* (Fourth edition) (Delhi: Oxford University Press, 1994), p. 738; etc.
2. Stanley A. Wolpert, *Tilak and Gokhale: Revolution and Reform in the Making of Modern India* (Berkeley and Los Angeles: University of California Press, 1962), p. 3. Wolpert goes on to add that 'this myth would appear to indicate that the original Chitpavans came to India by sea from the west'.
3. See M.K. Gandhi, *Gokhale: My Political Guru* (Ahmedabad: Navajivan Publishing House, 1955).
4. T.V. Parvate, *Gopal Krishna Gokhale* (Ahmedabad: Navajivan Publishing House, 1959), p. iii.
5. Ibid., Also see Wolpert, pp. 143–4.

6. Parvate, p. 9.
7. Ibid., p. 10.
8. Ibid., p. 12.
9. Ibid., p. 15.
10. Ibid., p. 187.
11. Wm. Theodore de Bary, ed., *Sources of Indian Tradition* (New York and London: Columbia University Press, 1958), Vol. II, p. 143.
12. Ibid., p. 187.
13. Ibid., p. 187.
14. Ibid., p. 188.
15. Ibid., p. 195.
16. Parvate, p. 73. According to Wolpert's account (p. 116) two Indian women were said to have done so.
17. de Bary, p. 165.
18. Parvate, p. 73.
19. Ibid., p. 78.
20. Ibid., p. 86.
21. Ibid., p. 86.
22. Wolpert, pp. 130–2.
23. Ibid., p. 130.
24. Cited, ibid., p. 131, italics in original.
25. Parvate, p. 409.
26. Wolpert, pp. 271–2.
27. de Bary, pp. 146–7.
28. Glyn Richards, ed., *A Source-Book of Modern Hinduism* (London: Curzon Press, 1985), p. 132.
29. *Ramdhari Singh Dinkar, Bharatiya Saniskriti Ike Cara Adhyaya* (Patna: Udayacala, 1977; in Hindi), p. 692.
30. Richards, pp. 126–8.
31. Ibid., pp. 128–9.
32. Parvate, pp. 193–4.
33. Ibid., pp. 191–3.
34. Ibid., p. 188.
35. Ibid., p. 189.

Bal Gangadhar Tilak
(1856–1920)

Life

The remark of a prospective publisher of a biography of Tilak to the author is telling: 'Is your book anti-British? You know, Mr. Tilak was the greatest enemy of our empire.'[1] With the generation represented by Tilak, Indian opinion regarding the British presence began to undergo a change, a fact reflected in the life and thought of many of that generation and after.

Tilak was born in Ratnagiri ('a mountain of jewels'),[2] a small town on the west coast of India. Like the British themselves who came from the West with their affinity to the sea, two main figures who challenged their rule, Tilak and Gandhi, were coincidentally born on the western coast of India.[3] Tilak was born there in 1856—the same year in which the University of Bombay was established from which he was destined to graduate—in the Chitapavan clan like Ranade and Gokhale before him,[4] but with a family-history of disaffection towards the British. His great-grandfather had fought under the Peshwas but when the British defeated them in 1818 he resigned, refusing to 'serve a foreign government'.[5] His grandfather became a *sannyāsī* in later life, dying in Banaras but perhaps not before sharing with him some of the 'most horrible, as well as some of the most inspiring deeds that took place in the Indian Mutiny',[6] which he had witnessed. His father, reluctant to seek favours with European officers, lived on a small salary, which he supplemented with earnings by writing textbooks. His fortunes survived the shock of his savings going down with an English entrepreneur and when his father died in 1872, Tilak, then sixteen years old, inherited a 'fair nest-egg'.[7] His mother had passed away when Tilak was ten, a loss he mourned in a Sanskrit poem composed at the time.

After an assertive childhood, during which he would shout correct answers to questions out of turn and once refused to be punished along with the class for the mess it had created because he was not individually responsible for it,[8] he joined the Deccan College in 1872. He, however, failed to make the grade in the first year because he decided to devote that year to building up his physique. He always stressed the importance of exercise in later life.[9] After a B.A. (1876) in which his favoured subjects were mathematics and astronomy, he also passed the LL.B. examination (1880), as he 'did not envisage a life without my coming into conflict with the British authorities'.[10]

By now he had reached the conclusion, along with some of his colleagues, that 'the salvation of our motherland lay in education and only in education, of the people'[11] (which, for him, had to be English education[12]). For furthering this cause they first discussed the idea of 'establishing private schools on the model of the missionary institutions',[13] and then succeeded in implementing it by founding the New English School without any help from the government, thereby establishing a model of education of the Indians, for the Indian and by the Indians, though not without arousing some governmental suspicion.[14] In furtherance of the same goals, at the popular level, he was instrumental in establishing two newspapers: *Kesari* in Marathi and *Mahratta* in English.

The success of the New English School as a private institution paved the way for its conversion into a public body as the Deccan Education Society, under whose auspices the Ferguson College (1885) was founded for training educational missionaries for all of Maharashtra. Although these educational efforts were so successful that for a time even the idea of handing over the management of the government-run Deccan College to them was entertained, differences arose within the Society over allowing its members to receive extramural emoluments, a point on which Tilak took a purist line and resigned. By now his differences with Gokhale, who had also joined the society in the meantime, were beginning to surface.[15]

Tilak was thus freed for fuller participation in public life, leading to further controversies. One of these centred on the work of Pandita Ramabai, a great Sanskrit scholar who became a widow, converted to Christianity and then set up Sharada Sadan, for educating 'destitute high-caste widows'. Tilak discovered that it was being covertly used to promote conversion to Christianity and exposed it as such, generating great commotion. Tilak himself told 'his friends (of course in a lighter vein) that he would arrange for the remarriage of a thousand widows on the day India gained political independence',[16] a statement which reveals where his priorities lay. His reaction to the proposed *Age of Consent Bill* (1890) also generated great controversy. The Bill proposed to raise the minimum age of cohabitation to 12, which seems harmless enough, but Tilak insisted, like Roy before him, that such changes should be brought about by education rather than legislation, and certainly not by legislation at the behest of the British government: 'Indian [social] problems must be solved by Indians.'[17] It became law in 1891 but when he invited its sponsors to join him in taking a public vow not to marry their daughters young 'surprisingly enough, those who were loudest in their support of the age of Consent Bill were the first to refuse to put their signatures to the resolution'.[18]

Tilak also took the offensive in generating self-confidence among the people by organizing festivals around the Hindu god Ganapati and the hero Shivaji, during the period stretching from 1893 to 1905.[19] These have been criticized as anti-Muslim in orientation on the one hand,[20] and on the other, defended as an attempt to consolidate Hindu identity in the face of the British government's pro-Muslim stance. Some have even suggested that while the Ganapati festival was religious in orientation that of Shivaji was 'secular',[21] though this has also been disputed. What has not been disputed is their success, exemplified by the following incident:

> The Ganapati procession was taking place, with thousands of young men and women singing devotional songs and playing music. Tilak was accompanying the procession when suddenly his attention was attracted by a shrill cry from a window in one of the houses on the processional route. He looked up and saw a boy of seven or eight crying loudly while his mother tried to pacify him. Tilak stopped to ask why the boy was crying. The mother did not know what to say—she was shy and timid, perhaps terrified. At last she told him that her son wanted his Ganapati to be taken to the river for the immersion ceremony along with other Ganapatis, but she dared not let him do this as her family belonged to the untouchable class. Tilak was moved to tears; he could not bear to see an innocent child suffer. He went into the house, took the Ganapati idol and placed it by the side of his own and the boy joined the procession holding on to Tilak's hand.[22]

The introduction of the festivals was succeeded by his controversial involvement in the government's handling of two disasters—a famine in 1896 and plague in 1897. The popular sentiment, that the former was handled inadequately and the latter insensitively, culminated in the assassination of a British officer, associated with plague relief policies, on 22 June 1897, chosen to coincide with the Diamond Jubilee of Queen Victoria's accession to the throne. Damodar Chapekar was executed for the crime. 'On the eve of his execution Damodar had to appeal to Tilak, for a copy of the "Song of the Lord", explaining that he had lost his own. Tilak complied, and it was his copy of the sacred book, which the young man carried to the gallows.'[23]

Tilak was also implicated in this episode and greeted as a hero upon his release. His subsequent participation in the agitation against the British government during 1905–8 further added to his stature. The occasion was provided by the decision of the British government to partition Bengal into two separate provinces. The government claimed that this was being done for administrative convenience; the Indian nationalists alleged that this was a deliberate attempt at 'divide and rule', as the division would virtually result in a 'Muslim' and a 'Hindu' Bengal. The agitation was spearheaded by the 'Lal-Bal-Pal triumvirate—an acronym for *Lala* Lajpat Rai of Punjab; *Bal* Gandadhar Tilak of Maharashtra and Bipin Chandra *Pal* of Bengal'. This agitation is considered by most historians as a turning point in the emergence of Indian nationalism. Tilak had already proposed a Swaraj Bill in 1895. The resulting radicalization of Indian politics caused a split in the Indian Congress when it met in Surat in 1907, which led to the expulsion of Tilak and his revolutionary group which included Aurobindo. The rift was only healed in 1914, when the Congress met in Lucknow, where Tilak finalized a pact with the Muslim League for a joint front against the British.

On 13 July 1908 Tilak found himself being tried for sedition because of an attempt on the life of Kingford, a British judge at Muzufferpore. This bomb outrage had 'offered the government a golden chance; it was the psychological moment for inaugurating an era of arrests, searches, prosecutions and persecutions'. In order to make its charge stick even in 1898 the government had to define 'disaffection' (most thought Jesuitically) as 'not so much a positive feeling of hatred against the government established by law as simply a want of affection'.[24] In any case this time he was sentenced for six years in prison, a sentence which even caught the attention of Lenin, who wrote in 1908: 'The despicable sentence passed on the Indian democrat, Tilak, gave rise to street demonstrations and a strike in Bombay', but not without a Marxist spin: 'The class conscious workers in Europe now have Asian comrades and their number will grow by leaps and bounds.'[25] It seems Tilak had been tipped off about his impending arrest, for when the police arrived he humorously chided them: 'I know the Presidency Magistrate signed the warrant of my arrest four hours ago and it's hardly a quarter of an hour's journey to Sardar Griha from your office. Why did you take so long?'[26]

Tilak was convicted for inciting disaffection against the government through his writings in Marathi but he claimed that the English renderings were defective. In making this claim Tilak was repeating a charge he had aleady levelled at the British government earlier. Stanley Wolpert notes:

In challenging the accuracy of translations from the Marathi, Tilak disputed fine shades of idiomatic meaning, which really did not affect the meaning of his statements. This line of argument, however, was significant since it provided fresh ammunition for the nationalist cause. Tilak's challenge cut to the heart of the question of a foreign people's capacity to rule over a land whose languages they neither spoke nor read with fluency. Tilak insisted that a judge and jury not reading Marathi, lacked the ability to try his case with intelligence. *This argument was to become the keynote of his second sedition trial defense as well,* and served to undermine the very premise of rule by Law, introducing the demand for svarajya into the courtroom and jury box of British India. Justice Strachey himself was obliged to concede that 'in a matter of this kind it is extremely difficult for the jury, who are not Marathi scholars, and for me also, to say what is the proper rendering of these passages. And I think I should consider the matter fully between this and tomorrow whether or not I should myself call a witness who is an expert in Marathi, to give an opinion as to some of these passages.'[27]

The trial ended in his incarceration. It was while in prison in Mandalay (Burma) that Tilak composed his influential commentary on the *Bhagavad Gītā,* under the following circumstances.

After a time, the order to allow all the books to remain in my possession was changed and I was allowed to have only four books at a time! When I complained about it to the Burma Government I was again allowed to have all the books I wanted with me as I was writing my *Gita Rahasya.* However, each book was carefully scrutinized and the pages counted, and their number was written on top on the frontispiece; underneath the Superintendent of the Jail used to sign. When I was released, the number of books in my possession was about four hundred. The paper which was given to me for writing was never in loose sheets. They were bound books with the pages counted and the number written as above. In the same way I was never given ink to write with, only lead pencils, and they too were sharpened beforehand. The only exception to this practice was when I wrote my monthly letter home. Then they gave me separated sheets of paper and also pen and ink.

Even before I was imprisoned, a conviction was growing on me that the meaning of the Gita, adumbrated by all the many commentaries and expositions, was not the correct one. I had long wanted to give a concrete shape to my ideas on the meaning of the Gita, together with a comparative study of the Eastern and Western philosophies. I could do that only at Mandalay. I have now written a book on this subject in Marathi; it took me four to six months to write but much time was spent in thinking out its plan and then again in revising it. The manuscript is with the Government—they did not give it to me at the time of my release.[28]

This commentary, which was subsequently published under the title *Gita Rahasya* or the Secret of the Gita, was completed in 1911. He wrote on March 2:

> I have just finished writing my book on the Gita and have given it the title *Gita Rahasya*. In it I have expounded some original ideas, which, in many ways, will be presented to the people for the first time. I have shown in this book how the Hindu religious philosophy helps to solve the moral issues (involved in everyday life). To a certain extent my line of argument runs parallel to the line of thinking followed by Green in his book on Ethics. However I do not accept that the basis of morality is the greatest good of the greatest number or the human inspiration. What I have done in *Gita Rahasya* is to prove, by comparing the philosophy of the Gita and the philosophy of the West, that ours, to put it at the lowest, is in no way inferior to theirs. I had been thinking about the Gita for the last twenty years, and the ideas which I propose to expound are challenging—so far no one has dared to put them forward. I have yet to cite quite a few supporting arguments from books which are not with me at present, which I can do only after my release.[29]

Tilak was released from jail in 1914. 'If in 1898 he had returned from prison a martyred hero, with his restoration to India in June of 1914 he appeared to his followers as little less than the reincarnation of a deity.'[30] Chastened by his imprisonment, however, Tilak was now more conciliatory vis-à-vis the British. He founded the Indian Home Rule League, acknowledged the merits of British rule and supported the British war effort during the First World War. He also vainly sought legal redress against Sir Vincent Chirol for libel in England in 1919. Tilak died on 1 August 1920. Mahatma Gandhi was one of his pall-bearers.

Tilak also wrote two books on Vedic studies: *The Orion* (1893) and *The Arctic Home of the Vedas* (1903). In the former he argued for a very early date of the ṚgVeda (*c*. 4000 BC) on the basis of astronomical evidence and in the latter he sought to locate the original homeland of the Aryans in the interglacial period in the Arctic Circle on botanical grounds. Although his conclusions have not gained widespread currency, the intellectual effort embodied in the books remains consequential for modern Hindu thought. It signalled the use of science (as distinguished from the scientific method in its most general sense) for recovering the data in the history of Hinduism and it represented a major attempt by Hindus to reconstruct their own history, as distinguished from such work by Western scholars. It is sometimes alleged that Tilak buttressed the claims of Hindu chauvinism through such scholarship. Although this possibility cannot be ruled out, it is worth reflecting that Tilak never questioned the view that the Aryans entered India from beyond India. This is important because the claim that the Aryans are indigenous to India enjoys almost the status of dogma in Hindu nationalist circles today.

Not only in Hindu studies but in terms of Hindu thought and even Indian politics, Tilak continues to remain a significant factor. His life marked the cusp of the transformation of Kipling's 'meek and mild Indian' (read Hindu), 'the most loyal and law-abiding citizen in the world',[31] into a person who would take the law into his or her own nationalistic hands and shift his or her loyalty from the British to the country over which the British were ruling.

It was for his role in this transformation that he merits the title: 'father of Indian unrest', a description interpreted approvingly by Indians and pejoratively by the British. Thereby hangs an anecdote.

> By the time Tilak returned to India in November the McNalty family had learned enough about Indian food and Indian cooking to be able to open an Indian restaurant. Mr. Parikh, an old Indian resident who recently died in London, used to tell a story about this restaurant, which displayed the sign: UNDER THE BLESSINGS OF LOKAMANYA TILAK, 'FATHER OF INDIAN UNREST'. One day, Sir Valentine Chirol, who had acquired a taste for hot Indian dishes, went to McNalty's Restaurant and was surprised to read the sign so prominently displayed. He asked to see the proprietor, but he was out; so he asked the head waiter to take down the sign. This he refused to do. It was, of course, Chirol himself who, in his book had called Tilak 'The father of Indian unrest'. But he had used it in a derogatory sense. What he objected to now was seeing it used as a commendation of Tilak.[32]

A Dialogue Among Friends

A key issue Hindu thought had to address in this period was: should striving for political independence follow social and economic reform as the moderates maintained or should it precede it as the 'extremists' argued, until they merged in the Gandhian dispensation. The following conversational record of Tilak with his comrades, Upasani and Agarkar, is revealing in this respect.

A Dialogue

TILAK: Tonight let's talk about the line of action we propose to follow when we leave college. It's nearly three years since we first started thinking and talking about it.

UPASANI: Why worry, Tilak, at this stage? Passing our examinations should be enough preparation for the future.

AGARKAR: Frankly, Upasani, I don't regard passing examinations as anything more than a stepping stone which will give us a more honourable and effective part in the service of the country. Of course, I have given some time and thought to considering the work before us. But I must say my ideas are still forming themselves, though I think, on the whole, that social reform should have priority over political reform.

UPASANI: Obviously, you haven't changed much since we discussed this matter in Bombay last year.

TILAK: That does not matter. Let us see if we can arrive at some common platform in spite of the apparent differences in our points of view. I suggest we confine our discussion to finding our common ideals. Well, then, Agarkar, I take it you stick to your view that social reform must come before political reform?

AGARKAR: Yes, that's how I feel. I have thought about it deeply and long, and have come to this conclusion. Tilak, leave aside our individual cases, but what do we see around us? Most of our Hindu community is soaked through and through in ignorance, superstition and dreadful social practices. I shudder to see people performing ridiculous ceremonies like offering coconuts and new-laid eggs before a railway engine to get a safe journey; those awful funeral precessions and worst of all—but how can I express the horror and agony I feel at the disfiguring of the widows? I simply cannot bear to think of the horrid custom. Tilak, say what you like but my war-cry will be social reform first and last, and all the time.

TILAK: Look here, don't imagine that I am opposed to social reform. Who does not love his home? Like your favourite poet Shelley, our Saint Ramadas says, 'Do your duty to the family first.' Agarkar, you can shout your social reform from the housetop, but what will you say to a peasant if he comes to you and says, 'You ask me to put my house in order. All right, but where is the house?' then you will have to give him a house first! You see all our activities must lead to providing homes for the homeless. What I say is, give the people the homes and then ask them to put them in order. Will you agree with me that the English came here for the benefit of their homes in England and not so much to emancipate us?

AGARKAR: Of course, I agree with you. I am not a fool to shut my eyes to hard facts. But I must say I feel differently from you. I think man's ideal should be set very high, even if it meant he had to take hundreds of years to achieve one tenth of it. You attach too much importance to this material life; it has influenced your way of thinking and obscured your vision. I do not think the heavenly family happiness and eternal bliss described in our Sanskrit epics are beyond the reach of man. I do grant you, though, that we cannot ignore the political realities as they are in India today. What I insist on is that politics must not become an obsession with us. After all, our political condition is an outward symptom of our social existence. All the same, call it political or social, I will not quarrel with you over words. I use these terms in their accepted meaning. I hope, Tilak, you don't misunderstand me.

TILAK: Of course not. I think it's a lucky day today. We have been discussing things quietly and without heat—and surely that in itself is an achievement! Agarkar, I am convinced each of us will serve the country in his own way and our service will be of the highest order. My friend, I am in complete agreement with your original proposition that all our activities must tend to the betterment of our homes, in other words the reform of our society. Although I do not look upon the home with your poet's vision, I think of it as the firm foundation of our well-being. But let us not forget that whatever ideals we preach, they should be attainable by the common people. We have to think in terms of the man in the street and examine the circumstances which condition his life and action. We must look back to the year 1632 and forward to 1930. Political circumstances, as you say, are only a part of the whole, but they come into everything. Well, whether you give the first place in the home to the family deity or to the children, the fact remains that under foreign rule our children do not get fresh milk and proper nourishment. Can anyone deny that our cattle are exported to foreign countries and our land taxes are increased every thirty years, making the farmer poorer and poorer? You know what kind of education is given to the children. I call it rubbish. There are a hundred and one terrible superstitions and dirty habits in our country, masquerading as religion. But has the Government done anything about it? It must be our job to teach our men and women our own religion and its true meaning. What we expect from the Government is financial help, but we should not allow them power to interfere in our religious practices; they can never understand their real meaning. Think of their belief that 'a cow has no soul'. Disgusting! Agarkar, if you are bent on social reform, well, follow your choice by all means. I say, begin at once. Talk will get you nowhere. Once you start on the campaign of social reform you will soon find out for yourself that at every step you come into conflict with the Government.

AGARKAR: Yes, if I have to fight I will fight. But do you realize, Tilak, that you will have to fight against ignorance just as much as against the Government?[33]

Tilak and Journalism

One important feature of the nationalist movement was the fillip it gave to journalism in the Indian languages. This emerges clearly in the following comments of Tilak in an interview with Kaka Kalelkar.

When I started *Kesari*, people asked me why I was going to publish it in Marathi. They said, 'No one will read it.' But I was determined to publish it in Marathi, and I replied that my decision was final. They then asked me to reserve at least two columns for English material. Again I replied categorically that it was impossible; *Kesari* was for the people and the people were sure to give it a rousing reception. Today the *Mahratta* (which is an English weekly) has to be financed from the funds of *Kesari*. When we started *Kesari* we had to make almost a new language. In the old Marathi there was plenty of writing on devotion and philosophy; also the ballad writers had introduced an element of heroics into it. But to discuss serious matters of politics, to attack and rebut opponents, to crush them with satire and ridicule, for all this the old Marathi was of very little use. And so we were forced to develop a new terminology to make our writings effective. A man who feels intensely, who is burning with new ideas, finds words to express them. He becomes, indeed, capable of creating a new language.[34]

On Untouchability

In 1918 Tilak addressed a conference of Untouchables in Bombay as follows.

If God were to tolerate untouchability I would not recognise Him as God at all . . . . Although I have appeared amongst you in person for the first time, believe me, you have been in my mind all the time . . . . I do not deny that it was the Brahman rule that introduced the practice of untouchability. This is a cancer in the body of Hindu society and we must eradicate it at all costs.[35]

On Being Sentenced

Tilak made the following comment on being convicted for sedition. His sentence was invoked as a precedent in the subsequent sentencing of Mahatma Gandhi on a similar charge.

All I wish to say is that in spite of the verdict of the jury I maintain that I am innocent. There are higher powers that rule the destiny of things and it may be the will of Providence that the cause which I represent is to prosper more by my suffering than by my remaining free.[36]

Tenets of the New Party

The fight between the Moderates and the Extremists, carried on in the political arena, split the Indian National Congress. The formation of the Extremist Party led to the following formulation of its tenets.

Two new words have recently come into existence with regard to our politics, and they are *Moderates* and *Extremists*. These words have a specific relation to time, and they, therefore, will change with time. The Extremists of today will be Moderates tomorrow, just as the Moderates of today were Extremists yesterday. When the National Congress was first started and Mr. Dadabhai's views, which now go for Moderates, were given to the public, he was styled an Extremist, so that you will see that the term Extremist is an expression of progress. We are Extremists to-day and our sons will call themselves Extremists and us Moderates. Every new party begins as Extremists and ends as Moderates. The sphere of practical politics is not unlimited. We cannot say what will or will not happen 1,000 years hence—perhaps during that long period, the whole of the white race will be swept away in another glacial period. We must, therefore, study the present and work out a programme to meet the present condition.

It is impossible to go into details within the time at my disposal. One thing is granted, viz., that this Government does not suit us. As has been said by an eminent statesman—the government of one country by another can never be a successful, and therefore, a permanent Government. There is no difference of opinion about this fundamental proposition between the Old and New schools. One fact is that this alien Government has ruined the country. In the beginning, all of us were taken by surprise. We were almost dazed. We thought that everything that the rulers did was for our good and that this English Government had descended from the clouds to save us from the invasions of Tamerlane and Chengis Khan, and, as they say, not only from foreign invasions but from internecine warfare, or the internal or external invasions, as they call it. We felt happy for a time, but it soon came to light that the peace which was established in this country did this, as Mr. Dadabhai has said in one place—that we were prevented from going at each other's throats, so that a foreigner might go at the throat of us all. Pax Britannica has been established in this country in order that a foreign Government may exploit the country. That this is the effect of this Pax Britannica is being gradually realized in these days. It was an unhappy circumstance that it was not realized sooner. We believed in the benevolent intentions of the Government, but in politics there is no benevolence. Benevolence is used to sugar-coat the declarations of self-interest and we were in those days deceived by the apparent benevolent intentions under which rampant self-interest was concealed. That was our state then. But soon a change came over us. English education, growing poverty, and better familiarity with our rulers, opened our eyes and our leaders, especially the venerable leader who presided over the recent Congress was the first to tell us that the drain from the country was ruining it, and if the drain was to continue, there was some great disaster awaiting us. So terribly convinced was he of this that he went over from here to England and spent 25 years of his life in trying to convince the English people of the injustice that is being done to us. He worked very hard. He had conversations and interviews with Secretaries of State, with Members of Parliament— and with what result? He has come here at the age of 82 to tell us that he is bitterly disappointed.

Your industries are ruined utterly, ruined by foreign rule: your wealth is going out of the country and you are reduced to the lowest level which no human being can occupy. In this state of things, is there any remedy by which you can help yourself? The remedy is not petitioning but boycott. We say prepare your forces, organize your power, and then go to work so that they cannot refuse you what you demand. A story in *Mahabharata* tells that Sri Krishna was sent to effect a compromise, but the Pandavas and Kauravas were both organizing their forces to meet the contingency of failure of the compromise. This is politics. Are you prepared in this way to fight if your demand is refused? If you are, be sure you will not be refused; but if you are not, nothing can be more certain than that your demand will be refused, and perhaps, for ever. We are not armed, and there is no necessity for arms either. We have a stronger weapon, a political weapon, in boycott. We have perceived one fact, that the whole of this administration, which is carried on by a handful of Englishmen, is carried on with our assistance. We are all in subordinate service. This whole Government is carried on with our assistance and they try to keep us in ignorance of our power of cooperation between ourselves by which that which is in our own hands at present can be claimed by us and administered by us. The point is to have the entire control in our hands. I want to have the key of my house, and not merely one stranger turned out of it. Self-Government is our goal; we want a control over our administrative machinery. We don't want to become clerks and remain [clerks]. At present, we are clerks and willing instruments of our own oppression in the hands of an alien Government, and that Government is ruling over us not by its innate strength but by keeping us in ignorance and blindness to the perception of this fact. Professor Seely shares this view. Every Englishman knows that they are a mere handful in this country and it is the business of every one of them to befool you in believing that you are weak and they are strong. This is politics. We have been deceived by such policy so long. What the New Party wants you to do is to realize the fact that your future rests entirely in your own hands. If you mean to be free, you can be free; if you do not mean to be free, you will fall and be for ever fallen. So many of you need not like arms; but if you have not the power of active resistance, have you not the power of self-denial and self-abstinence in such a way as not to assist this foreign Government to rule over you? This is boycott and this is what is meant when we say, boycott is a political weapon. We shall not give them assistance to collect revenue and keep peace. We shall not assist them in fighting beyond the frontiers or outside India with Indian blood and money. We shall have our own courts, and when time comes we shall not pay taxes. Can you do that by your united efforts? If you can, you are free from to-morrow.[37]

On Hinduism

B.G. Tilak addressed the Bharata Dharma Mahamandala (All-India Religious Association) on 3 January 1906 at Banaras. The address contains Tilak's answer to a question people have been asking ever since the word Hinduism was first coined early in the nineteenth century—what is Hinduism?

I am sorry I cannot address you in any other language except Marathi and English. English should be boycotted for religious purposes. But I cannot help and hope you will excuse me. I shall speak a few words on the importance of Hindu religion, its present condition and efforts that are being made to preserve it from decay. What is Hindu religion? If you go to the different parts of India, you will find different views about Hindu religion entertained by different people. Here you are mostly Vaishnavas or followers of Shri Krishna. If you go to the south, you will meet followers of Ramanuja and such others. What is Hindu religion then? Bharata Dharma Mahamandala cannot be a Mahamandala unless it includes and co-ordinates these different sections and parts. Its name can only be significant if different sections of Hindu religion are united under its banner. All these different sects are so many branches of the Vedic religion. The term Sanatana Dharma shows that our religion is very old—as old as the history of the human race itself. Vedic religion was the religion of the Aryans from a very early time. But you all know no branch can stand by itself. Hindu religion as a whole is made up of different parts co-related to each other as so many sons and daughters of one great religion. If this idea is kept in view and if we try to unite the various sections it will be consolidated in a mighty force. So long as you are divided amongst yourselves, so long as one section does not recognise its affinity with another, you cannot hope to rise as Hindus. Religion is an element in nationality. The word dharma means a tie and comes from the root dhri to bear or hold. What is there to hold together? To connect the soul with God, and man with man. Dharma means our duties towards God and duty towards man. Hindu religion as such provides for a moral as well as social tie. This being our definition we must go back to the past and see how it was worked out. During Vedic times India was a self-contained country. It was united as a great nation. That unity has disappeared bringing on us great degradation and it becomes the duty of the leaders to revive that union. A Hindu of this place is as much a Hindu as the one from Madras or Bombay. You might put on a different dress, speak a different language, but you should remember that the inner sentiments which move you all are the same. The study of the Gita, Ramayana and Mahabharata produce the same ideas throughout the country. Are not these—our common heritage? If we lay stress on it forgetting minor differences that exist between different sects, then by the grace of Providence we shall ere long be able to consolidate all the different sects into a mighty Hindu nation.

This ought to be the ambition of every Hindu. If you thus work to unite, you will find within a few years one feeling and one thought actuating and dominating all people throughout the country. This is the work we have to do. The present condition of our religion is not at all one that is desirable. We think ourselves separated and the feeling of that unity which was at the root of our advancement in the past is gone. It is certainly an unfortunate circumstance that we should have so many sections and sub-sections. It is the duty of an association like the Bharata Dharma Mahamandala to work to restore the lost and forgotten union. In the absence of unity India cannot claim its place among the nations of the world. For some two hundred years India was in the same condition as it is to-day. Buddhism flourished and attacks were made on Hindu religion by Buddhists and Jains. After 600 years of chaos rose one great leader, Shankaracharya and he brought together all the common philosophical elements for our religion and proved and preached them in such a way that Buddhism was swept away from the land.

We have the grand and eternal promise Shri Krishna has given in the Gita that whenever there is a decay of dharma, He comes down to restore it. When there is a decay owing to disunion when good men are persecuted, then Shri Krishna comes down to save us. There is no religion on the face of the earth except the Hindu religion wherein we find such a hopeful promise that God comes to us as many times as necessary. After Mahomed no prophet is promised, and Jesus Christ comes once for ever. No religion holds such promise full of hope. It is because of this that the Hindu religion is not dead. We are never without hope. Let heretic (sic) say what they may. A time will come when our religious thoughts and our rights will be vindicated. Each man is doing his best, and as the association is doing its best, every Hindu is welcome to assist it and carry it to its goal. If we do not find men coming forward let us hope they will do so in the next generation. We are never without hope; no other religion has such a definite and sacred promise as we have of Shri Krishna. It is based on truth and truth never dies. I say it and I am prepared to prove this statement. I believe that truth is not vouchsafed to one only. The great characteristic of truth is that it is universal and catholic. It is not confined to any particular race. Hindu religion tolerates all religions. Our religion says that all religions are based on truth, 'you follow yours, I mine.'

Shri Krishna says that the followers of other religions worship God though not in a proper form. Shri Krishna does not say that the followers of other religions would be doomed to eternal hell. I challenge anybody to point out to me a similar text from the scriptures of other religions. It cannot be found in any other religion, because they are partial truth while our Hindu religion is based on the whole, the Sanatan truth, and therefore it is bound to triumph in the end. Numerical strength also is a great strength. Can the religion which counts its followers by crores die? Never, unless the crores of our fellow-followers are suddenly swept away our religion will not die. All that is required for our glorious triumph and success is that we should unite all the different sects on a common platform and let the stream of Hindu religion flow through one channel with mighty consolidated and concentrated force. This is the work which the Bharat Dharma Mandala has to do and accomplish. Let us be all united. Because a particular man wears a particular dress, speaks a different tongue, worships a particular *devata*, is that any reason for our withdrawing our hands of fellowship to our Hindu brother? The character of our Hindu religion is very comprehensive—as comprehensive as its literature itself; we have a wonderful literature. Wisdom, as is concentrated in Gita and epitomized in about 700 verses, that wisdom, I am confident, cannot be defeated or overcome by any philosophy, be it Western or any other. Now I turn to the forces that are arrayed against us. There are mainly two forces of (1) science and (2) Christianity. If our religion is threatened with any hostile criticism, it comes from these two. As for the first, a great change is coming over the West and truths that are discovered by them were known to our Rishis. Modern science is gradually justifying and vindicating our ancient wisdom. With the establishment of Physical Research Societies and the expansion of scientific knowledge they have come to understand that the fundamental principles of our religion are based on truth that can be proved. Take an instance. Chaitanya pervades everything. It is strictly a Hindu theory. Professor Bose has recently shown that this Vedantic doctrine is literally true according to modern science. Take the doctrine of the survival of soul independent of the body.

Doctrines of Karma and Re-incarnation go with it. Spencer never believed in these. But recently it has been our great privilege to see that Sir Oliver Lodge and Mayor and others have declared that the soul does not die with body; so much now they are convinced of. Modern science accepts the doctrine of karma if not of re-incarnation. But it is not the belief of Christianity. They hold that God gives a new soul each and every time. Thus it would be seen that a change is coming over the West. Our enemies are fast disappearing before the teachings of modern science, take courage and work hard for the final triumph. If you make a little effort and aim at union, you have a bright future before you. Now-a-days, Vedanta is not only read but sudied by Americans. No European doctor believes that the beating of the heart can be voluntarily stopped. But it has been proved to the contrary. Vedanta and yoga have been fully vindicated by modern science and these aim at giving you spiritual union. It is our clear duty, therefore, to follow truth and re-edit our scriptures and place them before the world in the light of modern science that they may be acceptable to all. But I will tell you again unity is necessary for such work. You would be wanting in duty to yourself and to your ancestors if you do not give up provincial prejudices and promote unity that underlies all sects. We have been very idle. We have grown so stupid owing to our idleness that we are required to be told by foreigners that our treasures conceal gold and not iron. Modern science and education are prepared to help you if you take advantage of them, and time will come when instead of Christians preaching Christianity here we shall see our preachers preaching Sanatan Dharma all over the world. Concentrate all your forces. The idea of a Hindu University where our old religion will be taught along with modern science is a very good one and should have the support of all. In conclusion, I would again draw your attention to bring about a harmonious union of all sects and rightly claim and obtain our rightful place among the nations of the world.[38]

Interpretation of the Bhagavad Gita

The following is a summary of the speech on Gita Rahasya *delivered by B.G. Tilak in Amroati in 1917.*

Let me begin by telling you what induced me to take up the study of *Bhagavad Gita*. When I was quite a boy, I was often told by my elders that strictly religious and really philosophic life was incompatible with the hum-drum life of everyday. If one was ambitious enough to try to attain Moksha, the highest goal a person could attain, then he must divest himself of all earthly desires and renounce this world. One could not serve two masters, the world and God. I understood this to mean that if one would lead a life which was the life worth living, according to the religion in which I was born, then the sooner the world was given up the better. This set me thinking. The question that I formulated for myself to be solved was: does my religion want me to give up this world and renounce it before I attempt to, or in order to be able to, attain the perfection of manhood? In my boyhood I was also told that *Bhagavad Gita* was universally acknowledged to be a book containing all the principles and philosophy of the Hindu religion, and I thought if this be so I should find an answer in this book to my query; and thus began my study of the *Bhagavad Gita*. I approached the book with a mind prepossessed by no previous ideas about any philosophy, and had no theory of my own for which I sought any support in the *Gita*. A person whose mind is prepossessed by certain ideas reads the book with a prejudiced mind, for instance, when a Christian reads it he does not want to know what the *Gita* says but wants to find out if there are any principles in the *Gita* which he has already met with in the Bible, and if so the conclusion he rushes to is that the *Gita* was copied from the Bible. I have dealt with this topic in my book *Gita Rahasya* and I need hardly say much about it here, but what I want to emphasise is this, that when you want to read and understand a book, especially a great work like the *Gita*—you must approach it with an unprejudiced and unprepossessed mind. To do this, I know, is one of the most difficult things. Those who profess to do it may have a lurking thought or prejudice in their minds which vitiates the reading of the book to some extent. However I am describing to you the frame of mind one must get into if one wants to get at the truth and however difficult it be, it has to be done. The next thing one has to do is to take into consideration the time and the circumstances in which the book was written and the purposes for which the book was written. In short the book must not be read devoid of its context. This is especially true about a book like *Bhagavad Gita*. Various commentators have put as many interpretations on the book, and surely the writer or composer could not have written or composed the book for so many interpretations being put on it. He must have but one meaning and one purpose running through the book, and that I have tried to find out. I believe I have succeeded in it, because having no theory of mine for which I sought any support from the book so universally respected, I had no reason to twist the text to suit my theory. There has not been a commentator of the *Gita* who did not advocate a pet theory of his own and has not tried to support the same by showing that the *Bhagavad Gita* lent him support. The conclusion I have come to is that the *Gita* advocates the performance of action in this world even after the actor has achieved the highest union with the Supreme Deity by Gnana (knowledge) or Bhakti (Devotion). This action must be done to keep the world going by the right path of evolution which the Creator has destined the world to follow. In order that the action may not bind the actor it must be done with the aim of helping his purpose, and without any attachment to the coming result. This I hold is the lesson of the *Gita*. Gnanayoga there is, yes. Bhaktiyoga there is, yes. Who says not? But they are both subservient to the

Karmayoga preached in the *Gita*. If the *Gita* was preached to desponding Arjuna to make him ready for the fight—for the action—how can it be said that the ultimate lesson of the great book is Bhakti or Gnana alone? In fact there is blending of all these Yogas in the *Gita* as the air is not Oxygen or Hydrogen, or any other gas alone but a composition of all these in a certain proportion so in the *Gita* all these Yogas are blended into one.

I differ from almost all the commentators when I say that the *Gita* enjoins action even after the perfection in Gnana and Bhakti is attained and the deity is reached through these mediums. Now there is a fundamental unity underlying the Logos (Ishvara), man and world. The world is in existence because the Logos has willed it so. It is His Will that holds it together. Man strives to gain union with God: and when this union is achieved the individual Will merges in the mighty Universal Will. When this is achieved will the individual say: 'I shall do no action, and I shall not help the world'—the world which is because the Will with which he has sought union has willed it to be so? It does not stand to reason. It is not I who say so; the *Gita* says so. Shri Krishna himself says that there is nothing in all the three worlds that He need acquire, and *still* he acts. He acts because if He did not, the world's Will will be ruined. If man seeks unity with the Deity, he must necessarily seek unity with the interests of the world also, and work for it. If he does not, then the unity is not perfect, because there is union between two elements out of the three (man and Deity); and the third (the world) is left out. I have thus solved the question for myself and I hold that serving the world, and thus serving His Will, is the surest way of Salvation, and this way can be followed by remaining *in* the world and not going away from it.[39]

Tilak's Expanding Horizons

Tilak was, and is, a controversial figure and some of this controversy centres on the range and breadth of his sympathies. In this section his own statements, made from time to time, are cited to shed light on this issue.

1896

Tilak on the neglect of the sites associated with the life and death of Shivaji.

That the place of coronation and the tomb of that great man who gave the joy of independence to Maharashtra for two centuries should have been so utterly forgotten by the Marathas is indeed a misfortune.[40]

1899

Tilak on what unites Maharashtra with the rest of India.

The common factor in Indian Society is the feeling of *Hindutva* (Hinduness). I do not speak of Muslims and Christians at present because everywhere the majority of our society consists of Hindus. We say that the Hindus of the Punjab, Bengal, Maharashtra, Telangana (Andhra), and Dravida (Madras) are one, and the reason for this is only Hindu dharma. There may be different doctrines in the Hindu dharma, but certain principles can be found in common, and because of this alone a sort of feeling that we belong to one religion has remained among people speaking different languages in such a vast country. And this feeling of being one is still alive because in different provinces there are different institutions of the Hindu religion like temples, etc., or famous places of pilgrimage.[41]

1901

Tilak on what does not make them one nationally, even if ruled over as one.

Just as Pānini for some particular reason brought under one grammatical rule (*sutra*) the phrase, 'Dog, and Young Man, and Indra,' so too, it was only by accident within the mantle (*sutra*) of British rule that the Hindus, Muslims, Sikhs, Parsis, Bengalis, Madrasis, etc., all these people who once had different nationalities, have been brought together. Therefore, it is wrong to suppose from this that their nationality has become one.[42]

1904

Tilak speaking in terms of an Asian perspective.

The Chinese are the paper covering; and the Japanese are the nail joining the blades . . . . The Hindus are the blades in this fan.[43]

1905

If the coming of the British in India was a case of the flag following trade, then trade could also achieve the reverse in a global context.

We must establish national institutions, with various branches and try to learn about trade. These institutions must first consult with other business people and must try to learn how much produce is imported from England, and in what proportions; how to manufacture goods, and where in India to manufacture them; and if they cannot be manufactured here whether we can import them from non-English places. We must win the sympathy of traders in Germany, France, America, Japan, etc. We will also have to advise merchants here.[44]

1916

Tilak on a common Indian nationality which includes Hindus and Muslims.

That having regard to the fact that the great communities of India are the inheritors of ancient civilisations and have shown great capacity for Government and administration, and to progress in education and public spirit made by them during a century of British rule, and further having regard to the fact that the present system of Government does not satisfy the legitimate aspirations of the people and has become unsuited to the existing conditions and requirements, this Congress is of opinion . . . that a definite step should be taken towards self-government by granting the reforms contained in the scheme prepared by the All-India Congress Committee in concert with the Reform Committee appointed by the All-India Moslem League.[45]

Notes

1. D.V. Tahmankar, *Lokamanya Tilak: Father of Indian Unrest and Maker of Modern India* (London: John Murray, 1956), p. x.
2. Ibid., p. 9.
3. The following account is interesting and bears comparison with the one provided earlier when dealing with the life of Gokhale (ibid., p. 8). 'Bal Tilak was born into the clan or sect called Chitpavan, whose legendary origin recalls the Greek myth of the phoenix. This miraculous bird, when it grew old, burnt itself on a funeral pile and rose from the ashes with fresh youth and strength. In a similar way the Chitpavans are said to have been raised by the god Parashuram from the ashes of seven dead men. According to legend the ageing Parashuram, wanting to carry out some religious rites, could find no Brahmans to help in their performance. But as he wandered along the seashore, seven bodies were washed up in front of him, which he collected together and cremated, and then out of the glowing ashes brought the seven men back to life. These were the original Chitpavans (chita=ashes; pavan=pure) who did Parashuram a service by carrying out the religious rites for him. Legend says that the descendants of these men who were cremated and restored to life are the present-day Chitpavan Brahmans.

The legend also tells how Parashuram utterly destroyed the despotic and oppressive Kshatriyas (warrior lords) and brought back the people from the woods and jungles where they had taken refuge from the oppressors. Thus he restored peace and prosperity to the country. Many historians consider Parashuram to have been the founder of the first Aryan settlement in the Konkan on the West coast of the modern Bombay State, and to this day he is honoured as a family deity by many Brahman families in this part of India.'

4. Ibid., p. 10.
5. Ibid.
6. Ibid., p. 11.
7. Ibid., p. 13.
8. Ibid., p. 15.
9. Ibid., p. 17.
10. Ibid., p. 23.
11. Ibid., p. 37.
12. Ibid., p. 22.
13. Ibid., pp. 33–4.
14. Ibid., p. 33.
15. Ibid., pp. 48–9.
16. Ibid., p. 48.
17. Ibid.
18. Ibid., p. 47.
19. It has been proposed that these were suggested that the Olympian Games of the Greeks, ibid., p. 60.
20. Wolpert, pp. 68–71.
21. Tahmankar, p. 63.
22. Ibid., p. 49.
23. Wolpert, p. 89.
24. Stanley A. Wolpert, *Tilak and Gokhale* . . . (Berkeley and Los Angeles: University of California Press, 1962), p. 101.
25. Quoted in Tahmankar, p. 171.
26. Tahamankar, *Lokmanya Tilak* (London: John Murray, 1956), pp. 177–8.
27. Wolpert, p. 100, emphasis added.
28. Tahmankar, p. 196.
29. Ibid., p. 204.
30. Wolpert, p. 263.
31. See Tahamankar, p. 91.
32. Ibid., p. 287, note 1
33. Cited in ibid., pp. 18–21.
34. Ibid., p. 41.
35. Ibid., pp. 49–50.
36. Ibid., p. 183.
37. Richards, pp. 109–11.

38. *Bal Gangadhar Tilak: His Writings and Speeches* (third edition) (Madras: Ganesh & Co. 1922), pp. 35–41
39. Ibid., pp. 231–5.
40. Cited, Wolpert, p. 80.
41. Cited, ibid., p. 135.
42. Cited, ibid., p. 136.
43. Cited, ibid., p. 151.
44. Cited, ibid., p. 167.
45. Cited, ibid., p. 281.

Sree Narayana Guru
(1856–1928)

Life

The life of Sree Narayana Guru provides the background for presenting a slice of 'subaltern' contribution to modern Hindu thought, inasmuch as he hailed from Kerala (as compared to the metropolitan areas of British India) and from among the Ezhavas, who are considered low caste (*śūdra*)[1] to the point that in some of his biographies they are (erroneously) characterized as (former) untouchables.[2] It is particularly significant here that the Guru once asked rhetorically, 'What is the greatest need for India today?' and answered: 'Liberation from the competition among castes and religions,'[3] an insight which led him to epigrammatically summarize his teachings in the slogan: 'One Caste, One Religion, and One God for Man.'[4]

Sree Narayana Guru was born in Chempazhanthi, a hamlet near Trivandrum, on 26 August 1856 and given the name Narayana, which led to his being known by the diminutive 'Nanoo'.[5] During a robust childhood, he once consumed sweets offered at the domestic shrine, explaining it as an act surely pleasing to God.[6] He spent three years of his life (1876–79) as an acolyte of a Sanskrit scholar,[7] until a bout of dysentry compelled him to return home.[8] This should dispel the myth that classical Sanskrit (as distinguished from Vedic) learning is traditionally forbidden to the *śūdras*. Even the denial to Vedic learning was later challenged in a book entitled *Vedādhikāranirūpaṇa* by his associate Chattampi Swamikal, whom he befriended soon after becoming a recluse. He abandoned an arranged marriage which was probably never consummated[9]—a pattern which recurs so often in the lives of modern Hindu thinkers as to deserve special study. He had been married off to curb his ascetic tendencies, but the marriage resulted in intensifying his spiritual quest to the point of renunciation,[10] abetted by the death of his father.[11]

He now began leading a life devoted to austerities, during which he freely mingled with people of all castes, sects and religions and spent considerable time 'in a cave at Pillathadom [at] the crest of the mountain known as Maruthwamalai in the [now] Kanyakumari district of Tamil Nadu'.[12] He subsequently lived for a while at Aruvippuram near Trivandrum, where in 1888 he consecrated a temple to Śiva, in the following manner.

> At dead of night, Swami had a dip in the river. He came up after sometime with a *sivalingam* in his hands, and walked into the makeshift temple and stood there with his eyes closed in deep meditation, his hands holding the *sivalingam* to his chest, tears flowing down his cheeks, completely lost to the world. For full three hours, he stood motionless in that posture, while the entire crowd rent the midnight air with continuous cries of '*Om Namah Sivayah*', '*Om Namah Sivayah*' for full three hours. The whole lot of them seemed to have only one mind, one thought, one prayer, among them: 'Om Namah Sivayah'.[13]

This was unusual, to say the least, but when challenged on his right to do so by Brahmin priests, he explained : 'I've installed only a Ezhava Śiva.'[14] The centenary of this installation was celebrated in 1988.[15]

Sree Narayana Guru soon acquired a following and composed the *Atmopeśaśatam*, an original work on Advaita philosophy, in 1897.[16] In 1904 he settled down at Sivagiri and it remained the centre of his activities until he died in 1928. During this period he was visited by Rabindranath Tagore, who paid him a handsome tribute,[17] and by Mahatma Gandhi in the course of his drive against untouchability. Parts of his conversation with Mahatma Gandhi are excerpted later. During this period, he also visited Ramana Maharshi whom he celebrated as a *jīvanmukta* (a person who achieves premortem liberation).[18] This interaction among the holy men of India during the Independence movement makes one wonder whether it also involved a celestial conspiracy of sorts.

It is striking that Sree Narayana Guru, unlike other leaders of modern Hinduism, was actively engaged in temple construction. During a phase in his life not only did Sree Narayana Guru promote it,[19] he even went to the extent of demolishing and rededicating shrines, devoted to the worship of certain goddesses, to Śiva.[20] This is highly unusual in modern Hinduism. Temple building in general is said to have contributed to raising Ezhava self-esteem.[21] He, however, gradually so enlarged the concept of the temple that it became a centre of spiritual and educational activity in general.[22]

It was not always smooth going. On one occasion a rift developed among his followers on the question of image-worship, leading him to install a mirror with the sacred syllable *aum* etched on it.[23] In another less edifying instance, two contending groups of Ezhavas united against him in excluding the untouchables from the temple.[24]

Sree Narayana Guru consistently worked for the elimination of caste discrimination and caste distinctions and encouraged the all-round development of all communities, as vouched for by such aphorisms as 'educate to be free', 'organise to be strong' and 'thrive through industry'.[25]

Sree Narayana Guru died on 20 September 1928. Among the last verses recited to him was the following:

> Into the sea of Thy Glory profound
> Let us all plunge,
> And flourish ever,
> Flourish, in happiness flourish.

It was from one of his own compositions.[26]

Narayana Guru and Mahatma Gandhi: A Conversation on Untouchability

Mahatma Gandhi initiated a major Satyāgraha to affirm the right of untouchables to enter Hindu temples in 1924 at Vaikom, as a result of which 'Vaikom, of which until then hardly anyone outside Travancore had heard, suddenly leapt to fame'.[27] In the course of this celebrated and ultimately successful Satyāgraha, Mahatma Gandhi visited Sree Narayana Guru at Sivagiri. The following segment from their conversation might interest the reader.

GANDHI: Has Swamiji come across any injunction in the Hindu scriptures in favour of untouchability?

GURU: None.

GANDHI: Has Swamiji any reservations about the Satyagraha against untouchability at Vaikom?

GURU: No, none at all.

GANDHI: Does Swamiji desire anything else to be added to that movement or something deleted?

GURU: I understand it turns out well. No change is called for.

GANDHI: Besides removing untouchability, what else should be done to improve the lot of the depressed sections?

GURU: They should be educated. Also they should earn enough for their needs. I don't think inter-caste marriage and inter-dining are to be done immediately. Give them equal opportunities for betterment— along with everyone else.

GANDHI: Some consider non-violent satyagraha of no use; that force is to be used, for wresting these rights. What is Swamiji's view?

GURU: I don't consider force desirable.

GANDHI: Do the codes of Hinduism recommend force?

GURU: In the Puranas force seems to be the prerogative of kings. They wielded it too. But, for the common people, use of force is improper.

GANDHI: There is a view that people should change their religion, that it is the effective means to be free. Does Swamiji approve of this line of thinking?

GURU: We find people, who got converted, enjoying more freedom. As such we cannot blame those who hold such a view.

GANDHI: Does Swamiji think that the Hindu faith is adequate for one's spiritual salvation?

GURU: Other religions, too, show the paths to salvation.

GANDHI: Let alone other religions for the time being. Is Hinduism helpful enough to gain salvation?

GURU: Of course. Hinduism affords avenues of spiritual freedom. But people hanker more after worldly freedom.

GANDHI: That's true as far as disabilities arising from untouchability etc. are concerned. But does Swamiji feel that conversion is a must for spiritual freedom?

GURU: No. Conversion is not necessary for spiritual freedom.

GANDHI: We have been striving for material freedom. Would it prove futile?

GURU: No. Certainly not. It'll never be futile. But Mahatmaji may have to be born again to get it in its fullness. The problem is so complex.

GANDHI: (Laughing) I do hope it'll be realised in my life-time itself. . . . Untouchability is practised among the depressed classes also . . . . Are all people allowed entry in Swamiji's temples?

GURU: Yes. All are allowed. At Sivagiri, Pulaya and Pariah children live and study along with other children and they worship and pray together.

GANDHI: That's heartening news indeed.[28]

Cow Protection

The Hindus tend to look upon the cow as the foster-mother of humanity, which therefore evokes great concern in most of them. Both Dayānanda Sarasvatī and Mahatma Gandhi were advocates of cow protection. The following exchange suggests that Sree Narayana Guru's sentiments may also have lain in the same direction.

DEVOTEE: We drink the milk of the goat and cow. Why not eat their meat also? Is it harmful?

GURU: What harm? (He queried with a mischievous smile) Is your mother alive?

DEVOTEE: No, she is no more.

GURU: Did you bury her or eat her?[29]

On Conversion

The following two conversations of Sree Narayana Guru on the topic of conversion will perhaps resonate with most modern Hindus. The first one commences with his asking a European missionary his age:

PRIEST: Thirty years.

GURU: For your information, I became a Christian before you were born. Now say what you would like me to believe afresh.

PRIEST: You must believe that Jesus was born to redeem humanity from sin.

GURU: In that case, with Christ's birth, all sins have been washed away. And so everybody has been redeemed. Is it not so?

PRIEST: Yes.

GURU: As you are already free of sin, does it make any difference, whether you have faith or not or whether you are a Christian or not?

PRIEST: That's not right: the sins of those not baptised in Christ's name have not been washed away.

GURU: You mean to say only some were saved by Christ's birth?

PRIEST: No. Everyone was saved. That is the basic thing.

GURU: None left out?

PRIEST: That is it.

GURU: If that is so everybody has already been saved, and no need any more for faith.

PRIEST: That is not right. Salvation comes only to the faithful.

GURU: Everyone has not been saved by Christ's birth? Non-believers are excluded?[30]

II

Sahodaran Ayyappan was in favour of the wholesale conversion of Ezhavas to Buddhism to escape caste disabilities. His meeting with Sree Narayana Guru on this topic unfolded as follows:

GURU: Ayyappan, Doctor (Dr Palpu) talks about conversion.

AYYAPPAN: Some people are inclined to do so.

GURU: Is it not better for the individual to change? Well, will it not lead to change in the creed itself? How could they conceive of any other kind of change?

AYYAPPAN: Buddhism affords more opportunities for advancement.

GURU: Are all Buddhists good men? I understand that among them are many who eat fish, drink and practise inequality.

AYYAPPAN: It has to be admitted that among Buddhists nowadays good men are too few.

GURU: Is that so? I too came across that sad state. Buddhist monks are expected to subsist on whatever is given to them. So, will they not slowly begin relishing the taste of meat? People would choose to give them what they themselves liked best. Is this proper?

AYYAPPAN: Buddhism also has been corrupted. Still Lord Buddha's teachings are the best means for people to better themselves.

GURU: Aren't the teachings of Christ good? The teachings of Muhammad Nabi are equally good. But are all their followers good? The crux of the problem is this: whatever be one's religion, an individual should go on striving to improve himself. Otherwise he would slide down. Pure should be his deeds. So also thoughts and words. There should be no lapse with regard to these essentials. Mind should be pure that it tolerates not any compromise on these counts. That is the state of Jeevan Mukta (released soul).

AYYAPPAN: Buddhists call it Nirvana.

GURU: May be. Caste has established its sway amongst men. Sankaracharya himself has erred in this regard. Vyasa who wrote Bhagavad

Gita and Brahma Sutra mentions the four varnas in two places differently. Caste has to be done away with. Otherwise there will be no escape. All human beings belong to the same community. To re-establish that true state of existence, caste has to be done away with. What are the views of Kumaran Asan?[31]

AYYAPPAN: Asan thinks it would be a public insult to Swami, to change religion without getting Swami's consent.

GURU: Well, is it so?

AYYAPPAN: Asan says Swami's opinion should be sought first.

GURU: Is not my view known so far? Do you know my view?

AYYAPPAN: I know. Swami has no antipathy towards any religion. I know that Swami desires human beings to live as one integrated group whatever be the variations in religion, dress or language.

GURU: That's what I wish. Religion is an opinion. Whatever be the differences in religion, men can live together. Caste differentiation ought not to exist. Such a state of affairs can be established. I am sure of that. Take for example Sathyavrathan. He has no caste, no prejudice, has he?

AYYAPPAN: No, not a trace of it.

GURU: Probably it is difficult to reach that level. Even to Lord Buddha, in this matter of caste: I'm not sure. Satyavrathan is a man who does not discriminate. All can become like him. What is wrong with Hinduism? Aryasamajists and Brahmasamajists are Hindus. They don't observe caste.

AYYAPPAN: They are not Hindus. They call themselves Hindus just to feel strong. Aryasamajists swear by the Vedas. They acknowledge their authority after giving a new interpretation to them.

GURU: Is that so?

AYYAPPAN: Some of them pay homage to Swami hoping that Thiyas[32] will soon join their fold.

GURU: (Smiling) That is good. At least they know how to respect people!

AYYAPPAN: Some ask: why change religion? Isn't Sree Narayana Dharma good enough for us? Still, they are not happy when told to take Narayana Guru's opinion.

GURU: Let them have any religion they like. One must have the liberty to believe in the religion of one's choice.

AYYAPPAN: This was Swami's earlier view.

GURU: I still stick to it. When the need to change religion is genuinely felt, you should certainly do so. The freedom for it should be yours. Religion to each is different. Son may not like his father's faith. There should be freedom of faith for all. That's my view. Do you all feel so?

AYYAPPAN: Yes, we do. Recently in a registered deed, I entered Buddhism as my religion.

GURU: (Smiling) You didn't note your caste, did you? Well, that was good. Caste shouldn't be mentioned anywhere. Men should live together as of one caste. This view should get universal approval. Well, what defects do the advocates of conversion see in Hinduism?

A DISCIPLE: They point out that Hindu religious writing is rotten. For instance, the Vedas and the Gita sponsor animal sacrifice, worship of multiple gods and the caste system.

GURU: The Vedas may be doing that. But in them there are also sublime concepts. Those who follow a religion which has in its literature such wonderful concepts—what is objectionable is the way they conduct themselves, their way of life. What can the Vedas do if men are depraved? Men should reform themselves. They should cultivate purity of thought, word and deed. Whatever be one's spiritual creed, one should essentially be noble. That's how I view it.[33]

One Caste, One Religion and One God for Man

This statement epitomizes the teachings of Sree Narayana Guru. The following elaboration of this compact statement in the form of a conversation reconstructed by C.V. Kunjuraman, a disciple of the Guru, in which the disciple speaks in the first person, goes a long way towards shedding light on it.

'One religion'—An Elucidation

The discourse between Sree Narayana Guru Swami Thrippadangal and myself detailed below did not take place exactly as given here. But there is nothing in it extraneous to the discussions on religion we had on diverse occasions, during which I had the privilege of hearing his views and also of voicing my reactions to them. The points which surfaced in my talks have been organized and arranged according to the themes involved. Its end-product is what is given here. After writing down in this manner, I myself read it out first of all to Swami Bodhanandan and then to the conclave of monks which met at

Sivagiri recently. Finally through Swami Sathiavrathan this was read out to Swami Thrippadangal himself and is now published with his approval. Some of Swami Thrippadangal's views on these questions have been voiced by Swami Sathiavrathan in his welcome address to the All Religions Conference at Alwaye. Points made explicit in that speech are not repeated here.

Discourse

I: Your Holiness's inspired exhortation, 'One caste, One religion and One God for Man' is held aloft by your disciples as their watchword and chief slogan. Still a few doubt whether it is a valid piece of advice; certain others decry it. Even Mahatma Gandhi, during his visit to the Ashram, expressed his dissent. Not only that. People interpret this slogan differently. After listening to many of these, Kumaran Asan prayed, 'Save us from these interpreters.' He did not however attempt a correct explanation himself. Your Holiness may kindly give an exact elucidation. Even if we, disciples, explain reasonably, people won't be pleased.

SWAMI: Let me see how Kunjuraman interprets it.

I: 'One caste for man'—its meaning is easy to grasp.

> Humanness marks out the human kind
> As bovinity proclaims cowness.

That is how Your Holiness had clinched it. Being human, all men belong to the same caste. This conclusion is unacceptable to none. About this, therefore, there is no difference of opinion. Again 'One God for Man'. Those who believe in God cannot disagree. 'One Religion'—it's about this that most people are sceptical. Your Holiness had declared that

Not knowing that the essence

> Of religions different is the same,
> And sponsoring assumptions several,
> Like the blind, the ignorant go astray.

But this does not seem to be enough to remove doubts regarding this idea. That's why a further clarification is called for.

SWAMI: 'The essence of religions different is the same'—does anyone deny that?

I: It may be that there is dissent about that also. The essence of theistic and atheistic religions is not the same.

SWAMI: The plethora of meanings of the word 'religion' is the cause of this mistake. Atheism is only the 'opinion', 'point of view' put forward by certain individuals. It has never been the religion of an organised society.

I: Some people consider Buddhism as an atheistic religion.

SWAMI: Is it justified? Aren't you all champions of Buddhism?

I: What I feel about this charge against Buddhism is this. It is the accusation of those who don't know what is real faith in God. Such people do not know what they believe in. They do not understand what is faith or who is it that they have faith in.

SWAMI: Buddhism could not possibly have been an atheistic religion. Impossible that such a huge mass of humanity believed for so long a period in an exclusively atheistic creed . . . . On the basis of your present convictions, has Kunjuraman assessed yourself whether a theist or an atheist?

I: Yes. My firm conviction is that I am a theist.

SWAMI: It is heard that you propagate atheism.

I: Not surprising that such is the report on me. I have crossed swords with both the atheists who argued against the theists and the theists who contended with the atheists.

SWAMI: Don't argue for argument's sake. It is right to argue to clear doubts and to elucidate concepts . . . . Do the theistic religions differ only in external details? Are they different intrinsically?

I: When certain aspects are taken into account, it is to be admitted that there is divergence in their internal core also.

SWAMI: Well, what is the difference?

I: Certain religions hold that this Universe was made by the Creator. Others aver, as the evolutionists claim that the five elements like sky, fire, air arose out of Brahman and as a result of their interaction and relativity, in course of time, the Universe came into being. Likewise it is said that the Soul was made by the Creator from nothing. Or it is a part of the Universal Soul or even Itself. There is rebirth and there is not. Belief in Karma is right and not justified. Thus, as regards basic postulates, there is an ocean of difference!

SWAMI: Though divergent in concepts, is there basic dichotomy in the goal of these different religions?

I: It may be said that there is difference in that also. Certain religions hold the reaching of Heaven as the final goal. Others aim at Salvation which is superior to Heaven.

SWAMI: Is it not quite natural that one who has managed to reach Heaven sets his heart on a higher state of existence?

I: He should.

SWAMI: He will. Certainly he will. The religion which speaks of Salvation does not deny the existence of Heaven. From this earth, it is supposed, seven worlds have to be ascended. Afterwards the steps to *moksha* or Salvation are *Salokya, Sameepya, Sarupya* and *Sayoojya*. To one who has reached any of these steps, don't you think, he would be desirous of the next higher step?

I: But all religions do not recognise these steps.

SWAMI: What of that? Does any religion sponsor descending instead of ascending?

I: No, none.

SWAMI: The goal of all religions is the same. Once the rivers reach the ocean, is there difference like the shallow and the deep? Religion has the role of creating in human souls the trend to ascend. Once that is there, they themselves will seek and find the ultimate Truth. Religions are only the guides to help one seek rightly. To those who have attained the Supreme, religion is not at all authority; they themselves are authority to religion. Did Lord Buddha preach the path to Nirvana after studying Buddhism? He sought and found the way to Salvation and then preached. It subsequently became Buddhism. Did Buddhism do any good to Lord Buddha?

I: No.

SWAMI: Christ too did not gain anything from Christianity. The same could be said of other religions also. However, Buddhists gained through Buddhism and Christians too by Christianity. Likewise, all religions are of use to those who follow them.

I: But Hindus claim otherwise.

SWAMI: Well, what do they say?

I: They swear by the Vedas. According to them, Vedas are suprahuman creations. They emanated from the lips of Brahma. Hence there could be no authority superior to the Vedas. That's how they contend.

SWAMI: What do Christians claim about their Ten Commandments? That too emanated from God?

I: Yes. That's how they think about it.

SWAMI: Jehova knew only Hebrew and Brahma was conversant with Vedic Sanskrit alone? Is it so? When it is said that Vedas are suprahuman, what is to be understood is this—we do not know who wrote them—all these Vedic Hymns; or it may be that the concepts emerging out of the Vedas are beyond human inventiveness.

I: Lord Buddha has denied the authority of the Vedas. *Mundakopanished* also points out that the philosophy in the Vedas is inferior.

SWAMI: Don't take any of them as the sole authority. All of them may be made handy tools in the search for Truth. This advice, however, is valid only for those with an inquiring mind, with thirst for knowledge. To the common people, the text which is basic to the religion they believe in, should remain as authority.

I: If such basic texts have pieces of advice which go contrary to righteousness, it happens that common people come to believe in such advice.

SWAMI: Teachers of religion should take care that this did not happen. Swami Dayananda Saraswathi accepts the authority of the Vedas. Does he not, however, discard as spurious those portions which are absurd? That is what all teachers of religion ought to do.

I: Texts of religions should be studied with discrimination. Shall I take it as your Holiness's advice? Am I right?

SWAMI: Yes, that's the gist of my message. We have declared so at the time of the All Religions Conference at Alwaye. Quarrels between nations and peoples end when one of them overcomes the other. Fighting between religions will have no end. One religion cannot win over another. If this war of religions should end, with self-control all have to learn about all religions. Then it will become clear that, as far as basic tenets are concerned, there are no substantial differences. The religion which thus evolves is the 'One religion' that we advocate.

I: There is yet another doubt.

SWAMI: Well. What is that?

I: Interest in conversion is now on the increase in our community. Some say Buddhism is good, others prefer Christianity. Yet others say Aryasamaj is the right thing. Thus, this enthusiasm manifests in different forms. And there are those who say conversion is not necessary.

SWAMI: Religion has two faces—internal and external; which of these is sought to be changed? If enthusiasm is for the external, it is not change of religion, only change in the outward manifestations of it. Change in the internal sense, no doubt, slowly manifests itself, among those who think. It takes place naturally with the increase in understanding; none can order it. One who is identified as follower of a religion known by the specialised nomenclature of Hinduism or Christianity realises that he has lost faith in his then he should give it up. To carry on with a religion you have no faith in is cowardice as well as hypocrisy. Change of religion will do him good: it will also be good for the religion he has lost faith in. Increase in the number of non-believers is not in the interests of a religion.

I: Those who choose to continue as Hindus also say that Hinduism, as it exists to-day, is not good.

SWAMI: In that case what they say is that not only Hindus need change but also Hinduism. There is no such religion as Hinduism. Foreigners referred to the inhabitants of Hindustan as Hindus. If the assumption is that the religion of those who live in Hindustan is Hinduism, then the religion of Christians and Muslims living in Hindustan is also Hinduism. None says so nor agrees with it. Hinduism is the general name for those religions, except Christianity and Islam of foreign origin, which took shape in Hindustan itself. That is why some claim that Buddhism and Jainism etc are also part of Hinduism. If it is not illogical to call so many distinctly different religions like the Vedic, Puranic, Sankya, Vaiseshika, Meemamsaka, Dvaita, Advaita, Visishtadvaita, Saiva, Vaishnva etc by the common generic name of Hinduism, why attribute lack of logic in designating all the religions of the world, which, with slight differences arising from place and time, were taught for the salvation of all mankind by diverse teachers, by the appellation 'One Religion' with a single unambiguous goal?

I: Disputes engendered by wrong understanding arise not only among Hindus, but also among non-Hindus. Bringing under the umbrella of Christianity the teachings of Moses and Solomon who lived before Christ and those of St. Paul who came after him, is what Christians have done.

SWAMI: Adherents of all religions have done more or less the same thing. If the religious speculations of many are put under a particular teacher's name and be called a religion, why not blend so many religions sponsored by different teachers and designate it by the general nomenclature of a single religion of One religion or Human Religion or Dharma of Humanity? If to do so is illogical and absurd, this illogicality and absurdity are part and parcel of all the extant religions. It is surprising that those who wax eloquent about unity in diversity and diversity in unity of his own religion are incapable of taking humanity's religion as a single unit and observe its unity in diversity and diversity in unity. When Mahatmaji visited this place, in his address he pointed out a tree in the precincts of the Ashram and observed how its branches and leaves differed widely from each other: like so, individuals among the species also differ. As long as this difference exists, humanity's religions too are bound to differ. What Mahatmaji said is true. But if the line is followed logically it has to be admitted that each individual is bound to have his own brand of religion. If that is so, Rama who is a Hindu, and Krishna who is also a Hindu, do not believe in the same religion. It will lead to 20 crores of Hindus having 20 crores of religion. Though that is the fact, they are deemed members of the same religion, as there are certain common factors in the religious faith of these 20 crores. Like that, since the creeds of all religions have certain common elements, all human beings belong to the same religion. No religion can survive unless it has a hard core of certain eternal truths, Dharma. Islam gives primacy to brotherhood and Christianity to Love. But ignorant of the fact that Brotherhood is rooted in Love and Love is built on Brotherhood, claims are made that Brotherhood is superior or Love is all in all. Is it not a ridiculous dispute? Eternal values are of equal significance. Owning to factors in time and place, it becomes necessary to give priority to one or the other. In a time and place where violence is rampant, world teachers bestow primacy to non-violence over other dharmas. During Lord Buddha's times, killing was widespread. Consequently he allotted priority to the principle of non-killing. May be in Arabia, during Muhammad

Nabi's times, it was incumbent to give pride of place to Brotherhood. Hence in his religion the preeminence of brotherhood. What is India's need today? Deliverance from the conflicts between castes and religions. Let us all study and understand all religions with open minds and equal attention and try to lovingly give each other the wisdom so gained. Thus would we realise that conflict was due not to religion but to pride. Then the enthusiasm for conversion also will disappear.

I: In that case, those who believe in Hinduism, Buddhism, Christianity and Islam would be admitted into the circle of Your Holiness's disciples?

SWAMI: We have no objection to that.

I: I have more faith in and admiration for Buddhism than other religions.

SWAMI: That doesn't mean that you hate other religions?

I: Not at all.

SWAMI: Have you read Buddhist scriptures?

I: Read some in translation.

SWAMI: Translations too help to understand.

I: I've resolved to read them in the original.

SWAMI: Why is it that you are so fascinated by Buddhism?

I: In these hard times of ours, it is impossible not to feel drawn towards the teachings of Lord Buddha. To save people from caste and religious squabbles, Buddhism, I believe strongly, is better qualified than the other religions.

SWAMI: Do you intend joining our Order of Monks?

I: I desire to, but only if it is sanyasa of the Buddhist style.

SWAMI: Haven't we declared at Alwaye that Sanyasa of the Buddhist model was also adequate?

I: The Buddhist Order does not admit asthmatics into their sect.

SWAMI: Do they give sanyasa to those with nervous disorders?

I: I don't know.

SWAMI: All religious dispensations retain certain interesting oddities.

I: I've vowed to accept sanyasa only from your Holiness's hand: from none else.[34]

Notes

1. K. Sreenivasan, *Sree Narayana Guru* (Trivandrum: Jayasree Publications, 1989), pp. 13–14.
2. V.T. Samuel, *One Caste One Religion One God: A Study of Sree Narayana Guru* (New Delhi: Sterling Publishers, 1977), passim.

3. Sreenivasan, p. ix.
4. Ibid., p. 3.
5. Ibid., p. 13.
6. Ibid., p. 15.
7. Ibid., p. 19.
8. Ibid., p. 18.
9. Ibid., p. 19.
10. This motif recurs in the life of several saints of modern Hinduism.
11. Sreenivasan, p. xi.
12. Ibid., p. 21.
13. Murkoth Kunhappa as cited in K. Sreenivasan.
14. Ibid., p. 44, with Ezhave changed to Ezhava.
15. Ibid., p. 45.
16. See Nataraja Guru, tr., *One Hundred Verses on Self-Instruction by Narayana Guru* (Varkala, Kerala: Gurukula Publishing House, 1969).
17. Sreenivasan, pp. 4–5.
18. Ibid., p. 31.
19. Ibid., chapter 7.
20. Ibid., pp. 54–5.
21. Ibid., p. 56. He is said to have established over a hundred temples (ibid., p. 59).
22. Ibid., p. 65.
23. Ibid., p. 61.
24. Ibid., pp. 100–1.
25. Ibid., p. 93.
26. Ibid., pp. 173, 138.
27. M.K. Gandhi, *The Removal of Untouchability* (Ahmedabad: Navajivan Publishing House, 1954), p. 105.
28. Sreenivasan, pp. 108–9.
29. Ibid., p. 121.
30. Ibid., pp. 113–14.
31. Another person who favoured Buddhism, ibid., p. 114.
32. Another name for Ezhavas, ibid., p. 114.
33. Ibid., pp. 115–18.
34. Ibid., pp. 127–36.

Rabindranath Tagore
(1861–1941)

Life

Rabindranath Tagore belonged to a Brahmin family, which could 'claim descent from five orthodox Brahmins said to have been invited into Bengal by a Hindu king [Ballala Sen] after he had taken Bengal from a Buddhist ruler possibly around AD 1000'.[1] They belonged to the sub-caste known as Pirali, or Pir Ali, Brahmins, so-called as the result of an incident which occurred during the period of Muslim rule over Bengal, which superseded the Hindu.

It all began with a joke, some time in the fifteenth century when the Delhi Sultanate controlled Bengal, before the rise of the Mughals. During Ramadan, when Muslims fast, two brothers, Brahmins, were sitting in the court of Mohammed Tahir Pir Ali, the vizier of the governor of Jessore. (Jessore lies roughly half-way between Calcutta and Dhaka, and is now in Bangladesh.) Pir Ali, though a Muslim had been born a Brahmin; he had converted to Islam in order to further his career and because he was in love with a Muslim girl. As they talked, a gardener appeared with a large lemon, freshly plucked. When Pir Ali held it to his nose and exclaimed, 'How fragrant!', one of the Brahmin brothers remarked that Pir Ali had violated his fast—for smelling is half eating according to Hindu scriptures, which Pir Ali had once obeyed. The taunt provoked Pir Ali to get his revenge. He invited the brothers to a meal, ensured that they smelt beef being cooked, and forced them to taste it. Subsequently converted to Islam, the former Brahmins were given land near Jessore.

Their relatives were still Hindus, however, and deemed by Hindu society to be polluted. From one of them came the ancestors of the Tagores. Known from then on as 'Pirali' Brahmins, they were unmarriageable by orthodox Hindus. This ostracism was so serious that, around 1902, an orthodox Brahmin who ate with a Pirali Brahmin had to pay 50,000 rupees—a king's ransom—for readmission to caste; and in 1852, when the nephew of a leading Brahmin married a cousin of Rabindranath Tagore, the boy was expelled from his family.[2]

A split occurred in the family during this period of British rule, which superseded Muslim rule over Bengal, in the eighteenth century.

Some time after Nilmoni's [the great-great-grandfather of Rabindranath] return to Calcutta, the family developed a rift. The cause was money. Around 1784 (the year before Warren Hastings left Bengal), Nilmoni walked out of the family house at Pathuriaghat accompanied by his three sons and a daughter, holding in one hand, so they say, the *shalagram* or sacred image of his household deity, and in the other hand a bag containing one lakh (100,000) rupees. On a plot of land at Jorasanko, a little away from the river, he began to build the house where Rabindranath would be born three quarters of a century later. From then on, especially during the high noon of Empire in India after 1857, the two branches of the Tagores at Pathuriaghat and Jorasanko would have little to do with each other.[3]

Rabindranath's grandfather, Dwarkanath Tagore (1794–1846), took the tide of rising British presence at the flood and did so well that when 'he travelled to Europe in 1843 (in his own steamer), his reputation for munificence increased still further, and he became known as "Prince" Dwarkanath Tagore, friend of both Queen Victoria and King Louis-Philippe. At the end of one party in Paris the "Prince" draped a fine Indian shawl over the shoulders of every lady present as she left the room.'[4] He also kept a diary during his visit (since lost),[5] in which among other things he also jotted down scandals involving Christian clerics. One wonders if his close friendship with Raja Rammohun Roy, who regularly jousted with missionaries and whom he enthusiastically supported, has anything to do with it. In fact, like the wives of Raja Rammohun Roy, his wife also in 'her later years shunned all contact with her husband because of his intercourse with Europeans'.[6] She died fairly young—'from a chill caught through excessive bathing, apparently'.[7]

Dwarkanath's eldest son, Devendranath Tagore (1817–1905), 'to the dismay of Dwarkanath, largely lost interest in the family firm in 1838 at the age of twenty-one. Inspired by the example of Dwarkanath's friend Rammohun Roy, Debendranath revived the Brahmo Samaj and began a search for true religion all over northern India. Upon Dwarkanath's death (in London in 1846), his son scandalised the rest of the family by refusing to perform the usual idolatrous funeral rituals.'[8]

If Rabindranath only makes an entry into the account now, it is because he cannot be isolated from his background. Three of his own brothers 'were remarkable men, even when compared with Rabindranath, who was the youngest'.[9] Thus a life of wealth and cultural distinction came naturally to Rabindranath, which may account for his aesthetic approach to Hinduism, often contrasted with Gandhi's more ascetic approach.[10] Moreover, while Gandhi wore his religion on his chest, Tagore wore it as a vest.

Biographers note an attempt, on the part of Rabindranath, to distance himself from his grandfather.[11] That attitude, however, he does not extend to his father, whom he accompanied on his journey through north India with evident relish: 'My father had marked his favourite verses in his copy of the *Bhagavad Gita*. He asked me to copy these out for him, with their translation. At home I had been a boy of no account, but here, when these important functions were entrusted to me, I felt the glory of the situation.'[12]

Tagore's *Reminiscences* dwell on his early acquaintance with the stories of the *Rāmāyaṇa* and the *Mahābhārata*,[13] noting at one point when introduced to a Punjabi that 'We had the same reverence for the whole Punjabi nation as we had for Bhima and Arjuna of the *Mahābhārata*. They were warriors, and if they had sometimes lost the fight, that was clearly the enemy's fault.'[14] He recalls undergoing the thread ceremony,[15] and repeating the Gāyatrī *mantra*.[16] The reaction of the young Tagore in the company of his father to the Golden Temple is worth citing:

> The Golden Temple of Amritsar comes back to me like a dream. On many a morning I accompanied my father to this *gurudarbar* of the Sikhs in the middle of the lake. There the sacred chanting continually resounds. My father, seated amidst the throng of worshippers, would sometimes add his voice to the hymn of praise and, finding a stranger joining in their devotions they would welcome him most cordially, and we would return loaded with sanctified offerings of sugar crystals and other sweets . . . .
>
> When evening fell, my father would sit out on the verandah facing the garden. He would summon me to sing to him. I can see the moon risen; its beams, passing through the trees, falling on the verandah floor; and I am singing in raga Behag:
>
> O Companion in the darkest passage of life. . .
>
> My father with bowed head and clasped hands listens intently. I recall the evening scene quite clearly.[17]

Tagore was to write later that the period of his life 'from fifteen or sixteen to twenty-two or twenty-three, was one of utter disarray'.[18] One is led to wonder about the extent to which the ferment in the intelligentsia in Bengal at the time contributed to this sense of confusion. According to him, at the time the 'educated men fell into two classes':

One class would always thrust itself forward with unprovoked argument to cut all belief in God to pieces. Like the hunter whose hands itch to kill a living creature as soon as he spies it on a tree, these people, whenever they learn of a harmless belief lurking in fancied security, feel stirred to sally forth and demolish it. We had a tutor for a short time for whom this was a pet diversion. I was only a boy, but I could not escape his onslaughts. His attainments were not of any account, neither were his opinions the result of any enthusiastic search for truth, being gathered mostly from others' lips. But though I fought him with all my strength, I was no match and I suffered many a bitter defeat. Sometimes I felt so mortified I wanted almost to cry.

The second class consisted not of believers but religious epicureans, who found comfort and solace in gathering together and steeping themselves in pleasing sights, sounds and scents galore, under the garb of religious ceremonial; they luxuriated in the paraphernalia of worship. In neither of these classes were doubt or denial the outcome of the travail of their quest.

Though such religious aberrations pained me, I do not say I was entirely uninfluenced by them. With the intellectual impudence of youth I revolted. The religious services held in our family I would have nothing to do with, because I did not accept them. I busied myself in fanning a flame with the bellows of my emotions. This was only fire worship, the giving of oblations to increase the flame—with no other aim. And because my efforts had no purpose in mind they had no limit, always reaching beyond any prescription.

In religion and in my emotional life I felt no need for any underlying truth; excitement was everything. It brings to mind some lines by a poet of that time:

> My heart is mine
> I have sold it to none,
> Be it tattered and torn and worn away,
> My heart is mine.

In truth the heart need not worry itself so, for nothing compels it to wear itself to tatters. Sorrow is not truly to be coveted, but taken in isolation from life sorrow's poignancy may appear pleasurable. Our poets have often made much of this forgetting the god they intended to worship. This is a childishness our country has not yet rid itself of. So today we often fail to see the truth of religion and indulge instead in aesthetic gratification. Equally, much of our patriotism is not genuine service of the motherland, but simply emotional gratification.[19]

By the time Tagore was twenty-seven, his humanism was being tested by both Christianity and Hinduism. This is revealed by the poem *Dharma Prachar* (Mission-Work).

This poem was based on a reported incident in 1888 in which some Bengalis, Hindu revivalists, launched a cowardly assault on a Salvation Army preacher. At the time such British preachers dressed as sannyasis (Hindu ascetics) and adopted Indian standards of life. Ironically, by doing so, they both attracted the ire of 'true Aryans' (i.e. Hindu fundamentalists who saw themselves as descendants of the Aryan invaders of ancient India), and deprived themselves of the protection afforded by European dress. Until the policy changed, many lives were needlessly sacrificed in these attacks. Although Tagore had little sympathy with Christian missionaries as a group, he had not a grain of sympathy for their Hindu assailants.[20]

Herein lie the roots of a problem which persists to this day.[21]

Rabindranath was soon drawn into the vortex of nationalism, which began to gather force in the first decade of the twentieth century, and brought the issue of race relations to the fore. In 1904 he summarized the story of his novel-to-come, *Gora*, for a European guest. Its 'basic situation concerns a fair-faced boy (*gora* means fair-faced), brought up as an orthodox Hindu, who rejects the Brahmo Samaj but falls in love with a Brahmo girl; caught between worlds, he finally learns that he is not a Hindu at all but an adopted son whose real father was an Irishman killed in the Mutiny of 1857 and whose real mother died in childbirth.'[22]

The European guest he summarized the story for was none other than Sister Nivedita.

She was a Hindu convert, and Irishwoman, Margaret Noble, who took the name Sister Nivedita ('the dedicated') and worked with Swami Vivekananda, the disciple of Ramakrishna, in Calcutta. She was a ferocious champion of Hinduism, celebrated in her time both in India and in Britain. Tagore admired Sister Nivedita's devotion to India and her love for Indians, but found her narrow-minded. She, for her part, was angry with his story, telling him that he did wrong to Hindu women. Perhaps that was why he changed the ending when he published *Gora* in 1910.[23]

This novel 'at bottom *is* about the Indian predicament: whether modern India under the impact of the West, can be anything but an imitation of the West. The debate is alive today as it was in 1924 or in 1873.'[24]

Rabindranath's biographers characterize the phase of life from 1900 to 1905 as 'narrowly nationalistic'.[25] This was also a period filled with personal bereavement: he lost two close nephews in 1899 and 1902, his wife in 1902, his daughter Renuka in 1903, his father in 1905 and his youngest son Samindranath in 1907. The death rate in Bengal at the time was twice that in Britain and rising rather than falling as in Britain. Even so, Tagore was unlucky.[26]

In mid-1905 the Partition of Bengal caused a political storm. Tagore countered the Partition of Bengal by Lord Curzon by declaring it the Day of *Rakhibandhan* (The Tying of the *Rakhi*). 'On the way back from this celebration Rabindranath and his party saw ostlers at work in local stables. Rabindranath plunged in and tied the thread around their wrists; the rest of the party hung back, afraid of a row since the ostlers were Muslims. But nothing happened. After that the poet tied *Rakhis* even on the wrists of the mullahs in the main mosque on the Chitpur Road. They smiled.'[27] Was it an earnest of things to come? A poem of Tagore is today the National Anthem of the Islamic Republic of Bangladesh!

Tagore withdrew from the movement when it took on what for him was an excessively nationalistic character, as when a boycott of the British was organized. 'According to Tagore's son, who was a student in 1905, "the genius in him was fundamentally creative"—boycotts held no appeal',[28] either then or later in the 1920s when Gandhi organized them.

He withdrew into creative work. 'In the next few years . . . before his historic visit to the West, he produced some of his most famous fictional works: poetry (*Gitanjali*), a novel (*Gora*) and a play (*Dakghar*, translated as *The Post Office*). These years also saw the publication of his memoirs *Jibansmriti* (*My Reminiscences*), his wonderful letters to his niece written in the 1890s, *Chhinnapatra* (*Glimpses of Bengal*) and, not least, some further powerful essays.'[29]

The award of the Nobel Prize for Literature in 1913 for the English version of *Gitanjali* brought global recognition. From the point of view of modern Hindu thought these poems are revealing in their universalism. Nowhere is it more obvious than the way the book ends:

> Where the mind is without fear and the head is held high;
> Where knowledge is free;
> Where the world has not been broken up into fragments by narrow domestic walls;
> Where words come out from the depth of truth;
> Where tireless striving stretches its arms towards perfection;
> Where the clear stream of reason has not lost its way into the dreary desert sand of dead habit;
> Where the mind is led forward by thee into everwidening thought and action—
> Into that heaven of freedom, my Father, let my country awake.[30]

When the First World War was over by 1920, India found itself in the throes of a struggle against British imperialism, led by Mahatma Gandhi. By 1926 Tagore was writing to Romain Rolland: 'I can no longer hide it from myself that we'—he and Gandhi—'are radically different in our apprehension and pursuit of truth. Today to disagree with the Mahatma and yet to find rest in one's surroundings in India is not possible . . . .'[31] Small wonder that he soon embarked on a European tour. He returned by the end of the year, to leave again in 1927 for the Dutch East Indies. There, in Bali, something interesting happened.

> On Bali Rabindranath found himself in a car with a local chief and no interpreter. Unable to communicate, he looked out of the window at the luscious beauty of the island. Suddenly there was a glimpse of the ocean through a gap in the forest, and the chief uttered the word *samudra*—Sanskrit for 'sea'. Seeing that his eminent guest was both surprised and pleased, the chief went on to repeat the Sanskrit synonyms, following them with *sapta-samudra* (the seven seas), *sapta-parvata* (the seven mountains), *sapta-vana* (the seven forests) and *sapta-akasha* (the seven skies). Then he pointed to a hill and, having given the Sanskrit for 'hill', recited the names of mountains: Sumeru, Himalaya, Vindhya, Malaya, Rishyamukha. When they came to a river, he continued: Ganga, Yamuna, Narmada, Godaveri, Kaveri, Saraswati (all except the last being names of modern rivers in India).[32]

The incident reminded the international poet, as if he needed such reminding, that Hinduism too had been an international religion.

Then came a visit to the USA in 1929, which was cut short by his experience of racism. As he tried to enter USA from Canada,

> At the immigration office in Vancouver, a US official, aware of who he was, nevertheless kept him standing for half an hour and then asked him the stock questions: who had paid for his passage, had he been to jail, was he going to settle permanently in the USA? (A London paper claimed that Tagore was even asked if he could write.) After giving one lecture in Southern California, he abruptly cancelled his visit and sailed for Japan.[33]

In the meantime, as the nationalist movement had gained strength, Tagore's sentiments against it became more pronounced, resulting in serious disagreements with Gandhi. Reconciliation was achieved when the humanistic pole of Gandhian thought seemed to merge with the nationalistic in 1932, during the fast to death over the communal award and for the cause of the Untouchables. Here again, while he was physically present at the end of the first of the two fasts, he had reservations about the second.

> But of all the aspects of Tagore's life in the year or so following Gandhi's 1932 fast, the most fascinating was his reaction to Gandhi's second fast in May 1933. The first fast Tagore had faith in, albeit with a trembling heart; the second, which lasted twenty-one days (though not in prison),

he felt to be misguided. He supported it only under great duress. Most of those around Gandhi, including his long-suffering wife, agreed with Tagore.

Why this switch in attitude? The answer lay in Gandhi's stated purpose for each fast. In September 1932, Gandhi wanted to move the hearts of millions of Hindus who clung to an immoral belief; in May 1933, he said: 'The fast is intended to remove bitterness, to purify hearts and to make it clear that the movement [against Untouchability] is wholly moral, to be prosecuted by wholly moral persons . . . Whether I survive the fast or not, is a matter of little moment. Without it I would, in all probability, have been useless for further service of Harijans, and for that matter, any other service.'

This seemed wrong to Rabindranath. Both he and Gandhi were inspired by the *Isopanishad*, but whereas Gandhi believed in 'renounce and rejoice', Tagore put the phrase the other way round. Gandhi's second fast, entirely ascetic and cathartic in principle, therefore made little appeal to Tagore: he saw it, at root, as life-denying not life-affirming. And its potentially disastrous consequences for India frightened him.[34]

Perhaps it is fair to say that while Gandhi's Hinduism was forged on the anvil of India-versus-Britain, that of Tagore was shaped by the East-West axis. Hence his recurrent concern with synthesis, a theme not absent in Gandhi but less prominent in the din of the actual struggle of India against Britain. It is therefore interesting that Tagore detected on more than one occasion, 'An outburst of irritation *even among some Americans* at the idea of India ever dreaming of political severence of [its] British connection'.[35] The racism implicit in this—as in many Hindu attitudes and institutions—is what Tagore's attention was directed to more than anything else. The reconciliation of the East and the West was an abiding theme with him.

> The idea of India as a land with a genius for the synthesis of East and West, which had been present in his writing as far back as 1878, grew to dominate his thinking. He had never been interested in the dynastic history of India and its violent political struggles: always in writing about Indian history he stressed what he saw as its spiritual unity, incarnated in the Buddha. In Tagore's eyes, Buddha combined both contemplative spirituality and active spirituality—East and West so to speak. From the 1890s onwards there were more and more references to him in Tagore's works. In his seventies he would hail the Buddha as 'the greatest man ever born on this earth'.[36]

In one respect, however, his thought parallels Gandhi in that both moved gradually towards an increasingly liberal position on the caste system.[37] In general, however, if Tagore's life was that of a poet, Gandhi's life was more like a poem, an epic poem.

Tagore travelled widely during a five-year period, 1932–37, under the influence of '*wanderlust*—a word that might have been coined by Rabindranath', and out of the desire to raise funds for Shantiniketan, the name of an educational institution of a new kind he had been developing since 1901. Its cultural agenda is encapsulated in its original circumstance: 'Of the five teachers, three were Christians, two of them Roman Catholics. This, in a school that was supposed to be reproducing in modern form the glories of ancient Indian *tapaovana* (forest hermitage)!'[38] The last years of his life were devoted to its development.

Tagore died on 7 August 1941—in Calcutta, although he had longed to die at Shantiniketan.[39]

> When I go from hence, let this be my parting word,
> That what I have seen is unsurpassable[40]

To close with a sentiment and statement quintessentially Tagorean, and quintessentially Hindu.[41]

Ultimate Reality: Personal or Impersonal?

One of the issues endlessly debated in Hinduism, from the earliest times to this day, is whether the ultimate reality, is personal or impersonal. In the following conversation with Professor Albert Einstein, which took place on the afternoon of 14 July 1930 at the Professor's residence in Kaputh, Tagore confirms what is obvious from his writings: that for him, ultimate reality is personal.

E.: Do you believe in the Divine as isolated from the world?

T.: Not isolated. The infinite personality of Man comprehends the Universe. There cannot be anything that cannot be subsumed by the human personality, and this proves that the truth of the Universe is human truth. I have taken a scientific fact to illustrate this—Matter is composed of protons and electrons, with gaps between them; but matter may seem to be solid. Similarly humanity is composed of individuals, yet they have their interconnection of human relationship, which gives living solidarity to man's world. The entire universe is linked up with us in a similar manner, it is a human universe. I have pursued this through art, literature and the religious consciousness of man.

E.: There are two different conceptions about the nature of the universe: (1) The world as a reality dependent on humanity, (2) The world as a reality independent of the human factor.

T.: When our universe is in harmony with Man, the eternal, we know it as truth, we feel it as beauty.

E.: This is a purely human conception of the universe.

T.: Yes, one eternal entity. We have to realize it through our emotions and activities. We realize the Supreme Man who has no individual limitations through our limitations. Science is concerned with that which is not confined to individuals; it is the impersonal human world of truths. Religion realizes these truths and links them up with our deeper needs; our individual consciousness of truth gains universal significance. Religion applies values to truth, and we know truth as good through our own harmony with it.

E.: Truth, then, or Beauty, is not independent of Man?

T.: No.

E.: If there would be no human beings any more, the Apollo of Belvedere would no longer be beautiful?

T.: No.

E.: I agree with regard to this conception of Beauty, but not with regard to Truth.

T.: Why not? Truth is realized through man.

E.: I cannot prove that my conception is right, but that is my religion.

T.: Beauty is in the ideal of perfect harmony which is in the Universal Being; truth the perfect comprehension of the Universal Mind. We individuals approach it through our own mistakes and blunders, through our accumulated experience, through our illumined consciousness—how, otherwise, can we know Truth?

E.: I cannot prove scientifically that truth must be conceived as a truth that is valid independent of humanity; but I believe it firmly. I believe, for instance, that the Pythagorean theorem in geometry states something that is approximately true, independent of the existence of man. Anyway, if there is a *reality* independent of man there is also a truth relative to this reality; and in the same way the negation of the first engenders a negation of the existence of the latter.

T.: Truth, which is one with the Universal Being, must essentially be human, otherwise whatever we individuals realize as true can never be called truth—at least the truth which is described as scientific and can only be reached through the process of logic, in other words, by an organ of thought which is human. According to Indian Philosophy there is Brahman the absolute Truth, which cannot be conceived by the isolation of the individual mind or described by words, but can only be realized by completely merging the individual in its infinity. But such a truth cannot belong to Science. The nature of truth which we are discussing is an appearance—that is to say what appears to be true to the human mind and therefore is human, and may be called *máyá*, or illusion.

E.: So according to your conception, which may be the Indian conception, it is not the illusion of the individual, but of humanity as a whole.

T.: In science we go through the discipline of eliminating the personal limitations of our individual minds and thus reach that comprehension of truth which is in the mind of the Universal Man.

E.: The problem begins whether Truth is independent of our consciousness.

T.: What we call truth lies in the rational harmony between the subjective and objective aspects of reality, both of which belong to the Super-personal man.

E.: Even in our everyday life we feel compelled to ascribe a reality independent of man to the objects we use. We do this to connect the experiences of our senses in a reasonable way. For instance, if nobody is in this house, yet that table remains where it is.

T.: Yes, it remains outside the individual mind, but not outside the universal mind. The table which I perceive is perceptible by the same kind of consciousness which I possess.

E.: Our natural point of view in regard to the existence of truth apart from humanity cannot be explained or proved, but it is a belief which nobody can lack—no primitive beings even. We attribute to Truth a super-human objectivity; it is indispensable for us, this reality which is independent of our existence and our experience and our mind— though we cannot say what it means.

T.: Science has proved that the table as a solid object is an appearance, and therefore that which the human mind perceives as a table would not exist if that mind were naught. At the same time it must be admitted that the fact, that the ultimate physical reality of the table is nothing but a multitude of separate revolving centres of electric forces, also belongs to the human mind.

In the apprehension of truth there is an eternal conflict between the universal human mind and the same mind confined in the individual. The perpetual process of reconciliation is being carried on in our science and philosophy, and in our ethics. In any case, if there be any truth absolutely unrelated to humanity then for us it is absolutely non-existing.

It is not difficult to imagine a mind to which the sequence of things happens not in space, but only in time like the sequence of notes in music. For such a mind its conception of reality is akin to the musical reality of literature. For the kind of mind possessed by the moth, which eats that paper, literature is absolutely non-existent, yet for Man's mind literature has a greater value of truth than the paper itself. In a similar manner, if there be some truth which has no sensuous or rational relation to the human mind it will ever remain as nothing so long as we remain human beings.

E.: Then I am more religious than you are!

T.: My religion is in the reconciliation of the Super-personal Man, the Universal human spirit, in my own individual being. This has been the subject of my Hibbert Lectures, which I have called 'The Religion of Man'.[42]

The Vision

Under this title Tagore recounts his own religious autobiography in capsule form.

I hope that my readers have understood, as they have read these pages, that I am neither a scholar nor a philosopher. They should not expect from me fruits gathered from a wide field of studies or wealth brought by a mind trained in the difficult exploration of knowledge. Fortunately for me the subject of religion gains in interest and value by the experience of the individuals who earnestly believe in its truth. This is my apology for offering a part of the story of my life which has always realized its religion through a process of growth and not by the help of inheritance or importation.

Man has made the entire geography of the earth his own, ignoring the boundaries of climate; for, unlike the lion and the reindeer, he has the power to create his special skin and temperature, including his un-scrupulous power of borrowing the skins of the indigenous inhabitants and misappropriating their fats.

His kingdom is also continually extending in time through a great surplus in his power of memory, to which is linked his immense facility of borrowing the treasure of the past from all quarters of the world. He dwells in a universe of history, in an environment of continuous remembrance. The animal occupies time only through the multiplication of its own race, but man through the memorials of his mind, raised along the pilgrimage of progress. The stupendousness of his knowledge and wisdom is due to their roots spreading into and drawing sap from the far-reaching area of history.

Man has his other dwelling-place in the realm of inner realization, in the element of an immaterial value. This is a world where from the subterranean soil of his mind his consciousness often, like a seed, unexpectedly sends up sprouts into the heart of a luminous freedom, and the individual is made to realize his truth in the universal Man. I hope it may prove of interest if I give an account of my own personal experience of a sudden spiritual outburst from within me which is like the underground current of a perennial stream unexpectedly welling up on the surface.

I was born in a family which, at that time, was earnestly developing a monotheistic religion based upon the philosophy of the Upanishad. Somehow my mind at first remained coldly aloof, absolutely uninfluenced by any religious teaching merely because people in my surroundings believed it to be true. I could not persuade myself to imagine that I had a religion because everybody whom I might trust believed in its value.

Thus my mind was brought up in an atmosphere of freedom— freedom from the dominance of any creed that had its sanction in the definite authority of some scripture, or in the teaching of some organized body of worshippers. And, therefore, the man who questions me has every right to distrust my vision and reject my testimony. In such a case, the authority of some particular book venerated by a large number of men may have greater weight than the assertion of an individual, and therefore I never claim any right to preach.

When I look back upon those days, it seems to me that unconsciously I followed the path of my Vedic ancestors, and was inspired by the tropical sky with its suggestion of an uttermost Beyond. The wonder of the gathering clouds hanging heavy with the unshed rain, of the sudden sweep of storms arousing vehement gestures along the line of coconut trees, the fierce loneliness of the blazing summer noon, the silent sunrise behind the dewy veil of autumn morning, kept my mind with the intimacy of a pervasive companionship.

Then came my initiation ceremony of Brahminhood when the *gayatri* verse of meditation was given to me, whose meaning, according to the explanation I had, runs as follows:

Let me contemplate the adorable splendour of Him who created the earth,
the air and the starry shores, and sends the power of comprehension within
our minds.

This produced a sense of serene exaltation in me, the daily
meditation upon the infinite being which unites in one stream of
creation my mind and the outer world. Though to-day I find no
difficulty in realizing this being as an infinite personality in whom
the subject and object are perfectly reconciled, at that time the idea
to me was vague. Therefore the current of feeling that it aroused in
my mind was indefinite, like the circulation of air—an atmosphere
which needed a definite world to complete itself and satisfy me. For it
is evident that my religion is a poet's religion, and neither that of an
orthodox man of piety nor that of a theologian. Its touch comes to
me through the same unseen and trackless channel as does the
inspiration of my songs. My religious life has followed the same
mysterious line of growth as has my poetical life. Somehow they are
wedded to each other and, though their betrothal had a long period
of ceremony, it was kept secret to me.

When I was eighteen, a sudden spring breeze of religious experience
for the first time came to my life and passed away leaving in my memory
a direct message of spiritual reality. One day while I stood watching at
early dawn the sun sending out its rays from behind the trees, I suddenly
felt as if some ancient mist had in a moment lifted from my sight, and
the morning light on the face of the world revealed an inner radiance
of joy. The invisible screen of the commonplace was removed from all
things and all men, and their ultimate significance was intensified in
my mind; and this is the definition of beauty. That which was memorable
in this experience was its human message, the sudden expansion of my
consciousness in the super-personal world of man. The poem I wrote
on the first day of my surprise was named 'The Awakening of the
Waterfall'. The waterfall, whose spirit lay dormant in its ice-bound
isolation, was touched by the sun and, bursting in a cataract of freedom,
it found its finality in an unending sacrifice, in a continual union with
the sea. After four days the vision passed away, and the lid hung down
upon my inner sight. In the dark, the world once again put on its disguise
of the obscurity of an ordinary fact.

When I grew older and was employed in a responsible work in
some villages I took my place in a neighbourhood where the current
of time ran slow and joys and sorrows had their simple and elemental
shades and lights. The day which had its special significance for me
came with all its drifting trivialities of the commonplace life. The

ordinary work of my morning had come to its close, and before going to take my bath I stood for a moment at my window, overlooking a marketplace on the bank of a dry river bed, welcoming the first flood of rain along its channel. Suddenly I became conscious of a stirring of soul within me. My world of experience in a moment seemed to become lighted, and facts that were detached and dim found a great unity of meaning. The feeling which I had was like that which a man, groping through a fog without knowing his destination, might feel when he suddenly discovers that he stands before his own house.

I still remember the day in my childhood when I was made to struggle across my lessons in a first primer, strewn with isolated words smothered under the burden of spelling. The morning hour appeared to me like a once-illumined page, grown dusty and faded, discoloured into irrelevant marks, smudges and gaps, wearisome in its moth-eaten meaninglessness. Suddenly I came to a rhymed sentence of combined words, which may be translated thus—'It rains, the leaves tremble'. At once I came to a world wherein I recovered my full meaning. My mind touched the creative realm of expression, and at that moment I was no longer a mere student with his mind muffled by spelling lessons, enclosed by classroom. The rhythmic picture of the tremulous leaves beaten by the rain opened before my mind the world which does not merely carry information, but a harmony with my being. The unmeaning fragments lost their individual isolation and my mind revelled in the unity of a vision. In a similar manner, on that morning in the village the facts of my life suddenly appeared to me in a luminous unity of truth. All things that had seemed like vagrant waves were revealed to my mind in relation to a boundless sea. *I felt sure that some Being who comprehended me and my world was seeking his best expression in all my experiences, uniting them into an ever-widening individuality which is a spiritual work of art.*

To this Being I was responsible; for the creation in me is his as well as mine. It may be that it was the same creative Mind that is shaping the universe to its eternal idea; but in me as a person it had one of its special centres of a personal relationship growing into a deepening consciousness. I had my sorrows that left their memory in a long burning track across my days, but I felt at that moment that in them I lent myself to a travail of creation that ever exceeded my own personal bounds like stars which in their individual fire bursts are lighting the history of the universe. It gave me a great joy to feel in my life detachment at the idea of a mystery of a meeting of the two in a creative comradeship. *I felt that I had found my religion at last, the religion of Man, in which the infinite became defined in humanity and came close to me so as to need my love and co-operation.*

This idea of mine found at a later date its expression in some of my poems addressed to what I called *Jivan devata*, the Lord of my life. Fully aware of my awkwardness in dealing with a foreign language, with some hesitation I give a translation, being sure that any evidence revealed through the self-recording instrument of poetry is more authentic than answers extorted through conscious questionings.

> Thou who art the innermost Spirit of my being, art thou pleased,
>   Lord of my Life?
> For I gave to thee my cup
> filled with all the pain and delight
> that the crushed grapes of my heart had surrendered,
> I wove with the rhythm of colours and songs the cover for thy bed,
> and with the molten gold of my desires
> I fashioned playthings for thy passing hours.
> I know not why thou chosest me for thy partner,
>   Lord of my life!
> Didst thou store my days and nights,
> my deeds and dreams for the alchemy of thy art,
> and string in the chain of thy music my songs of autumn and spring,
> and gather the flowers from my mature moments for thy crown?
> I see thine eyes gazing at the dark of my heart,
>   Lord of my Life,
> I wonder if my failures and wrongs are forgiven.
> For many were my days without service
> and nights of forgetfulness;
> futile were the flowers that faded in the shade not offered to thee.
> Often the tired strings of my lute
> slackened at the strain of thy tunes.
> And often at the ruin of wasted hours
> my desolate evenings were filled with tears.
> But have my days come to their end at last,
>   Lord of my life,
> while my arms round thee grow limp,
> my kisses losing their truth?
> Then break up the meeting of this languid day.
> Renew the old in me in fresh forms of delight;
> and let the wedding come once again
> in a new ceremony of life.[43]

Notes

1. Krishna Dutta and Andrew Robinson, *Rabindranath Tagore: The Myriad-Minded Man* (New York: St. Martin's Press, 1995), p. 17.
2. Ibid., pp. 17–18. For another account see W.J. Wilkins, *Modern Hinduism* (Calcutta: Rupa & Co., 1975; first published 1887), p. 277.
3. Dutta and Robinson, pp. 18–19. 'Rabindranath never once referred to this split directly. (There was not even a hint of it in his memoirs.) It surfaced instead in a moving short story he wrote in 1911 . . .' (ibid.).
4. Andrew Robinson, in Introduction to Rabindranath Tagore, *My Reminiscences* (London: Macmillan, 1991), p. 3.
5. Dutta and Robinson, p. 24.
6. Ibid., p. 21.
7. Ibid.
8. Robinson, p. 4.
9. Ibid.
10. See Wm. Theodore de Bary, et al, *Sources of Indian Tradition* (New York and London: Columbia University Press, 1958), Vol. II, pp. 230–1.
11. Dutta and Robinson, p. 25.
12. Tagore, *My Reminiscences*, p. 70.
13. Ibid., pp. 21, 23, 33, 66, 83.
14. Ibid., p. 59.
15. Ibid., p. 61.
16. Ibid., p. 62.
17. Ibid., p. 72.
18. Ibid., p. 129. Tagore's mother passed away when he was twenty-three. His reaction to her death is worth citing (ibid., pp. 177–9): 'We came out into the verandah and saw my mother lying on a bedstead in the courtyard. Nothing in her appearance showed death to be terrible. The aspect it wore in that morning light was as lovely as a calm and peaceful sleep, and the gulf between life and absence of life was not brought home to us.

    'Only when her body was taken out through the main gateway and we followed the procession to the cremation ground did a storm of grief pass through me at the thought that Mother would never return by this door and again take her accustomed place in the affairs of the household. The day wore on, we returned from the cremation, and as we turned into our lane I looked up towards my father's rooms on the third storey. He was still sitting in the front verandah, motionless in prayer.

    . . .

    'The acquaintance I made with Death at the age of twenty-three was a permanent one, and its blow reverberates with each succeeding bereavement in ever-expanding wreathes of tears. An infant can skip away from the greatest of calamities, but with the coming of age evasion is not so easy. The shock of that day I had to face full-on.

'That there could be any gap in life's succession of joys and sorrows was something of which I had no idea. I had seen nothing beyond life, and accepted it as the ultimate truth. When death suddenly came, and in a moment tore a gaping rent in life's seamless fabric, I was utterly bewildered. All around, the trees, the soil, the water, the sun, the moon, the stars, remained as immovably true as before, and yet the person who was as truly there, who, through a thousand points of contact with life, mind and heart, was so very much more true for me, had vanished in an instant like a dream. What a perplexing contradiction! How was I ever to reconcile what remained with that which had gone?

'The terrible darkness disclosed to me through this rent, continued to lure me night and day as time went by. I would constantly return to it and gaze at it, wondering what was left to replace what had departed. Emptiness is a thing man cannot bring himself to believe in: that which is *not*, is untrue; that which is untrue, is not. So our efforts to find something where we see nothing are unceasing.

'Just as a young plant confined in darkness stretches itself, on tiptoe as it were, to reach the light, so the soul, when death surrounds it with negation, tries and tries to rise into affirmatory light. What sorrow is deeper than to be trapped in a darkness that prevents one from finding a way out of darkness?

'Yet amid unbearable grief, flashes of joy sparkled in my mind on and off in a way which quite surprised me. The idea that life is not a fixture came as tidings that helped to lighten my mind.'

19. Ibid., pp. 133–4.
20. Dutta and Robinson, p. 105.
21. The Vishva Hindu Parishad (VHP) objects, for instance, to the use of 'Hindu' names by Christians.
22. Dutta and Robinson, p. 154.
23. Ibid., p. 154. Other factors could account for the change as well (ibid.).
24. Ibid., p. 155.
25. Ibid., p. 151.
26. Ibid., p. 137.
27. Ibid., p. 145.
28. Ibid.
29. Ibid., p. 151.
30. Cited, Wm. Theodore de Bary, p. 236.
31. Ibid., p. 265.
32. Ibid., p. 278.
33. Ibid., p. 284. Another Nobel laureate from Bengal, Amartya Sen, was reportedly subjected to similar harassment in Europe recently.
34. Ibid., p. 311.
35. Dutta and Robinson, p. 301, emphasis added.
36. Ibid., p. 151.
37. Ibid., pp. 135, 156.
38. Ibid., p. 135.

39. Ibid., p. 308.
40. Cited, Dutta and Robinson, p. 167.
41. See S. Radhakrishnan, *The Philosophy of Rabindranath Tagore* (London: Macmillan & Co., 1918). The book is curiously not listed in the bibliography in Dutta and Robinson.
42. Rabindranath Tagore, *The Religion of Man* (London: George Allen & Unwin, 1931), pp. 222–5.
43. Ibid., pp. 90–8.

Mahatma Gandhi
(1869–1948)

Life

Hinduism, in general, emphasizes the connection between life and thought; and Mahatma Gandhi, arguably the most influential Hindu of modern times, epitomized this connection when he declared: 'My life is my message.'

Mahatma Gandhi was born on 2 October 1869, at Porbandar in Saurashtra, in western India, into a family which had served as ministers to one of the princely states that dotted that region. Significantly, unlike Bengal, this region was under *indirect* British rule. He was married at the age of thirteen, which was to make him, in later life, a severe critic of child marriage. He set great store by two virtues he imbibed early in life, by watching their dramatic enactments celebrated in Hindu lore: (1) truthfulness and (2) filial piety. In his early teens he acquired the then current version of drug addiction, namely, smoking on the sly. He could not, however, live with the idea of deceiving his parents. So one day he decided to make a clean breast of it, in a combined display of these two virtues.

> I decided at last to write out the confession, to submit it to my father, and ask his forgiveness. I wrote it on a slip of paper and handed it to him myself. In this note not only did I confess my guilt, but I asked adequate punishment for it, and closed with a request to him not to punish himself for my offence. I also pledged myself never to steal in future.
>
> I was trembling as I handed the confession to my father. He was then suffering from a fistula and was confined to bed. His bed was a plain wooden plank. I handed him the note and sat opposite the plank.
>
> He read it through, and pearl-drops trickled down his cheeks, wetting the paper. For a moment he closed his eyes in thought and then tore up

the note. He had sat up to read it. He again lay down. I also cried. I could see my father's agony. If I were a painter I could draw a picture of the whole scene today. It is still so vivid in my mind.

Those pearl-drops of love cleansed my heart, and washed my sin away. Only he who has experienced such love can know what it is. As the hymn says:

Only he
Who is smitten with the arrows of love,
Knows its power.

This was, for me, an object-lesson in *Ahimsa*. Then I could read in it nothing more than a father's love, but today I know that it was pure *Ahimsa*. When such *Ahimsa* becomes all-embracing, it transforms everything it touches. There is no limit to its power.

This sort of sublime forgiveness was not natural to my father. I had thought that he would be angry, say hard things, and strike his forehead. But he was so wonderfully peaceful, and I believe this was due to my clean confession. A clean confession, combined with a promise never to commit the sin again, when offered before one who has the right to receive it, is the purest type of repentance. I know that my confession made my father feel absolutely safe about me, and increased his affection for me beyond measure.[1]

Gandhi's *truthfulness* had been tested successfully but in his own estimate he always considered himself to have been tested and found wanting in filial piety. He was traumatized by the fact that he was in the arms of his wife when his father died, even though she was then in an advanced stage of pregnancy.

It was 10-30 or 11 p.m. I was giving the massage. My uncle offered to relieve me. I was glad and went straight to the bed-room. My wife, poor thing, was fast asleep. But how could she sleep when I was there? I woke her up. In five or six minutes, however, the servant knocked at the door. I started with alarm. 'Get up,' he said, 'Father is very ill.' I knew of course that he was very ill, and so I guessed what 'very ill' meant at that moment. I sprang out of bed.

'What is the matter? Do tell me!'

'Father is no more.'

So all was over! I had but to wring my hands. I felt deeply ashamed and miserable. I ran to my father's room. I saw that, if animal passion had not blinded me, I should have been spared the torture of separation from my father during his last moments. I should have been massaging him, and he would have died in my arms. But now it was my uncle who had had this privilege. He was so deeply devoted to his elder brother that he had earned the honour of doing him the last services! My father had forebodings of the coming event. He had made a sign for pen and paper, and written: 'Prepare for the last rites.' He had then snapped the amulet off his arm and also his gold necklace of *tulasi*-beads and flung them aside. A moment after this he was no more.

The shame, to which I have referred in a foregoing chapter, was this shame of my carnal desire even at the critical hour of my father's death, which demanded wakeful service. It is a blot I have never been able to efface or forget, and I have always thought that, although my devotion to my parents knew no bounds and I would have given up anything for it, yet it was weighed and found unpardonably wanting because my mind was at the same moment in the grip of lust. I have therefore always regarded myself as a lustful, though a faithful, husband. It took me long to get free from the shackles of lust, and I had to pass through many ordeals before I could overcome it.

Before I close this chapter of my double shame, I may mention that the poor mite that was born to my wife scarcely breathed for more than three or four days. Nothing else could be expected. Let all those who are married be warned by my example.[2]

It was also around this time that he started questioning the Hindu practice of untouchability, when his parents tried to prevent him from befriending the untouchable boy Uka, a problem to which his orthodox mother devised an ingenious solution. 'Very respectfully [Gandhi] suggested to his parents that they were wrong to regard the scavenger in this way: an accidental touch could not be a sin and Uka was a man like other men. His mother reminded him that it was not necessary to perform one's ablutions after touching a scavenger: instead, one could touch a Muslim, thus transferring the pollution to someone who was free of the taboos of the Hindu religion.'[3]

Around the age of eighteen he decided to go to England to study for the bar. At first his mother objected, as she had heard that Indian boys went astray in the West, but later relented when he agreed to abstain from meat, wine and sex during his sojourn abroad. These vows were formally administered to him by a Jaina monk, although his family was Vaiṣnava, that is, worshippers of the Hindu God Viṣṇu. He had to raise part of the fare to go to England by selling his wife's jewellery.

By the time he returned to India his mother had passed away. While still casting around for something to do he was invited in 1893 by a firm of Muslim Indians in South Africa to represent them. During this brief stay in India, prior to leaving for South Africa, Gandhi had already had his first bitter taste of what it meant to be a subject people. The British resident had him physically evicted from his chamber, and Gandhi concludes his autobiographical chapter which details this incident with a simple but epochal remark: 'This shock changed the course of my life.'[4]

More shocks were in store for him before he could reach his clients in Pretoria in South Africa. He was ejected from a first-class compartment although he had a ticket, as only whites were allowed the use of it and was left shivering on the platform in the cold. His train of thought after the incident is revealing in its sublime sobriety:

> I began to think of my duty. Should I fight for my rights or go back to India, or should I go on to Pretoria without minding the insults, and return to India after finishing the case? It would be cowardice to run back to India without fulfilling my obligation. The hardship to which I was subjected was superficial—only a symptom of the deep disease of colour prejudice. I should try, if possible, to root out the disease and suffer hardships in the process. Redress for wrongs I should seek only to the extent that would be necessary for the removal of the colour prejudice.[5]

By the time he made it to Pretoria he had also been beaten up while travelling by coach. The case he had been summoned for was quickly settled but as he was preparing to leave, the South African government announced the introduction of legislative measures, which the Indian community considered unjust. He was prevailed upon to stay to lead the struggle. He finally left South Africa for good only in 1915.

South Africa turned out to be a mini-laboratory for Gandhi for his political and moral experiments, which he was to try out on a grander scale in India. It was here that he perfected the technique of *satyāgraha* or non-violent resistance. The word means holding on to truth and Gandhi preferred it to the earlier term 'passive resistance', which he found misleading.

It was also in South Africa that Gandhi became both a committed and a reformist Hindu, as well as a firm proponent of Hindu-Muslim unity. He describes in detail the religious ferment he experienced,[6] whereupon he sought the guidance of a Jaina scholar, Raychand by name, who on their very first meeting had impressed him with a prodigious display of his mnemonic powers and later almost overwhelmed him by his saintly disposition.[7]

> I expressed my difficulties in a letter to Raychandbhai. I also corresponded with other religious authorities in India and received answers from them. Raychandbhai's letter somewhat pacified me. He asked me to be patient and to study Hinduism more deeply. One of his sentences was to this effect: 'On a dispassionate view of the question I am convinced that no other religion has the subtle and profound thought of Hinduism, its vision of the soul, or its charity.'[8]

The conversion of Gandhi from a private citizen to a public worker was accompanied by a moral transformation, during the course of which he

simplified his life-style, turned celibate,[9] and began treating all human beings irrespective of caste and class as equals—although this caused serious
differences with his wife, including a notorious scene in which he virtually
dragged her out of the house for not cleaning the chamber pot of an untouch-
able-turned-Christian, 'cheerfully'. [10]

Gandhi had made the acquaintance of Gokhale on his earlier visits to
India and looked upon him as his mentor. Upon his return to India, and on
Gokhale's advice, he spent the first few years acquainting himself with the
country.

After some early skirmishes with the British, Gandhi burst on the national
scene in 1919, when Indians rose in protest against draconian British measures
to curb post-War unrest. His impact is best conveyed in the words of Pandit
Nehru, who later on became India's first prime minister.

> And then came Gandhi. Political freedom took new shape then and
> acquired a new content. Much that he said we only partially accepted or
> sometimes did not accept at all. But all this was secondary. The essence of
> his teaching was fearlessness and truth and action allied to these, always
> keeping the welfare of the masses in view. The greatest gift for an individual
> or a nation, so we have been told in our ancient books, was *abhaya*,
> fearlessness, not merely bodily courage but the absence of fear from the
> mind. Janaka and Yajnavalka had said, at the dawn of our history, that it
> was the function of the leaders of a people to make them fearless. But the
> dominant impulse in India under British rule was that of fear. Pervasive,
> oppressing, strangling fear; fear of the army, the police, the widespread
> secret service; fear of the official class; fear of laws meant to suppress, and
> of prison; fear of the landlord's agent, fear of the moneylender; fear of
> unemployment and starvation, which were always on the threshold. It
> was against this all-pervading fear that Gandhi's quiet and determined
> voice was raised: Be not afraid.
>
> Was it so simple as all that? Not quite. And yet fear builds its phantoms
> which are more fearsome than reality itself, and reality when calmly
> analysed and its consequences willingly accepted loses much of its terror.
>
> So, suddenly as it were, that black pall of fear was lifted from the
> people's shoulders, not wholly, of course, but to an amazing degree. As
> fear is close companion to falsehood, so truth follows fearlessness. The
> Indian people did not become much more truthful than they were, nor
> did they change their essential nature overnight; nevertheless a sea
> change was visible as the need for falsehood and furtive behaviour
> lessened. It was a psychological change, almost as if some expert in
> psychoanalytical method had probed deep into the patient's past, found
> out the origins of his complexes, exposed them to his view, and thus rid
> him of that burden.[11]

Gandhi, to the consternation of everybody except perhaps the British, called off his campaign amidst reports of violence in 1922, after which he was tried and sentenced.

In his struggle against the British, Gandhi employed the allied measures of non-violent non-cooperation, which meant refusal to cooperate with an evil regime, and civil disobedience, which involved rebellion against the laws of an unjust state. The climax came in 1930 when he launched his salt *satyāgraha*—a term which encompasses both these senses. It is to an intrepid American correspondent, Webb Miller, that we owe the following unforgettable account of the campaign as it unfolded on May 21.

> Mme. Naidu called for prayer before the march started and the entire assemblage knelt. She exhorted them: 'Gandhi's body is in jail but his soul is with you. India's prestige is in your hands, you must not use any violence under any circumstances. You will be beaten but you must not resist; you must not even raise a hand to ward off blows.' Wild, shrill cheers terminated her speech.
>
> Slowly and in silence the throng commenced the half-mile march to salt-deposits. A few carried ropes for lassoing the barbed-wire stockade around the salt pans. About a score who were assigned to act as stretcher-bearers wore crude, hand-painted red crosses pinned to their breasts, their stretchers consisted of blankets. Manilal Gandhi, second son of Gandhi, walked among the foremost of the marchers. As the throng drew near the salt pans they commenced chanting the revolutionary slogan, *Inqilab Zindabad*, intoning the two words over and over.
>
> The salt-deposits were surrounded by ditches filled with water and guarded by four hundred native Surat Police in Khaki shorts and brown turbans. Half a dozen British officials commanded them. The Police carried *lathis*—five foot clubs tipped with steel. Inside the stockade twenty-five native rifle-men were drawn up.
>
> In complete silence the Gandhi men drew up and halted a hundred yards from the stockade. A picked column advanced from the crowd, waded the ditches, and approached the barbed-wire stockade, which the Surat Police surrounded, holding clubs, at the ready. Police officials ordered the marchers to disperse under a recently imposed regulation which prohibited gathering of more than five persons in any one place. The column silently ignored the warning and slowly walked forward. I stayed with the main body about a hundred yards from the stockade.
>
> Suddenly, at a word of command, scores of native police rushed upon the advancing marchers and rained blows on their heads with their steel-shod *lathis*. Not one of the marchers even raised an arm to fend off the blows. They went down like ten-pins. From where I stood I heard the sickening whacks of the clubs on unprotected skulls. The waiting crowd

of watchers groaned and sucked in their breaths in sympathetic pain at every blow.

Those struck down fell sprawling, unconscious or writhing in pain with fractured skulls or broken shoulders. In two or three minutes the ground was quilted with bodies. Great patches of blood widened on their white clothes. The survivors, without breaking ranks, silently and doggedly marched on until struck down. When everyone of the first column had been knocked down, stretcher-bearers rushed up unmolested by the Police and carried off the injured to a thatched hut which had been arranged as a temporary hospital.

Then another column formed while the leaders pleaded with them to retain their self-control. They marched slowly towards the police. Although everyone knew that within a few minutes he would be beaten down, perhaps killed, I could detect no signs of wavering or fear. They marched steadily with heads up, without the encouragement of music or cheering or any possibility that they might escape serious injury or death. The police rushed out and methodically and mechanically beat down the second column. There was no fight, no struggle; the marchers simply walked forward until struck down. There were no outcries, only groans after they fell. There were not enough stretcher-bearers to carry off the wounded; I saw eighteen injured being carried off simultaneously, while forty-two still lay bleeding on the ground awaiting stretcher-bearers. The blankets used as stretchers were sodden with blood.[12]

This agitation led to certain political concessions. In the meantime, Gandhi continued to carry out his fight against untouchability with great vigour and almost lost his life during a fast, when the British tried to capitalize on this Hindu social evil.[13] In an almost Christ-like fashion he tried to atone for the sin of his fellow Hindus with another fast, on which he embarked under mystical inspiration. He writes:

I had gone to sleep the night before without the slightest idea of having to declare a fast next morning. At about twelve o'clock in the night something wakes me up suddenly, and some voice—within or without, I cannot say—whispers, 'Thou must go on a fast.' 'How many days?' I ask. The voice again says, 'Twenty-one days.' 'When does it begin?' I ask. It says, 'You begin tomorrow.' I went off to sleep after making the decision. I did not tell anything to my companions until after the morning prayers.[14]

This incident is worth mentioning to highlight the mystical dimension of Gandhi's life, which has generally been overlooked.

During the Second World War, Gandhi tried to lead a campaign in 1942 to dislodge the British. It was crushed. After the War, however, the British finally decided to quit India. In the meantime Muslim political identity had rapidly coalesced and the Muslims demanded the right to self-determination. Gandhi's dream of Hindu–Muslim unity lay in shambles when India was divided into two countries, India and Pakistan, in August 1947, amidst unprecedented rioting which Gandhi did his best to contain. Gandhi was not the only person left disillusioned by the collapse of the dream of a united India. Some held him personally responsible for the tragedy, and attempts began to be made on his life.

On 29 January 1948 he told his grandniece, around 10 p.m., when she was massaging his head with oil:

> If I were to die of a lingering disease, or even from a pimple, then you must shout from the housetops to the whole world that I was a false Mahatma. Then my soul, wherever it might be, will rest in peace. If I die of an illness, you must declare me to be a false or hypocritical Mahatma, even at the risk of people cursing you. And if an explosion takes place, as it did last week, or if someone shot at me and I received his bullet in my bare chest without a sigh and with Rama's name on my lips, only then should you say that I was a true Mahatma.[15]

The next day at around 5.15 p.m., Gandhi lay dead, shot to death on his way to his prayer meeting, struck down by bullets on his bare chest, with the name of Rama on his lips.

Mahatma Gandhi on Religion

In 1936 Professors S. Radhakrishnan and J. H. Muirhead edited a volume entitled Contemporary Indian Philosophy *for the Muirhead Library of Philosophy, a series of which Professor H. D. Lewis was the general editor. The first and shortest self-statement it contains is by M. K. Gandhi, popularly known as Mahatma Gandhi.*

I have been asked by Sri S. Radhakrishnan to answer the following three questions:
(1) What is your Religion?
(2) How are you led to it?
(3) What is its bearing on social life?
My religion is Hinduism which for me, is the religion of humanity and includes the best of all the religions known to me.

I take it that the present tense in the second question has been purposely used instead of the past. I am being led to my religion through Truth and Non-violence, i.e. love in the broadest sense. I often describe my religion as Religion of Truth. Of late, instead of saying God is

Truth I have been saying Truth is God, in order more fully to define my Religion. I used, at one time, to know by heart the thousand names of God which a booklet in Hinduism gives in verse form and which perhaps tens of thousands recite every morning. But nowadays nothing so completely describes my God as Truth. Denial of God we have known. Denial of Truth we have not known. The most ignorant among mankind have some truth in them. We are all sparks of Truth. The sum total of these sparks is indescribable, as-yet-unknown-Truth, which is God. I am being daily led nearer to It by constant prayer.

The bearing of this religion on social life is, or has to be, seen in one's daily social contact. To be true to such religion one has to lose oneself in continuous and continuing service of all life. Realisation of Truth is impossible without a complete merging of oneself in, and identification with, this limitless ocean of life. Hence, for me, there is no escape from social service, there is no happiness on earth beyond or apart from it. Social service here must be taken to include every department of life. In this scheme there is nothing low, nothing high. For, all is one, though we *seem* to be many.[16]

Hind Swaraj

The Collected Works of Mahatma Gandhi cover almost a hundred volumes and render an anthologist's task somewhat daunting. One would feel lost at sea were it not for an early port of call in the form of the book called Hind Swaraj. *Gandhi wrote this book of 30,000 words originally in Gujarati (ambidextrously, when one hand began to fail) during the course of a voyage between 13 November and 22 November 1909 from England to South Africa, on the steamer's stationery in 271 pages.[17] Gandhi was forty at the time. Although, 'when Gokhale read it, he thought it so crude and hastily conceived that he prophesied that Gandhi himself would destroy the book after spending a year in India'; but Gandhi took a very different view of it. He observed years later that 'except for withdrawing the word "prostitute" used in connection with the British Parliament which annoyed an English lady, I wish to make no change at all'.[18]*

The book remains curiously relevant and has recently been reissued. It provides the blueprint on which the grand architectonics of Gandhian thought rests. It is a remarkably clear blueprint. The book is in the form of a dialogue between the reader and the editor. Since the basic context of Gandhi's life was provided by the Indian struggle for Independence against British rule, and since Gandhi's unique contribution in this context consisted of his doctrine of satyāgraha (which he preferred to translate as 'civil disobedience' rather than 'passive resistance'), the first extract deals with the enunciation of this doctrine. In the discussion leading up to this section the reader urges that the British can only be dislodged with the same 'brute force'[19] *they used to gain control over India. Gandhi as the editor then responds as follows:*

EDITOR: Your reasoning is plausible. It has deluded many. I have used similar arguments before now. But I think I know better now, and I shall endeavour to undeceive you. Let us first take the argument that we are justified in gaining our end by using brute force because the English gained theirs by using similar means. It is perfectly true that they used brute force and that it is possible for us to do likewise, but by using similar means we can get only the same thing that they got. You will admit that we do not want that. Your belief that there is no connection between the means and the end is a great mistake. Through that mistake even men who have been considered religious have committed grievous crimes. Your reasoning is the same as saying that we can get a rose through planting a noxious weed. If I want to cross the ocean, I can do so only by means of a vessel; if I were to use a cart for that purpose, both the cart and I would soon find the bottom. 'As is the God, so is the votary', is a maxim worth considering. Its meaning has been distorted and men have gone astray. The means may be likened to a seed, the end to a tree; and there is just the same inviolable connection between the means and the end as there is between the seed and the tree. I am not likely to obtain the result flowing from the worship of God by laying myself prostrate before Satan. If, therefore, anyone were to say: 'I want to worship God; it does not matter that I do so by means of Satan,' it would be set down as ignorant folly. We reap exactly as we sow. The English in 1833 obtained greater voting power by violence. Did they by using brute force better appreciate their duty? They wanted the right of voting, which they obtained by using physical force. But real rights are a result of performance of duty; these rights they have not obtained. We, therefore, have before us in England the force of everybody wanting and insisting on his rights, nobody thinking of his duty. And, where everybody wants rights, who shall give them to whom? I do not wish to imply that they do no duties. They don't perform the duties corresponding to those rights; and as they do not perform that particular duty, namely, acquire fitness, their rights have proved a burden to them. In other words, what they have obtained is an exact result of the means they adopted. They used the means corresponding to the end. If I want to deprive you of your watch, I shall certainly have to fight for it; if I want to buy your watch,

I shall have to pay you for it; and if I want a gift I shall have to plead for it; and, according to the means I employ, the watch is stolen property, my own property, or a donation. Thus we see three different results from three different means. Will you still say that means do not matter?

Now we shall take the example given by you of the thief to be driven out. I do not agree with you that the thief may be driven out by any means. If it is my father who has come to steal I shall use one kind of means. If it is an acquaintance I shall use another; and in the case of a perfect stranger I shall use a third. If it is a white man, you will perhaps say you will use means different from those you will adopt with an Indian thief. If it is a weakling, the means will be different from those to be adopted for dealing with an equal in physical strength; and if the thief is armed from top to toe, I shall simply remain quiet. Thus we have a variety of means between the father and the armed man. Again, I fancy that I should pretend to be sleeping whether the thief was my father or that strong armed man. The reason for this is that my father would also be armed and I should succumb to the strength possessed by either and allow my things to be stolen. The strength of my father would make me weep with pity; the strength of the armed man would rouse in me anger and we should become enemies. Such is the curious situation. From these examples we may not be able to agree as to the means to be adopted in each case. I myself seem clearly to see what would be done in all these cases, but the remedy may frighten you. I therefore hesitate to place it before you. For the time being I will leave you to guess it, and if you cannot, it is clear you will have to adopt different means in each case. You will also have seen that any means will not avail to drive away the thief. You will have to adopt means to fit each case. Hence it follows that your duty is *not* to drive away the thief by any means you like.

Let us proceed a little further. That well-armed man has stolen your property; you have harboured the thought of his act; you are filled with anger; you argue that you want to punish that rogue, not for your own sake, but for the good of your neighbours; you have collected a number of armed men, you want to take his house by assault; he is duly informed of it, he runs away; he too is incensed. He collects his brother-robbers, and sends you a defiant message that he will commit robbery in broad daylight. You are strong, you do not fear him, you are prepared to receive him. Meanwhile, the robber pesters your neighbours. They complain before you. You reply that you are doing all for their sake, you do not mind that your own goods have been stolen. Your neighbours reply that the robber never pestered them before, and that he commenced his depredations only after you declared hostilities against him. You are between Scylla and Charybdis. You are full of pity for the poor men. What they say is true. What are you to do? You will be disgraced if you now leave the robber alone. You, therefore, tell the poor men: 'Never mind. Come, my wealth is yours, I will give you arms, I will teach you how to use them; you should belabour the rogue; don't you leave him alone.' And so the battle grows; the robbers increase in numbers; your neighbours have deliberately put themselves to inconvenience. Thus the result of wanting to take revenge upon the robber is that you have disturbed your own peace; you are in perpetual fear of being robbed and assaulted; your courage has given place to cowardice. If you will patiently examine the argument, you will see that I have not overdrawn the picture. This is one of the means. Now let us examine the other. You set this armed robber down as an ignorant brother; you intend to reason with him at a suitable opportunity: you argue that he is, after all, a fellow man; you do not know what prompted him to steal. You, therefore, decide that, when you can, you will destroy the man's motive for stealing. Whilst you are thus reasoning with yourself, the man comes again to steal. Instead of being angry with him, you take pity on him. You think that this stealing habit must be a disease with him. Henceforth, you, therefore, keep your doors and windows open, you change your sleeping-place, and you keep your things in a manner most accessible to him. The robber comes again and is confused as all this is new to him; nevertheless, he takes away your things. But his mind is agitated. He inquires about you in the village, he comes to learn about your broad and loving heart, he repents, he begs your pardon, returns you your things, and leaves off the stealing habit. He becomes your servant, and you find for him honourable employment. This is the second method. Thus, you see, different means have brought about totally different results. I do not wish to deduce from this that robbers will act in the above manner or that all will have the same pity and love like you, but I only wish to show that fair means alone can produce fair results, and that, at least in the majority of cases, if not indeed in all, the force of love and pity is infinitely greater than the force of arms. There is harm in the exercise of brute force, never in that of pity.

Now we will take the question of petitioning. It is a fact beyond dispute that a petition, without the backing of force, is useless. However, the late Justice Ranade used to say that petitions served a useful purpose because they were a means of educating people. They give the latter an idea of their condition and warn the rulers. From this point of view, they are not altogether useless. A petition of an equal is a sign of courtesy; a petition from a slave is a symbol of his slavery. A petition backed by force is a petition from an equal and, when he transmits his demand in the form of a petition, it testifies to his nobility. Two kinds of force can back petitions. 'We shall hurt you if you do not give this,' is one kind of force; it is the force of arms, whose evil results we have already examined. The second kind of force can thus be stated: 'If you do not concede our demand, we shall be no longer your petitioners. You can govern us only so long as we remain the governed; we shall no longer have any dealings with you.' The force implied in this may be described as love-force, soul-force, or, more popularly but less accurately, passive resistance. This force is indestructible. He who uses it perfectly understands his position. We have an ancient proverb which literally means: 'One negative cures thirty-six diseases.' The force of arms is powerless when matched against the force of love or the soul.

Now we shall take your last illustration, that of the child thrusting its foot into fire. It will not avail you. What do you really do to the child? Supposing that it can exert so much physical force that it renders you powerless and rushes into fire, then you cannot prevent it. There are only two remedies open to you—either you must kill it in order to prevent it from perishing in the flames, or you must give your own life because you do not wish to see it perish before your very eyes. You will not kill it. If your heart is not quite full of pity, it is possible that you will not surrender yourself by preceding the child and going into the fire yourself. You, therefore, helplessly allow it to go into the flames. Thus, at any rate, you are not using physical force. I hope you will not consider that it is still physical force, though of a low order, when you would forcibly prevent the child from rushing towards the fire if you could. That force is of a different order and we have to understand what it is. Remember that, in thus preventing the child, you are minding entirely its own interest, you are exercising authority for its sole benefit. Your example does not apply to the English. In using brute force against the English you consult entirely your own, that is the national, interest. There is no question here either of pity or of love. If you say that the actions of the English, being evil, represent fire, and that they proceed to their actions through ignorance, and that therefore they occupy the position of a child and that you want to protect such a child, then you will have to overtake every evil action of that kind by whomsoever committed and, as in the case of the evil child, you will have to sacrifice yourself. If you are capable of such immeasurable pity, I wish you well in its exercise.

Chapter XVII: Passive Resistance

READER: Is there any historical evidence as to the success of what you have called soul-force or truth-force? No instance seems to have happened of any nation having risen through soul-force. I still think that the evil-doers will not cease doing evil without physical punishment.

EDITOR: The poet Tulsidas has said: 'Of religion, pity, or love, is the root, as egotism of the body. Therefore, we should not abandon pity so long as we are alive.' This appears to me to be a scientific truth. I believe in it as much as I believe in two and two being four. The force of love is the same as the force of the soul or truth. We have evidence of its working at every step. The universe would disappear without the existence of that force. But you ask for historical evidence. It is, therefore, necessary to know what history means. The Gujarati equivalent means: 'It so happened.' If that is the meaning of history, it is possible to give copious evidence. But, if it means the doings of kings and emperors, there can be no evidence of soul-force or passive resistance in such history. You cannot expect silver ore in a tin mine. History, as we know it, is a record of the wars of the world, and so there is a proverb among Englishmen that a nation which has no history, that is, no wars, is a happy nation. How kings played, how they became enemies of one another, how they murdered one another, is found accurately recorded in history, and if this were all that had happened in the world, it would have been ended long ago. If the story of the universe had commenced with wars, not a man would have been found alive today. Those people who have been warred against have disappeared as, for instance, the natives of Australia of whom hardly a man was left alive by the intruders. Mark, please, that these natives did not use soul-force in self-defence, and it does not require much foresight to know that the Australians will share the same fate as their victims. 'Those that take the sword shall perish by the sword.' With us the proverb is that professional swimmers will find a watery grave.

The fact that there are so many men still alive in the world shows that it is based not on the force of arms but on the force of truth or love. Therefore, the greatest and most unimpeachable evidence of the success of this force is to be found in the fact that, in spite of the wars of the world, it still lives on.

Thousands, indeed tens of thousands, depend for their existence on a very active working of this force. Little quarrels of millions of families in their daily lives disappear before the exercise of this force. Hundreds of nations live in peace. History does not and cannot take note of this fact. History is really a record of every interruption of the even working of the force of love or of the soul. Two brothers quarrel; one of them repents and re-awakens the love that was lying dormant in him; the two again begin to live in peace; nobody takes note of this. But if the two brothers, through the intervention of solicitors or some other reason take up arms or go to law—which is another form of the exhibition of brute force—their doings would be immediately noticed in the Press, they would be the talk of their neighbours and would probably go down to history. And what is true of families and communities is true of nations. There is no reason to believe that there is one law for families and another for nations. History, then, is a record of an interruption of the course of nature. Soul-force, being natural, is not noted in history.

READER: According to what you say, it is plain that instances of this kind of passive resistance are not to be found in history. It is necessary to understand this passive resistance more fully. It will be better, therefore, if you enlarge upon it.

EDITOR: Passive resistance is a method of securing rights by personal suffering; it is the reverse of resistance by arms. When I refuse to do a thing that is repugnant to my conscience, I use soul-force. For instance, the Government of the day has passed a law which is applicable to me. I do not like it. If by using violence I force the Government to repeal the law, I am employing what may be termed body-force. If I do not obey the law and accept the penalty for its breach, I use soul-force. It involves sacrifice of the self.

Everybody admits that sacrifice of self is infinitely superior to sacrifice of others. Moreover, if this kind of force is used in a cause that is unjust, only the person using it suffers. He does not make others suffer for his mistakes. Men have before now done many things which were subsequently found to have been wrong. No man can claim that he is absolutely in the right or that a particular thing is wrong because he thinks so, but it is wrong for him so long as that is his deliberate judgment. It is therefore meet that he should not do that which he knows to be wrong, and suffer the consequence whatever it may be. This is the key to the use of soul-force.

READER: You would then disregard laws—this is rank disloyalty. We have always been considered a law-abiding nation. You seem to be going even beyond the extremists. They say that we must obey the laws that have been passed, but that if the laws be bad, we must drive out the law-givers even by force.

EDITOR: Whether I go beyond them or whether I do not is a matter of no consequence to either of us. We simply want to find out what is right and to act accordingly. The real meaning of the statement that we are a law-abiding nation is that we are passive resisters. When we do not like certain laws, we do not break the heads of law-givers but we suffer and do not submit to the laws. That we should obey laws whether good or bad is a new-fangled notion. There was no such thing in former days. The people disregarded those laws they did not like and suffered the penalties for their breach. It is contrary to our manhood if we obey laws repugnant to our conscience. Such teaching is opposed to religion and means slavery. If the Government were to ask us to go about without any clothing, should we do so? If I were a passive resister, I would say to them that I would have nothing to do with their law. But we have so forgotten ourselves and become so compliant that we do not mind any degrading law.

A man who has realized his manhood, who fears only God, will fear no one else. Man-made laws are not necessarily binding on him. Even the Government does not expect any such thing from us. They do not say: 'You must do such and such a thing,' but they say: 'If you do not do it, we will punish you.' We are sunk so low that we fancy that it is our duty and our religion to do what the law lays down. If man will only realize that it is unmanly to obey laws that are unjust, no man's tyranny will enslave him. This is the key to self-rule or home rule.

It is a superstition and ungodly thing to believe that an act of a majority binds a minority. Many examples can be given in which acts of majorities will be found to have been wrong and those of minorities to have been right. All reforms owe their origin to the initiation of minorities in opposition to majorities. If among a band of robbers a knowledge of robbing is obligatory, is a pious man to accept the obligation? So long as the superstition that men should obey unjust laws exists, so long will their slavery exist. And a passive resister alone can remove such a superstition.

To use brute-force, to use gunpowder, is contrary to passive resistance, for it means that we want our opponent to do by force that which we desire but he does not. And if such a use of force is justifiable, surely he is entitled to do likewise by us. And so we should never come to an agreement. We may simply fancy, like the blind horse moving in a circle round a mill, that we are making progress. Those who believe that they are not bound to obey laws which are repugnant to their conscience have only the remedy of passive resistance open to them. Any other must lead to disaster.

READER: From what you say I deduce that passive resistance is a splendid weapon of the weak, but that when they are strong they may take up arms.

EDITOR: This is gross ignorance. Passive resistance, that is, soul-force, is matchless. It is superior to the force of arms. How, then, can it be considered only a weapon of the weak? Physical-force men are strangers to the courage that is requisite in a passive resister. Do you believe that a coward can ever disobey a law that he dislikes? Extremists are considered to be advocates of brute force. Why do they, then, talk about obeying laws? I do not blame them. They can say nothing else. When they succeed in driving out the English and they themselves become governors, they will want you and me to obey their laws. And that is a fitting thing for their constitution. But a passive resister will say he will not obey a law that is against his conscience, even though he may be blown to pieces at the mouth of a cannon.

What do you think? Wherein is courage required—in blowing others to pieces from behind a cannon, or with a smiling face to approach a cannon and be blown to pieces? Who is the true warrior— he who keeps death always as a bosom-friend, or he who controls the death of others? Believe me that a man devoid of courage and manhood can never be a passive resister.

This, however, I will admit: that even a man weak in body is capable of offering this resistance. One man can offer it just as well as millions. Both men and women can indulge in it. It does not require the training of an army; it needs no jiu-jitsu. Control over the mind is alone necessary, and when that is attained, man is free like the king of the forest and his very glance withers the enemy.

Passive resistance is an all-sided sword, it can be used anyhow; it blesses him who uses it and him against whom it is used. Without drawing a drop of blood it produces far-reaching results. It never rusts and cannot be stolen. Competition between passive resisters does not exhaust. The sword of passive resistance does not require a scabbard. It is strange indeed that you should consider such a weapon to be weapon merely of the weak.

READER: You have said that passive resistance is a speciality of India. Have cannons never been used in India?

EDITOR: Evidently, in your opinion, India means its few princes. To me it means its teeming millions on whom depends the existence of its princes and our own.

Kings will always use their kingly weapons. To use force is bred in them. They want to command, but those who have to obey commands do not want guns: and these are in a majority throughout the world. They have to learn either body-force or soul-force. Where they learn the former, both the rulers and the ruled become like so many madmen; but where they learn soul-force, the commands of the rulers do not go beyond the point of their swords, for true men disregard unjust commands. Peasants have never been subdued by the sword, and never will be. They do not know the use of the sword, and they are not frightened by the use of it by others. That nation is great which rests its head upon death as its pillow. Those who defy death are free from all fear. For those who are labouring under the delusive charms of brute-force, this picture is not overdrawn. The fact is that, in India, the nation at large has generally used passive resistance in all departments of life. We cease to co-operate with our rulers when they displease us. This is passive resistance.

I remember an instance when, in a small principality, the villagers were offended by some command issued by the prince. The former immediately began vacating the village. The prince became nervous, apologized to his subjects and withdrew his command. Many such instances can be found in India. Real Home Rule is possible only where passive resistance is the guiding force of the people. Any other rule is foreign rule.

READER: Then you will say that it is not at all necessary for us to train the body?

EDITOR: I will certainly not say any such thing. It is difficult to become a passive resister unless the body is trained. As a rule, the mind, residing in a body that has become weak by pampering, is also weak, and where there is no strength of mind there can be no strength of soul. We shall have to improve our physique by getting rid of infant marriages and luxurious living. If I were to ask a man with a shattered body to face a cannon's mouth, I should make a laughing-stock of myself.

READER: From what you say, then, it would appear that it is not a small thing to become a passive resister, and, if that is so, I should like you to explain how a man may become one.

EDITOR: To become a passive resister is easy enough but it is also equally difficult. I have known a lad of fourteen years become a passive resister;

I have also known sick people do likewise; and I have also known physically strong and otherwise happy people unable to take up passive resistance. After a great deal of experience it seems to me that those who want to become passive resisters for the service of the country have to observe perfect chastity, adopt poverty, follow truth, and cultivate fearlessness.

Chastity is one of the greatest disciplines without which the mind cannot attain requisite firmness. A man who is unchaste loses stamina, becomes emasculated and cowardly. He whose mind is given over to animal passions is not capable of any great effort. This can be proved by innumerable instances. What, then, is a married person to do is the question that arises naturally; and yet it need not. When a husband and wife gratify the passions, it is no less an animal indulgence on that account. Such an indulgence, except for perpetuating the race, is strictly prohibited. But a passive resister has to avoid even that very limited indulgence because he can have no desire for progeny. A married man, therefore, can observe perfect chastity. This subject is not capable of being treated at greater length. Several questions arise: How is one to carry one's wife with one, what are her rights, and other similar questions. Yet those who wish to take part in a great work are bound to solve these puzzles.

Just as there is necessity for chastity, so is there for poverty. Pecuniary ambition and passive resistance cannot well go together. Those who have money are not expected to throw it away, but they *are* expected to be indifferent about it. They must be prepared to lose every penny rather than give up passive resistance.

Passive resistance has been described in the course of our discussion as truth-force. Truth, therefore, has necessarily to be followed and that at any cost. In this connection, academic questions such as whether a man may not lie in order to save a life, etc., arise, but these questions occur only to those who wish to justify lying. Those who want to follow truth every time are not placed in such a quandary; and if they are, they are still saved from a false position.

Passive resistance cannot proceed a step without fearlessness. Those alone can follow the path of passive resistance who are free from fear, whether as to their possessions, false honour, their relatives, the government, bodily injuries or death.

These observances are not to be abandoned in the belief that they are difficult. Nature has implanted in the human breast ability to cope with any difficulty or suffering that may come to man unprovoked. These qualities are worth having, even for those who do not wish to serve the country. Let there be no mistake, as those who want to train themselves in the use of arms are also obliged to have these qualities more or less. Everybody does not become a warrior for the wish. A would-be warrior will have to observe chastity and to be satisfied with poverty as his lot. A warrior without fearlessness cannot be conceived of. It may be thought that he would not need to be exactly truthful, but that quality follows real fearlessness. When a man abandons truth, he does so owing to fear in some shape or form. The above four attributes, then, need not frighten anyone. It may be as well here to note that a physical-force man has to have many other useless qualities which a passive resister never needs. And you will find that whatever extra effort a swordsman needs is due to lack of fearlessness. If he is an embodiment of the latter, the sword will drop from his hand that very moment. He does not need its support. One who is free from hatred requires no sword. A man with a stick suddenly came face to face with a lion and instinctively raised his weapon in self-defence. The man saw that he had only prated about fearlessness when there was none in him. That moment he dropped the stick and found himself free from all fear.[20]

Such non-violent resistance had to be national. But is India a nation, specially if we look upon it as consistently of two large religious communities—the Hindus and the Muslims. The reader asks pointedly: 'How can they be one nation? Hindus and Mahomedans are old enemies. Our very proverbs prove it. Mahomedans turn to the West for worship, whilst Hindus turn to the East. The former look down on the Hindus as idolaters. The Hindus worship the cow, the Mahomedans kill her. The Hindus believe in the doctrine of non-killing, the Mahomedans do not. We thus meet with differences at every step. How can India be one nation?'[21] Gandhi answers as follows by way of the editor:

EDITOR: Your last question is a serious one and yet, on careful consideration, it will be found to be easy of solution. The question arises because of the presence of the railways, of the lawyers and of the doctors. We shall presently examine the last two. We have already considered the railways. I should, however, like to add that man is so made by nature as to require him to restrict his movements as far as his hands and feet will take him. If we did not rush about from place to place by means of railways and such other maddening conveniences, much of the confusion that arises would be obviated. Our difficulties are of our own creation. God set a limit to man's locomotive ambition in the construction of his body. Man immediately proceeded to discover means of overriding the limit. God gifted man with intellect that he might know his Maker. Man abused it so that he might forget his Maker. I am so constructed that I can only serve my immediate neighbours, but in my conceit I pretend to have discovered that I must with my body serve every individual in the Universe. In thus attempting the impossible, man comes in contact with different natures, different religions, and is utterly confounded. According to this reasoning, it must be apparent to you that railways are a most dangerous institution. Owing to them, man has gone further away from his Maker.

READER: But I am impatient to hear your answer to my question. Has the introduction of Mahomedanism not unmade the nation?

EDITOR: India cannot cease to be one nation because people belonging to different religions live in it. The introduction of foreigners does not necessarily destroy the nation; they merge in it. A country must have a faculty for assimilation. India has ever been such a country. In reality, there are as many religions as there are individuals; but those who are conscious of the spirit of nationality do not interfere with one another's religion. If they do, they are not fit to be considered a nation. If the Hindus believe that India should be peopled only by Hindus, they are living in dreamland. The Hindus, the Mahomedans, the Parsis and the Christians who have made India their country are fellow countrymen, and they will have to live in unity, if only for their own interest. In no part of the world are one nationality and one religion synonymous terms; nor has it ever been so in India.

READER: But what about the inborn enmity between Hindus and Mahomedans?

EDITOR: That phrase has been invented by our mutual enemy. When the Hindus and Mahomedans fought against one another, they certainly spoke in that strain. They have long since ceased to fight. How, then, can there be any inborn enmity? Pray remember this too, that we did not cease to fight only after British occupation. The Hindus flourished under Moslem sovereigns and Moslems under the Hindu. Each party recognized that mutual fighting was suicidal, and that neither party would abandon its religion by force of arms. Both parties, therefore, decided to live in peace. With the English advent quarrels re-commenced.

The proverbs you have quoted were coined when both were fighting; to quote them now is obviously harmful. Should we not remember that many Hindus and Mahomedans own the same ancestors and the same blood runs through their veins? Do people become enemies because they change their religion? Is the God of the Mahomedan different from the God of the Hindu? Religions are different roads converging to the same point. What does it matter that we take different roads as long as we reach the same goal? Wherein is the cause for quarrelling?

Moreover, there are deadly proverbs as between the followers of Shiva and those of Vishnu, yet nobody suggests that these two do not belong to the same nation. It is said that the Vedic religion is different from Jainism, but the followers of the respective faiths are not different nations. The fact is that we have become enslaved and, therefore, quarrel and like to have our quarrels decided by a third party. There are Hindu iconoclasts as there are Mahomedan. The more we advance in true knowledge, the better we shall understand that we need not be at war with those whose religion we may not follow.

READER: Now I would like to know your views about cow-protection.

EDITOR: I myself respect the cow, that is, I look upon her with affectionate reverence. The cow is the protector of India because, being an agricultural country, she is dependent on the cow. The cow is a most useful animal in hundreds of ways. Our Mahomedan brethren will admit this.

But, just as I respect the cow, so do I respect my fellow-men. A man is just as useful as a cow no matter whether he be a Mahomedan or a Hindu. Am I, then, to fight with or kill a Mahomedan in order to save a cow? In doing so, I would become an enemy of the Mahomedan as well as of the cow. Therefore, the only method I know of protecting the cow is that I would approach my Mahomedan brother and urge him for the sake of the country to join me in protecting her. If he would not listen to me I should let the cow go for the simple reason that the matter is beyond my ability. If I were overfull of pity for the cow, I should sacrifice my life to save her but not take my brother's. This, I hold, is the law of our religion.

When men become obstinate, it is a difficult thing. If I pull one way, my Moslem brother will pull another. If I put on superior airs, he will return the compliment. If I bow to him gently, he will do it much more so; and if he does not, I shall not be considered to have done wrong in having bowed. When the Hindus became insistent, the killing of cows increased. In my opinion, cow-protection societies may be considered cow-killing societies. It is a disgrace to us that we should need such societies. When we forgot how to protect cows, I suppose we needed such societies.

What am I to do when a blood-brother is on the point of killing a cow? Am I to kill him, or to fall down at his feet and implore him? If you admit that I should adopt the latter course, I must do the same to my Moslem brother.

Who protects the cow from destruction by Hindus when they cruelly ill-treat her? Whoever reasons with the Hindus when they mercilessly belabour the progeny of the cow with their sticks? But this has not prevented us from remaining one nation.

Lastly, if it be true that the Hindus believe in the doctrine of non-killing and the Mahomedans do not, what, pray, is the duty of the former? It is not written that a follower of the religion of Ahimsa (non-killing) may kill a fellow-man. For him the way is straight. In order to save one being, he may not kill another. He can only plead—therein lies his sole duty.

But does every Hindu believe in Ahimsa? Going to the root of the matter, not one man really practises such a religion because we do destroy life. We are said to follow that religion because we want to obtain freedom from liability to kill any kind of life. Gnerally speaking, we may observe that many Hindus partake of meat and are not, therefore, followers of Ahimsa. It is, therefore, preposterous to suggest that the two cannot live together amicably because the Hindus believe in Ahimsa and the Mahomedans do not.

These thoughts are put into our minds by selfish and false religious teachers. The English put the finishing touch. They have a habit of writing history; they pretend to study the manners and customs of all peoples. God has given us a limited mental capacity, but they usurp the function of the Godhead and indulge in novel experiments. They write about their own researches in most laudatory terms and hypnotize us into believing them. We in our ignorance then fall at their feet.

Those who do not wish to misunderstand things may read up the *Koran*, and they will find therein hundreds of passages acceptable to the Hindus; and the *Bhagavad Gita* contains passages to which not a Mahomedan can take exception. Am I to dislike a Mahomedan because there are passages in the *Koran* I do not understand or like? It takes two to make a quarrel. If I do not want to quarrel with a Mahomedan, the latter will be powerless to foist a quarrel on me; and, similarly, I should be powerless if a Mahomedan refuses his assistance to quarrel with me.

An arm striking the air will become disjointed. If everyone will try to understand the core of his own religion and adhere to it, and will not allow false teachers to dictate to him there will be no room left for quarrelling.

READER: But will the English ever allow the two bodies to join hands?

EDITOR: This question arises out of your timidity. It betrays our shallowness. If two brothers want to live in peace, is it possible for a third party to separate them? If they were to listen to evil counsels we would consider them to be foolish. Similarly, we Hindus and Mahomedans would have to blame our folly rather than the English, if we allowed them to put us asunder. A clay pot would break through impact, if not with one stone, then with another. The way to save the pot is not to keep it away from the danger point but to bake it so that no stone would break it. We have then to make our hearts of perfectly baked clay. Then we shall be steeled against all danger. This can be easily done by the Hindus. They are superior in numbers; they pretend that they are more educated; they are, therefore, better able to shield themselves from attack on their amicable relations with the Mahomedans.

There is mutual distrust between the two communities. The Mahomedans, therefore, ask for certain concessions from Lord Morley. Why should the Hindus oppose this? If the Hindus desisted, the English would notice it, the Mahomedans would gradually begin to trust the Hindus, and brotherliness would be the outcome. We should be ashamed to take our quarrels to the English. Everyone can find out for himself that the Hindus can lose nothing by desisting. That man who has inspired confidence in another has never lost anything in this world.

I do not suggest that the Hindus and the Mahomedans will never fight. Two brothers living together often do so. We shall sometimes have our heads broken. Such a thing ought not to be necessary, but all men are not equitable. When people are in a rage, they do many foolish things. These we have to put up with. But when we do quarrel, we certainly do not want to engage counsel and resort to English or any law-courts. Two men fight; both have their heads broken, or one only. How shall a third party distribute justice amongst them? Those who fight may expect to be injured.[22]

An important aspect of Gandhian thought is its critique of modern civilization. In terms of Gandhian thought it is not so much the case that the British had enslaved the Indians; the reality was that both had equally been enslaved by modern civilization and stood in need of being liberated from it. Gandhi regarded doctors, lawyers and machinery as typical of modern civilization and its ills. A summary statement on this point, which Gandhi made in a letter to a friend, must suffice to cover it in place of an extended extract from the book. The points in this letter in a way summarize the book itself.

1. There is no impassable barrier between East and West.
2. There is no such thing as western or European civilization, but there is a modern civilization which is purely material.
3. The people of Europe, before they were touched by modern civilization, had much in common with the people of India, and even today the Europeans who are not touched by modern civilization, are far better able to mix with Indians than the off-spring of that civilization.
4. It is not the British people who are ruling India, but it is modern civilization, through its railways, telegraph, telephone, and almost every invention which has been claimed to be a triumph of civilization.
5. Bombay, Calcutta, and other chief cities of India are the real plague-spots.
6. If British rule were replaced tomorrow by Indian rule based on modern methods, India would be no better, except that she would be able to retain some of the money that is drained away to England; but then India would only become a second or fifth nation of Europe or America.
7. East and West can really meet when the West has thrown overboard modern civilization, almost in its entirety. They can also seemingly meet when East has also adopted modern civilization, but that meeting would be an armed truce, even as it is between, say, Germany and England, both of which nations are living in the Hall of Death in order to avoid being devoured, the one by the other.
8. It is impertinence for any man or any body of men to begin or to contemplate reform of the whole world. To attempt to do so by means of highly artificial and speedy locomotion, is to attempt the impossible.
9. Increase of material comforts, it may be generally laid down, does not in any way whatsoever conduce to moral growth.
10. Medical science is concentrated essence of black magic. Quackery

is infinitely preferable to what passes for high medical skill as such.

11. Hospitals are the instruments that the Devil has been using for his own purpose, in order to keep his hold on his kingdom. They perpetuate vice, misery, and degradation and real slavery. I was entirely off the track when I considered that I should receive medical training. It would be sinful for me in any way whatsoever to take part in the abominations that go in the hospitals. If there were no hospitals for venereal diseases, or even for consumptives, we should have less consumption, and less sexual vice amongst us.

12. India's salvation consists in unlearning what she has learnt during the past fifty years or so. The railways, telegraphs, hospitals, lawyers, doctors, and such like have all to go, and the so-called upper classes have to learn to live consciously and religiously and deliberately the simple life of a peasant knowing it to be a life giving true happiness.

13. India should wear no machine-made clothing whether it comes out of European mills or Indian mills.

14. England can help India to do this and she will have justified her hold on India. There seems to be many in England today who think likewise.

15. There was true wisdom in the sages of old having so regulated society as to limit the material conditions of the people: the rude plough of perhaps five thousand years ago is the plough of the husbandman today. Therein lies salvation. People live long under such conditions, in comparative peace much greater than Europe has enjoyed after having taken up modern activity, and I feel that every enlightened man, certainly every Englishman, may, if he chooses, learn this truth and act according to it.[23]

Gandhi and the Caste System

The fact that Gandhi could still, years after writing it, hark back to Hind Swaraj *as a valid statement of his principles should not be taken to mean that Gandhian thought was either monolithic or static, because it was neither. Its dynamic quality, in contrast to its staying power, is illustrated by Gandhi's position over the years on the caste system. I am indebted to Professor Mark Lindley for the following selections which illustrate this point.*

1920

I believe that caste has saved Hinduism from disintegration. But like every other institution it has suffered from excrescences. I consider the four divisions alone to be fundamental, natural and essential. The innumerable sub-castes are sometimes a convenience, often a hindrance. The sooner there is fusion, the better . . . .

One of my correspondents suggests that we should abolish the caste [system] but adopt the class system of Europe—meaning thereby, I suppose, that the idea of heredity in caste should be rejected. I am inclined to think that the law of heredity is an eternal law and any attempt to alter that law must lead us, as it has before led [others], to utter confusion . . . . If Hindus believe, as they must believe, in reincarnation [and] transmigration, they must know that Nature will, without any possibility of mistake, adjust the balance by degrading a Brahmin, if he misbehaves himself, by reincarnating him in a lower division, and translating one who lives the life of a Brahmin in his present incarnation to Brahminhood in his next. (C, XIX, 83f)[24]

1920

The beauty of the caste system is that it does not base itself upon distinctions of wealth-possession. Money, as history has proved, is the greatest disruptive force in the world . . . . Caste is but an extension of the principle of the family. Both are governed by blood and heredity. Western scientists are busy trying to prove that heredity is an illusion and that milieu is everything. The . . . experience of many lands goes against the conclusions of these scientists; but even accepting their doctrine of milieu, it is easy to prove that milieu can be conserved and developed more through caste than through class . . . . As we all know, change comes very slowly in social life, and thus, as a matter of fact, caste has allowed new groupings to suit the changes in lives. But these changes are [as] quiet and easy as a change in the shape of the clouds. It is difficult to imagine a better harmonious human adjustment.

Caste does not connote superiority or inferiority. It simply recognizes different outlooks and corresponding modes of life. But it is no use denying the fact that a sort of hierarchy has been evolved in the caste system, but it cannot be called the creation of the Brahmins. When all castes accept a common [religious] goal of life, a hierarchy is inevitable, because all castes cannot realize the ideal in equal degree. (C, XIX, 174ff)

1921–1922

I believe that if Hindu society has been able to stand, it is because it is founded on the caste system . . . . A community which can create the caste system must be said to possess unique power of organization . . . .

To destroy the caste system and adopt the Western European social system means that Hindus must give up the principle of hereditary occupation which is the soul of the caste system. [The] hereditary principle is an eternal principle. To change it is to create disorder . . . . It will be a chaos if every day a Brahmin is to be changed into a Shudra and a Shudra is to be changed into a Brahmin. The caste system is a natural order of society . . . . I am opposed to all those who are out to destroy the caste system. (A, IX, 275f)[25]

1925

There is no harm if a person belonging to one varna acquires the knowledge of science and art specialized in by persons belonging to other varnas. But as far as the way of earning his living is concerned, he must follow the occupation of the varna to which he belongs, which means he must follow the hereditary profession of his forefathers.

The object of the varna system is to prevent competition and class struggle and class war. I believe in the varna system because it fixes the duties and occupations of persons . . . . Varna means the determination of a man's occupation before he is born. . . . In the varna system no man has any liberty to choose his profession. (A, IX, 277)

1925

For me there is no question of superiority or inferiority. A Brahmin who regards himself as [a] superior being born to look down upon the other castes is not a Brahmin. If he is first [in status] he is so by right of [spiritual] service. (C, XXVI, 289)

1926

In accepting the fourfold division I am simply accepting the laws of Nature, taking for granted what is inherent in human nature and the law of heredity . . . . It is not possible in one birth entirely to undo the results of our past doings. (C, XXIX, 410f)

1927

In [my] conception of the law of varna no one is superior to any other.
. . . A scavenger has the same status as a Brahmin. (C, XXXV, 260)

1927

I remember in 1915 the Chairman of the Social Conference in Nellore
suggesting that formerly all were Brahmins, and that now too all should
be recognized as such and that the other varnas should be abolished.
It appeared to me then, as it appears to me now, as a weird suggestion.
It is the so-called superior that has to descend from his heights, if the
reform is to be peaceful. (C, XXXV, 262f)

1931

I do not believe in caste in the modern sense. It is an excrescence and
a handicap on progress. Nor do I believe in inequalities between human
bings. We are all absolutely equal. But equality is of souls and not bodies
. . . . We have to realize equality in the midst of this apparent inequality.
Assumption of superiority by any person over any other is a sin against
God and man. Thus caste, in so far as it connotes distinctions in status,
is an evil.

I do however believe in varna which is based on hereditary occupations. Varnas are four to mark four universal occupations—imparting
knowledge, defending the defenceless, carrying on agriculture and
commerce, and performing service [to other humans] through physical
labour. These occupations are common to all mankind, but Hinduism,
having recognized them as the law of our being, has made use of this in
regulating social relations and conduct. Gravitation affects us all whether
one knows its existence or not. But scientists who knew the law have
made it yield results that have startled the world. Even so has Hinduism
startled the world by its discovery and application of the law of varna.

[Yet] according to my definition of varna there is no varna in
operation at present in Hinduism. The so-called Brahmins have ceased
to impart knowledge. They take to various other occupations. This is
more or less true of the other varnas. (C, XLVI, 302)

1932

My own opinion is that the varna system has just now broken down.
There is no true Brahmin or true Kshatriya or Vaishya. We are all
Shudras, i.e. one varna. If this position is accepted, then the thing

becomes easy. If this does not satisfy our vanity, then we are all Brahmins. Removal of untouchability does mean root-and-branch destruction of the idea of superiority and inferiority. (C, LI, 199f)

1932

No matter what was the position in ancient times, no one can nowadays go through life claiming to belong to a high class. Society will not willingly admit any such claim to superiority, but only under duress. The world is now wide awake . . . .

When it is suggested that everyone should practise his father's profession, the suggestion is coupled with the condition that the practitioner of every profession will earn only a living wage and no more . . . . The lawyer or doctor ought by practising his profession to earn only a living wage. And such was actually the case formerly . . . .

Boys [between 9 and 16 years of age] should be taught their parents' vocation in such a way that they will by their own choice obtain their livelihood by practising the hereditary craft. This does not apply to girls . . . . [From] 16 to 25 . . . every young person should have an education according to his or her wishes and circumstances. (C, L, 233)

If eradication of castes means the abolition of varna I do not approve of it. But I am with you if your aim is to end the innumerable caste distinctions. (C, LI, 264)

1933

AMBEDKAR: There will be outcastes as long as there are castes, and nothing can emanicipate the outcaste except the destruction of the caste system.

GANDHI: Dr Ambedkar is bitter, he has every reason to feel so . . . . [Yet] I do not believe the caste system, even as distinguished from Varnashrama, to be an 'odious and vicious dogma'. It has its limitations and defects, but there is nothing sinful about it, as there is about untoucahbility, and if [untouchability] is a by-product of the system, it is only in the same sense that an ugly growth is of a body, or weeds of crop. (T, III, 192f)[26]

1934

INTERVIEWER: Do you not think that in ancient India there was much difference in economic status and social privileges between the four varnas?

GANDHI: That may be historically true. But misapplication or an imperfect understanding of the law must not lead to the ignoring of the law itself. By constant striving we have to enrich the inheritance left to us. (C, LIX, 319)

1935

Caste Has To Go. Varnashrama of the shastras is today nonexistent in practice. The present caste system is the very antithesis of Varnashrama. The sooner public opinion abolishes it the better.

. . . Prohibition there is [in varnashrama] of change of one's hereditary occupation for purposes of gain. The existing practice is therefore doubly wrong in that it has set up cruel restrictions about interdining and intermarriage and tolerates anarchy about choice of occupation . . . .

The most effective, quickest and the most unobtrusive way to destroy caste is for reformers to begin the practice with themselves and, where necessary, take the consequences of social boycott. The change will be gradual and imperceptible. (C, LXII, 121f)

1945

In my opinion a man daily moves either forward or backward. He never stands still. The whole world is moving and there is no exception . . . .

Where are the four varnas of 'he Gita today? . . . There prevails only one varna today, that is, of 'Shudras', or, you may call it, 'Ati-Shudras' . . . . If I can bring round the Hindu society to my view, all our internal quarrels will come to an end . . . .

A man should consider himself not the owner of his property but its trustee . . . for the service of society. He will accept only that much for himself as he has earned with his [physical] labour. If that happens, no one will be poor and no one rich. In such a system, all religions will naturally be held equal. Therefore all quarrels arising [today] out of religion, caste and economic differences will be ended.

This is the swaraj of my dreams. I yearn for that. I want to live for the attainment of it. I am devoting every breath of my life to that effort.

The reader is therefore requested to discard anything in this book which may appear to him incompatible with my views given above. (C, LXXX, 222ff)

1946

You should become like Ambedkar. You should work for the removal of untouchability and caste. Untouchability must go at any cost.

1946

(AS REPORTED): 'He said he was trying to create a classless and casteless India. He yearned for the day when there would be only one caste and Brahmins would marry Harijans. "I am a social revolutionist," he asserted. "Violence is bred by inequality, non-violence by equality." ' (F, 425)[27]

1946

[Q.] In your recent correspondence . . . you have said that caste ought to go root and branch if untouchability is to be completely eradicated. Then, why do you not make anti-untouchability work part of a wider crusade against the caste system itself? If you dig out the root, the branches will wither by themselves.

[A.] It is one thing for me to hold certain views and quite another to make my views acceptable in their entirety to society at large. My mind, I hope, is ever growing, ever moving forward. All may not keep pace with it. I have therefore to exercise the utmost patience and be satisfied with hastening slowly . . . . I am wholly in agreement with you in principle. If I live up to 125 years, I do expect to convert the entire Hindu society to my view. (C, LXXXV, 24)

1947

(AS REPORTED): '[The] vocational organization of society, held Gandhi, may be vertical and competitive, or horizontal and cooperative. Under the former, remuneration is . . . on the basis of the law of supply and demand; in the latter all occupations are paid equal wages . . . [and] a person will choose an occupation, not because of the personal prospects it offers, but because he has special skill or aptitude for it. And since skills and aptitudes generally follow the line of heredity more or less, the average person in the normal course would, if there were no inequalities of remuneration to lure him away from it, tend to follow the occupation he is born in . . . . Would that mean that one would be debarred from changing his hereditary occupation, if he felt a special urge? "No," said Gandhiji, "not so long as one does not depend on it [the new occupation] for one's living." Such cases will naturally be few. Thus Buddha was [by heredity] a ruling prince, Socrates the prince of philosophers and St. Paul an apostle; but not one of them regarded their calling as a means of livelihood.' (P, I 541f)[28]

1947

Indian society may never reach the goal [equal wages for all] but it is the duty of every Indian to set his sail towards that goal and no other if India is to be a happy land. (C, LXXXVII, 10)

Mahatma Gandhi on Religion and Politics

Mahatma Gandhi ostensibly took the rather surprising stand that religion and politics cannot be separated from each other. His position runs the risk of being misunderstood unless it is clearly recognized that for Gandhi morality was the essence of religion.[29] One must therefore take religion to mean morality, when religion and politics are described as inseparable in the middle of the following text.

The entire selection constitutes Gandhi's farewell to the readers of his autobiography.

Farewell

The time has now come to bring these chapters to a close.

My life from this point onward has been so public that there is hardly anything about it that people do not know. Moreover, since 1921 I have worked in such close association with the Congress leaders that I can hardly describe any episode in my life since then without referring to my relation with them. For though Shraddhanandji, the Deshabandhu, Hakim Saheb and Lalaji are no more with us today, we have the good luck to have a host of other veteran Congress leaders still living and working in our midst. The history of the Congress, since the great changes in it that I have described above, is still in the making. And my principal experiments during the past seven years have all been made through the Congress. A reference to my relations with the leaders would therefore be unavoidable, if I set about describing my experiments further. And this I may not do, at any rate for the present, if only from a sense of propriety. Lastly, my conclusions from my current experiments can hardly as yet be regarded as decisive. It therefore seems to me to be my plain duty to close this narrative here. In fact my pen instinctively refuses to proceed further.

It is not without a wrench that I have to take leave of the reader. I set a high value on my experiments. I do not know whether I have been able to do justice to them. I can only say that I have spared no pains to give a faithful narrative. To describe truth, as it had appeared to me, and in the exact manner in which I have arrived at it, has been my ceaseless effort. The exercise has given me ineffable mental peace, because, it has been my fond hope that it might bring faith in Truth and Ahimsa to waverers.

My uniform experience has convinced me that there is no other God than Truth. And if every page of these chapters does not proclaim to the reader that the only means for the realization of Truth is Ahimsa, I shall deem all my labour in writing these chapters to have been in vain. And, even though my efforts in this behalf may prove fruitless, let the readers know that the vehicle, not the great principle, is at fault. After all, however sincere my strivings after Ahimsa may have been, they have still been imperfect and inadequate. The little fleeting glimpses, therefore, that I have been able to have of Truth can hardly convey an idea of the indescribable lustre of Truth, a million times more intense than that of the sun we daily see with our eyes. In fact what I have caught is only the faintest glimmer of that mighty effulgence. But this much I can say with assurance, as a result of all my experiments, that a perfect vision of Truth can only follow a complete realization of Ahimsa.

To see the universal and all-pervading Spirit of Truth face to face one must be able to love the meanest of creations oneself. And a man who aspires after that cannot afford to keep out of any field of life. That is why my devotion to Truth had drawn me into the field of politics; and I can say without the slightest hesitation, and yet in all humility, that those who say that religion has nothing to do with politics do not know what religion means.

Identification with everything that lives is impossible without self-purification; without self-purification the observance of the law of Ahimsa must remain an empty dream; God can never be realized by one who is not pure of heart. Self-purification therefore must mean purification in all the walks of life. And purification being highly infectious, purification of oneself necessarily leads to the purification of one's surroundings.

But the path of self-purification is hard and steep. To attain to perfect purity one has to become absolutely passion-free in thought, speech and action; to rise above the opposing currents of love and hatred, attachment and repulsion. I know that I have not in me as yet that triple purity, in spite of constant ceaseless striving for it. That is why the world's praise fails to move me, indeed it very often stings me. To conquer the subtle passions seems to me to be far harder than the physical conquest of the world by the force of arms. Ever since my return to India I have had the experiences of the dormant passions lying hidden within me. The knowledge of them has made me feel humiliated though not defeated. The experiences and experiments have sustained me and given me great joy. But I know that I have still before me a difficult path to traverse. I must reduce myself to zero. So long as a man does not of his own free will put himself last among his fellow creatures, there is no salvation for him. Ahimsa is the farthest limit of humility.

In bidding farewell to the reader, for the time being at any rate, I ask him to join with me in prayer to the God of Truth that He may grant me the boon of Ahimsa in mind, word and deed.[30]

Mahatma Gandhi on Varna and Āśrma

The caste system, as Mahatma Gandhi found it prevailing in Hindu society, was characterized by the following features at least in theory and often in practice: (1) occupation by birth-ascription; (2) marriage restricted to within one's caste; (3) a similar restriction on interdining; (4) hierarchy among the castes; and (5) the existence of untouchables, whose touch was considered polluting.

Gandhi, even in his teens, rejected untouchability, and regarded the idea of inferiority and superiority of castes as a distortion of the system. His thinking gradually evolved in the direction of first the mitigation and then elimination of commensality and endogamy. Hence, finally, the only element of the traditional caste system which Gandhi retained in his own idealized version of it was the hereditary determination of occupation. To the natural question: what if one's natural gifts do not coincide with one's birth-ascribed occupation he offered a typically Gandhian response—these must be made available to society free of charge. For Gandhi, what the so-called caste system, which he regarded as a misnomer for the Hindu varna system, meant was that one is entitled to earning one's livelihood only through the occupation of one's birth. For Gandhi, in this lay the solution to the modern problem of ruthless economic competition.

Gandhi was quite forceful in his advocacy of his understanding of the 'caste' system.

Varna and Ashrama

So far as I know anything at all of Hinduism, the meaning of *varna* is incredibly simple. It simply means the following on the part of us all of the hereditary and traditional calling of our forefathers, in so far as the traditional calling is not inconsistent with fundamental ethics, and this only for the purpose of earning one's livelihood. I regard this as the law of our being, if we would accept the definition of man given in all religions. Of all the animal creation of God, man is the only animal who has been created in order that he may know his Maker. Man's aim in life is not therefore to add from day to day to his material prospects and to his material possessions but his predominant calling is from day to day to come nearer his own Maker, and from this definition it was that the *rishis* of old discovered this law of our being. You will realize that if all of us follow this law of *varna* we would limit our material ambition, and our energy would be set free for exploring those vast fields whereby and wherethrough we can know God. You will at once then see that nine-tenths of the activities that are today going on throughout the world and which are engrossing our attention would fall into disuse. You would then be entitled to say that *varna* as we observe it today is a travesty of the *varna* that I have described to you. And so it undoubtedly is, but just as we do not hate truth because untruth parades itself as truth, but we sift untruth from truth and cling to the latter, so also we can destroy the distortion that passes as *varna*, and purify the state to which the Hindu society has been reduced today.

Ashrama is a necessary corollary to what I have stated to you, and if *varna* today has become distorted, *ashrama* has altogether disappeared. *Ashrama* means the four stages in one's life, and I wish the students who have kindly presented their purses to me—the Arts and Science students and the Law College students—were able to assure me that they were living according to the laws of the first *ashrama*, and that they were *brahmacharis* in thought, word and deed. The *brahmacharya ashrama* enjoins that only those who live the life of a *brahmachari*, at least up to 25 years, are entitled to enter the second *ashrama* i.e. the Grihasthashrama. And because the whole conception of Hinduism is to make man better than he is and draw him nearer to his Maker, the *rishis* set a limit even to the *grihasthashrama* stage and imposed on us the obligation of *vanaprastha* and *sannyasa*. But today you will vainly search throughout the length and breadth of India for a true *brahmachari*, for a true *grihastha*, not to talk of a *vanaprastha* and *sannyasi*. We may, in our elongated wisdom, laugh at this scheme of life, if we wish to. But I have no doubt whatsoever that this is the secret of the great success of Hinduism. The Hindu civilization has survived the Egyptian, the Assyrian and the Babylonian. The Christian is but two thousand years old. The Islamic is but of yesterday. Great as both these are they are still in my humble opinion in the making. Christian Europe is not at all Christian, but is groping, and so in my opinion is Islam still groping for its great secret, and there is today a competition, healthy as also extremely unhealthy and ugly, between these three great religions.

As years go by, the conviction is daily growing upon me that *varna* is the law of man's being and therefore as necessary for Christianity and Islam, as it has been necessary for Hinduism and has been its saving. I refuse, therefore, to believe that *varnashrama* has been the curse of Hinduism, as it is the fashion nowadays in the South on the part of some Hindus to say. But that does not mean that you and I may tolerate for one moment or be gentle towards the hideous travesty of *varnashrama* that we see about us today. There is nothing in common between *varnashrama* and caste. Caste, if you will, is undoubtedly a drag upon Hindu progress, and untouchability is, as I have already called it or described it, an excrescence upon *varnashrama*. It is a weedy growth fit only to be weeded out, as we weed out the weeds that we see growing in wheat fields or rice fields. In this conception of *varna*, there is absolutely no idea of superiority and inferiority. If I again interpret the Hindu spirit rightly all life is absolutely equal and one. It is therefore an arrogant assumption on the part of the *brahmana* when he says, 'I am superior to the other three *varnas.*' That is not what the *brahmanas* of old said. They commanded homage not because they claimed superiority, but because they claimed the right of service through and through without the slightest expectation of a reward. The priests, who today arrogate to themselves the function of the *brahmana* and distort religion, are no custodians of Hinduism or *brahmanism*. Consciously or unconsciously they are laying the axe at the root of the very tree on which they are sitting, and when they tell you that *shastras* enjoin untouchability and when they talk of pollution distance, I have no hesitation in saying that they are belying their creed and that they are misinterpreting the spirit of Hinduism. You will now perhaps understand why it is absolutely necessary for you Hindus who are here and listening to me to energize yourselves and rid yourselves of this curse. You should take pride in leading the way of reform, belonging as you do to an ancient Hindu State. So far as I can read the atmosphere around you here, the moment is certainly propitious for you if you will sincerely and energetically undertake this reform.[31]

Appendix

The thought and practice of Mahatma Gandhi has gained global recognition. This raises the question of its applicability in non-Indian conditions, even when the issues involved appear similar to those faced by him in India. Readers might find the following responses to his suggestions, one of them by a person no less in stature than the famous Jewish scholar Martin Buber himself, stimulating in this context. They might also welcome this opportunity of seeing modern Hindu thought in 'dialogue' with other traditions.

Mahatma Gandhi and the Jewish Question

The success of the Gandhian technique of non-violent agitation in securing India's independence, although assisted no doubt by a cluster of other factors, remains a remarkable accomplishment. This raises the question of its limitations—one of which was provided by its inability to prevent the partition of the country. Even if one is tempted to dismiss this as a domestic quirk of the Indian situation, the larger issue of the context in which such a struggle is viable continues to be relevant, as illustrated by the situation of the African Americans in the USA. The issue surfaces with great force and clarity in the following selection, which consists of two letters addressed to Mahatma Gandhi—one by Martin Buber and the other by J. L. Magnes, in response to his statement of 26 November 1938, which appears first.[32]

I

Gandhi's Statement
From *Harijan*, 26 November 1938

Several letters have been received by me asking me to declare my views about the Arab-Jew question in Palestine and the persecution of the Jews in Germany. It is not without hesitation that I venture to offer my views on this very difficult question.

My sympathies are all with the Jews. I have known them intimately in South Africa. Some of them became lifelong companions. Through these friends, I came to learn much of their age-long persecution. They have been the untouchables of Christianity. The parallel between their treatment by Christians and the treatment of untouchables by Hindus is very close.

Religious sanction has been invoked in both cases, for the justification of the inhuman treatment meted out to them. Apart from the friendships, therefore, there is the more common universal reason for my sympathy for the Jews.

But my sympathy does not blind me to the requirements of justice. The cry for the national home for the Jews does not make much appeal to me. The sanction for it is sought in the Bible and the tenacity with which the Jews have hankered after return to Palestine.

Why should they not like other peoples of the earth, make that country their home where they are born and where they earn their livelihood?

Palestine belongs to the Arabs in the same sense that England belongs to the English, or France to the French. It is wrong and inhuman to impose the Jews on the Arabs.

What is going on in Palestine today cannot be justified by any moral code of conduct. The mandates have no sanction but that of the last war. Surely it would be a crime against humanity to reduce the proud Arabs so that Palestine can be restored to the Jews partly or wholly as their national home.

The nobler course would be to insist on a just treatment of the Jews wherever they are born and bred. The Jews born in France are French in precisely the same sense that Christians born in France are French.

If the Jews have no home but Palestine, will they relish the idea of being forced to leave the other parts of the world in which they are settled? Or do they want a double home where they can remain at will? This cry for the National Home affords a colourable justification for the German expulsion of the Jews.

But the German persecution of the Jews seems to have no parallel in history. The tyrants of old never went so mad as Hitler seems to have gone. And he is doing it with religious zeal. For he is propounding a new religion of exclusive and militant nationalism, in the name of which any inhumanity becomes an act of humanity to be rewarded here and hereafter. The crime of an obviously mad but intrepid youth is being visited upon his whole race with unbelievable ferocity. If there ever could be justifiable war in the name of and for humanity, a war against Germany, to prevent the wanton persecution of a whole race, would be completely justified. But I do not believe in any war. A discussion of the pros and cons of such a war is therefore outside my horizon or province.

But if there can be no war against Germany, even for such a crime as is being committed against the Jews, surely there can be no alliance between a nation which claims to stand for justice and democracy and one which is the declared enemy of both? Or is England drifting towards armed dictatorship and all it means?

Germany is showing to the world how efficiently violence can be worked when it is not hampered by any hypocrisy or weakness masquerading as humanitarianism. It is also showing how hideous, terrible and terrifying it looks in its nakedness.

Can the Jews resist this organised and shameless persecution? Is there a way to preserve their self-respect, and not to feel helpless, neglected and forlorn? I submit there is. No person who has faith in a living God need feel helpless or forlorn. Jehovah of the Jews is a God more personal than the God of the Christians, the Mussalmans or the Hindus, though as a matter of fact in essence, He is common to all and one without a second and beyond description. But as the Jews attribute personality to God and believe that He rules every action of theirs, they ought not to feel helpless.

If I were a Jew and were born in Germany and earned my livelihood here I would claim Germany as my home even as the tallest gentile German may, and challenge him to shoot me or cast me in the dungeon; I would refuse to be expelled or to submit to discriminating treatment. And for doing this I should not wait for the fellow Jews to join me in civil resistance, but would have confidence that in the end the rest are bound to follow my example. If one Jew or all the Jews were to accept the prescription here offered, he or they cannot be worse off than now. And suffering voluntarily undergone will bring them an inner strength and joy which no number of resolutions of sympathy passed in the world outside Germany can. Indeed even if Britain, France and America were to declare hostilities against Germany, they can bring no inner joy, no inner strength.

The calculated violence of Hitler may even result in the general massacre of the Jews by way of his first answer to the declaration of such hostilities. But if the Jewish mind could be prepared for *voluntary suffering*, even the massacre I have imagined could be turned into a day of thanksgiving and joy that Jehovah had wrought deliverance of the race even at the hands of the tyrant. For the God-fearing, death has no terror.

It is hardly necessary for me to point out that it is easier for the Jews than for the Czechs to follow my prescription. And they have in the Indian *satyagraha* campaign in South Africa an *exact parallel*. There the Indians occupied precisely the same place that the Jews occupy in Germany. The persecution had also a religious tinge. President Kruger used to say that the white Christians were the chosen of God and Indians were inferior beings created to serve the whites. A fundamental clause in the Transvaal Constitution was that there should be no equality between the whites and coloured races, including Asiatics. There too the Indians were consigned to ghettos described as locations. The other disabilities were almost of the same type as those of the Jews in Germany. The Indians, a mere handful, resorted to *satyagraha* without any backing from the world outside or the Indian Government. Indeed, the British officials tried to dissuade the satyagrahis from their contemplated step. World opinion and the Indian Government came to their aid after eight years of fighting. And that too was by way of diplomatic pressure, not of a threat of war.

But the Jews of Germany can offer *satyagraha* under definitely better auspices than the Indians of South Africa. The Jews are a compact, homogeneous community in Germany. They are far more gifted than the Indians of South Africa. And they have organised world opinion behind them. I am convinced that if someone with courage and vision can arise among them to lead them in non-violent action, the winter of their despair can in the twinkling of an eye be turned into the summer of hope. And what has today become a degrading man-hunt can be turned into a calm and determined stand offered by unarmed men and women possessing the strength of suffering given to them by Jehovah. It will be then a truly religious resistance offered against the godless fury of dehumanized man. The German Jews will score a lasting victory over the German Gentiles in the sense that they will have converted the latter to an appreciation of human dignity. They will have rendered service to fellow Germans and proved their title to be the real Germans as against those who are today dragging, however unknowingly, the German name into the mire. And now a word to the Jews in Palestine. I have no doubt that they are going about it the wrong way. The Palestine of the Biblical conception *is not a geographical tract. It is in their hearts.* But if they must look to the Palestine of geography as their National Home, it is wrong to enter it under the shadow of the *British gun*. A religious act cannot be performed with the aid of the bayonet or the bomb. They can settle in Palestine only by the goodwill of the Arabs. They should seek to convert the Arab heart. The same God rules the Arab heart who rules the Jewish heart. They can offer *satyagraha* in front of the Arabs and offer themselves to be shot or thrown into the Dead Sea without raising a little finger against them. They will find world opinion in their favour in their religious aspiration. There are hundreds of ways of reasoning with the Arabs, if they will only discard the help of the British bayonet. As it is, they are co-sharers with the British in despoiling a people who have done no wrong to them.

II
Letter to Mahatma Gandhi from Martin Buber

He who is unhappy lends a deaf ear when idle tongues discuss his fate amongst themselves. But when a voice that he has long known and honoured, a great voice and an earnest one, pierces the vain clamour and calls him by his name, he is all attention. Here is a voice, he thinks, which can but give good counsel and genuine comfort: for he who speaks knows what suffering is: he knows that the sufferer is more in need of comfort than of counsel: and he has both the wisdom to counsel rightly and that simple union of faith and love which alone is the open-sesame to true comforting. But what he hears—containing though it does elements of a noble and most praiseworthy conception such as he expects from this speaker—is yet barren of all application to his peculiar circumstances. These words are in truth not applicable to him at all. They are inspired by most praiseworthy general principles; but the listener is aware that he, the speaker, has cast not a single glance at the situation of him whom he is addressing, that he sees him not nor does he know him and the straits under which he labours. Moreover, intermingled with the counsel and the comfort, a third voice makes itself heard drowning both the others, the voice of reproach. It is not that the sufferer disdains to accept reproach in this hour from the man he honours: on the contrary, if only there were mingled with the good counsel and the true comfort a word of just reproach giving to the former a meaning and a reason, he would recognise in the speaker the bearer of a message. But the accusation voiced is another altogether from that which he hears in the storm of events and in the hard beating of his own heart: it is almost the opposite of this. He weighs it and examines it—no, it is not a just one! And the armour of his silence is pierced. The friendly appeal achieves what the enemy's storming has failed to do: he must answer. He exclaims: let the lords of the ice-inferno affix my name to a cunningly constructed scare crow; this is the logical outcome of their own nature and the nature of their relations to me. But you, the man of good will, do you not know that you must see him whom you address, in his place and circumstance, in the throes of his destiny?

Jews are being persecuted, robbed, maltreated, tortured, murdered. And you, Mahatma Gandhi, say that their position in the country where they suffer all this is an exact parallel to the position of Indians in South Africa at the time when you inaugurated your famous 'Force of Truth' or 'Strength of the Soul' (Satyagraha) campaign. There the Indians occupied precisely the same place and the persecution there also had a religious tinge. There also the constitution denied equality of rights to the white and the black race including the Asiatics: there also the Indians were assigned to ghettos and the other disqualifications were, at all events, almost of the same type as those of the Jews in Germany. I read and reread these sentences in your article without being able to understand. Although I know them well, I reread your South African speeches and writings and called to mind, with all the attention and imagination at my command, every complaint which you made therein; and I did likewise with the accounts of your friends and pupils at that time; but all this did not help me to understand what you say about us. In the first of your speeches with which I am acquainted, that of 1896, you quoted two particular incidents to the accompaniment of the hisses of your audience: *first*, that a band of Europeans had set fire to an Indian village shop causing some damage; and *second*, that another band had thrown burning rockets into an urban shop. If I oppose to this the thousands on thousands of Jewish shops, destroyed and burnt-out, you will perhaps answer that the difference is only one of quantity and that the proceedings were almost of the same type. But, Mahatma, are you not aware of the burning of Synagogues and scrolls of the Law? Do you know nothing of all the sacred property of the community—in part of great antiquity, that has been destroyed in the flames? I am not aware that Boers and Englishmen in South Africa ever injured *anything sacred to the Indians*. I find further only one other concrete complaint quoted in that speech, namely, that three Indian school-teachers, who were found walking in the streets after 9 p.m. contrary to orders, were arrested and only acquitted later on. That is the only incident of the kind you bring forward. Now do you know or do you not know, Mahatma, what a concentration camp is like and what goes on there? Do you know of the torments in the concentration camp, of its methods of slow and quick slaughter? I cannot assume that you know of this; for then this tragi-comic utterance 'almost of the same type' could scarcely have crossed your lips. Indians were despised and despicably treated in South Africa: but they were not deprived of rights, they were not outlawed, they were not hostages for the coveted attitude of foreign powers. And do you think perhaps that a Jew in Germany could pronounce in public one single sentence of a speech such as yours without being knocked down? Of what significance is it to point to a certain something in common when such differences are overlooked? It does not seem to me convincing when you base your advice to us to observe Satyagraha in Germany on these similarities of circumstance. In the five years which I myself spent under the present regime, I observed many instances of *genuine Satyagraha among the Jews*, instances showing a strength of spirit wherein there was no question of bartering their rights or of being bowed down, and where neither force nor cunning was used to escape the consequences of their behaviour. Such action, however, exerted apparently not the slightest influence on their opponents. All honour indeed to those who displayed such strength of soul! But I cannot recognise herein a parole for the general behaviour of German Jews which might seem suited to exert an influence on the oppressed or on the world. An effective stand may be taken in the form of non-violence against unfeeling human beings in the hope of gradually bringing them thereby to their senses; but a diabolic universal steam-roller cannot thus be withstood. There is a certain situation in which from the 'Satyagraha' of the strength of the spirit no 'Satyagraha' of the power of truth can result. The word 'Satyagraha' signifies testimony. Testimony without acknowledgement, ineffective, unobserved martyrdom, a martyrdom cast to the winds— that is the fate of innumerable Jews in Germany. God alone accepts their testimony, God 'seals' it, as is said in our prayers. But no maxim for suitable behaviour can be deduced therefrom. Such martyrdom is a deed—but who would venture to *demand it?*

But your comparing of the position of the Jews in Germany with that of the Indians in South Africa, compels me to draw your attention to a yet more essential difference. True, I can well believe that you were aware of this difference, great as it is, when you drew the exact parallel. It is obvious that when you think back to your time in South Africa it is a matter of course for you that then as now you always had this great Mother India. That fact was and still is so taken for granted that apparently you are entirely unaware of the fundamental differences existing between nations having such a *mother* (it need not necessarily be such a great Mother, it may be a tiny motherkin, but yet a mother, a mother's bosom and a mother's heart) and a nation that is orphaned, or to whom one says in speaking of his country: 'This is no more your mother!'

When you were in South Africa, Mahatma, there were living there 150,000 Indians. But in India there were far more than 200 millions! And this fact nourished the souls of the 150,000, whether they were conscious of it or not: they drew from this source their strength to live and their courage to live. Did you ask then as you ask the Jews now, whether they want a double home where they can remain at will? You say to the Jews: if Palestine is their home, they must accustom themselves to the idea of being forced to leave the other parts of the world in which they are settled. Did you also say to the Indians in South Africa that if India is their home, they must accustom themselves to the idea of being compelled to return to India? Or did you tell them that India was not their home? And if—though indeed it is inconceivable that such a thing could come to pass—the hundreds of millions of Indians were to be scattered tomorrow over the face of the earth; and if the day after to-morrow another nation were to establish itself in India and the Jews were to declare that there was yet room for the establishment of a national home for the Indians, thus giving to their diaspora a strong organic concentration and a living centre; should then a Jewish Gandhi—assuming there could be such—answer them, as you answered the Jews; this cry for the national home affords a *colourable justification for your expulsion?* Or should he teach them, as you teach the Jews: that the India of the Vedic *conception is not a geographical tract, but that it is in your hearts?* A land about which a sacred book speaks to the sons of the land is never merely in their hearts; a land can never become a mere symbol. It is in the heart because it is the prophetic image of a promise to mankind: but it would be a vain metaphor if Mount Zion did not actually exist. This land is called 'Holy'; but this is not the holiness of an idea. It is the holiness of a piece of earth. That which is merely an idea and nothing more cannot become holy; but a piece of earth can become holy just as a mother's womb can become holy.

Dispersion is bearable: it can even be purposeful, if somewhere there is ingathering, a growing home centre, a piece of earth wherein one is in the midst of an ingathering and not in dispersion and from whence the spirit of ingathering may work its way out to all the places of the dispersion. When there is this, there is also a striving, common life, the life of a community which dares to live to-day because it hopes to live to-morrow. But when this growing centre, this increasing process of ingathering is lacking, *dispersion becomes dismemberment. On this criterion the question of our Jewish destiny is indissolubly bound up with the possibility of ingathering and this in Palestine.*

You ask: 'Why should they not, like other nations of the earth, make that country their home where they are born and where they earn their livelihood?' Because their destiny is different from that of all other nations of the earth: it is a destiny which in truth and justice should not be imposed on any nation on earth. For their destiny is dispersion, not the dispersion of a fraction and the preservation of the main substance as in the case of other nations; it is dispersion without the living heart and centre; and every nation has a right to demand the possession of a living heart. It is different, because a hundred adopted homes without one original and natural one render a nation sick and miserable. It is different, because although the well-being and the achievement of the individual may flourish on step-mother soil, the nation as such must languish. And just as you, Mahatma, wish that not only should all Indians be able to live and work, but that also Indian substance, Indian wisdom and Indian truth should prosper and be fruitful, so do we wish this for the Jews. For you there is no need to be aware, that the Indian substance could not prosper without the Indian's attachment to the mother-soil and without this ingathering therein. But we know what is the essential: we know it because it is just this that is denied us or was, at least, up to the generation which has just begun to work at the redemption of the mother-soil.

But this is not all: because for us, for the Jews who think as I do, painfully urgent as it is, it is indeed not the decisive factor. You say, Mahatma Gandhi, that to support the cry for a national home which 'does not make much appeal to you,' a sanction is 'sought in the Bible'. No—this is not so. We do not open the Bible and seek therein sanction. The opposite is true: the promises of return, of re-establishment, which have nourished the yearning hope of hundreds of generation, give those of to-day an elementary stimulus, recognised by few in its full meaning but effective also in the lives of many who do not believe in the message of the Bible. Still this too is not the determining factor for us who, although we do not see divine revelation in every sentence of Holy Scripture, yet trust in the spirit which inspired their speakers. *Decisive for us is not the promise of the Land—but the command, the fulfilment of which is bound up with the land*, with the existence of a free Jewish community in this country. For the Bible tells us and our inmost knowledge testifies to it, that once, more than 3000 years ago, our entry into this land was in the consciousness of a mission from above to set up a just way of life through the generations of our people, such a way of life as can be realised not by individuals in the sphere of their private existence but only by a nation in the establishment of its society: communal ownership of the land, regularly recurrent levelling of social distinctions, guarantee of the independence of each individual, mutual help, a common Sabbath embracing serf and beast as beings with equal claim, a Sabbatical year whereby, letting the soil rest, everybody is admitted to the free enjoyment of its fruits. These are not practical laws thought out by wise men; they are measures which the leaders of the nation, apparently themselves taken by surprise and overpowered have found to be the set task and condition for taking possession of the land. No other nation has ever been faced at the beginning of its career with such a mission. Here is something which allows of no forgetting, and from which there is no release. At that time we did not carry out what was imposed upon us: we went into exile with our task unperformed: but the command remained with us and it has become more urgent than ever. We need our own soil in order to fulfil it: we need the freedom of ordering our own life: no attempt can be made on foreign soil and under foreign statute. It may not be that the soil and the freedom for fulfilment be denied us. We are not covetous, Mahatma: our one desire is that at last we may obey.

Now you may well ask whether I speak for the Jewish people when I say 'we'. I speak only for those who feel themselves entrusted with the commission of fulfilling the command of justice delivered to Israel of the Bible. Were it but a handful—these constitute the pith of the nation and the future of the people depends on them; for the ancient mission of the nation lives on in them as the *cotyledon* in the core of the fruit. In this connection I must tell you that *you are mistaken when you assume that in general the Jews of today believe in God* and derive from their faith guidance for their conduct. Jewry of to-day is in the throes of a serious crisis in the matter of faith. It seems to me that the lack of faith of present-day humanity, its inability truly to believe in God, finds its concentrated expression in this crisis of Jewry; here all is darker, more fraught with danger, more fateful than anywhere else in the world. Neither is this crisis resolved here in Palestine; indeed we recognise its severity here even more than elsewhere among Jews. But at the same time we realise that here alone can it be resolved. There is no solution to be found in the life of isolated and abandoned individuals, although one may hope that the spark of faith will be kindled in their great need. The true solution can only issue from the life of a community which begins to carry out the will of God, often without being aware of doing so, without believing that God exists and this is His will. It may be found in this life of the community if believing people support it who neither direct nor demand, neither urge nor preach, but who share the life, who help, wait and are ready for the moment when it will be their turn to give the true answer to the enquirer. This is the innermost truth of the Jewish life in the Land; perhaps it may be of significance for the solution of this crisis of faith not only for Jewry but for all humanity. The contact of this people with this Land is not only a matter of sacred ancient history: we sense here a secret still more hidden.

You, Mahatma Gandhi, who know of the connection between tradition and future, should not associate yourself with those who pass over our cause without understanding or sympathy.

But you say—and I consider it to be the most significant of all the things you tell us—that Palestine belongs to the Arabs and that it is therefore 'wrong and inhuman to impose the Jews on the Arabs'.

Here I must add a personal note in order to make clear to you on what premises I desire to consider this matter.

I belong to a group of people who, from the time when Britain conquered Palestine, have not ceased to strive for the concluding of genuine peace between Jew and Arab.

By a genuine peace we inferred and still infer that both peoples should together develop the Land without the one imposing his will on the other. In view of the international usages of our generation this appeared to us to be very difficult but not impossible. We were well aware and still are, that in this unusual—yea unexampled case, it is a question of seeking new ways of understanding and cordial agreement between the nations. Here again we stood and still stand under the sway of a commandment.

We *considered it a fundamental point, that in this case two vital claims are opposed to each other*, two claims of a different nature and a different origin, which cannot be pitted one against the other and between which no objective decision can be made as to which is just or unjust. We considered and still consider it our duty to understand and to honour the claim which is opposed to ours and to endeavour to reconcile both claims. We cannot renounce the Jewish claim; something even higher than the life of our people is bound up with the Land, namely the work which is their divine mission. But we have been and still are convinced that it must be possible to find some form of agreement between this claim and the other; for we love this land and we believe in its future; and, seeing that such love and such faith are surely present also on the other side, a union in the common service of the Land must be within the range of the possible. Where there is faith and love, a solution may be found even to what appears to be a tragic contradiction.

In order to carry out a task of such extreme difficulty—in the recognition of which we have to overcome an internal resistance on the Jewish side, as foolish as it is natural—we are in need of the support of well-meaning persons of all nations, and we had hope of such. But now you come and settle the whole existential dilemma with the simple formula; 'Palestine belongs to the Arabs'.

What do you mean by saying that a land belongs to a population? Evidently you do not intend only to describe a state of affairs by your formula, but to declare a certain right. You obviously mean to say that a people, being settled on the land, has such an absolute claim to the possession of this land that whoever settles in it without the permission of this people, has committed a robbery. But by what means did the Arabs attain to the right of ownership in Palestine? Surely by conquest and, in fact, a conquest by settlement. You therefore admit that this being so, it constitutes for them an exclusive right of possession; whereas the subsequent conquests of the Mamelukes and the Turks which were not conquests with a view to settlement, do not constitute such in your opinion, but leave the former conquering nation in rightful ownership. Thus settlement by force of conquest justifies for you a right of ownership of Palestine; whereas a settlement such as the Jewish one—the methods of which, it is true, though not always doing full justice to Arab ways of life, were, even in the most objectionable cases, far removed from those of conquest—do not justify in your opinion any participation in this right of possession. These are the consequences which result from your statement in the form of an axiom that a land belongs to its population. In an epoch of migration of nations you would first support the right of ownership of the nation that is threatened with dispossession or extermination; but were this once achieved, you would be compelled, not at once, but after the lapse of a suitable number of generations, to admit that the land belongs to the usurper.

Possibly the time is not far removed when—perhaps after a catastrophe the extent of which we cannot yet estimate—the representatives of humanity will have to come to some agreement on the re-establishment of relations between peoples, nations and countries, on the colonisation of thinly populated territories as well as on a communal distribution of the necessary raw materials and on a logical intensification of the cultivation of the globe in order to prevent a new, enormously extended migration of nations which would threaten to destroy mankind. Is then the dogma of 'possession', of the inalienable right of ownership, of the sacred status quo to be held up against the men who dare to save the situation? For surely, we are witness of how the feeling, penetrating deep into the heart of national life, that this dogma must be opposed, is disastrously misused; but do not those representatives of the most powerful states share the guilt of this misuse, who consider every questioning of the dogma as a sacrilege?

And what if it is not the nations who migrate, but one nation? And what if this migrating nation should yearn towards its ancient home where there is still room for a considerable section of it, enough to form a centre side by side with the people to whom the land now 'belongs'? And what if this wandering nation, to whom the land once belonged, likewise on the basis of a settlement by force of conquest—and who were once driven out of it by mere force of domination, should now strive to occupy a free part of the land, or a part that might become free without encroaching on the living room of others, in order at last to acquire again for themselves a national home—a home where its people could live as a nation? Then you come, Mahatma Gandhi, and help to draw the barriers and to declare 'Hands off! This land does not belong to you!' Instead of helping to establish a genuine peace, giving us what we need without taking from the Arabs what they need, on the basis of a fair adjustment as to what they would really make use of and what might be admitted to satisfy our requirements!

Such an adjustment of the required living room for all is possible if it is brought into line with an all-embracing intensification of the cultivation of the whole soil in Palestine. In the present, helplessly primitive state of fellah agriculture the amount of land needed to produce nourishment for a family is ever so much larger that it otherwise would be. Is it right to cling to ancient forms of agriculture which have become meaningless, to neglect the potential productivity of the soil, in order to prevent the immigration of new settlers without prejudice to the old? *I repeat: without prejudice.* This should be the basis of the agreement for which we are striving.

You are only concerned, Mahatma, with the 'right of possession' on the one side: you do not consider the right to a piece of free land on the other side—for those who are hungering for it. But there is another of whom you do not enquire and who in justice, i.e. on the basis of the whole perceptible reality, would have to be asked: this other is the soil itself. *Ask the soil what the Arabs have done for her in 1300 years and what we have done for her in 50!* Would her answer not be weighty testimony in a just discussion as to whom this land 'belongs'?

It seems to me that God does not give any one portion of the earth away so that the owner thereof may say as God does in the Holy Script: 'Mine is the Land'. Even to the conqueror who has settled on it, the conquered land is, in my opinion, only lent—and God waited to see what he will make of it.

I am told however, I should not respect the cultivated soil and despise the desert. I am told, the desert is willing to wait for the work of her children: we who are burdened with civilisation are not recognised by her any more as her children. I have a veneration of the desert; but I do not believe in her absolute resistance for I believe in the great marriage between man (Adam) and earth (Adama). *The land recognises us, for it is fruitful through us: and through its fruit-bearing for us it recognises us*. Our settlers do not come here as do the colonists from the Occident, with natives to do their work for them: they themselves set their shoulders to the plow, and they spend their strength and their blood to make the land fruitful. But it is not only for ourselves that we desire its fertility. The Jewish peasants have begun to teach their brothers, the Arab peasants, to cultivate the land more intensively; we desire to teach them further: together with them we want to cultivate the land—to 'serve' it as the Hebrew has it. The more fertile this soil becomes, the more space there will be for us and for them. We have no desire to dispossess them: we want to live with them. We do not want to rule, we want to serve with them.

You once said, Mahatma, that politics enmesh us nowadays as with serpent's coils from which there is no escape however hard one may try. You said you desired, therefore, to wrestle with the *serpent. Here is the serpent in the fullness of its power*! Jews and Arabs both have a claim to this land; but these claims are in fact reconcilable as long as they are restricted to the measure which life itself allots, and as long as they are limited by the desire for conciliation—that is, if they are translated into the language of the needs of living people for themselves and their children. But instead of this they are turned through the serpent's influence into claims of principle and politics, and are represented with all the ruthlessness which politics instils into those that are led by her. Life with all its realities and possibilities disappears as does the desire for truth and peace: nothing is known and sensed but the political parole alone. The serpent conquers not only the spirit but also life. Who would wrestle with her?

In the midst of your arguments, Mahatma, there is a fine word which we gratefully accept. We should seek, you say, *to convert the heart of the Arab. Will they—help us to do so*! Among us also there are many foolish hearts to convert—hearts that have fallen a prey to that nationalist egoism which only admits its own claims. We hope to achieve this ourselves. But for the other task of conversion we need your help. Instead, your admonition is only addressed to the Jews, because they allow British bayonets to defend them against the bomb-throwers. Your attitude to the latter is much more reserved: you say you wish the Arabs had chosen the way of non-violence; but, according to the accepted canons of right and wrong there is nothing to be said against their behaviour. How is it possible that in this case, you should give credence—if only in a limited form—to the accepted canons, whereas you have never done so before! You reproach us, that, having no army of our own, we consent to the British army preventing an occasional blind murder. But in view of the accepted canons you cast a lenient eye on those who carry murder into our ranks every day without even noticing who is hit. Were you to look down on all, Mahatma, on what is done and what is not done on both sides—would you not admit that we certainly are not least in need of your help?

We began to settle in the land anew, 35 years *before* the 'shadow of the British gun' was cast upon it. We did not seek out this shadow; it appeared and remained here to guard British interests and not ours. We do not want force. But after the resolutions of Delhi, at the beginning of March 1922, you yourself, Mahatma Gandhi, wrote: 'Have I not repeatedly said that I would have India become free even by violence rather than that she should remain in bondage?' This was a very important pronouncement on your part: you asserted thereby that non-violence is for you a faith and not a political principle—and that the *desire for the freedom of India is even stronger in you than your faith.* And for this, I love you. We do not want force. We have not proclaimed, as did Jesus, the son of our people, and as you do, the teaching of non-violence, because we believe that a man must sometimes use force to save himself or even more his children. But from time immemorial we have proclaimed the teaching of justice and peace: we have taught and we have learnt that peace is the aim of all the world and that justice is the way to attain it. Thus we cannot desire to use force. No one who counts himself in the ranks of Israel can desire to use force.

But, you say, our non-violence is that of the helpless and the weak. This is not in accordance with the true state of affairs. You do not know or you do not consider what strength of soul, what Satyagraha has been needed for us to restrain ourselves here after years of ceaseless deeds of blind violence perpetrated against us, our wives and our children, and not to answer with like deeds of blind violence. And on the other hand you, Mahatma, wrote in 1922 as follows: 'I see that our non-violence is skin-deep . . . . This non-violence seems to be due merely to our helplessness . . . . Can true voluntary non-violence come out of this seeming forced non-violence of the weak?' When I read those words at that time, my reverence for you took birth—a reverence so great that even your injustice towards us cannot destroy it.

You say it is a stigma against us that our ancestors *crucified* Jesus. I do not know whether that actually happened; but I consider it possible. I consider it just as possible as that the Indian people under different circumstances should condemn you to death—if your teachings were more strictly opposed to their own tendencies ('India', you say, 'is by Nature non-violent'). *Not infrequently do nations swallow up the greatness to which they have given birth.* How can one assert, without contradiction, that such action constitutes a stigma! I would not deny however, that although I should not have been among the crucifiers of Jesus, I should also not have been among his supporters. For I cannot help withstanding evil when I see that it is about to destroy the good. I am forced to withstand the evil in the world just as the evil within myself. I can only strive not to have to do so by force. I do not want force. But if there is no other way of preventing the evil destroying the good, I trust I shall use force and give myself up into God's hands.

'India', you say, 'is by Nature non-violent.' It was not always so. The Mahabharata is an epos of warlike, disciplined force. In the greatest of its poems, the Bhagavad Gita, it is told how Arjuna decides on the battlefield that he will not commit the sin of killing his relations who are opposed to him and he lets fall his bow and arrow. But the God reproaches him saying that such action is unmanly and shameful; there is nothing better for a knight in arms than a just fight.

Is that the truth? If I am to confess what is truth to me, I must say: There is nothing better for a man than to deal justly—unless it be to love; we should be able even to fight for justice—but to *fight lovingly*.

I have been very slow in writing this letter to you, Mahatma. I made repeated pauses—sometimes days elapsing between short paragraphs—in order to test my knowledge and my way of thinking. Day and night I took myself to task, searching whether I had not in any one point overstepped the measure of self-preservation allotted and even prescribed by God to a human community, and whether I had not fallen into the *grievous error of collective egoism.* Friends and my own conscience have helped to keep me straight whenever danger threatened. Weeks have now passed since then and the time has come, when negotiations are proceeding in the capital of the British Empire on the Jewish-Arab problem—and when, it is said, a decision is to be made. But the true decision in this matter can only come from within and not from without.

I take the liberty therefore of closing this letter without waiting for the result in London.

Jerusalem, February 24th 1939   Martin Buber

III

Letter from J.L. Magnes

Dear Mr. Gandhi,

What you have said recently about the Jews is the one statement I have yet seen which needs to be grappled with fundamentally. Your statement is a challenge, particularly to *those of us who have imagined ourselves your disciples*.

I am sure you must be right in asserting that the Jews of Germany can offer Satyagraha to the 'godless fury of their dehumanized oppressors'.

But how and when? You do not give the answer. You may say that you are not sufficiently acquainted with the German persecution to outline the practical technique of Satyagraha for use by the German Jews. But one of the great things about you and your doctrine has been that you have always emphasized the chance of practical success if Satyagraha be offered. Yet to the German Jews you have not given the practical advice which only your unique experience could offer, and I wonder if it is helpful merely in general terms to call upon the Jews of Germany to offer Satyagraha. I have heard that many a Jew of Germany has asked himself how and when Satyagraha must be offered, without finding the answer. *Conditions in Germany are radically different from those that have prevailed in South Africa and in India.* Those of us who are outside Germany must, I submit, think through most carefully the advice we proffer the unfortunates who are caught in the claws of the Hitler beast.

If you take the sentences of your statement as to what you would do were you a German Jew, you will find, I believe, that not only one German Jew, as you require has had 'courage and vision', but many whose names are known and many more who have borne witness to their faith without their names being known.

'I would claim Germany as my home'. There has never been a community more passionately attached to its home than the German Jews to Germany. The thousands of exiles now to be found everywhere are so thoroughly German mentally, psychologically, in their speech, manners, prejudices, their outlook, that we wonder how many generations it may take before this is uprooted. The history of the Jews in Germany goes back to at least Roman times and though the Jews throughout their history there have been massacred and driven out on diverse occasions, one thing or the other has always brought them back there.

'I would challenge him to shoot me or to cast me into the dungeon.'

Many Jews—hundreds, thousands—have been shot. Hundreds, thousands have been cast into the dungeon. *What more can Satyagraha give them?* I ask this question in humility, for I am sure that you can give a constructive answer.

'I would not wait for fellow Jews to join me in civil resistance, but would have confidence that in the end the rest are bound to follow my example.' But the question is how can Jews in Germany offer civil resistance? The slightest sign of resistance means killing or concentration camps or being done away with otherwise. It is usually in the dead of night that they are spirited away. No one, except their terrified families, is the wiser. It makes not even a ripple on the surface of German life. The streets are the same, business goes on as usual, the casual visitor sees nothing. Contrast this with a single hunger strike in an American or English prison, and the public commotion that this arouses. Contrast this with one of your fasts, or with your salt march to the sea, or a visit to the Viceroy, when the whole world is permitted to hang upon your words and be witness to your acts. Has not this been possible largely because, despite all the excesses of its imperialism, England is after all a democracy with a Parliament and a considerable measure of free speech? I wonder if even you would find the way to public opinion in totalitarian Germany, where life is snuffed out like a candle, and no one sees or knows the light is out.

'If one Jew or all the Jews were to accept the prescriptions here offered, he or they cannot be worse off than now.' Surely you do not mean that those Jews who are able to get out of Germany are as badly off as those who must remain? You call attention to the unbelievable ferocity visited upon all the Jews because of the crime of 'one obviously mad but intrepid youth'. But the attempt at civil resistance on the part of even one Jew in Germany, let alone the community, would be regarded as an infinitely greater crime and would probably be followed by a repetition of this unbelievable ferocity, or worse.

'And suffering voluntarily undergone will bring them an inner strength and joy.' I wonder that no one has drawn your attention to the fact that those German Jews who are faithful to Judaism—and they are the majority—have in large measure the inner strength and joy that comes from suffering for their ideals. It is those unfortunate 'non-Aryans', who have a trace of Jewish blood but who have been brought up as German Christians, who are most to be pitied. They are made to suffer, and they do not know why. Many of them have been raised to despise Jews and Judaism, and now this despised people, this scorned religion is, in their eyes, the cause of their suffering. What a tragedy for them.

But as to the Jews—I do not know if there is a *deeper and more widespread history of martyrdom*. You can read the story of it in any Jewish history book or, if you wish a convenient account, in the Jewish Encyclopedia published in New York a generation ago. To take Germany alone, you may be interested in one document that has come down to us from the middle ages. It is called the *Memorbuch of Nuernberg*—Nuernberg of the Nuernberg laws, whose synagogue has just been torn down and a 15th century covering of a Scroll of the Law stolen and presented recently to the city's arch-fiend.

The Memorbuch gives a list of the places where massacres took place in Germany during the Crusades from 1096 to 1298. There are some fifty of these massacres entered chronologically. There is a further entry of some 65 large pages containing dates and places with the names of those martyred from 1096 to 1349. Take what happened in this very Nuernberg on Friday the 22nd of Ab 5058 of the Jewish calendar, the 1st August 1298 of the Christian calendar. We find the names of 628 men, women and children, whole families, old and young, strong and sick, rabbis and scholars, rich and poor, slaughtered on that day—burned, drowned, put to the sword, strangled, broken on the wheel and on the rack. In some places the elders killed the young, and then put an end to their own lives.

In Spain and Portugal where Jews were given the chance of conversion to Christianity, what usually happened in a stricken town was, that about a third converted, and a third succeeded in escaping, and always at least a third accepted their agony with the praise of God and his Unity on their lips. Our Hebrew literature is in many ways a literature of martyrdom. Our Talmud, which covers a period of about 1000 years is a literature that grew up in large measure under oppression, exile and martyrdom, and it contains discussions, traditions and rules bearing upon our duty to accept martyrdom rather than yield to 'idolatry, immorality, or the spilling of blood'. The Hebrew liturgy throbs with elegies in which poets and teachers commemorate the martyrs of one generation after another.

If ever a people was a people of non-violence through century after century, it was the Jews. I think they need learn but little from anyone in faithfulness to their God and in their readiness to suffer while they Sanctify His Name.

What is new and great about you has seemed to me this, that you have exalted non-violence into the dominant principle of all of life, both religious, social and political, and that you have made it into a practical technique both of communing with the Divine and of battling for a newer world of justice and mercy and of respect for the human personality of even the most insignificant outcast. What you could give to help the Jew add to his precious contribution to mankind, 'the surpassing contribution of non-violent action', is not as much the exhortation to suffer voluntarily, as the practical technique of Satyagraha.

You would have the right to say that some Jew should do this. But we have no one comparable to you as religious and political leader.

There are, as I am aware, other elements besides non-violence in Satyagraha. There is non-cooperation and the renunciation of property, and the disdain of death.

The Jews are a people who exalt life, and they can hardly be said to disdain death. Lev. 18, 5 says: 'my judgements which if a man do he shall live in them', and the interpretation adds as a principle of Jewish life 'and not die through them'. For this reason I have often wondered if we are fit subjects for Satyagraha. And as to property, it is but natural that Jews should want to take along with them a minimum of their property from Germany or elsewhere so as not to fall a burden upon others. It would, I am sure, give you satisfaction to see how large numbers of refugees who in Germany were used to wealth, comfort, culture, have without too much complaint and very often cheerfully buckled down to a new life in Palestine and elsewhere, many of them in the fields or in menial employment in the cities.

It is in the matter of non-cooperation that I have a question of importance to put to you.

A plan is being worked out between the Evian Refugee Committee and the German Government which appears to be nothing short of devilish. The details are not yet known. But it seems to amount to this: The German Government is to confiscate all German Jewish property and in exchange for increased foreign trade and foreign currency they will permit a limited number of Jews to leave Germany annually for the next several years. The scheme involves the sale of millions of pounds of debentures to be used by a Refugee or Emigration Bank that is to be created. Whether Governments are to subscribe to these debentures, I do not know. But certainly the whole Jewish world will be called upon to do so.

Here is the dilemma: If one does not subscribe, no Jews will be able to escape from this prison of torture called Germany. If one does subscribe one will be cooperating with that Government, and be dealing in Jewish flesh and blood in a most modern and up-to-date slave market. I see before me here in Jerusalem a child who is happy now that he is away from the torment there, and his brother, or parent, or grandparent. One of the oldest of Jewish sayings is : 'Who saves a single soul in Israel is as if he had saved a whole world.' Not to save a living soul? And yet to cooperate with the powers of evil and darkness? Have you an answer?

You touch upon a vital phase of the whole subject when you say that '*if there* ever could be a justifiable war in the name of and for humanity, a war against Germany, to prevent the wanton persecution of a whole race, would be completely justified. But I do not believe in any war. A discussion of the pros and cons of such a war is therefore outside my horizon and province.'

But it is on 'the pros and cons of such a war' that I would ask your guidance. The question gives me no rest, and I am sure there are many like myself. Like you I do not believe in any war. I have pledged myself never to take part in a war. I spoke up for pacifism in America during the world war alongside of many whose names are known to you. That war brought the 'peace' of Versailles and the Hitlerism of today. But my pacifism, as I imagine the pacifism of many others, is passing through a *pitiless crisis*. I ask myself: Suppose America, England, France are dragged into a war with the Hitler bestiality, what am I do and what am I to teach? This war may destroy a large part of the life of the youth of the world and force those who remain alive to lead the lives of savages. Yet I know I would pray with all my heart for the defeat of the Hitler inhumanity; and am I then to stand aside and let others do the fighting? During the last war I prayed for a peace without defeat or victory.

The answer given by Romain Rolland in his little book 'Par la revolution la paix' (1935), seems to be, that while he himself as an individual continues to refuse to bear arms, he will do everything he can to help his side (in this case, Russia) to win the war. That is hardly a satisfying answer.

I ask myself how I might feel if I were not a Jew. Is the Hitler iniquity really as profound as I imagine? I recall that during the last war the arguments against Germany were much the same as these of today. I took no stock in those arguments then. Perhaps it is the torture of my own people that enrages me unduly? Yet it is my conviction that, being a Jew, my sense of outrage at injustice may, perhaps, be a bit more alive than the average and therefore more aware of the evils that the Hitler frenzy is bringing upon all mankind. The Jew, scattered as he is, is an outpost, bearing the brunt earlier of an action against mankind, and bearing it longest. For a dozen reasons he is a convenient scapegoat. I say this in order to make the point that if the Jew is thoroughly aroused about an evil such as the Hitler madness, his excitement and indignation are apt to be based not only on personal hurt but on a more or less authentic appraisal of the evil that must be met.

If you will take the trouble of looking at the little pamphlet I am sending, 'Fellowship in War' (1936), you will see that I have an ineradicable belief that no war whatsoever can be a *righteous* war. The war tomorrow for the 'democracies' or for some other noble slogan will be just as unrighteous or as fatuous as was the 'war to save democracy' yesterday. Moreover, to carry on the war the democracies will perforce become totalitarian. Not even a war against the ghastly Hitler savagery can be called righteous, for we all of us have sinned, conquerors and conquered alike, and it is because of our sins, because of our lack of generosity and the spirit of conciliation and renunciation, that the Hitler beast has been enabled to raise its head. Even on the pages of the Nuernberg Memorbuch we find the words 'Because of our many sins' this and that massacre took place. There can be no war for something *good*. That is a contradiction in terms. The good is to be achieved through totally different means.

But a war *against* something *evil*? If the Hitler cruelty launches a war against you, what would you do, what will you do? Can you refrain from making a choice? It is a choice of evils—a choice between the capitalisms, the imperialisms, the militarisms of the western democracies and between the Hitler religion. Can one hesitate as to which is the lesser of these two evils? Is not a choice therefore imperative? I am all too painfully conscious that I am beginning to admit that if Hitler hurls his war upon us we must resist. For us it would thus become, not a righteous war, nor, to use your term, a justifiable war, but a *necessary* war, not *for* something good, but, because no other choice is left us, *against* the greater *evil*. Or do you know of some other choice?

I have already written you an inordinately long letter, but *I must abuse your patience further and refer to Palestine*, I hope in not too lengthy a way.

I am burdening you with a further pamphlet of mine called 'Like all the nations?' May I refer you to pages 14 and 15, and then to pages 29–32. You will see that on page 31 I say, that we must overcome all obstacles in Palestine 'through all the weapons of civilization except bayonets . . . brotherly, friendly weapons', and on p. 32, the Jew 'should not either will or believe in or want a Jewish Home that can be maintained in the long run only against the violent opposition of the Arab and

Moslem peoples.' There are other Jews who hold the same views and who regard the Mandate as suspect because, as you say, 'the Mandate has no sanction but that of the last war'. In an address in New York in May, 1919, I said: 'Palestine is, so they say, to be 'given' to the Jewish people. To my mind, no peace conference has the right to give any land to any people even though it be the land of Israel to the People of Israel. If self-determination be a true principle for other peoples, it is just as true for the Jewish people . . . . If we are to be true democrats we must be true democrats in Jewish life as well. Our new beginnings in Palestine are burdened by this gift' (p.60 of the above pamphlet).

But the attachment of Israel to Palestine is as old as the Bible, and there has been no period of history in which this attachment has not expressed itself, and, as we know more and more clearly from archaeological excavations and the recovery of lost documents, there has never been a time when Jewish settlements were utterly absent from the Holy Land.

Jewish life will always be lacking in an essential constant, if Judaism and the Jewish people have no spiritual and intellectual Centre in Palestine. *It is true they can exist without it, as history shows, but they have never ceased experiencing the deep need for such a Centre and of trying to establish it in Palestine on innumerable occasions.* Such a spiritual and religious Centre must, for the Jewish people, take on the qualities of a *National* Home. The Jewish people are not like the Catholic Church for whom the ecclesia is the supreme authority. Judaism is peculiar in this, that it derives its final authority out of the life, the sufferings, the aspirations, the accumulated traditions, the God-consciousness of a *people* composed of ordinary everyday, hard-working human beings. It is for this reason that the Jewish Centre cannot be composed only of priests and scholars. The Jewish Centre to fulfil its true functions should be endowed with all the problems and possibilities that life itself imposes, and, as no one knows better than yourself, life expresses itself in many forms, political and social, as well as religious and spiritual.

It is, I think, in recognition of all of this that 52 nations accepted the doctrine that the Jews are in Palestine as of 'right' and not just on sufferance. Do you not think that all of this, added to the barbarous treatment meted out to the Jews in all too many places, constitutes a kind of 'right' at least as valid as the other varieties of 'rights'?

But essential as this Centre, or National Home, seems to be, in the opinion of many, for Judaism and the Jews, I think you would find great numbers of Jews agreeing with you that 'it would be a crime against humanity to reduce the proud Arabs.'

The question is, what is meant by reduce and are the Arabs being reduced?

You say that 'Palestine belongs to the Arabs in the same sense that England belongs to the English.'

'Mine is the land' (Lev. 25, 23) saith the Lord.

May I point out at least two ways in which Palestine does not 'belong' to the Arabs as England does to the English?

Usually a land 'belongs' to that people which has conquered it. That is *an ugly fact*. The Jews conquered the land long ago. They lost to conquerors, who themselves lost it, and eventually the Arabs conquered it. But the Arabs lost it to the Crusaders, and they again to the Arabs, and they to the Mongols and to the Mameluks, and they to the Turks, from whom it was conquered by the Allied Powers, primarily by England. The Arabs do not therefore possess political sovereignty from conquest, and the land does not 'belong' to them in this sense.

Palestine does 'belong' to the Arabs in the sense that they have been in the land in large numbers since the Moslem conquest, that most (by no means all) of those working the land are Arabs, and most (by no means all) of those owning the land are Arab landholders (a comparatively small number), and Arabic is the chief spoken language.

But Palestine is different from England also in this, that it is a sacred land for three monotheistic religions, and in this, that a people, the Jews, who became a people in Palestine and whose great classic, the basis of whose life, the Bible, was produced there, have never throughout all the centuries forgotten the land and ceased to yearn for it.

That is a unique fact of no mean importance.

The basic problem is, as you put it, the need for the Jews of settling in Palestine 'with the goodwill of the Arabs', and not 'under the shadow of the British gun'.

I would not be honest if I conveyed the impression to you that in my opinion my people have always gone at this in the right way. They have done wonderful things in building up the land. They have planned intelligently and with high social ideals. They have borne sufferings and hardships willingly. They love the land and they have rescued it from further decay. They have revived the Hebrew tongue. In this sense the land also 'belongs' to them. But I am sure that it has been the tragic pressure of Jewish life in Central and Eastern Europe that has made my people impatient and often intolerant. The tragedy of the Jewish wanderer and refugee did not begin with Germany. We have had this problem with us always, and it was one of the chief reasons for the rise of modern Zionism. And now with the German barbarities, and what is impending in Poland and elsewhere, the pressure for space and a Home has grown to be almost unbearable.

During the past three years when the Jewish community here has been under continual attack, it is a fact that the Jewish community has been non-violent. Our young men and women are hot-blooded as are others. But there are very few recorded cases of attack on their part and there have been no ascertained reprisals. This *self-restraint, this 'Havlaga'*, as it is called, can be ascribed to many factors. But, as the never ceasing discussion of 'Havlaga' shows, a deep ethical passion has been the predominant factor in this non-violence.

I wonder therefore if the question of the Jews offering 'Satyagraha in front of the Arabs' arises in Palestine. The Jewish youth has had organised self-defence units which are now, for the most part, merged with the constituted forces of the country. *As far as I am aware, you do not advocate the abolition of police or military forces anywhere.* The record shows that in no single instance have the legalised Jewish forces in Palestine committed an act of aggression. I should like to know if you think that the Jewish settlements should have remained, or should now be, unarmed, and that when bands come into a town like Tiberias and murder and mutilate babes in their mother's arms, they should offer 'themselves to be shot or thrown into the Dead Sea without raising a little finger against them'. As I have understood *Satyagraha, it must, in order to be effective, be offered in front of Constituted Authority, and not in front of roving bandits.*

Will you not speak to the Arabs in terms of Satyagraha? That would also have a profound influence upon the Jews.

Great as is the need for finding a refuge in Palestine for persecuted Jews, and great as are the possibilities of spiritual and intellectual, social and political achievements in the Jewish National Home, there are very many who agree with you that we must not 'reduce' the Arabs. If I understand what you mean by the word 'reduce' I would give it as my opinion, after many years of residence in Palestine, that the Arabs have not been reduced. But that does not at all absolve the Jews from the primary duty and the vital necessity of 'seeking to convert the Arab heart'. Perhaps you could help us in this through suggestions?

Sincerely Yours,

J.I. Magnes

Jerusalem, February 26, 1939

P.S. You may be interested in a third pamphlet containing a recent address at the Hebrew University on the Jews of Bologna, Italy, particularly from page 8 onwards.

Notes

1. *Gandhi's Autobiography: The Story of My Experiments with Truth* by M. K. Gandhi, tr. Mahadev Desai (Washington, D.C., Public Affairs Press, 1940), pp. 41–2.
2. Ibid., p. 45.
3. Robert Payne, *The Life and Death of Mahatma Gandhi* (New York: E. P. Dutton & Co. Inc., 1969), p. 34.
4. *Gandhi's Autobiography*, p. 126.
5. Ibid., p. 141.
6. Ibid., pp. 169–72.
7. Ibid., pp. 112–14.
8. Ibid., p. 171.
9. Ibid., pp. 252–63.
10. Ibid., pp. 338–40.
11. Jawaharlal Nehru, *The Discovery of India* (Calcutta: The Signet Press, 1946), p. 311.
12. See R. C. Majumdar, ed., *Struggle for Freedom* (Bombay: Bharatiya Vidya Bhavan, 1969), pp. 471–2.
13. Payne, pp. 431–7.
14. Payne, p. 449.
15. Ibid., p. 579.
16. S. Radhakrishnan and J. H. Muirhead, eds., *Contemporary Indian Philosophy* (London: George Allen & Unwin Ltd. 1958), p. 21.
17. D.G. Tendulkar, *Mahatma: Life of Mohandas Karamchand Gandhi* (New Delhi: Government of India, The Publications Division, 1951), Vol. I, p. 105.
18. Ibid., p. 109.
19. *The Collected Works of Mahatma Gandhi* (New Delhi: The Publications Division, Government of India, 1963), Vol. X, p. 43.
20. Ibid., pp. 43–53.
21. Ibid., p. 28.
22. Ibid., pp. 28–9.
23. Tendulkar, Vol. I, pp. 107–8.
24. C stands for *The Collected Works of Mahatma Gandhi*.
25. As cited in Ambedkar, *Writings and Speeches* (Bombay, 1979–93).
26. T stands for D.G. Tendulkar, *Mahatma: Life of Mohandas Karamchand Gandhi* (Delhi; Second edition, 1962).
27. F stands for Louis Fischer, *The Life of Mahatma Gandhi* (New York, 1950).
28. P stands for Pyarelal, *Mahatma Gandhi—The Last Phase* (Ahmedabad, rev. ed., 1956–8).
29. *Gandhi's Autobiography*, p. 5.
30. Ibid., pp. 614–16.
31. M.K. Gandhi, *Hindu Dharma* (ed. Bharatan Kumarappa. Ahmedabad: Navajivan Press, 1958) pp. 323–5.
32. *The Bond: Two Letters to Gandhi* (Jerusalem: Rubin Mass, April 1939), pp. 1–44.

Aurobindo Ghose
(1872–1950)

Life

Aurobindo was born in 1872, in the heyday of the British empire, to an Anglophile Bengali doctor, and was shipped off to England at the age of seven to insulate him from Indian influences. He returned to India in 1893, at the age of twenty, after successfully completing his education at King's College, Cambridge, and after competing for the ICS unsuccessfully. He made it in through the toughest part, the competitive examination, but failed first to pass and later, even to appear for the various tests set up for him.[1] It makes one wonder whether there was something deliberate about this and whether he failed to pass them on purpose.

Upon his return he entered the civil service of the state of Baroda, whose ruler Sayaji Rao had the reputation of being one of the most enlightened of Indian princes. It was here that he once again familiarized himself with the religion and culture of his own country. Events, however, soon caught up with his peaceful existence. Lord Curzon announced the partition of Bengal in 1905, which caused unprecedented agitation against the British. Then, in 1907, came the split in the Congress between the moderates and the extremists led by Tilak. Aurobindo sided with Tilak and 'served as his right-hand man'. Aurobindo had by now given up his position at the Baroda College to join the agitation against the partition of Bengal, which he carried out journalistically through the English weekly called *Bande Mataram*.

He was arrested as a result of his activities and jailed at Alipore prison in 1908. During this incarceration he underwent a spiritual transformation, which was not as sudden as might appear at first sight. While at Baroda he had come in contact with a meditation master, Lele by name, and the stage had been set for the exploration of the spiritual dimension of life. As he was to write later on 5 August 1932:

> 'Sit in meditation,' he said, 'But do not think, look only at your mind; you will see thoughts *coming into it*; before they can enter throw these away from your mind till your mind is capable of entire silence.' I had never heard before of thoughts coming visibly into the mind from out-side, but I did not think either of questioning the truth or the possibility, I simply sat down and did it. In a moment my mind became silent as windless air on a high mountain summit and then I saw one thought and then another coming in a concrete way from outside; I flung them away before they could enter and take hold of the brain and in three days I was free.[2]

However, while at the Alipore jail, he underwent a profound mystical appearance. He received messages, which were probably an objectification of the inner workings of his own spirit, from the Beyond, which he disclosed in his famous Uttarapara speech.

> He tells us how one day, in a vision, he saw the spirit of God all around him in the prison compound and, later, again in the court. He also heard a definite message. It came to him in the familiar form of the *Bhagavān* of the *Gītā*, whom he saw everywhere, in place of the prison bars, the trees in the compound, the prisoners in chains and, later, in place of the judge and counsel, while he stood in the dock. A voice told him that he was being prepared for an altogether different kind of work, which he should undertake after his release.[3]

After his release on 6 May 1909, Aurobindo spent some time in Chundernagore, a French enclave near Calcutta, in order to avoid being detained by British authorities again. Finally, he left for and settled in the French enclave of Pondicherry in Madras, having got wind of an impending arrest. The popular belief that Sister Nivedita tipped him off either then or earlier is unfounded.[4] In Pondicherry he devoted himself to spiritual pursuits, publishing the outcome of his intellectual and spiritual endeavours in some of his journals, one of which was called *Arya*. A French writer, Paul Richard, had helped launch this journal in 1914. Later that year Paul Richard returned to Europe but his wife Mirra remained with Sri Aurobindo and later came to be known as the Mother, and carried on his work after Aurobindo passed away in 1950.

The extended period of spiritual practice led Śrī Aurobindo to reinterpret many traditional concepts of Hinduism, and to introduce some new ones, through his many works. The better known among them are *Savitri, Essays on the Gita,* and *The Foundations of Indian Culture; The Life Divine* is possibly the best known.[5]

First Advaitic Experience

Although Aurobindo was destined to move beyond the confines of Advaita Vedānta, his account of the initial experience is intriguing, as also the manner in which it was brought about and what it culminated in. The incident was recounted by him in May 1932.

The First Advaitic Experience

I think you have made too much play with my phrase 'an accident', ignoring the important qualification, 'it *seemed* to come by an accident'. After four years of Pranayam and other practices on my own, with no other result than an increased health and outflow of energy, some phycho-physical phenomena, a great outflow of poetic creation, a limited power of subtle sight (luminous patterns and figures, etc.) mostly with the waking eye, I had a complete arrest and was at a loss. At this juncture I was induced to meet a man without fame whom I did not know, a bhakta with a limited mind but with some experience and evocative power. We sat together and I followed with an absolute fidelity what he instructed me to do, not myself in the least understanding where he was leading me or where I was myself going. The first result was a series of tremendously powerful experiences and radical changes of consciousness which he had never intended—for they were Adwaitic and Vedantic and he was against Adwaita Vedanta— and which were quite contrary to my own ideas, for they made me see with a stupendous intensity the world as a cinematographic play of vacant forms in the impersonal universality of the Absolute Brahman. The final upshot was that he was made by a Voice within him to hand me over to the Divine within me enjoining an absolute surrender to its will—a principle or rather a seed force to which I kept unswervingly and increasingly till it led me through all the mazes of an incalculable Yogic development bound by no single rule or style or dogma or shastra to where and what I am now and towards what shall be hereafter. Yet he understood so little what he was doing that when he met me a month or two later, he was alarmed, tried to undo what he had done and told me that it was not the Divine but the devil that had got hold of me. Does not all that justify my phrase 'it seemed to come by an accident'? But my meaning is that the ways of the Divine are not like those of the human mind or according to our patterns and it is impossible to judge them or to lay down for Him what He shall or shall not do, for the Divine knows better than we can know. If we admit the Divine at all, both true reason and bhakti seem to me to be at one in demanding implicit faith and surrender. I do not see how without them there can be *avyabhicarini bhakti* (one-pointed adoration).[6]

Aurobindo also describes this experience elsewhere as follows.

The Experience of Nirvana

I have never said that things (in life) are harmonious now—on the contrary, with the human consciousness as it is harmony is impossible. It is always what I have told you, that the human consciousness is defective and simply impossible—and that is why I strive for a higher consciousness to come and set right the disturbed balance. I don't want to give you Nirvana (on paper) immediately because Nirvana only leads up to Harmony in my communication. I am glad you are getting converted to silence, and even Nirvana is not without its uses—in my case it was the first positive spiritual experience and it made possible all the rest of the sadhana; but as to the positive way to get these things, I don't know if your mind is quite ready to proceed with it. There are in fact several ways. My own way was by rejection of thought. 'Sit down,' I was told, 'look and you will see that your thoughts come into you from outside. Before they enter, fling them back.' I sat down and looked and saw to my astonishment that it was so; I saw and felt concretely the thought approaching as if to enter through or above the head and was able to push it back concretely before it came inside.

In three days—really in one—my mind became full of an eternal silence—it is still there. But that I don't know how many people can do. One (not a disciple—I had no disciples in those days) asked me how to do Yoga. I said: 'Make your mind quiet first.' He did and his mind became quite silent and empty. Then he rushed to me saying: 'My brain is empty of thoughts, I cannot think. I am becoming an idiot.' He did not pause to look and see where these thoughts he uttered were coming from! Nor did he realise that one who is already an idiot cannot become one. Anyhow I was not patient in those days and I dropped him and let him lose his miraculously achieved silence.

The usual way, the easiest if one can manage it at all, is to *call down* the silence from above you into the brain, mind and body.[7]

Aurobindo's Yoga and its Relation to the Doctrine of Maya (Mayavad), and Aurobindo's Novel Experiences

Now to reach Nirvana was the first radical result of my own Yoga. It threw me suddenly into a condition above and without thought, unstained by any mental or vital movement; there was no ego, no real world—only when one looked through the immobile senses, something perceived or bore upon its sheer silence a world of empty forms, materialised shadows without true substance. There was no One or many even, only just absolutely That, featureless, relationless, sheer, indescribable, unthinkable, absolute, yet supremely real and solely real. This was no mental realisation nor something glimpsed somewhere above—no abstraction—it was positive, the only positive reality—although not a spatial physical world, pervading, occupying or rather flooding and drowning this semblance of a physical world, leaving no room or space for any reality but itself, allowing nothing else to seem at all actual, positive or substantial. I cannot say there was anything exhilarating or rapturous in the experience, as it then came to me—(the ineffable Ananda I had years afterwards)—but what it brought was an inexpressible Peace, a stupendous silence, an infinity of release and freedom. I lived in that Nirvana day and night before it began to admit other things into itself or modify itself at all, and the inner heart of experience, a constant memory of it and its power to return remained until in the end it began to disappear into a greater Superconsciousness from above. But meanwhile realisation added itself to realisation and fused itself with this original experience. At an early stage the aspect of an illusionary world gave place to one in which illusion is only a small surface phenomenon with an immense Divine Reality behind it and a supreme Divine Reality above it and an intense Divine Reality in the heart of everything that had seemed at first only a cinematic shape or shadow. And this was no reimprisonment in the senses, no diminution or fall from supreme experience, it came rather as a constant heightening and widening of the Truth; it was the spirit that saw objects, not the senses, and the Peace, the Silence, the freedom in Infinity remained always with the world or all worlds only as a continuous incident in the timeless eternity of the Divine.

Now, that is the whole trouble in my approach to Mayavada. Nirvana in my liberated consciousness turned out to be the beginning of my realisation, a first step towards the complete thing, not the sole true attainment possible or even a culminating finale. It came unasked, unsought for, though quite welcome. I had no least idea about it before, no aspiration towards it, in fact my aspiration was towards just the opposite, spiritual power to help the world and to do my work in it, yet it came—without even a 'May I come in' or a 'By your leave'. It just happened and settled in as if for all eternity or as if it had been really there always. And then it slowly grew into something not less but greater than its first self. How then could I accept Mayavada or persuade myself to pit against the Truth imposed on me from above the logic of Shankara?

But I do not insist on everybody passing through my experience or following the Truth that is its consequence. I have no objection to anybody accepting Mayavada as his soul's truth or his mind's truth or their way out of the cosmic difficulty. I object to it only if somebody tries to push it down my throat or the world's throat as the sole possible, satisfying and all-comprehensive explanation of things. For it is not that at all. There are many other possible explanations; it is not at all satisfactory, for in the end it explains nothing; and it is—and must be unless it departs from its own logic—all-exclusive, not in the least all-comprehensive. But that does not matter. A theory may be wrong or at least one-sided and imperfect and yet extremely practical and useful. This has been amply shown by the history of Science. In fact, a theory whether philosophical or scientific, is nothing else than a support for the mind, a practical device to help it to deal with its object, a staff to uphold it and make it walk more confidently and get along on its difficult journey. The very exclusiveness and one-sidedness of the Mayavada make it a strong staff or a forceful stimulus for a spiritual endeavour which means to be one-sided, radical and exclusive. It supports the effort of the Mind to get away from itself and from Life by a short cut into superconscience. Or rather it is the Purusha in Mind that wants to get away from the limitations of Mind and Life into the superconscient Infinite. Theoretically, the way for that is for the mind to deny all its perceptions and all the preoccupation of the vital and see and treat them as illusions. Practically, when the mind draws from itself, it enters easily into a relationless peace in which nothing matters—for in its absoluteness there are no mental or vital values—and from which the mind can rapidly move towards that great short cut to the superconscient, mindless trance, *susupti*. In proportion to the thoroughness of that movement all the perceptions it had once accepted become unreal to it—illusion, Maya. It is on its road towards immergence.

Mayavada therefore with its sole stress on Nirvana, quite apart from its defects as a mental theory of things, serves a great spiritual end and, as a path, can lead very high and far. Even if the Mind were the last word and there were nothing beyond it except the pure Spirit, I would not be averse to accepting it as the only way out. For what the mind with its perceptions and the vital with its desires have made of life in this world, is a very bad mess, and if there were nothing better to be hoped for, the shortest cut to an exit would be the best. But my experience is that there is something beyond mind; Mind is not the last word here of the Spirit. Mind is an ignorance-consciousness and its perceptions cannot be anything else than either false, mixed or imperfect—even when true, a partial reflection of the Truth and not the very body of Truth herself. But there is a Truth-Consciousness, not static only and self-introspective, but also dynamic and creative, and I prefer to get at that and see what it says about things and can do rather that take the short cut away from things offered as its own end by the Ignorance.[8]

Shankara's Mayavada and Integral Yoga

I do not base my Yoga on the insufficient ground that the Self (not soul) is eternally free. That affirmation leads to nothing beyond itself, or, if used as a starting-point, it could equally well lead to the conclusion that action and creation have no significance or value. The question is not that but of the meaning of creation, whether there is a Supreme who is not merely a pure undifferentiated Consciousness and Being, but the source and support also of the dynamic energy of creation and whether the cosmic existence has for it a significance and a value. That is a question which cannot be settled by metaphysical logic which deals in words and ideas, but by a spiritual experience which goes beyond Mind and enters into spiritual realities. Each mind is satisfied with its own reasoning, but for spiritual purposes that satisfaction has no validity, except as an indication of how far and on what line each one is prepared to go in the field of spiritual experience. If your reasoning leads you towards the Shankara idea of the Supreme, that might be an indication that the Vedanta Adwaita (Mayavada) is your way of advance.

This Yoga accepts the value of cosmic existence and holds it to be a reality; its object is to enter into a higher Truth-Consciousness or Divine Supramental Consciousness in which action and creation are the expression not of ignorance and imperfection, but of the Truth, the Light, the Divine Ananda. But for that, surrender of the mortal mind, life and body to that Higher Consciousness is indispensable, since it is too difficult for the mortal human being to pass by its own effort beyond mind to a Supra-mental Consciousness in which the dynamism is no longer mental but of quite another power. Only those who can accept the call to such a change should enter into this Yoga.[9]

The Realistic and the Illusionist Adwaita

There is possible a realistic as well as an illusionist Adwaita. The philosophy of *The Life Divine* is such a realistic Adwaita. The world is a manifestation of the Real and therefore is itself real. The reality is the infinite and eternal Divine, infinite and eternal Being, Consciousness-Force and Bliss. This Divine by his power has created the world or rather manifested it in his own infinite Being. But here in the material world or at its basis he has hidden himself in what seem to be his opposites, Non-Being, Inconscience and Insentience. This is what we nowadays call the Inconscient which seems to have created the material universe by its inconscient Energy, but this is only an appearance, for we find in the end that all the dispositions of the world can only have been arranged by the working of a supreme secret Intelligence. The Being which is hidden in what seems to be an inconscient void emerges in the world first in Matter, then in Life, then in Mind and finally as the Spirit. The apparently inconscient Energy which creates is in fact the Consciousness-Force of the Divine and its aspect of consciousness, secret in Matter, begins to emerge in Life, finds something more of itself in Mind and finds its true self in a spiritual consciousness and finally a Supramental Consciousness through which we become aware of the Reality, enter into it and unite ourselves with it. This is what we call evolution of Consciousness and an evolution of the Spirit in things and only outwardly an evolution of species. Thus also, the delight of existence emerges from the original insentience, first in the contrary forms of pleasure and pain, and then has to find itself in the bliss of the Spirit or, as it is called in the Upanishads, the bliss of the Brahman. That is the central idea in the explanation of the universe put forward in *The Life Divine*.[10]

Shankara and Illusionism

Q: A writer in 'Prabuddha Bharata' states that your understanding of Shankara's philosophy is not right. Perhaps he bases his statement on the ground that you have missed the indications of Brahmavada of Bhaktivada that Shankara brings in at places. I doubt if Vivekananda or Ramakrishna accepted Shankara's philosophy in toto.

A: They want to show that Shankara was not so savagely illusionist as he is represented—that he gave a certain temporary reality to the world, admitted Shakti, etc. But these (supposing he made them) are concessions inconsistent with the logic of his own philosophy which is that only the Brahman exists and the rest is ignorance and illusion. The rest has only a temporary and therefore an illusory reality in Maya. He further maintained that Brahman could not be reached by works. If that was not his philosophy, I should like to know what was his philosophy. At any rate that was how his philosophy has been understood by people. Now that the general turn is away from the rigorous Illusionism, many of the Adwaitists seem to want to hedge and make Shankara hedge with them.

Vivekananda accepted Shankara's philosophy with modifications, the chief of them being Daridra-Narayan-Seva which is a mixture of Buddhist compassion and modern philanthropy.[11]

New Elements in Sri Aurobindo's Yoga

By transformation I do not mean some change of the nature—I do not mean, for instance, sainthood or ethical perfection or Yogic siddhis (like the Tantrik's) or a transcendental (*chinmaya*) body. I use transformation in a special sense, a change of consciousness radical and complete and of a certain specific kind which is so conceived as to bring about a strong and assured step forward in the spiritual evolution of the being of a greater and higher kind and of a larger sweep and completeness than what took place when a mentalised being first appeared in a vital and material animal world. If anything short of that takes place or at least if a real beginning is not made on that basis, a fundamental progress towards this fulfilment, then my object is not accomplished. A partial realisation, something mixed and inconclusive, does not meet the demand I make on life and Yoga.

Light of realisation is not the same thing as Descent. Realisation by itself does not necessarily transform the being as a whole; it may bring only an opening or heightening or widening of the consciousness at the top so as to realise something in the Purusha part without any radical change in the parts of Prakriti. One may have some light of realisation at the spiritual summit of the consciousness but the parts below remain what they were. I have seen any number of instances of that. There must be a descent of the light not merely into the mind or part of it but into all the being down to the physical and below before a real transformation can take place. A light in the mind may spiritualise or otherwise change the mind or part of it in one way or another, but it need not change the vital nature; a light in the vital may purify and enlarge the vital movements or else silence and immobilise the vital being, but leave the body and the physical consciousness as it was, or even leave it inert or shake its balance. And the descent of Light is not enough, it must be the descent of the whole higher consciousness, its Peace, Power, Knowledge, Love, Ananda. Moreover the descent may be enough to liberate, but not to perfect, or it may be enough to make a great change in the inner being, while the outer remains an imperfect instrument, clumsy, sick or unexpressive. Finally transformation effected by the sadhana cannot be complete unless it is a supramentalisation of the being. Psychicisation is not enough, it is only a beginning; spiritualisation and the descent of the higher consciousness is not enough, it is only a middle term; the ultimate achievement needs the action of the Supramental Consciousness and Force. Something less than that may very well be considered enough by the individual, but it is not enough for the earth-consciousness to take the definitive stride forward it must take at one time or another.

I have never said that my yoga was something brand new in all its elements. I have called it the integral Yoga and that means that it takes up the essence and many processes of the old Yogas—its newness is in its aim, standpoint and the totality of its method. In the earlier stages which is all I deal with in books like the 'Riddle' or the 'Lights' or in the new book to be published there is nothing in it that distinguishes it from the old Yogas except the aim underlying its comprehensiveness, the spirit in its movements and the ultimate significance it keeps before it—also the scheme of its psychology and its working: but as that was not and could not be developed systematically or schematically in these letters, it has not been grasped by those who are not already acquainted with it by mental familiarity or some amount of practice. The detail or method of the later stages of the Yoga which go into little known or untrodden regions, I have not made public and I do not at present intend to do so.

I know very well also that there have been seemingly allied ideals and anticipations—the perfectibility of the race, certain Tantric sadhanas, the effort after a complete physical siddhi by certain schools of Yoga, etc., etc. I have alluded to these things myself and have put forth the view that the spiritual past of the race has been a preparation of Nature not merely for attaining the Divine beyond the world, but also for the very step forward which the evolution of the earth-consciousness has still to make. I do not therefore care in the least— even though these ideals were, up to some extent parallel, yet not identical with mine—whether this Yoga and its aim and method are accepted as new or not; that is in itself a trifling matter. That it should be recognised as true in itself by those who can accept or practise it and should make itself true by achievement is the one thing important; it does not matter if it is called new or a repetition or revival of the old which was forgotten. I laid emphasis on it as new in a letter to certain sadhaks so as to explain to them that a repetition of the aim and idea of the old Yogas was not enough in my eyes, that I was putting forward a thing to be achieved that has not yet been achieved, not yet clearly visualised, even though it is one natural but still secret outcome of all the past spiritual endeavour.

It is new as compared with the old Yogas:

(1) Because it aims not at a departure out of world and life into Heaven or Nirvana, but at a change of life and existence, not as something subordinate or incidental, but as a distinct and central object. If there is a descent in other Yogas, yet it is only an incident on the way or resulting from the ascent—the ascent is the real thing. Here the ascent is the first step, but it is a means for the descent. It is the descent of the new consciousness attained by the ascent that is the stamp and seal of the sadhana. Even the Tantra and Vaishnavism end in the release from life; here the object is the divine fulfilment of life.

(2) Because the object sought after is not an individual achievement of divine realisation for the sake of the individual, but something to be gained for the earth-consciousness here, a cosmic, not solely a supra-cosmic achievement. The thing to be gained also is the bringing in of a Power of Consciousness (the Supramental) not yet organised or active directly in earth-nature, even in the spiritual life, but yet to be organised and made directly active.

(3) Because a method has been precognized for achieving this purpose which is as total and integral as the aim set before it, viz., the total and integral change of the consciousness and nature, taking up old methods but only as a part action and present aid to others that are distinctive. I have not found this method (as a whole) or anything like it professed or realised in the old Yogas. If I had, I should not have wasted my time in hewing out paths and in thirty years of search and inner creation when I could have hastened home safely to my goal in an easy canter over paths already blazed out, laid down, perfectly mapped, macadamised, made secure and public. Our Yoga is not a retreading of old walks, but a spiritual adventure.[12]

Transformation and Purification
(1)

'Transformation' is a word that I have brought in myself (like 'Supermind') to express certain spiritual concepts and spiritual facts of the integral Yoga. People are now taking them up and using them in senses which have nothing to do with the significance which I put into them. Purification of the nature by the 'influence' of the Spirit is not what I mean by transformation; purification is only part of a psychic change or a psycho-spiritual change—the word besides has many senses and is very often given a moral or ethical meaning which is foreign to my purpose. What I mean by the spiritual transformation is something dynamic (not merely liberation of the Self or realisation of the One which can very well be attained without any descent). It is a putting on of the spiritual consciousness dynamic as well as static in every part of the being down to the subconscient. That cannot be done by the influence of the Self leaving the consciousness fundamentally as it is with only purification, enlightenment of the mind and heart and quiescence of the vital. It means a bringing down of the divine Consciousness static and dynamic into all these parts and the entire replacement of the present consciousness by that. This we find unveiled and unmixed above mind, life and body. It is a matter of the undeniable experience of many that this can descend and it is my experience that nothing short of its *full* descent can thoroughly remove the veil and mixture and effect the full spiritual transformation. No metaphysical or logical reasoning in the voids as to what the Atman 'must' do or can do or needs or needs not to do is relevant here or of any value; I may add that transformation is not the central object of other paths as it is of this Yoga—only so much purification and change is demanded by them as will lead to liberation and the beyond-life. The influence of the Atman can no doubt do that—a full descent of a new consciousness into the whole nature from top to bottom to transform life here is not needed at all for the spiritual escape from life.[13]

Aurobindo and Guruhood

One interesting aspect of modern Hinduism consists in the fact that some of its major representatives did not possess a Guru. Mahatma Gandhi did not have a Guru, neither did Aurobindo. Both were influenced by remarkable people like Raychandbhai and Lele but they were not their Gurus. In the case of Ramana Mahariṣi even such influence is difficult to identify.

In the light of this fact the following remarks of Śrī Aurobindo are of particular interest.

Deficiencies of the Human Guru

It is not the human defects of the Guru that can stand in the way when there is the psychic opening, confidence and surrender. The Guru is the channel or the representation or the manifestation of the Divine, according to the measure of his personality or his attainment; but whatever he is, it is the Divine that one opens to, in opening to him; and if something is determined by the power of the channel, more is determined by the inherent and intrinsic attitude of the receiving consciousness, and element that comes out in the surface mind as simple trust or direct unconditional self-giving, and once that is there, the essential things can be gained even from one who seems to others than the disciple an inferior spiritual source, and the rest will grow up in the sadhak of itself, by the Grace of the Divine, even if the human being in the Guru cannot give it. It is this that K [Krishamurti] appears to have done perhaps from the first; but in most nowadays this attitude seems to come with difficulty, after much hesitation and trouble. In my own case, I owe the first decisive turn of my inner life to one who was infinitely inferior to me in intellect, education, capacity and by no means spiritually perfect or supreme; but having seen a power behind him and decided to turn there for help I gave myself entirely into his hands and followed with an automatic passivity the guidance. He himself was astonished and said to others that he had never met anyone before who could surrender himself so absolutely and without reserve or question to the guidance of the helper. The result was a series of transmuting experiences of such a radical character that he was unable to follow and had to tell me to give myself up in future to the Guide within with the same completeness of surrender as I had shown to the human channel. I give this example to show how these things work; it is not in the calculated way the human reason wants to lay down, but by a more mysterious and greater law.[14]

Aurobindo and the Vedas

Aurobindo came from a thoroughly Western educational background. By contrast, Swami Dayānanda's background was traditional through and through. It is, therefore, of more than passing interest that, in Aurobindo's opinion, Dayānanda did not go far enough in his original interpretation of the Vedas, when most orthodox and Western scholars claim that he went too far!

There is then nothing fantastical in Dayānanda's idea that the Veda contains truths of science as well as truths of religion. I will even add my own conviction that the Veda contains other truths of a science which the modern world does not at all possess, and, in that case, Dayānanda has rather understated than overstated the depth and range of the Vedic wisdom.

Immediately the character of the Veda is fixed in the sense Dayānanda gave to it, the merely ritual, mythological, polytheistic interpretation of Sayanacarya collapses, and the merely mateological and materialistic European interpretation collapses. We have, instead, a real scripture, one of the world's sacred books and the divine word of a lofty and noble religion.[15]

Uttarpara Speech

This speech was delivered at Uttarpara on 30 May 1909 under the auspices of the Dharma Rakshini Sabha, just after Śrī Aurobindo's acquittal in the Alipore Bomb Case.

When I was asked to speak to you at the annual meeting of your Sabha, it was my intention to say a few words about the subject chosen for today, the subject of the Hindu religion. I do not know now whether I shall fulfil that intention; for as I sat here, there came into my mind a word that I have to speak to you, a word that I have to speak to the whole of the Indian nation. It was spoken first to myself in jail and I have come out of jail to speak it to my people.

It was more than a year ago that I came here last. When I came I was not alone; one of the mightiest prophets of Nationalism sat by my side. It was he who then came out of the seclusion to which God had sent him, so that in the silence and solitude of his cell he might hear the word that He had to say. It was he that you came in your hundreds to welcome. Now he is far away, separated from us by thousands of miles. Others whom I was accustomed to find working beside me are absent. The storm that swept over the country has scattered them far and wide. It is I this time who have spent one year in seclusion, and now that I come out I find all changed. One who always sat by my side and was associated in my work is a prisoner in Burma; another is in the north rotting in detention. I looked round when I came out, I looked round for those to whom I had been accustomed to look for counsel and inspiration. I did not find them.

There was more than that. When I went to jail the whole country was alive with the cry of Bande Mataram, alive with the hope of a nation, the hope of millions of men who had newly risen out of degradation. When I came out of jail I listened for that cry, but there was instead a silence. A hush had fallen on the country and men seemed bewildered; for instead of God's bright heaven full of the vision of the future that had been before us, there seemed to be overhead a leaden sky from which human thunders and lightnings rained. No man seemed to know which way to move, and from all sides came the question. 'What shall we do next? What is there that we can do?' I too did not know which way to move, I too did not know what was next to be done. But one thing I knew, that as it was the Almighty Power of God which had raised that cry, that hope, so it was the same Power which had sent down that silence. He who was in the shouting and the movements was also in the pause and the hush. He has sent it upon us, so that the nation might draw back for a moment and look into itself and know His will. I have not been disheartened by that silence, because I had been made familiar with silence in my prison and because I knew it was in the pause and the hush that I had myself learned this lesson through the long year of my detention. When Bepin Chandra Pal came out of jail, he came with a message, and it was an inspired message. I remember the speech he made here. It was a speech not so much political as religious in its bearing and intention. He spoke of his realisation in jail, of God within us all, of the Lord within the nation, and in his subsequent speeches also he spoke of a greater than ordinary force in the movement and a greater than ordinary purpose before it. Now I also meet you again, I also come out of jail, and again it is you of Uttarpara who are the first to welcome me, not at a political meeting but at a meeting of a society for the protection of our religion. That message which Bepin Chandra Pal received in Buxar jail, God gave to me in Alipore. That knowledge He gave to me day after day during my twelve months of imprisonment and it is that which He has commanded me to speak to you now that I have come out.

I knew I would come out. The year of detention was meant only for a year of seclusion and of training. How could anyone hold me in jail longer than was necessary for God's purpose? He had given me a word to speak and a work to do, and until that word was spoken I knew that no human power could hush me, until that work was done no human power could stop God's instrument, however weak that instrument might be or however small. Now that I have come out, even in these few minutes, a word has been suggested to me which I had no wish to speak. The thing I had in my mind He has thrown from it and what I speak is under an impulse and a compulsion.

When I was arrested and hurried to the Lal Bazar Hajat I was shaken in faith for a while, for I could not look into the heart of His intention. Therefore I faltered for a moment and cried out in my heart to Him, 'What is this that has happened to me? I believed that I had a mission to work for the people of my country and until that work was done, I should have Thy protection. Why then am I here and on such a charge?' A day passed and a second day and a third, when a voice came to me from within, 'Wait and see.' Then I grew calm and waited, I was taken from Lal Bazar to Alipore and was placed for one month in a solitary cell apart from men. There I waited day and night for the voice of God within me, to know what He has to say to me, to learn what I had to do. In this seclusion the earliest realisation, the first lesson came to me. I remembered then that a month or more before my arrest, a call had come to me to put aside all activity, to go into seclusion and to look into myself, so that I might enter into closer communion with Him. I was weak and could not accept the call. My work was very dear to me and in the pride of my heart I thought that unless I was there, it would suffer or even fail and cease; therefore I would not leave it. It seemed to me that He spoke to me again and said, 'The bonds you had not the strength to break, I have broken for you, because it is not my will nor was it ever my intention that that should continue. I have had another thing for you to do and it is for that I have brought you here, to teach you what you could not learn for yourself and to train you for my work.' Then He placed the Gita in my hands. His strength entered into me and I was able to do the Sadhana of the Gita. I was not only to understand intellectually but to realise what Sri Krishna demanded of Arjuna and what He demands of those who aspire to do His work, to be free from repulsion and desire, to do work for Him without the demand for fruit, to renounce self-will and become a passive and faithful instrument in His hands, to have an equal heart for high and low, friend and opponent, success and failure, yet not to do His work negligently. I realised what the Hindu religion meant. We speak often of the Hindu religion, of the Sanatan Dharma, but few of us really know what that religion is. Other religions are preponderatingly religions of faith and profession, but the Sanatan Dharma is life itself; it is a thing that has not so much to be believed as lived. This is the Dharma that for the salvation of humanity was cherished in the seclusion of this peninsula from of old. It is to give this religion that India is rising. She does not rise as other countries do, for self or when she is strong, to trample on the weak, she is rising to shed the eternal light entrusted to her over the world. India has always existed for humanity and not for herself and it is for humanity and not for herself that she must be great.

Therefore this was the next thing He pointed out to me—He made me realise the central truth of the Hindu religion. He turned the hearts of my jailors to me and they spoke to the Englishman in charge of the jail, 'He is suffering in his confinement; let him at least walk outside his cell for half an hour in the morning and in the evening.' So it was arranged, and it was while I was walking that His strength again entered into me. I looked at the jail that secluded me from men and it was no longer by its high walls that I was imprisoned; no, it was Vasudeva who surrounded me. I walked under the branches of the tree in front of my cell but it was not the tree, I knew it was Vasudeva, it was Sri Krishna whom I saw standing there and holding over me his shade. I looked at the bars of my cell, the very grating that did duty for a door and again I saw Vasudeva. It was Narayana who was guarding and standing sentry over me, or I lay on the coarse blankets that were given me for a couch and felt the arms of Sri Krishna around me, the arms of my Friend and Lover. This was the first use of the deeper vision He gave me. I looked at the prisoners in the jail, the thieves, the murderers, the swindlers, and as I looked at them I saw Vasudeva, it was Narayana whom I found in these darkened souls and misused bodies. Amongst these thieves and dacoits there were many who put me to shame by their sympathy, their kindness, the humanity triumphant over such adverse circumstances. One I saw among them especially, who seemed to me a saint, a peasant of my nation who did not know how to read and write, an alleged dacoit sentenced to ten years' rigorous imprisonment, one of those whom we look down upon in our Pharisaical pride of class as Chhotalok. Once more He spoke to me and said, 'Behold the people among whom I have sent you to do a little of my work. This is the nature of the nation I am raising up and the reason why I raise them.'

When the case opened in the lower court and we were brought before the Magistrate I was followed by the same insight. He said to me, 'When you were cast into jail, did not your heart fail and did you not cry out to me, where is Thy protection? Look now at the Magistrate, look now at the Prosecuting Counsel.' I looked and it was not the Magistrate whom I saw, it was Vasudeva, it was Narayana who was sitting there on the bench. I looked at the Prosecuting Counsel and it was not the Counsel for the prosecution that I saw; it was Sri Krishna who sat there, it was my Lover and Friend who sat there and smiled. 'Now do you fear?' He said, 'I am in all men and I overrule their actions and their words. My protection is still with you and you shall not fear. This case which is brought against you, leave it in my hand. It is not for you. It was not for the trial that I brought you here but for something else. The case itself is only a means for my work and nothing more.' Afterwards when the trial opened in the Sessions Court, I began to write many instructions for my Counsel as to what was false in the evidence against me and on what points the witnesses might be cross-examined. Then something happened which I had not expected. The arrangements which had been made for my defence were suddenly changed and another Counsel stood there to defend me. He came unexpectedly—a friend of mine, but I did not know he was coming. You have all heard the name of the man who put away from him all other thoughts and abandoned all his practice, who sat up half the night day after day for months and broke his health to save me—Srijut Chittaranajan Das. When I saw him, I was satisfied, but I still thought it necessary to write instruction. Then all that was put away from me and I had the message from within, 'This is the man who will save you from the snares put around your feet. Put aside those papers. It is not you who will instruct him. I will instruct him.' From that time I did not of myself speak a word to my Counsel about the case or give a single instruction, and if ever I was asked a question, I always found that my answer did not help the case. I had left it to him and he took it entirely into his hands, with what result you know. I knew all along what He meant for me, for I heard it again and again, always I listened to the voice within; 'I am guiding, therefore fear not. Turn to your own work for which I have brought you to jail and when you come out, remember never to fear, never to hesitate. Remember that it is I who am doing this, not you nor any other. Therefore whatever clouds may come, whatever impossibilities, there is nothing impossible, nothing difficult. I am in the nation and its uprising and I am Vasudeva, I am Narayana, and what I will, shall be, not what others will. What I choose to bring about no human power can stay.'

Meanwhile He had brought me out of solitude and placed me among those who had been accused along with me. You have spoken much today of my self-sacrifice and devotion to my country. I have heard that kind of speech ever since I came out of jail, but I hear it with embarrassment, with something of pain. For I know my weakness, I am a prey to my own faults and back slidings. I was not blind to them before and when they all rose up against me in seclusion, I felt them utterly. I knew then that I the man was a mass of weakness, a faulty and imperfect instrument, strong only when a higher strength entered into me. Then I found myself among these young men and in many of them I discovered a mighty courage, a power of self-effacement in comparison with which I was simply nothing. I saw one or two who were not only superior to me in force and character—very many were that—but in the promise of that intellectual ability on which I prided myself. He said to me, 'This is the young generation, the new and mighty nation that is arising at my command. They are greater than yourself. What have you to fear? If you stood aside or slept, the work would still be done. If you were to cast aside tomorrow, here are the young men who will take up your work and do it more mightily than you have ever done. You have only got some strength from me to speak a word to this nation which will help to raise it.' This was the next thing He told me.

Then a thing happened suddenly and in a moment I was hurried away to the seclusion of a solitary cell. What happened to me during that period I am not impelled to say, but only this that day after day, He showed me His wonders and made me realise the utter truth of the Hindu religion. I had had many doubts before. I was brought up in England amongst foreign ideas and an atmosphere entirely foreign. About many things in Hinduism I had once been inclined to believe that they were imaginations, that there was much of dream in it, much that was delusion and Maya. But now day after day I realised in the mind, I realised in the heart, I realised in the body the truths of the Hindu religion. They became living experiences to me, and things were opened to me which no material science could explain. When I first approached Him, it was not entirely in the spirit of the Bhakta, it was not entirely in the spirit of the Jnani. I came to Him long ago in Baroda some years before the Swadeshi began and I was drawn into the public field.

When I approached God at that time, I hardly had a living faith in Him. The agnostic was in me, the atheist was in me, the sceptic was in me and I was not absolutely sure that there was a God at all. I did not feel His presence. Yet something drew me to the truth of the Vedas, the truth of the Gita, the truth of the Hindu religion. I felt there must be a mighty truth somewhere in this Yoga, a mighty truth in this religion based on the Vedanta. So when I turned to the Yoga and resolved to practice it and find out if my idea was right, I did it in this spirit and with this prayer to Him, 'If Thou art, then Thou knowest my heart. Thou knowest that I do not ask for Mukti, I do not ask for anything which others ask for. I ask only for strength to uplift this nation, I ask only to be allowed to live and work for this people whom I love and to whom I pray that I may devote my life.' I strove long for the realisation of Yoga and at last to some extent I had it, but in what I most desired I was not satisfied. Then in the seclusion of the jail, of the solitary cell I asked for it again. I said, 'Give me Thy Adesh. I do not know what work to do or how to do it. Give me a message.' In the communion of Yoga two messages came. The first message said, 'I have given you a work and it is to help to uplift this nation. Before long the time will come when you will have to go out of jail; for it is not my will that this time either you should be convicted or that you should pass the time, as others have to do, in suffering for their country. I have called you to work, and that is the Adesh for which you have asked. I give you the Adesh to go forth and do my work.' The second message came and it said, 'Something has been shown to you in this year of seclusion, something about which you had your doubts and it is the truth of the Hindu religion. It is this religion that I am raising up before the world, it is this that I have perfected and developed through the Rishis, saints and Avatars, and now it is going forth to do my work among the nations. I am raising up this nation to send forth my word. This is the Sanatan Dharma, this is the eternal religion which you did not really know before, but which I have now revealed to you, the agnostic and the sceptic in you have been answered, for I have given you proofs within and without you, physical and subjective, which have satisfied you. When you go forth, speak to your nation always this word, that it is for the Sanatan Dharma that they arise, it is for the world and not for themselves that they arise. I am giving them freedom for the service of the world. When therefore it is said that India shall rise, it is the Sanatan Dharma that shall rise. When it is said that India shall be great, it is the Sanatan Dharma that shall be great. When it is said that India shall expand and extend herself, it is the Sanatan Dharma that shall expand and extend itself over the world. It is for the Dharma and by the Dharma that India exists. To magnify the religion means to magnify the country. I have shown you that I am everywhere and in all men and in all things, that I am in this movement and I am not only working in those who are striving for the country but I am working also in those who oppose them and stand in their path. I am working in everybody and whatever men may think or do they can do nothing but help in my purpose. They also are doing my work, they are not my enemies but my instruments.

In all your actions you are moving forward without knowing which way you move. You mean to do one thing and you do another. You aim at a result and your efforts subserve one that is different or contrary. It is Shakti that has gone forth and entered into the people. Since long ago I have been preparing this uprising and now the time has come and it is I who will lead it to its fulfilment.'

This then is what I have to say to you. The name of your society is 'Society for the Protection of Religion'. Well, the protection of the religion, the protection and upraising before the world of the Hindu religion, that is the work before us. But what is the Hindu religion? What is this religion which we call Sanatan, eternal? It is the Hindu religion only because the Hindu nation has kept it. Because in this Peninsula it grew up in the seclusion of the sea and the Himalayas, because in this sacred and ancient land it was given as a charge to the Aryan race to preserve through the ages. But it is not circumscribed by the confines of a single country, it does not belong peculiarly and for ever to a bounded part of the world. That which we call the Hindu religion is really the eternal religion, because it is the universal religion which embraces all others. If a religion is not universal, it cannot be eternal. A narrow religion, a sectarian religion, an exclusive religion can live only for a limited time and a limited purpose. This is the one religion that can triumph over materialism by including and anticipating the discoveries of science and the speculations of philosophy. It is the one religion which impresses on mankind the closeness of God to us and embraces in its compass all the possible means by which man can approach God. It is the one religion which insists every moment on the truth which all religions acknowledge that He is in all men and all things and that in Him we move and have our being. It is the one religion which enables us not only to understand and believe this truth but to realise it with every part of our being. It is the one religion which shows the world what the world is, that it is the Lila of Vasudeva. It is the one religion which shows us how we can best play our part in that Lila, its subtlest laws and its noblest rules. It is the one religion which does not separate life in any smallest detail from religion, which knows what immortality is and has utterly removed from us the reality of death.

This is the word that has been put into my mouth to speak to you today. What I intended to speak has been put away from me, and beyond what is given to me I have nothing to say. It is only the word that is put into me that I can speak to you. That word is now finished. I spoke once before with this force in me and I said then that this movement is not a political movement and that nationalism is not politics but a religion, a creed, a faith. I say it again today, but I put it in another way. I say no longer that nationalism is a creed, a religion, a faith; I say that it is the Sanatan Dharma which for us is nationalism. This Hindu nation was born with the Sanatan Dharma, with it it moves and with it it grows. When the Sanatan Dharma declines, then the nation declines, and if the Sanatan Dharma were capable of perishing, with the Sanatan Dharma it would perish. The Sanatan Dharma, that is nationalism. This is the message that I have to speak to you.[16]

Message on the Fifteenth of August 1947

Śrī Aurobindo's message to India on the attainment of Independence from British Rule on 15 August 1947:

Not Fortuitous

August 15 is my own birthday and it is naturally gratifying to me that it should have assumed this vast significance. I take this coincidence, not as a fortuitous accident, but as the sanction and seal of the Divine Force that guides my steps on the work with which I began life, the beginning of its full fruition. Indeed, on this day I can watch almost all the world-movements which I hoped to see fulfilled in my life-time, though then they looked like impracticable dreams, arriving at fruition or on their way to achievement. In all these movements free India may well play a large part and take a leading position.

The first of these dreams was a revolutionary movement which would create a free and united India; India today is free but she has not achieved unity. At one moment it almost seemed as if in the very act of liberation she would fall back into the chaos of separate States which preceded the British conquest. But fortunately it now seems probable that this danger will be averted and a large and powerful though not yet a complete union will be established. Also the wisely drastic policy of the Constituent Assembly has made it probable that the problem of the depressed classes will be solved without schism or fissure. But the old communal division into Hindus and Muslims seems now to have hardened into a permanent political division of the country. It is to be hoped that this settled fact will not be accepted as settled for ever or as anything more than a temporary expedient. For if it lasts, India may be seriously weakened, even crippled: civil strife may remain always possible, possible even a new invasion and foreign conquest, India's internal development and prosperity may be impeded, her position among the nations weakened, her destiny impaired or even frustrated. This must not be; the partition must go. Let us hope that that may come about naturally, by an increasing recognition of the necessity not only of peace and concord but of common action, by the practice of common action and the creation of means for that purpose. In this way unity may finally come about under whatever form—the exact form may have a pragmatic but not a fundamental importance. But by whatever means, in whatever way, the division must go; unity must and will be achieved, for it is necessary for the greatness of India's future.

Another dream was for the resurgence and liberation of the peoples of Asia and her return to her great role in the progress of human civilisation. Asia has arisen; large parts are now quite free or are at this moment being liberated: its other still subject or partly subject parts are moving through whatever struggles towards freedom. Only a little has to be done and that will be done today or tomorrow. There India has her part to play and has begun to play it with energy and ability which already indicate the measure of her possibilities and the place she can take in the council of the nations.

World Union

The third dream was a world-union forming the outer basis of a fairer, brighter and nobler life for all mankind. That unification of the human world is under way: there is an imperfect initiation organised but struggling against tremendous difficulties. But the momentum is there and it must inevitably increase and conquer. Here too India has begun to play a prominent part and, if she can develop that larger statesmanship which is not limited by the present facts and immediate possibilities but looks into the future and brings it nearer, her presence may make all the difference between a slow and timid and a bold and swift development. A catastrophe may intervene and interrupt or destroy what is being done, but even then the final result is sure. For unification is a necessity of Nature, an inevitable movement. Its necessity for the nations is also clear, for without it the freedom of the small nations may be at any moment in peril and the life even of the large and powerful nations insecure. The unification is therefore to the interests of all, and only human imbecility and stupid selfishness can pervert it; but these cannot stand for ever against the necessity of Nature and the Divine Will. But an outward basis is not enough; there must grow up an international spirit and outlook, international forms and institutions must appear, perhaps such developments as dual or multilateral citizenship, willed interchange or voluntary fusion of cultures. Nationalism will have fulfilled itself and lost its militancy and would no longer find these things incompatible with self-preservation and the integrality of its outlook. A new spirit of oneness will take hold of the human race.

Another dream, the spiritual gift of India to the world has already begun. India's spirituality is entering Europe and America in an ever increasing measure. That movement will grow; amid the disasters of the time more and more eyes are turning towards her with hope and there is even an increasing resort not only to her teachings, but to her psychic and spiritual practice.

Final Dream

The final dream was a step in evolution which would raise man to a higher and larger consciousness and begin the solution of the problems which have perplexed and vexed him since he first began to think and to dream of individual perfection and a perfect society. This is still a personal hope and an idea, an ideal which has begun to take hold both in India and in the West on forward-looking minds. The difficulties in the way are more formidable than in any other field of endeavour but difficulties were made to be overcome and if the Supreme Will is there, they will be overcome. Here too, if this evolution is to take place, since it must proceed through a growth of the spirit and the inner consciousness, the initiative can come from India and, although the scope must be universal, the central movement may be hers.

Such is the content which I put into this date of India's liberation; whether or how far this hope will be justified depends upon the new and free India.[17]

Notes

1. Peter Heehs, *Sri Aurobindo: A Brief Biography* (Delhi: Oxford University Press, 1989), pp. 16–17.
2. *Sri Aurobindo on Himself and on the Mother* (Pondicherry: Sri Aurobindo Ashram, 1953), pp. 132–3. For earlier experiences see pp. 84–5.
3. Ibid.
4. Ibid., pp. 115–19.
5. See Robert A. McDermott, *Six Pillars: Introduction to the Major Works of Sri Aurobindo* (Chambersburg, Pennsylvania: Wilson Books, 1974).
6. *Sri Aurobindo on Himself and on the Mother*, pp. 126–8.
7. Ibid., pp. 130–1.

8. *Sri Aurobindo on Himself and on the Mother* (Pondhicherry: Sri Aurobindo Ashram, 1953), pp. 153–8.

9. Ibid., pp. 158–9.

10. Ibid., pp. 159–61.

11. Ibid., pp. 161–2.

12. Ibid., pp. 162–8.

13. Ibid., pp. 168–9.

14. Ibid., pp. 128–30.

15. As cited in Haridas Bhattacharyya, ed., *The Cultural Heritage of India* (Calcutta: The Ramakrishna Mission Institute of Culture, 1956), Vol. IV, p. 634.

16. Śrī Aurobindo, *Karmayogin: Early Political Writings-2* (Birth Centenary Library, 1972), pp. 1–10.

17. Verinder Grover, ed., *Political Thinkers of Modern India* (New Delhi: Deep & Deep Publications, 1992), Vol. XI, pp. 286–8.

Sarvepalli Radhakrishnan
(1888–1975)

Life

S. Radhakrishnan was a man of many parts, but he was above all else a philosopher, and a philosopher of religion at that. But he was as much a philosopher of Hinduism and of comparative religion, as of religion per se.[1]

As the focus of his life remained primarily intellectual, and even academic, it can be conveniently divided into five phases.[2]

1888–1908: This phase commences with his birth and ends with the publication of his Master's thesis, in which he defended Vedānta against the charge that it lacked ethics: *The Ethics of the Vedanta and its Metaphysical Pre-Suppositions* (1908).

1908–1926: During this period he taught, wrote a book on Tagore illustrating his links to Hinduism and also published *The Reign of Religion in Contemporary Philosophy* (1921), *Indian Philosophy* (Vol. I, 1923), and *The Philosophy of the Upaniṣads* (1924).

1926–1945: This period represents the international phase of his academic life. Many of the major works of Radhakrishnan belong to this period. These include *The Hindu View of Life* (1926); *Indian Philosophy* (Vol. II, 1927); *Kalki or the Future of Civilization* (1929); *East and West in Religion* (1933); *Contemporary Indian Philosophy* (1936); *An Idealist View of Life* (1937); *Eastern Religions and Western Thought* (1939).

1945–1967: During this period Radhakrishnan served as the Vice-President and then President of India, and it represents, in that sense, the more political phase of his life. The following books belong to this period: *Religion and Society* (1947); *The Bhagavad Gītā* (1948); *The Principal Upaniṣads* (1953); *Recovery of Faith* (1956); *The Brahma Sūtra: The Philosophy of Spiritual Life* (1960).[3]

1967–1975: Retirement in Madras.

Personal Reflections of a Philosopher

Tagore shared with us the philosophical reflections of a poet; Radhakrishnan shares with us the personal reflections of a philosopher. One factor which emerges clearly in these reflections is the role the Christian critique of Hinduism played in his philosophical evolution.

The Undermining of Tradition

My teachers in Christian missionary institutions cured me of this faith and restored for me the primordial situation in which all philosophy is born. They were teachers of philosophy, commentators, interpreters, apologists for the Christian way of thought and life, but were not, in the strict sense of the term, seekers of truth. By their criticism of Indian thought they disturbed my faith and shook the traditional props on which I leaned.

While the undogmatic apprehensions and the discipline of mind which Hinduism provides as the essential means for the discovery of truth are established in a rigorously logical manner, while the great insights, fundamental motives and patterns of thought of Hindu religion have meaning for us even today, it has taken on in its long history many arbitrary and fanciful theories and is full of shackles which constrict the free life of the spirit. Besides, we live in a time when we have become the inheritors of the world's thought. We have accumulated much historical knowledge about religions and philosophies. We find that innumerable people before us have raised these questions about the nature of the universe, the principle of being and have given answers which they treated as final and absolute. The very multiplicity of these absolutisms makes it difficult for us to assume, if we are honest, that our absolutism is the true one and all others false. Faced by these conflicting and competing absolutisms, we become either traditionalists or sceptics. A critical study of the Hindu religion was thus forced on me.[4]

Hindu Tolerance

Radhakrishnan identified tolerance as a major feature of Hinduism and pointedly noted how Western religions suffer by contrast.

Hinduism does not support the sophism that is often alleged that to coerce a man to have the right view is as legitimate as to save one by violence from committing suicide in a fit of delirium. The intolerance of narrow monotheism is written in letters of blood across the history of man from the time when first the tribes of Israel burst into the land of Canaan. The worshippers of the one jealous god are egged on to aggressive wars against people of alien cults. They invoke divine sanction for the cruelties inflicted on the conquered. The spirit of old Israel is inherited by Christianity and Islam, and it might not be unreasonable to suggest that it would have been better for Western civilization if Greece had moulded it on this question rather than Palestine. Wars of religion which are the outcome of fanaticism that prompts and justifies the extermination of aliens of different creeds were practically unknown in Hindu India. Of course, here and there, there were outbursts of fanaticism, but Hinduism as a rule never encouraged persecution of unbelief. Its record has been a clean one, relatively speaking.[5]

Mysticism and Tolerance

It is one of Radhakrishnan's persistent claims that religion is an experience, and religious tolerance finds its basis in the unity of mystical experience.

The chief sacred scriptures of the Hindus, the Vedas, register the intuitions of the perfected souls. They are not so much dogmatic dicta as transcripts from life. They record the spiritual experiences of souls strongly endowed with the sense for reality. They are held to be authoritative on the ground that they express the experiences of the experts in the field of religion. If the utterances of the Vedas were uninformed by spiritual insight, they would have no claim to our belief. The truths revealed in the Vedas are capable of being re-experienced on compliance with ascertained conditions. We can discriminate between the genuine and the spurious in religious experience, not only by means of logic but also through life. By experimenting with different religious conceptions and relating them with the rest of our life, we can know the sound from the unsound.

The Vedas bring together the different ways in which the religious minded of that age experienced reality and describe the general principles of religious knowledge and growth. As the experiences themselves are of a varied character, so their records are many-sided (*viśvatomukham*) or 'suggestive of many interpretations' (*anekārthatām*).

It matters not whether the seer who has the insight has dreamed his way to the truth in the shadow of the temple or the tabernacle, the church or the mosque. Those who have seen the radiant vision of the Divine protest against the exaggerated importance attached to outward forms. They speak a language which unites all worshippers as surely as the dogmas of the doctors divide. The true seer is gifted with a universality of outlook, and a certain sensitiveness to the impulses and emotions which dominate the rich and varied human nature. He whose consciousness is anchored in God cannot deny any expression of life as utterly erroneous. He is convinced of the inexhaustibility of the nature of God and the infinite number of its possible manifestations.

The intellectual representations of the religious mystery are relative and symbolic. As Plato would say, our accounts of God are likely stories, but all the same legendary. Not one of them is full and final. We are like little children on the seashore trying to fill our shells with water from the sea. While we cannot exhaust the waters of the deep by means of our shells, every drop that we attempt to gather into our tiny shells is a part of the authentic waters. Our intellectual representations differ simply because they bring out different facets of one central reality. From the Ṛṣis, or seers, of the Upaniṣads down to Tagore and Gandhi, the Hindu has acknowledged that truth wears vestures of many colours and speaks in strange tongues. The mystics of other denominations have also testified to this. Boehme says: 'Consider the birds in our forests, they praise God each in his own way, in diverse tones and fashions. Think you God is vexed by this diversity and desires to silence discordant voices? All the forms of being are dear to the infinite Being Himself.' Look at this Sufi utterance in the translation of Professor Browne of Cambridge:

> Beaker or flagon, or bowl or jar,
> Clumsy or slender, coarse or fine;
> However the potter may make or mar,
> All were made to contain the wine:
> Should we seek this one or that one shun
> When the wine which gives them their worth is one?[6]

The Racial Problem

Radhakrishnan analyses the racial problem in the following passage and assesses the role of the caste system in this context positively.

Regarding the solution to the problem of racial conflicts the different alternatives which present themselves are those of extermination, subordination, identification or harmonization. The first course has been adopted often in the course of the history of the world. The trail of man is dotted with the graves of countless communities which reached an untimely end. But is there any justification for this violation of human life? Have we any idea of what the world loses when one racial culture is extinguished? It is true that the Red Indians have not made, to all appearance, any contribution to the world's progress, but have we any clear understanding of their undeveloped possibilities which, in God's good time, might have come to fruition? Do we know so much of ourselves and the world and God's purpose as to believe that our civilization, our institutions and our customs are so immeasurably superior to those of others, not only what others actually possess but what exists in them potentially? We cannot measure beforehand the possibilities of a race. Civilizations are not made in a day, and had the fates been kindlier and we less arrogant in our ignorance, the world, I dare say, would have been richer for the contributions of the Red Indians. Our civilization is quite recent when compared with the antiquity of man and the differentiation of human types. Some of the ancestors of the Great British people who are now in the vanguard of humanity were not much advanced as depicted by Julius Caesar. Who could understand the great potentialities of the savages of Britain dressed in skins at their religious worship burning man alive to appease their gods? No one acquainted with the ancestors of the Teutons would have anticipated for them their glorious contributions to music and metaphysics. Human potentiality is so great, and our knowledge of fundamental racial differences so little, that the cruel repression and extermination of races is not part of wisdom. A little understanding of human nature and history will enable us to sympathize with the savage and the primitive, the barbarous and the backward, and help us to see that they also in their imperfect fashions are struggling towards that abiding city which shines in dazzling splendour up the steep and narrow way. Every people, every tribe however little advanced in its stage of development, represents a certain psychic type or pattern. The interests of humanity require that every type should be assisted and educated to its adequate expression and development. No race lives to itself and no race dies to itself. Besides, the backwardness of races is due to environmental conditions, physical, social and cultural. Races show considerable powers of adaptation when an external stimulus is applied to them.

When extermination is impossible, the powerful races of the world adopt the second alternative of subordination. They act on the maxim, spare the slave and smash the rebel. The superior races of the world cannot have a clean conscience if they remember their dealings with the coloured ones on the Congo, in Brazil, in Peking at the time of the Boxer revolution, and in America today. For a man like Lord Milner the British Empire meant the *brotherhood* of communities of like *blood* and the mastery of the British race over the non-British dependencies. Civilization is not suppression of races less capable of or less advanced in culture by people of higher standing. God does not give us the right to destroy or enslave the weak and the unfit. One race may not be as clever or as strong as another, and yet the highest idealism requires that we should give equality of opportunity even to unequal groups. We must respect the independence of every people and lead the backward ones to a full utilization of the opportunities of their environment and a development of their distinctive natural characteristics.

Racial fusion on a large scale is an impossibility, if it is to be achieved in a short period of time. For long centuries of social tradition and natural inheritance have produced marked divergencies of temperament, mentality and physique which cannot be destroyed at a stroke. Nor is it necessary to do away with race individualities and differences to solve the race problem. Uniformity is not the meaning of unity.

In dealing with the problem of the conflict of the different racial groups, Hinduism adopted the only safe course of democracy, viz. that each racial group should be allowed to develop the best in it without impeding the progress of others. Every historical group is unique and specific and has an ultimate value, and the highest morality requires that we should respect its individuality. Caste, on its racial side, is the affirmation of the infinite diversity of human groups. Though the Vedic Aryans started their life in India with a rigid and narrow outlook, regarding themselves as a sort of chosen people, they soon became universal in intention and developed an ethical code applicable to the whole of humanity, a *mānava dharma*.[7]

The Religious Problem

Radhakrishnan repeatedly draws creative attention to the fact that the contemporary world may benefit from the solutions formulated by Hindus centuries ago. The Brahmasūtra (I.1.4) suggests that divergent passages in the scriptures should be interpreted harmoniously (samanvaya). Radhakrishnan extends this intrascriptural principle into an interscriptural one.

Today the *samanvaya* or harmonisation has to be extended to the living faiths of mankind. Religion concerns man as man and not man as Jew or Christian, Hindu or Buddhist, Sikh or Muslim. As the author of the . . . [Brahmasūtra] tried to reconcile the different doctrines prevalent in his time, we have to take into account the present state of our knowledge and evolve a coherent picture. Beliefs retain their vigour for a long time after their roots have withered or their sources have silted up. We must express our beliefs in the context and shape of the real questions and search of modern men. The way in which faith has hitherto expressed itself, the categories which it has evolved, the very nature of the world and the hope towards which faith directs its attention have lost their meaning and reality for the modern world. Our society is shaken to its foundations. The conventional call on the part of religions to believe in God, work for his glory and purpose has become open to question. Philosophy is not a mere intellectual pursuit labelling and classifying the contents of thought but the creation of a new awareness of oneself and the world. *Samanvaya* or reconciliation is the need of our age. The global, all-comprehensive changes which are taking place represent something new in the structure of human society, though they are not deviations from the normal course of history. The world community which we envisage can be sustained only by a community of ideals. We have to look beyond the political and economic arrangements to ultimate spiritual issues. We have to fashion a new type of man who uses the instruments he has devised with a renewed awareness that he is capable of greater things than mastery of nature.[8]

Notes

1. For an autobiographical note see P. Nagaraja Rao, K. Gopalaswami and S. Ramakrishnan, eds., *Radhakrishnan Reader: An Anthology* (Bombay: Bharatiya Vidya Bhavan, 1969), pp. 3–15.

2. Arvind Sharma, *The Concept of Universal Religion in Modern Hindu Thought* (London: Macmillan, 1998).
3. See K. Iswara Dutt, ed., *Sarvepalli Radhakrishnan: A Study of the President of India* (New Delhi: Popular Book Services, 1966), Appendix.
4. Nagaraja Rao et al, p. 21.
5. S. Radhakrishnan, *The Hindu View of Life* (London: Macmillan, 1927), pp. 40–1.
6. Ibid., pp. 14–15; 27–8.
7. Ibid., pp. 67–70.
8. S. Radhakrishnan, *The Brahma Sūtra: The Philosophy of Spiritual Life* (London: George Allen & Unwin Ltd., 1960), pp. 250–79.

Jiddu Krishnamurti
(1895–1986)

Life

One cannot talk about the life of J. Krishnamurti without first talking about the Theosophical Society. The Theosophical Society was founded in 1875 in New York, by Colonel Olcott and Madam Blavatsky, to promote the brotherhood of humanity and the equality of religions in general, and the dissemination of Eastern religions and esoteric occult and spiritual knowledge in particular. Its involvement with the latter led it to develop a messianic expectation, especially under the influence of the Buddhist concept of Maitreya or the Buddha to-be, to whom numerous rocks have been found dedicated in Central Asia with the evocative lapidary invocation: 'Come, Maitreya, come.'

The then leader of the Theosophical Society, Mrs Annie Besant, identified this messiah with a young man called Krishnamurti, the son of an Indian follower of the Theosophical Society, who was then groomed for his messianic role. In 1929, however, Krishnamurti, instead of stepping into the messianic shoes turned away from this role as a result of a decisive spiritual experience, when he 'renounced his role of coming messiah to travel the world as a teacher with his own religious philosophy, unattached to any orthodox religion or sect. The single object of his teaching was to set men free from all the cages which divide man from man, such as race, religion, nationality, class and tradition, and thereby bring about a transformation in the human psyche'.[1]

Krishnamurti soon attracted a globally dispersed following, despite the fact that 'all he claimed for his teaching was that it held up a mirror in which people could see themselves exactly as they were inwardly and outwardly, and if they did not like what they saw *change themselves*.[2] This was for grown-ups. Since children are typically free up to a point in their life from such distortions, he took a special interest in their education, which led him to found several schools of a special kind. He interacted with adults through a series of audiences, and its spin-offs in the form of audio-cassettes and other things. These audiences varied in size from 1000 to 5000 in number. He also met people in smaller groups or interacted with them individually.

Although he disclaimed the role of a guru, his personal magnetism cannot be denied. Here, for instance, are snippets of encounters with him by a follower.

It was the fall of 1965 in New Delhi. My wife had asked me to deliver something to Mrs Kitty Shiva Rao who had been very kind to her when she, four years earlier, had come to India as a volunteer from Canada. I went on my bicycle and came to a sudden stop in front of a very tall man sitting completely alone on a wicker chair on the porch of the Shiva Rao house. I wondered if Mrs Shiva Rao was in, and the man, who was extremely self-contained, said he would go in and look. Without any hurry, but without delay, he got up and went in, and returned to say that she was not in at that time, but I could wait until she came back. I do not recall why I could not wait; perhaps I had the usual haste of the young, especially of those recently returned from a long stay in the West. I handed over to him what I had to deliver to the lady of the house, and rode away on my bicycle. But I kept looking back at this unusual man with an extraordinary presence sitting on the porch, until I fell off my bicycle, having crashed into a woman carrying a large bundle on her head.

Several months later, at Rajghat in Varanasi, where an interview with Krishnamurti had been arranged for me, I was in a great turmoil; I became more and more agitated as four o'clock, the appointed time of the meeting, approached. I was not sure what I needed to ask him. I knew I needed a different kind of knowledge and education than I had obtained in the many schools and universities I had attended. I had become sadder and sadder the closer I had gotten to finishing my Ph.D.: the more I was certified as an educated man by the world, the clearer I was about my ignorance of myself. What little I had gathered about Krishnamurti, mostly from my wife who had taught for a year in one of his schools in India before we had met, and the little that I had read by him, had convinced me that he offered the sort of influence I needed. Here, at last, I was going to meet the great man himself. What was I going to say to him? What did I need to know? What should I ask him? Besides, how could he, or anybody else, say something that would really become a part of myself? After all, I had read what the Buddha had said, and I still behaved the way I did before. And what was I going to tell him about myself? What did I know of any value? What did I have of any value? What was my value? Why waste his time?

All these questions whirled around in my head, making me more and more restless as the time for my meeting with Krishnamurti approached. Then, suddenly, a great calm possessed me. I knew with certainty that I did not know, that nobody else could really tell me something deeply true unless I saw it myself directly, and that there was no escape from an encounter with myself, an encounter without fear and without self-importance. I had no idea what had brought about these realizations and the resulting calm; maybe it was the magic of this extraordinary man working even before I had met him. I walked over to his room with assurance, and precisely at the appointed hour he opened his door. I was surprised to discover that the man in front of me was the same man I had met on the porch in New Delhi. I had difficulty accepting his actual physical size; my first impression of him had no doubt been of his real spiritual height.

He asked me to sit down on the same divan on which he was sitting. Then, after a brief silence, he asked, 'What can I do for you?' 'Nothing,' I said with clarity. 'I have really nothing to ask you. I have come just to look at you.' He smiled; and we sat in silence for a long time, just looking at each other. Then, no doubt having noticed my attention wandering, he asked what I did and what interested me. I told him, and I also told him about my dissatisfaction with what I had learned. My clarity was dwindling and I was returning to my habitual and more discursive mode of thought. I asked him, 'Is there life after death?' He said: 'Why worry about death when you don't know anything about life?'

When it was time for me to leave, he took me to the window of his room perched over the river Ganga, overlooking the path which the Buddha had taken on his way to Sarnath after his enlightenment. That was the only time I understood why pilgrims over the centuries have regarded this river as sacred. There were dark, thick clouds over the majestic river, and a white bird was flying in and out of the clouds, sometimes disappearing completely and at other times showing clearly its innocent vulnerability. He put his hand on my shoulder and we stood there watching for a little while; then he said, pointing to the bird in the clouds over the river, 'Life is like that: sometimes you see it, sometimes you don't.' As I was leaving, he said simply, 'We shall meet again.'[3]

Krishnamurti represents a strand of modern Hindu thought which paradoxically manages to to be universal and esoteric at the same time. It is universal in the sense that it demonstrates how modern Hindu universalism results in a type of religious thinker who is Hindu to the point of being virtually non-Hindu, inasmuch as being a Hindu means identifying oneself with a specific religious tradition. It is esoteric in the sense that its teachings are 'not intended to bring comfort but to shake people into an awareness of the dangerous state of the world for which every individual was responsible since, every individual was the world in microcosm'.[4] Krishnamurti in the West and Ramaṇa Maharṣi in India typify this form of modern Hindu thought.

On Truth

The form of 'Hindu' thought represented by Krishnamurti has a brass tacks metaphysical quality, and an existential quality which is not existentialist in the Continental sense. The following talk of Krishnamurti lays it bare.

For most of us, our whole life is based on effort, some kind of volition. And we cannot conceive of an action that is not based on it. Our social, economic, and so-called spiritual life, is a series of efforts, always culminating in a certain result. We think effort is essential. So we are now going to find out if it is possible to live differently, without this constant battle.

Why do we make effort? Put simply, it is in order to achieve a result, to become something, to reach a goal, isn't it? If we do not make an effort, we think we shall stagnate. We have an idea about the goal towards which we are constantly striving; and this striving has become part of our life. If we want to alter, to bring about a radical change in ourselves, we make a tremendous effort to eliminate old habits, to resist the habitual environmental influences, and so on. So we are used to this series of efforts in order to find or achieve something, in order to live at all.

Now, is not all such effort the activity of the self? Is not effort self-centred activity? And, if we make an effort from the centre of the self, it must inevitably produce more conflict, more confusion, more misery. Yet we keep on making effort after effort; and very few of us realize that the self-centred activity of effort does not clear up any of our problems. On the contrary, it increases our confusion and our misery and our sorrow. Or we know this, and yet continue hoping somehow to break through this self-centred activity of effort, the action of the will.

This is our problem—Is it possible to understand anything without effort? Is it possible to see what is real, what is true, without introducing the action of will, which is essentially based on the self, the 'me?' and if we do not make an effort, is there not a danger of deterioration, of going to sleep, of stagnation? Perhaps, as I am talking, we can experiment with this individually, and see how far we can go through this question. For I feel that what brings happiness, quietness, tranquillity of the mind, does not come through any effort. A truth is not perceived through any volition, through any action of will. And if we can go into it very carefully and diligently, perhaps we shall find the answer.

How do we react when a truth is presented? Take, for example, the problem of fear. We realize that our activity and our being and our whole existence would be fundamentally altered if there were no fear of any kind in us. We may see that, we may see the truth of it; and thereby there is freedom from fear. But for most of us, when a fact, a truth, is put before us, what is our immediate response? Please, experiment with what I am saying; please do not merely listen. Watch your own reactions; and find out what happens when a truth, a fact, is put before you—such as 'any dependency in relationship destroys relationship'. Now, when a statement of that kind is made, what is your response? Do you see, are you aware of the truth of it, and does dependency thereby cease? Or have you an idea about the fact? Here is a statement of truth. Do we experience the truth of it, or do we create an idea about it?

If we can understand this process of the creation of idea, then we shall perhaps understand the whole process of effort. Because once we have created the idea, then effort comes into being. Then the problem arises, what to do, how to act? That is, we see that psychological dependency on another is a form of self-fulfilment; it is not love; in it there is conflict, fear, the desire to fulfil oneself through another, jealousy, and so on, which corrode. We see that psychological dependency on another embraces all these facts. Then, we proceed to create the idea, do we not? We do not directly experience the fact, the truth of it; but, we look at it, and then create an idea of how to be free from dependency. We see the implications of psychological dependence, and then we create the idea of how to be free from it. We do not directly experience the truth, which is the liberating factor. But out of the experience of looking at that fact we create an idea. We are incapable of looking at it directly, without ideation. Then, having created the idea, we proceed to put that idea into action. Then we try to bridge the gap between idea and action—in which effort is involved.

So can we not look at the truth without creating ideas? It is almost instinctive with most of us: when something true is put before us, we immediately create an idea about it. And I think if we can understand why we do this so instinctively, almost unconsciously, then perhaps we shall understand if it is possible to be free from effort.

Why then do we create ideas about truth? Surely that is important to find out, is it not? Either we see the truth nakedly, as it is, or we do not. But why do we have a picture about it, a symbol, a word, and image, which necessitates a postponement, the hope of an eventual result? So can we hesitantly and guardedly go into this process of why the mind creates the image, the idea—that I must be this or that, that I must be free from dependence, and so on? We know very well that when we see something very clearly, experience it directly, there is a freedom from it. It is that immediacy that is vital, not the picture or the symbol of the truth—on which all systems and philosophies and deteriorating organizations are built. So is it not important to find out why the mind, instead of seeing the thing directly and simply, and experiencing the truth of it immediately, creates an idea about it?

I do not know if you have thought about this. It may perhaps be something new. And to find the truth of it, please do not merely resist. Do not say, 'What would happen if the mind did not create the idea? It is its function to create ideas, to verbalize, to recall memories, to recognize, to calculate.' We know that. But the mind is not free; and it is only when the mind is capable of looking at the truth totally, completely, without any barrier, that there is freedom..

So our problem is—why does the mind, instead of seeing the thing immediately and experiencing it directly, indulge in all these ideas? Is this not one of the habits of the mind? Something is presented to us, and immediately there is the old habit of creating an idea, a theory about it. And the mind likes to live in habit. Because without habit the mind is lost. If there is not a routine, a habitual response to which it has become accustomed, it feels confused, uncertain.

That is one aspect. Also, does not the mind seek a result? Because in the result is permanency. And the mind hates to be uncertain. It is always seeking security in different forms—through beliefs, through knowledge, through experience. And when that is questioned there is a disturbance, anxiety. And so the mind, avoiding uncertainty, seeks security for itself by making efforts to achieve a result.

I hope you are actually observing your own minds in operation. If you are not, then you will not experience, your mind will remain on the verbal level. But—if I may suggest—if you can observe your own mind in operation, and watch how it thinks, how it reacts, when a truth is put before it, then you will experience step-by-step what I am talking about. Then there will be an extraordinary experience. And it is this direct approach, this direct experience of what truth is, that is so essential for bringing about a creative life.

So why does the mind create these ideas, instead of directly experiencing? Why does the mind intervene? As we have said, it is habit. Also, the mind wants to achieve a result. We all want to achieve a result. In listening to me, are you looking for a result? You are, aren't you? The mind is seeking a result; it sees that dependency is destructive, and therefore it wants to be free of it. But the very desire to be free creates the idea. The mind is not free; but the desire to be free creates the idea of freedom as the goal towards which it must work. And thereby effort comes into being. And that effort is self-centred; it does not bring freedom. Instead of depending on a person, you depend on an idea or on an image. So your effort is only self-enclosing; it is not liberating.

Now, can the mind, realizing that it is caught in habit, be free from habit—not have an idea that it should achieve freedom as an eventual goal, but see the truth that the mind is caught in habit, directly experience it? And similarly, can the mind see that it is pursuing incessantly a permanency for itself, a goal that it must achieve, a God, a truth, a virtue, a state of being, or whatever, and is thereby bringing about this action of will, with all its complications? And when we see that, is it not possible to experience the truth of something *directly* without all the paraphernalia of verbalization? You may objectively see a fact, in that there is no ideation, no creation of idea, symbol, desire. But subjectively, inwardly, it is entirely different. Because there we want a result; there is the craving to be something, to achieve, to become—in which all effort is born.

I feel that to see what is true from moment to moment, without any effort, but directly to experience it, is the only creative existence. Because it is only in moments of complete tranquillity that you discover something—not when you are making an effort, whether it is under the microscope or inwardly. It is only when the mind is not agitated, not caught in habit, not trying to achieve a result, not trying to become something—it is only when it is not doing these things, when it is really tranquil, when there is no effort, no movement—that there is a possibility of discovering something new.

Surely, that is freedom from the self, that is the abnegation of the 'me'—and not the outward symbols, whether you possess this or that virtue or not. But freedom comes into being only when you understand your own processes, conscious as well as unconscious. It is possible only when we go fully into the different processes of the mind. And as most of us live in a state of tension, in constant effort, it is essential to understand the complexity of effort, to see the truth that effort does not bring virtue, that effort is not love, that effort does not bring about the freedom that truth alone can give—which is a direct experiencing. For that, one has to understand the mind, one's own mind—not somebody else's mind, not what somebody else says about it. You may read all the volumes ever written but they will be utterly useless. For you must observe your own mind, and penetrate it more and more deeply, and experience the thing directly as you go along. Because *there* is the living quality, not in the things of the mind. And the mind, to find its own processes, must not be enclosed by its own habits, but must be free occasionally to look, therefore, it is important to understand this whole process of effort. For effort does not bring about freedom. Effort is only more and more self-enclosing, more and more destrucitve, outwardly as well as inwardly, in relationship with one or with many.[5]

On Truth and Actuality

This selection, which consists of a conversation between Krishnamurti and the scientist David Bohm,[6] is useful for three reasons. It is dialogical or even dialectical, and this is the favoured method of philosophical exposition and teaching in this form of Hinduism. It also recalls an earlier conversation between Rabindranath Tagore and Albert Einstein and bears comparison with it. Finally, its content is typical of this form of modern Hindu thought.

KRISHNAMURTI: I was thinking about the question of what truth is and what reality is and whether there is any relationship between the two, or whether they are separate. Are they eternally divorced, or are they just projections of thought? And if thought didn't operate, would there be reality? I thought that reality comes from *res*, thing, and that anything that thought operates on, or fabricates, or reflects on, is reality. And thought, thinking in a distorted, conditioned manner, is illusion, is self-deception, is distortion. I left it there, because I wanted to let it come rather than my pursuing it.

DAVID BOHM: The question of thought and reality and truth has occupied philosophers over the ages. It's a very difficult one. It seems to me that what you say is basically true, but there are a lot of points that need to be ironed out. One of the questions that arises is this: If reality is thought, does what thought thinks about, what appears in consciousness, go beyond consciousness?

K: Are the contents of consciousness reality?

DB: That's the question; and can we use thought as equivalent to consciousness in its basic form?

K: Yes.

DB: I wonder whether, just for the sake of completeness, we should also include in thought feeling, desire, will, and reaction. I feel we should, if we are exploring the connection between consciousness, reality and truth.

K: Yes.

DB: One of the points I'd like to bring up is: There is thought, there is our consciousness, and there is the thing of which we are conscious. And as you have often said, the thought is not the thing.

K: Yes.

DB: We have to get it clear, because in some sense the thing may have some kind of reality independent of thought; we can't go so far as to deny all that. Or do we go as far as some philosophers, like Bishop Berkeley, who has said that all is thought? Now I would like to suggest a possibly useful distinction between that reality which is largely created by our own thought, or by the thought of mankind, and that reality which one can regard as existing independently of this thought. For example, would you say nature is real?

K: It is, yes.

DB: And it is not just our own thoughts.

K: No, obviously not.

DB: The tree, the whole earth, the stars.

K: Of course, the cosmos.

DB: Yes. I was thinking the other day, illusion is real, in the sense that it is really something going on, to a person who is in a state of illusion.

K: To him it is real.

DB: But to us it is also real because his brain is in a certain state of electrical and chemical movement, and he acts from his illusion in a real way.

K: In a real way, in a distorted way.

DB: Distorted but real. Now it occurred to me that one could say that even the false is real but not true. This might be important.

K: I understand. For instance: Is Christ real?

DB: He is certainly real in the minds of people who believe in him, in the sense we have been discussing.

K: We want to find out the distinction between truth and reality. We said anything that thought thinks about, whether unreasonably or reasonably, is a reality. It may be distorted or reasoned clearly, it is still a reality. That reality, I say, has nothing to do with truth.

DB: Yes, but we have to say besides, that in some way reality involves more than mere thought. There is also the question of actuality. Is the thing actual? Is its existence an actual fact? According to the dictionary, the fact means what is actually done, what actually happens, what is actually perceived.

K: Yes, we must understand what we mean by the fact.

DB: The fact is the action that is actually taking place. Suppose, for example, that you are walking on a dark road and that you think you see something. It may be real, it may not be real. One moment you feel that it's real and the next moment that it's not real. But then you suddenly touch it and it resists your movement. From this action it's immediately clear that there is a real thing that you have contacted. But if there is no such contact you say that it's not real, that it was perhaps an illusion, or at least something mistakenly taken as real.

K: But, of course, that thing is still a reality that thought thinks about. And reality has nothing to do with truth.

DB: But now, let us go further with the discussion of 'the thing'. You see, the root of the English word *thing* is fundamentally the same as the German *bedingen*, to condition, to set the conditions or determine. And indeed we must agree that a thing is necessarily conditioned.

K: It is conditioned. Let's accept that.

DB: This is a key point. Any form of reality is conditioned. Thus, an illusion is still a form of reality that is conditioned. For example, the man's blood may have a different constitution because he's not in a balanced state. He is distorting, he may be too excited, and that could be why he is caught in illusion. So every thing is determined by conditions and it also conditions every other thing.

K: Yes, quite.

DB: All things are interrelated in the way of mutual conditioning, which we call influence. In physics that's very clear—the planets all influence one another, the atoms influence one another, and I wanted to suggest that maybe we could regard thought and consciousness as part of this whole chain of influence.

K: Quite right.

DB: So that everything can influence consciousness, and it in turn can work back and influence the shapes of things, as we make objects.

And you could then say that this is all reality, that thought is therefore also real.

K: Thought is real.

DB: And there is one part of reality influencing another part of reality.

K: Also, one part of illusion influences another part of illusion.

DB: Yes, but now we have to be careful because we can say there is that reality which is not made by man, by mankind. But that's still limited. The cosmos, for example, as seen by us is influenced by our own experience and therefore limited.

K: Quite.

DB: Any thing that we see, we see through our own experience, our own background. So that reality cannot possibly be totally independent of man.

K: No.

DB: It may be relatively independent. The tree is a reality that is relatively independent but it's our consciousness that abstracts the tree.

K: Are you saying that man's reality is the product of influence and conditioning?

DB: Yes, mutual interaction and reaction.

K: And all his illusions are also his product.

DB: Yes, they are all mixed together.

K: And what is the relationship of a sane, rational, healthy, whole man, to reality and to truth?

DB: Yes, we must consider that, but first may we look at this question of truth. I think the derivation of words is often very useful. The word *true* in Latin, which is *verus*, means 'that which is', the same as the English *was* and *were*, or German *wahr*. Now in English the root meaning the word *true* is honest and faithful; you see, we can often say that a line is true, or that a machine is true. There is a story I once read about a thread that ran so true, it was using the image of a spinning wheel with the thread running straight.

K: Quite.

DB: And now we can say that our thought, or our consciousness, is true to 'that which is', if it is running straight, if the man is sane and healthy. And otherwise it is not, it is false. So the falseness of consciousness is not just wrong information, but is actually running crookedly as a reality.

K: So you're saying, as long as man is sane, healthy, whole, and rational, his thread is always straight.

DB: Yes, his consciousness is on a straight thread. Therefore, his reality . . .

K: . . . is different from the reality of a man whose thread is crooked, who is irrational, who is neurotic.

DB: Very different. Perhaps the latter is even insane. You can see with insane people how different it is—they sometimes cannot even see the same reality at all.

K: And the sane, healthy, whole, holy man, what is his relationship to truth?

DB: If you accept the meaning of the word, if you say truth is that which is, as well as being true to that which is, then you have to say that he is all this.

K: So you would say the man who is sane, whole, is truth?

DB: He is truth, yes.

K: Such a man is truth. He may think certain things that would be reality, but he is truth. He can't think irrationally.

DB: Well, I wouldn't say quite that, I'd say that he can make a mistake.

K: Of course.

DB: But he doesn't persist in it. In other words, there is the man who has made a mistake and acknowledges it, changes it.

K: Yes, quite right.

DB: And there is also the man who has made a mistake but his mind is not straight and therefore he goes on with it. But we have to come back to the question: Does truth go beyond any particular man? Does it include other men, and nature as well?

K: It includes all that is.

DB: Yes, so the truth is one. But there are many different things in the field of reality. Each thing is conditioned, the whole field of reality is conditioned. But clearly, truth itself cannot be conditioned or dependent on things.

K: What then is the relationship to reality of the man who is truth?

DB: He sees all the things and, in doing this, he comprehends reality. What the word *comprehends* means is to hold it all together.

K: He doesn't separate reality. He says, 'I comprehend it, I hold it, I see it'.

DB: Yes, it's all one field of reality, himself and everything. But it has things in it that are conditioned and he comprehends the conditions.

K: And because he comprehends conditioning, he is free of conditioning.

DB: It seems clear then that all our knowledge, being based on thought, is actually a part of this one conditioned field of reality.

K: Now another question. Suppose I am a scholar; I'm full of such conditioned and conditioning knowledge. How am I to comprehend truth in the sense of holding it all together?

DB: I don't think you can comprehend truth.

K: Say I have studied all my life, I've devoted all my life to knowledge, which is reality.

DB: Yes, and it is also about a bigger reality.

K: And suppose you come along and say, 'Truth is somewhere else, it's not that'. I accept you, because you show it to me, and so I say, 'Please help me to move from here to that'. Because once I get *that*, I comprehend it. If I live *here*, then my comprehension is always fragmented. Therefore my knowledge tells me, 'This is reality but it is not truth'. And suppose you come along and say, 'No, it is not'. And I ask: Please tell me how to move from here to that.

DB: Well, we've just said we can't move . . .

K: I'm putting it briefly. What am I to do?

DB: I think I have to see that this whole structure of knowledge is inevitably false, because my reality is twisted.

K: Would you say the content of my consciousness is knowledge?

DB: Yes.

K: How am I to empty that consciousness and yet retain knowledge that is not twisted—otherwise I can't function—and reach a state, or whatever it is, that will comprehend reality. I don't know if I'm making myself clear.

DB: Yes.

K: What I'm saying is: My human consciousness is its content, which is knowledge; it's a messy conglomeration of irrational knowledge and some that is correct. Can that consciousness comprehend, or bring into itself, truth?

DB: No, it can't.

K: Therefore, can this consciousness go to that truth? It can't either. Then what?

DB: There can be a perception of the falseness in this consciousness. This consciousness is false, in the sense that it does not run true. Because of the confused content it does not run true.

K: It's contradictory.

DB: It muddles things up.

K: Not, 'muddles things up'; it is a muddle.

DB: It is a muddle, yes, in the way it moves. Now then, one of the main points of the muddle is that when consciousness reflects of itself, the reflection has this character: It's as if there were a mirror and consciousness were looking at itself through the mirror and the mirror is reflecting consciousness as if it were not consciousness but an independent reality.

K: Yes.

DB: Now therefore, the action that consciousness takes is wrong, because it tries to improve the apparently independent reality, whereas in fact to do this is just a muddle. I would like to put it this way: The whole of consciousness is somehow an instrument that is connected to a deeper energy. And as long as consciousness is connected in that way, it maintains its state of wrong action.

K: Yes.

DB: So on seeing that this consciousness is reflecting itself wrongly as independent of thought, what is needed is somehow to disconnect the energy of consciousness. The whole of consciousness has to be disconnected, so it would, as it were, lie there without energy.

K: You're saying don't feed it. My consciousness is a muddle, it is confused, contradictory, and all the rest of it. And its very contradiction, its very muddle, gives it its own energy.

DB: Well, I would say that the energy is not actually coming from consciousness, but that as long as the energy is coming, consciousness keeps the muddle going.

K: From where does it come?

DB: We'd have to say that perhaps it comes from something deeper.

K: If it comes from something deeper, then we enter into the whole field of gods and outside agency and so on.

DB: No, I wouldn't say the energy comes from an outside agency. I would prefer to say it comes from me, in some sense.

K: Then the 'me' is this consciousness?

DB: Yes.

K: So the content is creating its own energy. Would you say that?

DB: In some sense it is, but the puzzle is that it seems impossible for this content to create its own energy. That would be saying that the content is able to create its own energy.

K: Actually, the content is creating its own energy. Look, I'm in contradiction and that very contradiction gives me vitality. I have opposing desires. When I have opposing desires I have energy, I fight. Therefore, that desire is creating the energy—not God, or something profounder—it is still desire. This is the trick that so many played. They say there is an outside agency, a deeper energy—but then one's back in the old field. But I realize that the energy of contradiction, the energy of desire, of will, of pursuit of pleasure is the content of my consciousness; that is, consciousness is creating its own energy. Reality is this; reality is creating its own energy. I may say, 'I derive my energy deep down', but it's still reality.

DB: Yes, suppose we accept that, but the point is that seeing the truth of this . . .

K: . . . that's what I want to get at. Is this energy different from the energy of truth?

DB: Yes.

K: It is different.

DB: But let's try to put it like this: Reality may have many levels of energy.

K: Yes.

DB: But a certain part of the energy has gone off the straight line. Let's say the brain feeds energy to all the thought processes. Now, if somehow the brain didn't feed energy to the thought process that is confused, then the thing might straighten out.

K: That's it. If this energy runs along the straight thread it is a reality without contradiction. It's an energy that is endless because it has no friction. Now is that energy different from the energy of truth?

DB: Yes. They are different, and as we once discussed, there must be a deeper common source.

K: I'm not sure. You are suggesting that they both spring out of the same root.

DB: That's what I suggest. But for the moment there is the energy of truth that can comprehend the reality and . . .

K: . . . the other way it cannot.

DB: No, it cannot; but there appears to be some connection in the sense that when truth comprehends reality, reality goes straight. So there appears to be a connection at least one way.

K: That's right, a one-way connection—truth loves this, this doesn't love truth.

DB: But once the connection has been made, then reality runs true and does not waste energy or make confusion.

K: You see, that's where meditation comes in. Generally, meditation is from here to there, with practice and all the rest of it. To move from this to that.

DB: Move from one reality to another.

K: That's right. Meditation is actually seeing what is. But generally meditation is taken as moving from one reality to another.[7]

Notes

1. Mary Lutyens, The Life and Death of Krishnamurti (London: John Murray, 1990), p. xiv.
2. Ibid., p. xv.
3. Ravi Ravindra, Yoga and the Teaching of Krishna: Essays on the Indian Spiritual Traditions (Wheaton, Il.: The Theosophical Publishing House, 1998), p. 327–9.
4. Mary Lutyens, p. xvi.
5. J. Krishnamurti, On Truth (HarperSanFrancisco, 1995), pp. 24–9.
6. Mary Lutyens, p. xv. Krishnamurti was famously on friendly terms with famous men.
7. Krishnamurti, pp. 51–63.

Glossary

Abhaya	:	Fearlessness, especially as the psychological correlate of metaphysical nondualism, as fear only arises from an 'other'.
Ācāryas	:	Doctors of divinity.
Advaita	:	A school of Hindu philosophy known for its strict adherence to the proposition that the ultimate reality is singular (*advaita*).
Adyasakti (Ādyāśakti)	:	The primordial power which accounts for the universe, perceived as a feminine first principle.
Agnihotra	:	The fire altar, maintained by the family practising Vedic rituals.
Ahiṁsā	:	The word literally means non-violence but includes active compassion. In its contemporary resonance it also means struggling for one's rights non-violently even when a violent option may be available—a cardinal teaching of Mahatma Gandhi.
Ānanda	:	Bliss. Everlasting in nature, as distinguished from pleasure which alternates with pain. Its experience is associated with the realization of Brahman.
Anekārthatām	:	The hermeneutical principles that a scriptural passage is capable of simultaneously possessing and conveying several levels of meaning.
Apta (Āpta)	:	A person who can serve as a trustworthy intellectual or moral resource.
Arjuna	:	One of the five Pāṇḍava brothers who was known for his martial skill, and who is Kṛṣṇa's interlocutor in the Bhagavadgītā.

Arshagranthas (Ārṣagranthas)	:	Texts associated with the ṛṣis or sages to whom Vedic revelation was vouchsafed, as distinguished from the texts composed by those who came after them.
Artha	:	The acquisition of wealth as one of the four legitimate goals of human endeavor (puruṣārtha), along with the pursuit of pleasure (kāma), virtue (dharma) and salvation (mokṣa).
Arya	:.	The Sanskrit form of the word, Aryan. The word Aryan has acquired racial connotations in English which ring false in the Indic context, wherein the word ārya denotes nobility of character.
Aryavarta (Āryāvarta)	:	The land of the Aryans, classically described as the land lying between the Himalayas and the Vindhya mountains and extending from sea to sea (see Manusmṛti II. 22).
Astiks (Āstikas)	:	Literally, one who says yes. In the broad Hindu context it may mean one who believes in (1) after life; (2) God; (3) Vedic authority; (4) in all three. In a philosophical context it usually carries the third connotation.
Asura	:	Anti-gods or demons; an antonym for sura.
Ati-Shudras (Ati- Śūdras)	:	Former untouchables, now called 'dalits'. The word was coined in an attempt to find a place for them within the fourfold Hindu classification of varṇas, which are enumerated in following order: brāhmaṇa, kṣatriya, vaiśya, and śūdra. The untouchables would then comprise a group 'beyond the pale' of śūdras, and may therefore be called atiśūdras. Such usage, however, is a solecism according to the Manusmṛti (X. 4).
Ātman	:	The spiritually irreducible component of the human personality.
Avatars (Avatāras)	:	The form in which divinity manifests itself in the universe, periodically intervening to ensure its continued functioning in accordance with dharma.
Avyabhichāriṇī Bhakti	:	Unwavering devotion, which never strays from the object of devotion.
Bali	:	Offerings.
Bande Mataram (Vande Mātaram)	:	The title of a famous song found in the novel Ānanda Maṭha, which celebrates the holy land of India as Divine Mother.
Bhagavan (Bhagavān)	:	'The worshipful one.' An honorific, and in many Indian languages the word used to denote God.

Bhagavata (Bhāgavata)	:	Pertaining to God, especially to Viṣṇu or Kṛṣṇa. Worshippers of these Gods. Also the name of a famous Purāṇa which deals primarily with the early life of Kṛṣṇa.
Bhaktas	:	Individuals distinguished by their devotion to God.
Bhakti	:	An attitude of loving devotion towards God.
Bhartrihari (Bhartṛhari)	:	Sanskrit poet, famous for three compositions of over a hundred verses called *śatakas* devoted to morality, romance and renunciation.
Bhavamukha	:	The threshold of phenomenal existence.
Bhīma	:	One of the five Pāṇḍava brothers, known for his physical powers.
Brahma	:	See Brahman.
Brahmachari (Brahmacārī)	:	One who practices Brahmacarya.
Brahmacharya (Brahmacārya)	:	The word literally means a lifestyle devoted to the realization of Brahman, or the ultimate reality. As celibacy is often considered an important component of such a lifestyle the word primarily bears the meaning of celibacy. Since, in the Hindu scheme of things, the first quarter of one's life is meant to be spent as a celibate student, it is also used to denote that stage.
Brahmaji (Brahmājī)	:	God Brahmā. *Ji* is a common honorific suffix in several Indian languages.
Brahman	:	The word used to designate the ultimate reality in Hindu thought.
Brāhmaṇas	:	The first of the four classes of Hindu society which is traditionally said to consist of (1) Brāhmaṇas, the priestly class; (2) Kṣatriyas, the martial class; (3) Vaiśyas, the mercantile class; and (4) Śūdras, the labour class.
Brāhmaṇas	:	A section of Vedic literature, so called because it consists of the authoritative utterances of priests or *Brāhmaṇas*.
Brahma-Sūtra	:	An aphoristic formulation for the teachings of the Upaniṣads. The Brahma-Sūtrā, the Upaniṣads, and the Bhagavadgītā, constitute the triple canon of Vedānta.
Caitanya	:	Famous sixteenth century Vaiṣṇava saint of Bengal, known for his devotion to Kṛṣṇa. The Hare Krishna movement traces its origins back to him.
Chinmaya	:	Pervaded by consciousness.

Daksiṇā	:	The fees offered to the priest or a teacher out of regard for services rendered.
Daridra-Narayan-Seva (Daridra-Nārāyaṇa-Sevā)	:	Service towards the poor and the dispossessed as a form of worship.
Darshan (Darśana)	:	Literally, to 'see' a holy person, where 'seeing' is symbolic of perceptual interaction spiritually elevating in nature.
Dassue (Dasyu)	:	The historical or mythical antagonists of the Aryans in the Ṛg Veda. The word also denotes criminal elements in society in general.
Daya (Dayā)	:	The quality of compassion, especially as representing the essence of morality.
Dayabhaga (Dāyabhāga)	:	A system of Hindu law, especially governing inheritance, based on a treatise which bears the same name. This treatise, composed by Jīmūtavāhana (12th century) forms part of a larger corpus called Dharmaratna.
Dayatattwa (Dayātattva)	:	A section of the encyclopedic work of Raghunandana (c. 1518–1580) entitled Smṛtitattva, which deals with inheritance.
Devpuja (Devapūjā)	:	A religious ceremony performed formally in accordance with liturgical rules. It especially includes idol-worship.
Dharma	:	A multivalent word, considered untranslatable in English, which stands for cosmic order, normative order, law, morality and allied significations.
Dhishta (Dhiṣṭha)	:	A person of profound understanding.
Dhrubo (Dhruva)	:	A celebrated devotee of God, identified with the Pole Star, which also bears his name, and which symbolizes exemplary steadfastness of devotion.
Dvaita	:	A schol of Vedānta, known for its thoroughgoing dualism (i.e. plurlaism).
Gatha (Gāthā)	:	Song of praise, especially honouring a royal figure when it appears in the expression gāthānārāsaṁsī.
Gayatri (Gāyathrī)	:	A famous prayer in the Vedas (Ṛg Veda III. 62. 10) named after the metre in which it is composed, whose special recitation constitutes formal initiation into Vedic studies.
Gita (Gītā, Bhagavad Gītā)	:	A text of seven hundred verses in the form of a dialogue between Kṛṣṇa and Arjuna, widely revered within the Hindu tradition as the word of God. It constitutes part of the Mahābhārata.

Gita Rahasya	:	A celebrated commentary on the Gītā, originally written in Marathi by B.G. Tilak (1856–1920).
Grihsatha (Gṛhastha)	:	The second, and according to many texts sociologically the most important stage of life in the Hindu scheme of things, wherein one leads the life of a house-holder.
Gyana (Jñāna)	:	This Sanskrit word is basically analogous to the English word 'knowledge' but with a semantic tilt in favor of experiential or intuitive knowledge as distinguished from discursive knowledge.
Harivamsa (Harivaṃśa)	:	A substantial appendix to the epic Mahābhārata, which contains the genealogy of Kṛṣṇa.
Ishvara (Īśvara)	:	God, especially as the Lord of all creation.
Ishopanished (Iśopaniṣad)	:	A short but significant verse Upaniṣad, usually mentioned first in the traditional enumeration of the major Upaniṣads.
Itihas (Itihāsa)	:	Literally, 'thus it was'. The Sanskrit word used to translate the English word 'history'.
Janma	:	Birth, especially as a nexus in the chain of ongoing existence in *saṃsāra*.
Jeevan Mukta (Jīvanmukta)	:	A person who has experienced liberation while alive, as distinguished from a post-mortem experience.
Jimutavahana (Jīmūtavāhana)	:	A famous jurist of the twelfth century, whose work in inheritance, entitled the Dāyabhāga, was influential in the evolution of Hindu civil law.
Jnani (Jñānī)	:	One possessing, or seeking to attain, direct experiential knowledge of the ultimate reality.
Kali (Kālī)	:	Ultimate reality when conceived as a female principle, in the form of a Goddess, especially in her apparently destructive and eventually regenerative aspect.
Kalpa	:	An enormous duration of time, equivalent to a 'day of brahmā' or 4,320 million years.
Kāma	:	The pursuit of the pleasures of the senses, including sex, as one of the legitimate goals of human endeavor.
Kauravas	:	The rivals of the Pāṇḍavas in the fratricidal struggle for the throne—a struggle which constitutes the episodic core of the Mahābhārata.
Kayastha (Kāyastha)	:	A prominent class in Bengal, which enjoy a ritually low but educationally high status.
Kshatriya (Kṣatriya)	:	One of the four classes (*varṇas*), which, along with the Brāhmaṇas, the Vaiśyas and the Śūdras, constitute Hindu society.

Kulina Brahmans (Kulīna Brāhmaṇas)	:	A class of Brāhmaṇas in Bengal known for their strict observance of the rules of endogamy and exogamy, which resulted in a scarce pool of eligible males, culminating in the institution of polygamous alliances whose reform in due course became an important social issue, especially Bengal.
Lila (Līlā)	:	The idea that the universe is an expression of divine playfulness.
Maharshi (Maharṣi)	:	Literally, 'great sage'.
Maitreya	:	The name of the Buddha yet to come. Many Buddhists tend to look forward to this appearance with an air of messianic expectation.
Mānava Dharma	:	The normative conduct appropriate for a human being qua a human, irrespective of sexual or other differences.
Maya (Māyā)	:	A concept with many shades of meaning, basically involving an attempt to account for the mysterious relationship of the phenomenal world to the ultimate reality.
Mayavada (Māyāvāda)	:	The doctrine that the world experienced by us is unreal, possessing no higher ontological status than that of a mere dream.
Meemamsaka (Mīmāṁsaka)	:	The follower of the Hindu philosophical school known as Mīmāṁsā, which privileges a liturgical interpretation of the Vedas over the metaphysical.
Mitakshara (Mitākṣarā)	:	The name of a commentary on the Yājñavalkya-Smṛti by Vijñāneśvara (12th century), influential in the evolution of Hindu civil law.
Moksha (Mokṣa)	:	The summum bonum of human life in Hinduism. The word literally means freedom or emancipation and more concretely implies freedom from the cycle of rebirth, corresponding to salvation in Christian thought.
Mundakopanished (Muṇḍakopaniṣad)	:	One of the classical Upaniṣads, significant for its doctrine of two levels of knowledge.
Naraka	:	The Hindu analogue of the western 'hell', with the difference that doctrines of eternal damnation are rare in Hinduism.
Nava Vidhāna	:	The idea of a new dispensation, consummating the ones in the Old and the New Testaments, which plays a prominent role in the later thought of K.C. Sen.
Nigam (Nigama)	:	The collective name for the body of Vedic literature, wherein worship is mostly aniconic, especially when distinguished

		from liturgical manuals laying down rules of image-worship called Āgamas.
Nirguna (Nirguṇa)	:	An entity without distinguishing attributes, especially without a form. The worship of God could also be called *nigruṇa* if it did not involve image-worship.
Nirvana (Nirvāṇa)	:	The word used to indicate, specially in Buddhism, the final state of Realization.
Nirvikalpa Samadhi (Nirvikalpa Samādhi)	:	A state of absorption in which all traces of mental functioning cease.
Nivartak (Nivartaka)	:	Any action which attenuates further involvement in the process of *saṁsāra* or rebirth.
Niyoga	:	The practice of levirate as known in India, allowing the widow to bear the child of the brother of the deceased husband. Although disallowed in the present age, Swami Dayananda proposed its revival as a way of addressing the widow problem.
Om Tat Sat	:	An invocatory utterance in Hinduism.
Pancavati (Pañcavaṭī)	:	A grove consisting of five trees as a locus of Rāmakṛṣṇa's *sādhanā*.
Pāṇḍavas	:	The rivals of the Kauravas and the rightful heirs to the throne at Hastināpura. The struggle between the two constitutes the kernel of the Mahābhārata.
Paramahaṁsa	:	The supreme swan, a title accorded to one who has attained the highest spiritual flight possible for a human being to undertake.
Paramatma (Paramātmā)	:	God in general; in Sāṁkhya and Yoga, the supreme soul or God, as distinguished from the souls of ordinary beings bound to *saṁsāra*.
Parasuram (Paraśurāma)	:	Three figures in whose name the word 'rāma' appears are significant in Hindu mythology: Balarāma, the brother of Kṛṣṇa; Paraśurāma or Rāma with the axe and, Rāma (or Rāmacandra), son of king Daśrartha. Confusion is caused by the fact that sometimes all three apeear in various lists of divine incarnations. In his incarnation as Paraśurama, God is said to have mowed down the *kṣatriyas* repeatedly for deviating from the path of *dharma* instead of protecting it.
Paropkar (Paropakāra)	:	A cardinal virtue of doing good to others. According to many popular axioms, this is the quintessential virtue.

Pinda (Piṇḍa)	:	Balls of rice offered to ancestors in the ceremony called *śrāddha*.
Pishaca (Piśāca)	:	A class of goblin-like beings which inhabit the Hindu world.
Prahlada (Prahlāda)	:	Famous devotee of Viṣṇu.
Praja (Prajā)	:	The subjects in a kingdom as distinguished from the king or *rājā* .
Prakriti (Prakṛti)	:	A comprehensive category in Hindu thought analogous of that of 'nature' or 'matter'.
Prarthana (Prārthanā)	:	Prayer to God, specially in its petitionary aspect.
Pravartak (Pravartaka)	:	Any action which leads to further involvement in the process of *saṁsāra* or rebirth.
Prayaschit (Prāyaścitta)	:	An act of penance performed to atone for a sin.
Puranas (Purāṇas)	:	The class of texts in Hinduism dealing with the lives of saints and gods and other cosmic matters.
Purohita	:	The chaplain or leading priest.
Purusha (Puruṣa)	:	God as the Supreme Person.
Raghunandana	:	See Dayātattva.
Rakshasas (Rākṣasas)	:	Demonic beings.
Ramanuja (Rāmānuja)	:	Famous philosopher of the twelfth century, who offers a primarily theistic and devotional interpretation of Vedic thought.
Ṛg Veda	:	A foundational text of Hinduism, which, along with the Yajur Veda, the Sama Veda and the Atharva Veda, constitutes the corpus of revealed literature in Hinduism, otherwise called *śruti*.
Rishis (Ṛṣis)	:	A class of sages, especially those to whom the Vedas were revealed.
Sadhana (Sādhanā)	:	Spiritual practice especially directed towards the realization of God.
Sadhu (Sādhu)	:	A mendicant.
Saguna	:	An entity which possesses attributes, especially as distin-

(Saguṇa)		guished from one which doesn't. Thus physical objects are *saguṇa* in that they possess material attributes, but space, in which they exist, by comparison, is *nirguṇa* as it is immaterial in nature.
Sakti (Śakti)	:	The ultimate as the locus of feminine power.
Salokya, Sameepya, Sarupya, Sayooja (Sālokya, Sāmīpya, Sārūpya, Sāyujya)	:	Four degrees of closeness to God which the liberated souls may enjoy, each more intimate than the other: (1) residing in the world of God; (2) remaining in close proximity to God; (3) having the same form as God and (4) being in a state of unity with God.
Samanvaya	:	The Hindu hermeneutical proposition that the various apparently diverse passages in a scripture are meant to be interpreted consistently and harmoniously.
Sanatana Dharma (Sanātana Dharma)	:	'The eternal or immemorial religion'—Hinduism's name for itself.
Sankara (Śaṅkara)	:	See Śaṅkarācārya.
Sankhya (Sāṅkhya)		A school of Hindu thought which posits a fundamental dualism between *puruṣa* and *prakṛti* (or 'spirit' and 'matter').
Sanskara (Saṁskāra)	:	Habitual and latent patterns of thought and behavior as constructs of one's personality.
Sanyas (Sannyāsa)	:	The fourth and final stage of life in the Hindu scheme of things, known as the *āśramas*.
Sannyasin (Sannyāsin)	:	A person who has renounced the world; a monk. Any renunciant, especially one who has formally entered the fourth stage of life in Hinduism called *sannyāsa*.
Sapta-Samudra, Sapta- Parvata, Sapta-Vana, Sapta-Akasha (Ākāśa)	:	The 'seven seas', 'seven mountains', 'seven forests' and 'seven skies' as components of the sacred or sanctified geography of Hinduism.
Sarirak Mimamsa (Śārīraka Mīmāṁsā)	:	Another name for the Brahma-Sūtra, pertaining to the discussion of the embodied (*śārīraka*) *ātman*.
Shastra (Śāstra)	:	A comprehensive term including any body of work which possesses, or deserves the status of an authoritative work within the religious traditions of Indian origin, specifically Hinduism.
Satyagraha (Satyāgraha)	:	The word literally means 'clinging to truth' and in the Gandian vocabulary implies relying on the justness of one's cause rather than force to achieve one's goal.

Shakhas (Śākhās)	:	A 'branch' or school of the Veda. Vedic recitation and learning was carried out among different families resulting in the various branches or *śākhās* of recitation.
Shalagram (Ślagrāma)	:	A representation of Viṣṇu in the form of a conical stone (analogous to the *liṅga* as a representation of Śiva).
Shankaracarya (Śaṅkarācārya)	:	A celebrated exponent of Advaita Vedānta, usually placed in the eighth century.
Shishya (Śiṣya)	:	A disciple who receives instructions from a spiritual master or guru; the word Sikh is derived from it.
Shistachar (Śiṣṭācāra)	:	The conduct of the esteemed members of society, as paradigmatic for the rest of society.
Shraddha (Śrāddha)	:	A ceremony performed to honour one's ancestors.
Shri Guru Dattātreya	:	A popular deity, synthesizing aspects of Brahmā, Viṣṇu and Śiva.
Siddhis	:	Supernatural powers with which one is endowed or which may be attained while traversing the spiritual path.
Śiva-Liṅga	:	A conical symbol of Śiva, the form in which he is most often worshipped.
Śiva-Rātri	:	Night sacred to Śiva, on which his worshippers maintain a night-long vigil.
Sri Krishna	:	Lord Kṛṣṇa, especially as the gracious object of one's devotion.
Stuti	:	A litany in praise, especially in honour, of a god.
Shuddhi (Śuddhi)	:	The word literally means purity but has now come to symbolize the return, to the Hindu fold, of Hindu converts or their descendants to Islam or Christianity, through a rite of purification.
Sudra (Śūdra)	:	One of the four *varṇas* which constitute Hindu society.
Suṣupti	:	The state of dreamless sleep, especially as a state in which one is neither conscious of oneself nor of the universe.
Swadeshi (Svadeśī)	:	'Of one's own country'. An ideology which favours indigenous structures of production of goods or knowledge over those imported from abroad.
Swarga (Svarga)	:	Swarga is like the Christian heaven in that it follows upon good deeds in this world, but unlike Christianity, Hindus do not believe that the soul remains in heaven forever.

Tantra	:	A body of texts dealing with the modes of worshipping Viṣṇu, Śiva and Śakti. Also used to refer to the doctrines embodied in the texts. Sometimes the use of the word is restricted to the texts dealing with the worship of Śakti, especially as characterised by sexual techniques for gaining spiritual liberation.
Tilaka	:	A mark on the forehead made with powder or paste, often possessing a religious significance.
Tirthas (Tīrthas)	:	Places of pilgrimage, often at the confluence of rivers, as topographical points which are spiritually transformational.
Upadhyaya (Upādhyāya)	:	A respected teacher.
Upangas (Upāṅgas)	:	Vedic studies, as a formal field of study, is said to consist of six vedāṅgas: śikṣā (pronunciation); kalpa (ritual); nirukta (etymology); vyākaraṇa (grammar); chandas (metre) and jyotiṣa (astronomy). Fields of study ancillary to these vedāṅgas are called upāṅgas. These are four: purāṇa, nyāya, mīmāṁsā and dharmaśāstra.
Upaniṣads	:	Series of texts which constitute the last section of the four Vedas and provide the philosophical basis of much of Hindu thought.
Upasana (Upāsanā)	:	Worship.
Up-Vedas (Upa-Vedas)	:	Vedas ancillary to the four major Vedas involving more 'secular' forms of knowledge such as medicine (Ayur Veda), music and dance (Gandharva Veda), military science (Dhanur Veda) and architecture (Sthāpatya Veda).
Vaiseshika (Vaiśeṣika)	:	An orthodox school of Hindu thought characterized by atomistic pluralism.
Vaisnavism (Vaiṣṇavism)	:	A form of Hindu devotionalism which looks upon Viṣṇu as the supreme deity.
Vāmana	:	Incarnation of Viṣṇu as a dwarf.
Varṇa	:	The Hindu conceptual framework which views society as an aggregate of four classes: priests, intellectuals, etc. (brāhmaṇas); soldiers, bureaucrats, etc. (kṣatriyas); merchants, agriculturalists, etc. (vaiśyas); the labour class (śūdra).
Vānaprastha	:	One of the four stages of life in the Hindu scheme of things, in which one retires to the forest after having led the life of a householder.

Varnashram (Varṇāśrama)	:	The twin concepts of the four classes of society (*varṇa*) and the four stages of life (*āśrama*), as the distinguishing features of the Hindu way of life.
Vāsudeva	:	A name for Kṛṣṇa, 'son of Vasudeva'.
Vedānta	:	The term refers to the texts which constitute the concluding sections (*anta*) of the Vedas (otherwise known as the Upaniṣads) and derivatively, to the systems of philosophy based on them.
Vedanta Darsana (Vedānta Darśana)	:	The teachings of the Upaniṣads formulated as a pilosophical system.
Vedas	:	The foundational texts of Hinduism, four in number (Ṛg Veda, Yajur Veda, Sāma Veda and Atharva Veda).
Visishtadvaita (Viśiṣṭādvaita)	:	A school of Vedānta which differs from Advaita in regarding a personal God (rather than the impersonal Brahman) as the ultimate reality.
Viśvatomukham	:	The idea that scriptural passages are to be interpreted generously and universally rather than parochially and narrowly.
Yajamana (Yajamāna)	:	The patron on whose behalf the priest performs a sacrifice.
Yajur Veda	:	One of the four Vedas, which deals primarily with the sacrificial application of the hymns of the Ṛg Veda. It contains the earliest prose texts available in Sanskrit.
Yamas	:	The five 'restraints' involving adherence to non-violence, truthfulness, celibacy or chastity, 'non-stealing' and non-possession.
Yoga	:	A polysemic word which conveys a vast array of meanings in which the idea of spiritual practice or discipline to achieve a spiritual goal is paramount.
Yudhisthira (Yudhiṣṭhira)	:	The eldest of the five Pāṇḍavas known for his uncompromising commitment to virtue.

Index